The Scott and Laurie Oki Series in Asian American Studies

JUDGMENT
without Trial

Japanese American Imprisonment
during World War II

TETSUDEN KASHIMA

UNIVERSITY OF WASHINGTON PRESS

Seattle and London

This book is published with the assistance of a grant
from the Scott and Laurie Oki Endowed Fund
for the publication of Asian American Studies,
established through the generosity of Scott and Laurie Oki.

University of Washington Press
P.O. Box 50096
Seattle, WA 98145-5096, U.S.A.
www.u.washington.edu/uwpress

Library of Congress Cataloging-in-Publication Data
Kashima, Tetsuden, 1940–
Judgment without trial : Japanese American imprisonment
during World War II / Tetsuden Kashima.
p. cm — (The Scott and Laurie Oki series in Asian American studies)
Includes bibliographical references and index.
ISBN 0-295-98299-3 (alk. paper)
1. Japanese Americans—Evacuation and relocation, 1942–1945.
2. World War, 1939–1945—Japanese Americans.
I. Title.   II. Series
D769.8.A6K37 2003   940.53′17′08956073—DC21   2003040289

To Kanako, Daniel Tetsunori, James Tetsuro

&

Jeanie, Kenn Tetsuryo, Sara Ryoko

&

to the memory of my brother, Tetsuyo

CONTENTS

ABBREVIATIONS

ACLU	American Civil Liberties Union
AEC	Alien Enemy Control
CCC	Civilian Conservation Corp
CWRIC	Commission on the Wartime Relocation and Internment of Civilians
FBI	Federal Bureau of Investigation
INS	Immigration and Naturalization Service, Justice Department
JACL	Japanese American Citizens League
MID	Military Intelligence Division, U.S. Army
MIS	Military Intelligence Service, U.S. Army
ONI	Office of Naval Intelligence
SDU	Special Defense Unit, Justice Department
SWP	Special War Problems Division, State Department
UNIA	Universal Negro Improvement Association
WCCA	Wartime Civil Control Administration, U.S. Army
WDC	Western Defense Command, U.S. Army
WRA	War Relocation Authority
WRB	War Refuge Board

Preface and Acknowledgments

MY MOTHER ONCE TOLD ME that she placed a packed suitcase next to the living room sofa soon after December 7, 1941. My father believed that agents of the Federal Bureau of Investigation would eventually come to take him to jail, although he didn't know when it would happen—thus, the suitcase parked in the living room. It was not until I was an undergraduate student that my mother told me of her preparations—I was an infant in 1941—and it seemed strange that she had never mentioned it before. By then, my father had died, but she wouldn't or couldn't answer further questions about why a suitcase was necessary or why my father, who had been a Buddhist priest, a community leader, and a law-abiding person, would worry about being arrested. As it turned out, the FBI did not then or later arrest my father or other Buddhist priests in the San Francisco–Oakland Bay area, where we lived. Even the presiding bishop of the Buddhist Churches of America (headquartered in San Francisco) was left untouched, although Japanese religious leaders in other regions who were also, by all accounts, law-abiding persons—Buddhists, Christians, and those of other Japanese religious orders—were quickly arrested and imprisoned.

A few months into 1942, the U.S. Army ordered our entire family—my father, mother, brother, and myself—to leave Oakland and sent us to a place it called an "assembly center," at the Tanforan racetrack in south San Francisco. After a few months there, we were again moved, this time to a civilian-controlled "relocation camp." The name of our particular camp was Topaz, "A Jewel in the Desert"; it takes about three hours to get there now, traveling by car in a southwesterly direction from Salt Lake City. Here, seemingly in the middle of nowhere, surrounded by sweet-smelling sagebrush and far-off mountains, the government incarcerated some 10,000 persons, thereby creating a new desert community from 1942 to 1945. Altogether, nearly 117,116 persons of Japanese descent—citizens and permanent resident nationals alike—were eventually incarcerated in ten so-called relocation centers in desolate places in the interior United States during those wartime years.

Why my father should have expected his arrest was a question that bothered me for many years. If there is any one particular motive for my interest in the imprisonment of Japanese Americans, perhaps it was this question, to which I then had no answer.

One caveat should be noted: although the U. S. government imprisoned more than just the Japanese and their citizen children, my focus here will be upon this particular group. The experiences of interned German and Italian nationals are discussed when relevant. That subject, however, deserves separate treatment and analysis, because although many Germans and Italians had experiences similar to those of the Japanese, significant differences are evident. I leave that discussion for another time.

The first chapter introduces the thesis of the book and details the importance of the process whereby the U.S. government created a loosely structured imprisonment network during World War II. The second chapter examines the years before America's formal entry into the war and the preparations for internment that took place prior to it; the third chapter describes the arrest, detention, and internment of Japanese nationals just after December 7, 1941. The fourth and fifth chapters discuss the imprisonment process used outside the contiguous United States—in Alaska, Hawaii, and Latin American countries. The sixth deals with the camps run by the Justice Department's Immigration and Naturalization Service and the U.S. Army and what life was like for those internees. The seventh and eighth focus on lesser-known aspects of various types of camps operated by the War Relocation Authority. The ninth chapter examines the mistreatment of the prisoners—the abuses, beatings, and homicides—that occurred in various camps. The last chapter concludes with an analysis of the camp experience.

Data for this study come from a number of sources. First were the governmental archives: the records of the War Relocation Authority, Old Military and Civil Records, and Modern Military Records at the National Archives; Justice Department records at the National Archives and in the Department of Justice History Section; and the Federal Bureau of Investigation Archives. In addition, I perused materials at the Bancroft Library of the University of California, Berkeley; the University of Hawaii, Honolulu; the University of California, San Diego; and the Suzzallo and Law School Library of the University of Washington, Seattle. I also obtained and recorded a number of interviews with Issei internees or their Nisei children, as well as investigated the recollections of Issei who wrote about their experiences, mainly in the Japanese language.

This work would not have been possible without the invaluable help of many fine individuals. My long-term gratitude goes to Stanford M. Lyman for his constant encouragement and comments. In addition, Yasuko Iwai Takezawa was indispensable in interpreting and translating the Issei documents, and Arthur Hansen supplied invaluable editorial assistance. Patricia Draher Kiyono and Laura Iwasaki were consummate editors. I can only formally acknowledge a few others: Stephen S. Fugita, Scott Gitlen, Edwin Hamada, Aiko Yoshinaga-Herzig, Jack Herzig, Pau King Hung, Janet Inahara, Tamiko Iwashita, Ken Izumi, Otari Kaneko, Eugenia Kashima, S. Frank Miyamoto, Henry Miyatake, Henry Miyoshi, Donald T. and

Lynn Mizokawa, Dorothy Nakagawa, Kenichi Nakano, Masayuki and Shirley Shimada, and Hope Wenk. My sincerest thanks go to all the rest.

Since the start of this project, a number of individuals, some of whom were internees, have passed away. I can only remember them in this small way for their great support and encouragement: Edward Ennis, Roy Shin Hasegawa, Yasutaro Hibi, Kakuaki Kaneko, Taju Koide, Genji Mihara, Saburo Muraoka, Hajime Takemoto, Masato Uyeda, and Tadashi Yamaguchi.

My deep appreciation goes as well to all the fine staff members of the University of Washington Press. I appreciate the kind words and deep support of Naomi Pascal, associate director and editor-in-chief; Marilyn Trueblood, managing editor; and Donald Ellegood and Pat Soden, former and present directors.

I am also indebted to the Institute for Ethnic Studies in the United States, University of Washington, and the Motoda Foundation, Seattle, for financial support. These organizations made it possible to travel to libraries, gather materials, and conduct interviews of former internees.

Various librarians and libraries were extremely helpful to this study: Karl Matsushita at the Japanese American National Library, San Francisco; Richard Berner, Karyl Winn, Tom Kaasa, Teruko Chin, and Takika Yamada Lee at the University of Washington Libraries, Seattle; Constance Hagiwara at the Hawaii State Library, Honolulu; W. Robert Ellis Jr. and Frederick Romanski at the National Archives, Washington, D.C.; and Marion L. Smith at the Department of Justice, Immigration and Naturalization Service History Section, Washington, D.C.

Judgment without Trial

1

The Imprisonment Process

After sundown on December 10, 1941, a midsize tuna-fishing boat cruised northward from Mexican waters toward the San Pedro harbor to unload its catch at the Franco-American Cannery. A U.S. Navy ship intercepted the vessel and escorted it up the coast. At San Pedro, navy personnel directed the boat to a designated area and ordered everyone to stay on board overnight. Officers of the Immigration and Naturalization Service (INS) of the U.S. Department of Justice arrived the next morning. They talked to the ship's captain, who was a Nisei—an American of Japanese ancestry—and told him to pilot the vessel to the cannery. Once there, the INS agents ordered the crew on deck and started to interrogate each of them. Two crew members were Issei, or resident Japanese immigrants: Yasutaro Hibi, the captain's father, and Taju Koide. To the crew's astonishment the INS agents arrested both men and took them to the San Pedro INS station. There, they met seventy or eighty other Issei fishermen who had been similarly arrested.

The INS kept these Issei at San Pedro for two weeks without telling them the reason for their arrest. Later, the INS moved them to the Tuna Canyon Detention Station, located in Tujunga, California, where they joined other Issei from different areas around Southern California. The Issei stayed there for varying lengths of time, some for a few weeks and others for three months, before boarding a train equipped with blackout shades for the long ride to Missoula, Montana.

The INS kept the elder Hibi for more than half a year before he was paroled; he was released, however, only to enter another imprisonment center, although he was at least able to rejoin his family there. This time, the incarcerating authority was a civilian agency called the War Relocation Authority (WRA), which held Hibi and his family for three more years. The INS kept Koide, the other Issei fisherman, even longer, for more than a year. He was unable to see his family until he, too, was finally released to a WRA camp.[1]

Farther northward, in Seattle, on December 7, Tadashi Yamaguchi, an Issei and owner of the West Coast Importing Company, heard the news about the Japanese attack on Pearl Harbor. Although he initially could not believe such a disastrous event had taken place, he realized after a constant stream of radio announcements that America would probably enter the ongoing war in Europe and Asia. At around seven that night, he heard rapping on his front door and opened it to find two officials asking for admittance. Neither Yamaguchi nor his two Nisei sons recall their visitors showing any badges or warrants or giving any reason for their intrusion. They did ask if they could look around the house and, after obtaining oral permission, conducted a search of the premises. The search turned up nothing of interest, but the officials told Yamaguchi that he would have to accompany them to the Seattle INS station. Once he stepped out of the house, more than a year and half elapsed before he was able to rejoin his family.[2]

These stories show how three Issei were taken into captivity on and immediately after that fateful December day. It was, of course, imperial Japan's air attack on U.S. military forces at Pearl Harbor that caused this country fully and openly to enter the war in Europe and Asia. For weeks afterward, U.S. government agents arrested and interned German, Italian, Japanese, and a few other foreign nationals plus a number of American citizens and placed them in numerous holding centers. By this process, the Justice and War Departments interned 31,275 persons, of whom 17,477 were of Japanese ancestry.

Later, after President Franklin D. Roosevelt signed Executive Order 9066 on February 19, 1942, agents of the government took nearly 120,000 persons of Japanese ancestry, mostly from West Coast states, and incarcerated them in various parts of the country. These people were herded initially into fifteen temporary camps operated by the U.S. Army's Wartime Civil Control Administration (WCCA), which called the camps "assembly centers." The army then transported them to ten permanent "relocation centers" run by the WRA. Two-thirds of this group were American citizens. The actions of these agencies—the Justice Department, the WRA, and the army, plus others yet to be introduced—and the process used to imprison persons of Japanese ancestry constitute the focus of this book.

Significant as this calamitous experience was for Japanese Americans, their imprisonment attracted comparatively little attention at the time from the wider American society. Within the context of a world war, the American media, military leaders, politicians, and others were riveted by global events transpiring in the European and Asian arenas. When the military campaign concluded in the mid-1940s, the United States began to return to a peacetime normalcy.

From the end of World War II through the 1970s, increasing attention has been directed to what one scholar in 1945 called "our worst wartime mistake."[3] Most of the literature on the Japanese American imprisonment concentrates on the assembly centers and relocation centers. These two types of camps were emphasized for three reasons. First, they held the largest number of inmates. Second, these inmates were mostly American citizens, a fact that epitomizes the injustice of a government incarcerating its own citizens. Third, the most accessible government documents and other source materials pertain to these two types of centers. For these three reasons, there now exists a large corpus of works on the assembly and relocation centers.[4] It might appear that the entire imprisonment experience has been sufficiently examined. This, in fact, is not the case.

This book asserts that studies concentrating only or mainly on the assembly and relocation centers reveal but a partial picture of the imprisonment episode. It will examine the totality of the decision-making process by which persons of Japanese ancestry were imprisoned during World War II. In the aggregate, this group was quite large; it included almost an entire ethnoracial population on the West Coast and in the territory of Alaska, plus a few thousand others from the territory of Hawaii and certain Latin American countries.

This study shows that the decision to imprison persons of Japanese ancestry during the war was made before the attack on Pearl Harbor. There were differences of opinion over which persons or organizations ought to be investigated and who should later be imprisoned, but the decision was a product of rational deliberation; it was not necessarily made in haste or because of "hysteria," as perhaps the general populace and some authors may believe. Further, the failure to establish a single overarching authority for those interned or incarcerated led to considerable bureaucratic conflict and confusion. As persons of Japanese ancestry were placed in various imprisonment centers, flawed coordination of authority gave rise to anomalous situations and ad hoc rules that were erratically enforced.

THE IMPRISONMENT ORGANIZATION

This study thus demonstrates that the imprisonment experience was much larger and more complex, and involved many more agencies and types of camps, than the assembly and relocation centers. To achieve its purposes, the United States created what I assert to be an imprisonment organization composed of many different units from various sectors of the government and the military.

A central framework employed here maintains that a loosely coordinated imprisonment organization existed in incipient form years before December 1941. Beginning in the 1920s, agencies such as the Federal Bureau of Investigation (FBI), the Office of Naval Intelligence (ONI) under the Navy Department, and the U.S. Army's Military Intelligence Division (MID) engaged in mutually beneficial and coordinated actions that eventually resulted in a loosely structured imprisonment network. This network was formed initially to assess various groups as to their potential threat to national security, but it was later used to arrest, intern, incarcerate, and maintain control over its prisoners. This imprisonment organization was a meta-organization, since it was never formally consolidated in an official unit. Rather, separate governmental agencies engaged in cooperative activities for a common purpose. At other times, these same governmental units were involved in disputes and divisions among themselves over areas of jurisdictional responsibilities as they tried to gain power, justify larger budgets, or increase their personnel. I refer to this meta-organization as the *imprisonment organization* throughout this presentation.

President Roosevelt, as chief executive, was ultimately responsible for each segment of the imprisonment organization, but day-to-day responsibility rested in the hands of individual civilian directors and military commanders. The main elements of this organization included the War Department (the secretary of the army and his staff, the Western Defense Command and its Wartime Civil Control Administration, the provost marshal general's office, and the army's Military Intelligence Division [Intelligence Branch], which became the Military Intelligence Service [Counter Intelligence Corps]);[5] the Navy Department (the secretary of the navy and his staff and the Office of Naval Intelligence); the Justice Department (the attorney general and his staff, the Federal Bureau of Investigation, the Immigration and Naturalization Service, the Border Patrol, the Special Defense Unit, and the Alien Enemy Control Unit); the State Department (the secretary of state and his staff and the Special War Problems Division); and the civilian-run War Relocation Authority. Other agencies in the government were also involved—the Interior Department, the Bureau of Indian Affairs, and the Treasury Department—but they had less direct influence. All these agencies dealt with the handling, imprisonment, and disposition of almost all persons of Japanese ancestry residing in the continental United States and its territories, as well as selected resident German and Italian nationals and others brought here from Latin American countries.

Since the imprisonment organization was not a single entity, assignment of authority and administrative control was never resolved to the satisfaction of the agencies involved. Throughout the war, disputes arose over the jurisdiction of various agencies over prisoners, the disposition of certain persons, the application of particular rules (such as the 1929 Geneva Convention) to the prisoners, the relation of Issei internees to captured prisoners of war, definitions of acceptable actions on the part of prisoners, the right to leave camps, and the reuniting of families. The imprisonment organization was rife with internal competition, lack of coordination, and ad hoc decision making.

Although the imprisonment organization started before the war with but a few constituent parts, once the United States entered the conflict, it grew quickly as more and different types of prisoner populations came under its sway. Agency officials and workers were drawn from a wide variety of governmental units, and the level of training and expertise of administrators and personnel varied. Seasoned professionals from the Justice and State Departments conferring in Washington, D.C., contrasted with the inexperienced army private manning a guard tower at the Topaz WRA center in southwestern Utah. What they had in common was their almost total ignorance about people of Japanese ancestry. Into their hands, the government entrusted the fate of these people.

The history of the imprisonment organization encompasses a much longer time frame than that represented by the origin and demise of the assembly and relocation centers. The full period extends back decades before the United States entered the war and does not end until more than two years after peace was declared. The period before December 7, 1941, becomes crucial to understanding the imprisonment process. I contend that, not only did it result in the internment of nationals from enemy nations as well as some American citizens, it also led to the creation of the assembly and relocation camps. Decades before the war, high-level meetings were held and agreements were reached on what to do about persons of Japanese ancestry—both first-generation immigrants and their American-citizen descendants—in the event of a war with Japan.

First, all parties agreed to a careful and organized scrutiny of persons of Japanese descent residing in the contiguous United States and in the territories of Hawaii and Alaska. Second, a methodical plan was developed to intern various Japanese nationals and certain American citizens of Japanese ancestry on the mainland and in the territory of Hawaii. Third, pivotal high-level officials in Washington, D.C., and on the West Coast calmly discussed the need to remove and/or imprison the entire group in the event of a war with Japan. Although no particular large-scale mass incarceration plan existed prior to December 7, 1941, it was relatively easy for the army command on the West Coast to do so since it had already planned for the removal and internment of thousands of enemy nationals. The arrest and removal of this group from the West Coast just after December 7 and for months into 1942, then, was the product of a rational and deliberate decision-making process.

Certain continuing themes are found throughout this study. One concerns the problem of jurisdictional disputes among agencies as they fought to exert their organizational authority over intelligence and security; the many agencies involved worked both competitively and cooperatively with one another. Once the jurisdictional disputes were worked out, the main problem revolved around control of the prisoner population. Another theme concerns the way in which the imprisonment organization met unanticipated needs that arose in regard to the prisoners. Certain unplanned centers were created where authorities could hold anybody whom they wished to remove from existing camps. These were the internees and inmates the imprisonment organization defined as troublemakers, anti-WRA, or even anti-American.

Another theme concerns the actual control methods used in the centers. These government units had virtually unlimited power over the internees and inmates. They administered the entire imprisonment process as well as legitimated it socially and politically. All the constituent segments used psychological means of control, while many also frightened, coerced, and resorted to physical threats and reprisals to assure their command over the prisoners. Many employed brute force and assault, and at times homicides resulted from the use of arms. The organization not only arrested prisoners but concentrated them in large groups, selectively separated some, placed others in solitary confinement, "encouraged" American citizens to renounce their citizenship, transferred some into so-called isolation centers or segregation centers, and even created a secret camp. All these tactics had but one aim—to maintain docile and well-managed internee and inmate populations.

It is clear that all branches of the government were involved in the imprisonment process. This study highlights the actions of the executive branch of government because it was closely involved in the daily operations of the centers and camps. The important roles played by the judicial and legislative branches of government will be touched upon only lightly in this study.

It is important to understand what this book will *not* do. This study will not examine the underlying reasons for the imprisonment. Many works on the assembly and relocation camps discuss the major role played by early race prejudice in the incarceration of Japanese nationals and their citizen children after December 7. Rather than examine this cause, and without negating its influence in any way, I would assert that anti-Japanese sentiments constituted the backdrop for the investigations of Japanese immigrants and their children conducted by officials and military leaders from the 1920s. Thus, rather than looking at why the imprisonment occurred, this study will focus on *how* it occurred. I examine when and in what ways both the selective and the later mass incarcerations happened and who was involved.

TERMS AND EUPHEMISMS

During the war years, the government used various designations to identify the imprisonment centers. The most accurate overall descriptive term is *concentration camp*—that is, a barbed-wire enclosure where people are interned or incarcerated under armed guard. Some readers might object to the use of this term, believing that it more properly applies to the Nazi camps of World War II. Those European camps were more than just places of confinement, however; many were established to provide slave labor for the Nazi regime or to conduct mass executions. I contend that such camps are more properly called *Nazi slave camps* or *Nazi death camps*.

At the time, the U.S. government used its own euphemisms to identify its wartime camps and actions. Terms such as "assembly centers," "relocation camps," and "evacuation" mask the unpleasantness of people removed involuntarily from their homes and forced to live in flea-infested stables, dusty fairgrounds, and hastily and shoddily built barracks in desolate places. We usually think of an evacuation as the removal of a group to a safe place in order to escape from, or after suffering the devastation wrought by, floods, famines, and earthquakes. The word "evacuation," which the government used during World War II, sugarcoats the actions it took to rid itself of unwanted citizens and foreign nationals. These euphemisms do not convey the fact that the prisoners daily faced fear, anxiety, weariness, and despair. They could not predict or plan the future beyond any single day.

Three particular terms will be used throughout this study: *internment, incarcer-*

ation, and *imprisonment. Internment* designates the imprisonment of civilian enemy nationals; the word will be used to refer to the confinement of German, Italian, Japanese, and other nationals primarily by the Justice, State, and War Departments. As will be explained later, the authority by which these agencies interned people differed from that of the w r a. *Incarceration,* as a concept, applies to those imprisoned by the w r a and to the assembly camps created by the War Department. *Imprisonment* encompasses the overall process that includes both internment and incarceration. The reason for these distinctions is the lack of an agreed-upon vocabulary for the entire operation. Previous works on the wartime imprisonment experience have used *incarceration* and *internment* interchangeably when referring to some or all of these camps or centers. The term *imprisonment* also best expresses a salient feature of the process by which individuals were arrested without criminal charge, detained without trial, and placed inside primitive prisons. The words *camp* and *center* are treated as interchangeable here.

This three-part terminology also allows us to differentiate between the two types of prisoners. Those in the internment camps are called *internees,* and those in the incarceration centers will be referred to as *inmates.* The overarching term for both is *prisoners.* The government used its own euphemisms for the prisoners. The w r a referred to its inmates as "relocatees" or "evacuees" and to the American-citizen Nisei as "non-aliens" in a rather cumbersome avoidance of the obvious term. The Justice Department stated that those initially arrested were "detainees" who were held in "detention" no matter the length of their internment. Later, the word for a person kept in permanent confinement was changed to "internee." Because it is important to delineate the various prisoner populations, I will use the designations *internee, inmate,* and *prisoner.*

ISSEI, NISEI, KIBEI, SANSEI

Another important issue of terminology concerns the generational categories maintained by Japanese Americans. It appears to be a sociological fact that only those of Japanese and Korean ancestry use specific terms to distinguish succeeding generations from the original immigrant generation. Most immigrant groups in America identify the first generation and then clump all others into the category *American-born.* In 1940, there were 126,947 persons of Japanese ancestry in the contiguous forty-eight states and a larger population of 157,905 in the territory of Hawaii. In the mainland United States in 1940, the original immigrants from Japan, or the Issei (first generation), constituted about one-third of the American Japanese population—47,305 persons. Their American-born children, the Nisei (second generation), made up almost two-thirds of the group—79,642. The proportional breakdown by generations in the territory of Hawaii at that time was roughly the same. The Kibei constituted a smaller but important subgroup of the Nisei generation. A Kibei is a Nisei who spent a portion of his or her pre–World

War II childhood in Japan. The importance of this subgroup will be made clear later. The Issei generation's American-born grandchildren are called Sansei (third generation) and, according to one estimate, numbered 5,965 in the w R A camps in 1942.[6] In 2002, there are already Yonsei (fourth generation), Gosei (fifth generation), and Rokusei (sixth generation) Japanese Americans on the mainland and in Hawaii.

Although the Issei were Japanese nationals (from 1922, they were ineligible for naturalization), subsequent generations were American citizens by virtue of their birth on U.S. soil. In 1952, the Issei were eligible for citizenship, and many of them took advantage of the opportunity to become Americans. In this study, when discussing events before 1952, the term *Japanese American* usually refers to the Nisei; when the perspective shifts to the decades after the war, the term includes all generations—from the Issei onward. Another generic word used here is *Nikkei*, which refers to a person of Japanese ancestry and includes both immigrant and later generations.

TYPES OF IMPRISONMENT CAMPS

In 1940, before the United States formally entered the European war, the government maintained a few enclosures in which to hold stranded German and Italian seamen. This group of people constituted the first U.S. internee population of World War II. Beginning at that time and continuing until a few years after the war ended, the United States created ten different types of imprisonment camps or centers.

As shown in table 1.1, the first two types of camps formed by the Justice and War Departments after December 7, 1941, were detention stations and internment centers. These camps held German, Italian, and Japanese nationals as well as some American citizens of Japanese ancestry. Other Japanese nationals and their citizen children were brought to the United States from Latin American countries and the territories of Hawaii and Alaska. The third type of camp was the assembly center, operated by the wcca; inmates of these camps were Issei and Japanese American citizens. Most were transferred to the fourth type of imprisonment center, the relocation camp, which was administered by the w R A, a civilian agency. The w R A, assisted by guards from the army, also had jurisdiction and responsibility for four other types of camps: isolation and "pro-w R A" centers, a segregation center, institutions such as prisons and sanatoriums, and a European refugee camp. A ninth type, also a segregation center, was operated by the Justice Department. The State Department was responsible for the tenth type of camp, the internment hotel, which housed German, Italian, and Japanese diplomats, their families, and other civilians pending their exchange for Allied diplomatic personnel. These ten types of centers constitute the United States' World War II imprisonment camps.

Each type of center was represented by 1–125 actual sites during different phases

TABLE 1.1

Ten Types of U.S. Imprisonment Centers during World War II

Names	Responsible Agencies	Types of Prisoners
1. Detention stations	Justice (INS) and War Departments	Nationals
2. Internment camps	Justice (INS) and War Departments	Nationals
3. Assembly centers	War Department (WCCA)	Nationals and citizens
4. Relocation camps	WRA	Nationals and citizens
5. Isolation and "pro-WRA" centers	WRA	Citizens
6. Segregation center	WRA and U.S. Army	Nationals and citizens
7. Segregation center	Justice Department	Nationals
8. Institutions	WRA	Nationals and citizens
9. Refugee camps	WRA	Refugees (European)
10. Internment hotels	State Department	Diplomats and Nationals

of its existence. The number of prisoners in the centers varied—from less than 50 persons to more than 18,000 men and women and their children. The centers were in use for different lengths of time. Some opened and closed after only a few months, while most remained in operation for years; a few others were still holding internees two years after the war ended. In the following chapters, we will examine the centers in relation to the imprisonment process and explain how that process of rationalization and justification occurred.

Let us start this fateful journey with the years before December 7, 1941.

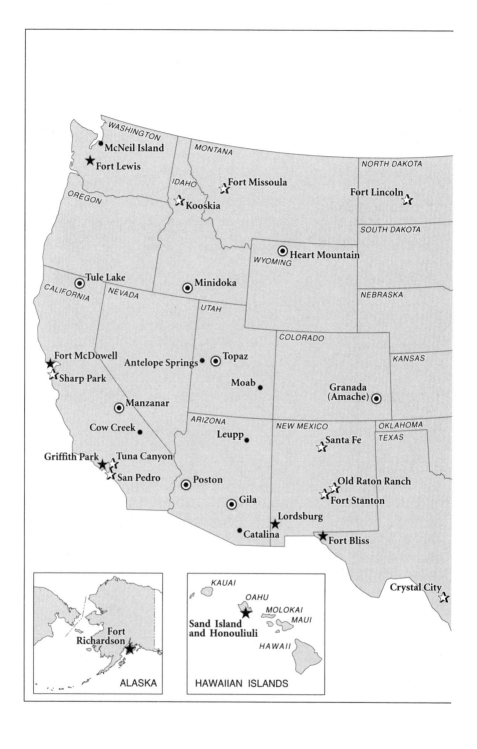

☆ Justice Department
★ U.S. Army Centers
⊙ WRA Centers
• Temporary WRA or other Facility

MAINE

MINNESOTA

WISCONSIN

MICHIGAN

VT.
N.H.

Fort
Ontario

MASS.
CONN.
R.I.

☆ Camp McCoy

NEW YORK

PENNSYLVANIA

N.J.

IOWA

ILLINOIS

INDIANA   OHIO

• Bridgeton
Fort Meade
DEL.

MD.

MISSOURI

WEST
VIRGINIA   D.C.

VIRGINIA

KENTUCKY

NORTH CAROLINA

TENNESSEE

ARKANSAS

★ Camp Forrest

SOUTH
CAROLINA

MISS.   ALABAMA   GEORGIA

Fort Sill
★   Stringtown
★

Rohwer ⊙

Jerome ⊙

LOUISIANA

FLORIDA

Seagoville ☆

Livingston ★

Fort Sam Houston
★

Kenedy ☆

N
W ⊙ E
S

0   400 Miles

2

Pre-World War II Preparations

Decades before 1941, certain governmental agencies considered the possibility of, and then actively prepared for, the country's entry into a future war. Immigrant nationals of potential enemy nations and their American-citizen children were of special concern to these agencies. This chapter describes the process used to gather information on these nationals, create lists of suspect individuals, and prepare for the outbreak of hostilities. The arrests—even those made during the attack on Pearl Harbor and for months into 1942—were not spontaneous happenings but were the culmination of coordinated preplanning by federal agencies. This was a rational process, not one conceived in haste or necessitated by administrative panic.

The prewar years are vitally important because the machinery of imprisonment had its genesis during this time. It is therefore imperative to set the stage. The mass removal of persons of Japanese ancestry from their West Coast homes and communities did not occur within a social vacuum; instead, this action must be understood within a long tradition of anti-Asian and anti-Japanese sentiment in this area of the United States.

PREWAR HISTORY OF THE ISSEI AND NISEI

In the United States, the majority of persons of Japanese ancestry lived along the Pacific coast and in the territory of Hawaii. On the mainland, the Issei and Nisei faced an almost continual barrage of racial animosity in the years before World War II. Anti-Japanese sentiments and actions coalesced especially, but not exclusively, in California from 1905 to 1924. For example, the San Francisco school segregation issue arose in 1906; in 1907–8, the Gentlemen's Agreement effectively cut off Japanese labor immigration; and the 1913 California Alien Land Law and the 1920 amendment were aimed at removing resident Japanese from farmlands. In addition, with the *Ozawa v. United States* case in 1922, the U.S. Supreme Court officially denied Japanese immigrants the right to naturalization, making them "aliens ineligible for citizenship."

The anti-Japanese movement was sustained through the efforts of influential groups and individuals. James D. Phelan, a California senator, for example, asserted in 1919 that the high birthrate of Japanese immigrants would eventually create overpopulation in the state. In 1921, Valentine S. McClatchy, publisher of the newspaper *Sacramento Bee,* castigated Japanese immigrants and the Nisei as unassimilable because, among other reasons, "in the mass, with opportunity offered, and even when born here, they have shown no disposition to do so [become citizens], but on the contrary, [have shown] pronounced antagonism."[1] These and other assertions were disseminated through magazine articles, radio commentaries, and editorials. America was told that Japan had evil designs on the United States and that the early facilitators of its intentions were the immigrants. Anti-Japanese groups espoused the idea that Japan meant to conquer California first and then move on to the rest of the country. These beliefs continued even after the suppression of virtually all Japanese immigration with the passage of the 1924 Immigration Act.

The Issei on the West Coast tried to fight the measures directed against them. They channeled their political efforts mainly through the Japanese Association (Nihonjinkai), which had branches in numerous towns along the Pacific coast. This association tried to educate Americans about the resident Japanese population and argued against the discriminatory laws proposed or legislated against them. The hostile social environment, coupled with a proclivity for group-oriented relationships, resulted in the formation of an insular ethnic group that had relatively few intimate social interactions with the wider American society.

From at least the 1920s, federal agencies grew concerned about Japanese immigrants in relation to internal security. They questioned whether these immigrants could or might be engaged in subversive activities. The U.S. Navy's commandant of the Twelfth Naval District on the West Coast expressed his fears about the Japanese if there were to be a future conflict. In July 1922, he wrote to the Office of Naval Intelligence:

> Many people know of the race movement and place little importance to it, as they do other things that are going on in the world, such as the Mexican situation, the German-American situation, the Russian Bolshevik agitation and the negro movement. They place little importance on them, passing off the subject as greatly exaggerated. But all of these things are growing, and behind all is the Japanese hand playing the powerful yet silent note. So in the time of emergency, especially when Japan will play a role on the stage, these agitory elements all united will not be a thing that "amounts to nothing."[2]

This fear was directed specifically toward Japanese immigrants. On the West Coast, the ONI "had concerned itself with this danger [of the possibility of subversive activities] in the event of a war against Japan. The Navy was particularly uncomfortable about the Japanese who had settled on Bainbridge Island making them close neighbors to the Bremerton, Washington, Naval Base."[3]

By 1930, U.S. officials were aware that the war clouds gathering in Asia and Europe would affect this country. After monitoring the Japanese invasion and occupation of Manchuria in September 1931, these officials increased their vigilance over the resident Japanese. They compiled files on individuals, documented their daily activities, and listed the various organizations to which they belonged. These officials considered the Issei to be an extremely dangerous group, and some believed the earlier propaganda branding them an advance party of the Japanese force. Some in the State Department, for example, felt by 1934 that the Issei were ready to assist Japan in the eventual war between the two countries: "When war breaks out, the entire Japanese population on the west coast will rise and commit sabotage. They will endeavor by every means to neutralize the West Coast and render it defenseless."[4]

This statement, applicable to "the entire Japanese population," reveals an issue that later became significant to the Nikkei on the mainland in that it fails to distinguish Japanese nationals from their citizen children. The inability or refusal to make a distinction between the two groups was also part of President Franklin D. Roosevelt's prewar perspective. On August 10, 1936, Roosevelt wrote to the chief of naval operations: "One obvious thought occurs to me—that every Japanese citizen or non-citizen on the Island of Oahu who meets these Japanese ships [arriving in Hawaii] or has any connection with their officers or men should be secretly but definitely identified and his or her name placed on a special list of those who would be the first to be placed in a concentration camp in the event of trouble."[5] Again, the Nisei are seen as no different from the Issei. Roosevelt also offers a suggestion on how to treat both groups in a future conflict between the United States and Japan.

International events in the mid-1930s led to war in Europe and Asia. Adolf Hitler became the German chancellor in 1933 and threatened Germany's neighbors with menacing words and military power. On July 7, 1937, the Japanese military engaged Chinese troops at the Marco Polo Bridge near Beijing, thereby initiating the Sino-Japanese War. In 1938, Germany annexed Austria and took control of Czechoslovakia. On September 1, 1939, Germany invaded Poland, and two days later, Britain and France declared war on Germany.

Although President Roosevelt proclaimed the neutrality of the United States on September 5, 1939, he nevertheless began preparing for America's entrance into the European war. On September 8, he declared a limited national emergency and increased the strength of the armed forces. On December 29, 1940, he publicly recognized the military successes of Nazi Germany as a threat to the United States: "The Nazi masters of Germany have made it clear that they intend not only to dominate all life and thought in their own country, but also to enslave the whole of Europe and then to use the resources of Europe to dominate the rest of the world."[6]

Throughout 1940 and 1941, Roosevelt provided aid to countries that were at war with Nazi Germany. Among other measures, the Lend-Lease Act released surplus military supplies to Britain in exchange for the right of U.S. destroyers to access English bases in the Atlantic Ocean. Roosevelt also proclaimed an unlimited national emergency on May 27, 1941, allowing for the further strengthening of the country's overall defenses.[7] Other acts that followed in 1941 emphasized aid to those in Europe instead of to those in Asia.

INTERNMENT OF GERMAN AND ITALIAN SEAMEN

The declaration of war in Europe had an immediate impact on the United States. In mid-December 1939, crew members of the German ocean liner SS *Columbus* scuttled their ship in the Atlantic Ocean rather than allow a British warship to capture it. The USS *Tuscaloosa* rescued the 576 officers and crew members, including one woman, and brought them to the Port of New York on December 20. After hearings conducted by the Board of Special Inquiry, 513 were transferred for temporary detention to the Justice Department's Immigration and Naturalization Service. The INS then transported them to Angel Island, in San Francisco Bay, expecting to repatriate the group to Germany via Asia. England refused to grant the Germans safe conduct passes, however, and they stayed at Angel Island. When it became apparent that their return to Germany was impossible, the U.S. government looked for a more permanent location for them. The INS renovated a former Civilian Conservation Corps campsite at Fort Stanton, New Mexico. The camp's capacity was enlarged from 200 to 450 persons, and 411 of the seamen were placed there on March 17, 1941.[8]

The conditions of their captivity were quite relaxed because the United States and Germany—which were not yet at war—maintained formal diplomatic ties. Fort Stanton did not even have a fence, and the ship's captain and a few INS Border Patrol officers maintained discipline. Only after the United States entered World War II, when nine sailors escaped and were retrieved, did the INS construct a ten-foot-high lighted steel fence.

In addition to the German seamen, the United States interned 483 Italian seamen from the SS *Count Biancamano* at an army post at Fort Missoula, Montana, on May 9, 1941. More Italian seamen continued to arrive, and there were 1,133 in confinement by October 14, 1942.

U.S. INTELLIGENCE AGENCIES AND INTERNAL SECURITY

National concern about internal security in the United States began well before the war. During World War I, a few officers from the Secret Service, a division of the Treasury Department, sought to counter German spy activity. In June 1919, John Edgar Hoover, later director of the FBI within the Justice Department, started to look into "subversive" activities when Attorney General A. Mitchell

Palmer appointed him to head the newly established General Intelligence Division. The division's mission was to examine subversive activities in the United States, compile files on persons with suspect political beliefs and associations, and develop and recommend policies to control such activities. Its initial targets were anarchists, communists, and members of the Industrial Workers of the World, a labor union organized in 1905.

From the 1920s, the activities of the Japanese in America drew Hoover's attention. His interest stemmed from the F B I's investigation of the Universal Negro Improvement Association (U N I A) and its founder, Marcus Garvey. Hoover displayed an early animus toward black protesters and their link with the American Communist Party. In a 1920 report, he wrote: "The Communist Party will carry on among negro workers agitation to unite them with all class conscious workers." It was Hoover's belief that in communism, "we see the cause of much of the racial trouble in the United States at the present time."[9]

His second reason for investigating the U N I A was his apparent fear that interethnic contacts might result in a militant coalition of America's racial and ethnic groups. An F B I agent said of an October 9, 1920, telephone conversation with Garvey, "My chief reason for making this appointment [with Garvey] is to try to question him diplomatically as to whether any Japanese are behind his movement or lending him any support."[10] Garvey did have a few Japanese among his early supporters. The F B I heard its U N I A informant express positive views on the Japanese:

Japan is a mighty nation today and is the pride of all the colored races. In our [U N I A] Convention in New York a couple of years ago, there were two Japanese delegates and a few Japanese visitors. . . . You know how the Japanese, Chinese and Koreans are treated in California and in other states of the Union. How can they help themselves from being against the whites? As the Japanese are trying to do, as our Association will do when it expands, as I said—*all the colored races should unite together against the white man's rule or their attempts to rule.* You know at the present our Association seems to have something to do only with the Negroes, but it means to and will in time have something to do and something to say about all the colored races. "Down with the Whites!" is our aim.[11]

The two Japanese delegates mentioned in the quotation above were probably Satohata "Major" Takahashi and his chief aide, Ashima Takis. There is little information about Takahashi (also known as Naka Nakana) prior to his apparent illegal entry into the United States from Canada in 1930 or 1932. The F B I, according to Karl Evanzz, reported that Takahashi left the West Coast and embarked on a campaign to influence notable black nationalist leaders and their organizations into taking a pro-Japan stance.[12]

Takahashi came to the attention of the O N I through the actions of Takis, described as a "Japanese student at Johns Hopkins University, [who] has been lecturing or speaking in a manner to arouse the colored citizens of America against their government."[13] In actuality, Takis was Mimo de Guzman or Policarpio Manansalas, a Filipino who had served in the U.S. Navy until 1920.

Takahashi and Takis contributed money to various black leaders and thereby gained entry into black organizations, where they preached an anti-American, pro-Japan message. Elijah Muhammad, leader of the Nation of Islam, apparently delivered repeated sermons on the superiority of the Japanese people compared to the "white man" and the need for African Americans to follow their lead. Takis gave the clearest summation of the pair's appeal: "Negroes of the United States: You are the most oppressed people on Earth. If you will join the Japanese and other colored races, you will be in command of the whites. In case of war between the United States and Japan, you must divorce yourselves from the whites, the United States commanding bosses, and join the Japanese yellow race, your only friends."[14] These ideas fell on fertile ground with those who were unable to find work during the depression years.

Since the Nation of Islam and other Black Nationalist groups considered any nonwhite individual to be a black person, Takahashi apparently had no problem gaining access to the leaders and their organizations. Black Mohammedans such as the American Moorish Science Temple as well as Garvey and the UNIA later were outspoken in their sympathy for Japan at the outset of World War II.[15]

Thus, there is reason to believe that U.S. intelligence agencies discussed the need to gather information on the connections between Japan, the overseas Japanese, and other American racial and minority groups.

COUNTERINTELLIGENCE FOR GERMANY AND JAPAN

Until the 1930s, there was no governmental agency with overall responsibility for counterintelligence and other security matters.[16] Ironically, this situation changed because of a complaint lodged with the State Department by the German ambassador. In March 1933, an American identified as Daniel Stern reportedly threatened the life of Chancellor Adolf Hitler. The ambassador's complaint was referred to the FBI for investigation. Although "Stern" was never discovered, the report on the rise of fascist organizations in America worried President Roosevelt. On May 9, 1934, Roosevelt met with the attorney general, the FBI, the secretaries of labor and the treasury, and the Secret Service to discuss investigating these groups and their activities. Roosevelt instructed Hoover to get evidence on "Nazi groups, with particular reference to anti-racial activities and any anti-American activities having any possible connection with official representatives of the German Government in the United States."[17]

During the 1930s, Nazi agents tried to introduce a number of spies into the United States. As a result, the FBI, the ONI, the army's Military Intelligence

Division (MID), and the State Department all became involved in counterintelligence activity. The FBI neutralized a number of these espionage efforts by, in a few cases, disseminating false information.[18]

No evidence exists that any Issei or Nisei resident of the United States or its territories ever committed an act of espionage or sabotage on behalf of Japan. This is not to say, however, that Japan did not try to obtain information, overtly in most cases, when diplomats collected trade journals, magazines, and newspapers and sent them back to Japan. In the area of covert intelligence, Japan's efforts appear to have been minimal, especially after meetings held between Japan and Germany:

> At a series of secret meetings in 1935, Colonel Nicolai [appointed by Hitler to accelerate the creation of a Nazi spy network in the United States] made a formal offer to the Japanese to pool their espionage resources. He pointed out that only Caucasians could do effective spying in the United States, since Oriental agents would be more easily detected. The Japanese bought the proposal, and Hitler appointed Eugene Ott, who would later become German ambassador to Japan, to coordinate activities between the two nations' secret services.[19]

Japan sent very few agents to America, and those who came worked in conjunction with the German network. Since it was difficult for Japanese agents to obtain covert information personally, they applied their efforts toward buying the services of non-Japanese individuals.[20] For example, in 1934, Harry T. Thompson, who had been a navy yeoman, sold military information to a Japanese naval officer. Thompson was convicted of conspiracy to violate the Espionage Act on July 3, 1936. His handler was also indicted but quickly left the country after Thompson's arrest.[21]

All other espionage arrests and convictions involved agents from or acting on behalf of European Axis countries. From 1938 to 1945, the U.S. government convicted some ninety-one people for espionage: "Sixty-four of them were American citizens betraying their own country. The greater number worked for the Hitler government because of loyalty to Germany. A few others were mere adventurers. A few were recruited by threats of death or injury to loved ones held by the Nazis. A few became enemy agents because they saw a need to make easy money."[22] Other countries were also interested in conducting espionage activity in the United States. In 1938, for example, the U.S. government tried four German nationals for attempting to turn over American defense secrets to the Union of Soviet Socialist Republics.[23]

The United States had its own agents working to acquire information. It is alleged, for example, that amateur intelligence gatherers, including Ernest Hemingway and Charles Lindbergh, were involved in pre–World War II raw-data collection.[24] Another American's exploit has come into question: earlier sources reported that in 1934, Moe Berg, catcher for the Washington Senators, was asked by the State Department to take photos of industrial facilities and warships in Tokyo Bay. These pictures were smuggled out of Japan and were said to figure in General James H. Doolittle's raid on Tokyo in 1942.[25] A later source asserts, however, that Berg's photography assignment was not ordered by any American intelligence agency and that his pictures did not play a role in the famous raid.[26]

Unquestionably, all the warring nations used professional agents to gather intelligence information; that fact is not disputed. FBI files, however, reveal no evidence of overt spying by the Issei or their citizen children. Had there been such evidence, the Justice Department and the FBI would have created case files and brought charges, as they did for other individuals. The few intelligence agents sent by Japan to the United States and Hawaii in the 1930s came for this purpose and were representatives of the Japanese government. They constitute a different category from the immigrant Issei who came to America for personal reasons between the late 1800s and early 1900s. The only similarity happens to be their ethnoracial ancestry.

THE FBI AND DOMESTIC INTELLIGENCE

During the 1930s, the FBI entered fully into the domestic intelligence realm. On August 24, 1936, President Roosevelt called FBI director Hoover and asked for information about the activities of Communist, Nazi, and Fascist organizations in the United States. No mention was made of the Issei or Nisei or of their organizations. Hoover replied that no government agency was then compiling such information and, moreover, that mere membership in these groups was not a violation of law. He did suggest that the 1936 Appropriation Act (Chap. 405, Title II, 49 Stat. 1322, May 15, 1936) allowed the Justice Department to conduct investigations if the State Department so requested such action of the attorney general. President Roosevelt then met with Hoover and Secretary of State Cordell Hull; Hoover's subsequent memo claimed it was the FBI's responsibility to investigate organizations and persons suspected of engaging in "subversive" activities.[27]

Hoover established the General Intelligence Section in order to "collect through investigative activity and other contacts and to correlate for ready reference information dealing with various forms of activities of either a subversive or a so-called intelligence type." After this act, Hoover again created lists of "dangerous" nationals, citizens, and political groups. By 1938, the FBI had identified and indexed some 2,500 names of individuals "engaged in activities of Communism, Nazism, and various forms of foreign espionage,"[28] along with 250 cases of purported espionage. As tensions increased in Europe, the number of investigations also increased, and a year later, the FBI reported 651 such occurrences and 16 convictions.[29]

Beginning in 1938, the FBI increased its efforts to gather names for a "suspects" list, and in June 1940, Hoover formally established the Custodial Detention Program. The program's purpose was to compile and maintain an intelligence file on those "who may become potential enemies to our internal security."[30] This file of "dangerous" persons who might be arrested included dossiers and addresses.

In 1939, an interagency dispute arose over who had primary intelligence jurisdiction in this internal area. Before the FBI could gather background information on persons other than American citizens, it had to obtain "specific authorization" from the State Department.[31] Hoover worked to undermine this division of authority and to gain increasing control for the FBI, by, for instance, working with the army's MID and the navy's ONI to exchange information about subversive organizations. The State Department countered by questioning the growing prominence of the FBI in the counterintelligence area.[32] Army and navy intelligence agencies sided with the FBI, and Hoover sent a memorandum to President Roosevelt arguing for the centralization of investigatory work. Roosevelt also supported the FBI and, on June 26, sent a confidential memorandum to his cabinet giving responsibility to the FBI and the intelligence divisions of the War Department and the navy to establish the Interdepartmental Intelligence Coordinating Committee. This committee would investigate "matters involving actually or potentially any espionage, counterespionage or sabotage."[33]

As Lee Kennett points out, American citizens became an important focus of attention: "The [Federal] Bureau [of Investigation], like the ONI and G-2, fixed aliens and 'hyphenated-Americans' with ties to potentially hostile countries as the most likely candidates for surveillance."[34] The three agencies, along with representatives from the State and Treasury Departments, held weekly meetings after June 1939 to discuss the establishment of procedures and coordination of information.[35] In this way, the FBI won an early jurisdictional battle in the intelligence field: it increased its activities in this area, made no distinction between foreign nationals and American citizens, and sidestepped the necessity of obtaining State Department approval for conducting such surveillance in the continental United States.

As concerns over internal security increased, President Roosevelt made public this confidential arrangement and issued a directive on September 6, 1940, stating that the FBI was to take charge of all intelligence-related matters.[36] The FBI thus became the major federal agency in charge of internal intelligence matters at the national level.[37]

With war raging in Europe and Asia, Congress passed the National Alien Registration Act, part of the Smith Act (54 Stat. 670), in June 1940. Under it, all foreign nationals were to be fingerprinted, registered, and prevented from possessing "firearms, explosives, or radio transmitting apparatus."[38] It also became illegal under the Smith Act to be a member of an organization promoting the destruction of the U.S. government. The government developed a questionnaire for aliens that requested information on citizenship status, occupation, residence, biographical data, and organizational memberships.[39] When the registration ended, the United States had rosters and life histories for 4,921,452 foreign nationals. This list constituted a significant data source from which the government could create sublists of particular groups and individuals and their locations.

The F B I began targeting the Issei and their citizen children from the late 1930s. This group had aroused occasional interest earlier, but individuals suspected of being Nazis, Communists, or Fascists were the objects of more consuming attention. Members of the Japanese immigrant group itself were an important source of information, including some Issei and even the Nisei: "As Mike Masaoka put it, his [Nisei] organization [the Japanese American Citizens League] passed on 'facts or rumors relating to [various people's] ostensible business and sympathies, family relationships, and organization ties.'"[40] Others also assisted the F B I and the navy's O N I: "Tokutaro Slocum [national J A C L leader] for one, proudly identified himself as a zealous source of intelligence. Numerous federal and local officials have testified that the Nisei were cooperative about providing information."[41]

It would be unfair to think that all Japanese Americans who talked with agents were informants for intelligence agencies.[42] That some Nisei did give such information, as Slocum admitted, is indisputable. An unspecified number of Issei are also believed to have cooperated. A former internee thought that one innocuous bit of information mentioned to him by the F B I was known by only one Issei, who, he suspected, revealed it to the F B I because the internee had bested him in a Japanese community organization's election. This accusation cannot be substantiated, yet, five decades later, such perceptions persist.[43]

The F B I also was not above using heavy-handed tactics to gather information. On October 21, 1941, for example, twelve F B I agents conducted nighttime raids of the Los Angeles Japanese Chamber of Commerce and the Central Japanese Association offices and seized membership lists and "almost a truckful" of other materials. The *Los Angeles Times* reported that the F B I was investigating various Japanese individuals and organizations and had been doing so for many months. The F B I questioned the officers of these two organizations, but they affirmed their loyalty to their adopted country. Gongoro Nakamura, then president of the Central Japanese Association said, "The Federal agents did not seize any 'propaganda' when books and records were taken because 'we had none'. . . . Our people are 100 percent loyal to America."[44] Regardless of their claims of innocence, when the United States entered the war, Nakamura and all the interrogated officers were arrested.[45]

AGREEMENTS BETWEEN THE JUSTICE AND WAR DEPARTMENTS

Many of the agreements made by federal agencies regarding foreign nationals during World War II are similar to those of earlier periods, so it is worthwhile to briefly examine past actions.

The Justice and War Departments both participated in the detention and internment of foreign nationals during World War I. At that time, the Justice Department arrested selected enemy nationals on orders of the attorney general and kept them until a disposition was made on each case. If the decision was for internment, a U.S. marshal took the internee to the army post at Fort Oglethorpe, Georgia, or Fort Douglas, Utah. The Justice Department initially arrested more than 6,300 persons and interned 2,300 of them.[46] The approximately 4,000 other arrested and detained individuals were eventually paroled or released. The army's participation in this internment process may be somewhat puzzling, since federal penitentiaries and jails were available, but the individuals' status as foreign nationals of newly declared enemy countries justified military involvement. This change allowed the United States to consider these civilians to be prisoners of war and thus properly under military jurisdiction. The same rationale would hold for the similar situation that arose in World War II.

Between 1940 and 1941, the Justice Department held a series of meetings with the War Department to discuss foreign nationals and U.S. citizens. The purpose of these meetings was to delineate, in broad strokes, the responsibilities of the two agencies for controlling selected individuals after the United States entered the ongoing war. In effect, the Justice and War Departments carved out respective jurisdictional areas, a measure that increased their cooperative activities and lessened the chances of interference from other agencies.

From the beginning, the two departments did not agree on the possible number of eventual internees. On July 19, 1940, the FBI estimated that after a declaration of war, it would be necessary to intern a minimum of 18,500 persons at twenty-two sites. Neither the identities of individuals nor groups were specified.[47] This estimate apparently bothered the army. Although the War Department agreed to intern foreign nationals after their arrest by the Justice Department, the army was not prepared to hold so many people. Moreover, it declined at that time to provide holding sites for foreign nationals still under investigation, those convicted of committing crimes, and American citizens who were merely under suspicion. These individuals, the army argued, would not normally come under its jurisdiction. The army, then, did not decline to intern arrested American citizens as long as their final disposition was clear.

After additional meetings, an important agreement for interning foreign nationals emerged between April 16 and July 18, 1941. The agreement was divided into two sections: the first applied to the responsibilities of the Justice Department and the second specified the responsibilities of the War Department.

The Justice Department's Portion of the Agreement

The Justice Department's initial task was to prepare a proclamation for the president to sign "immediately upon the declaration of war or if and when an invasion or predatory incursion is perpetrated, attempted or threatened against the territory of the United States by any foreign nation or government . . . [and] the President makes a public proclamation of the event."[48] This last phrase would become especially important later.

Once the proclamation was signed, after war was declared between the United States and a foreign nation, "natives, citizens, denizens, or subjects of the hostile nation," fourteen years or older, could be "apprehended, restrained, secured, and removed as alien enemies." This proclamation is based on what is known as the Alien Enemies Act (Section 21, Title 50, of the United States Code, April 16, 1918). The 1918 act rested in turn on the Alien Enemies Act of July 6, 1798, the third of the 1798 Alien and Sedition Acts.

The Justice and War Departments agreed that enemy nationals would be forbidden to enter or remain in Alaska, the Canal Zone, the Hawaiian Islands, or Puerto Rico, except under regulations issued by the attorney general or respective military commanders. In the Canal Zone, the Hawaiian Islands, and the Philippine Islands, the appropriate military commanders could intern enemy nationals and restrict possession of items of possible military use such as firearms, ammunition, and shortwave radio sets.

In addition, upon recommendation of the regional U.S. attorney and information from the F B I or "other informatory sources" in the United States, Alaska, Puerto Rico, and the Virgin Islands, enemy foreign nationals were subject to arrest by the F B I, using presidential warrants. In the Canal Zone, the Hawaiian Islands, and the Philippines, military authorities were authorized to make the arrests.

In May 1941, the War Department considered the question of its own authority to arrest civilians other than a designated "enemy alien" in the three areas over which it had authority. The military reasoned that it could legally arrest them, based on the Alien Enemies Act.[49] We see then that prior to December 7, the War Department, although without making specific plans, did discuss with the Justice Department its interpretation of possible actions concerning the arrest and removal of persons outside the purview of the Alien Enemies Act. The Justice Department disagreed with this interpretation, asserting that a civilian could be a citizen or a foreign national and the military had no jurisdiction over the former category.[50] This matter was not resolved, and it left some unknowing U.S. citizens and other foreign nationals in an ambiguous position.

According to the agreement, the Justice Department's internment process would begin with the F B I arresting designated foreign nationals and sending the case files to the regional U.S. attorney. The U.S. attorney would then compile a report for the attorney general on all arrested foreign nationals and make recommendations for the disposition of their cases—internment, parole with or without bond, or unconditional or conditional release. The report was to contain any pre- and post-arrest data from the F B I or other sources and information obtained from the arrested national as to citizenship, immigration status, alien registration number, and any evidence of loyalty to the United States.

In addition, the Justice Department agreed to craft a questionnaire for the arrested nationals "designed to elicit detailed information about the life, activities and associations of each interned alien enemy. . . . The completion of this statement may be made a condition precedent to any application for review of the circumstances for which his internment has been ordered."[51]

The Justice Department was also to create hearing boards to advise on the disposition of those taken. A hearing board would meet with the arrestee and then make one of four recommendations to the attorney general: outright release, parole, a request for more information, or permanent internment. If internment was advised, the U.S. attorney would notify the U.S. marshal to deliver the foreign national to the army corps area commander. Except for women and minors, who would remain under the control of the INS, all arrested persons were to be under the authority of the War Department. If the recommendation was for parole or release, the Justice Department, through the U.S. attorney, would take primary responsibility for the individual upon release.[52]

Initially, the U.S. marshal was to provide detention facilities normally used for federal prisoners, but the INS became the agency responsible for holding the detainees before their hearings. If adequate facilities were not available for some reason, the army corps area commander would furnish detention facilities. If the action took place outside the contiguous United States and the decision mandated permanent internment, the army consented to ship those nationals to the mainland for internment.

The Justice Department was also responsible for creating a review board to study each individual's case after the initial arrest. The agreement specified that the foreign national could receive another review after the initial recommendation, if so desired. The Justice Department did not specify a deadline for this second review, and more than a year usually passed before any reassessment took place.

The Justice Department also agreed to establish a planning and coordinating committee for the War and State Departments. The committee was assigned to develop plans for the civilian authorities designated as responsible for arrested foreign nationals; persons originating from areas under military control were not included. These plans resulted in the Justice Department's Alien Enemy Control Program, which formally went into effect in late December 1941.

The War Department's Portion of the Agreement

The second part of the 1941 agreement dealt with the responsibilities of the War Department, which consented to accept and hold all nationals recommended for internment. Initially, the nine army corps areas were supposed to detain the internees for three to five months until three permanent internment camps could be constructed—one each in the Southeast, the central South, and the Southwest. The army was to provide additional temporary detention facilities when needed.

The plan called for the War Department to arrest and intern foreign nationals outside the contiguous United States—that is, those in Alaska, the Canal Zone, the Hawaiian Islands, the Philippine Islands, and Puerto Rico—for later transfer to the continental United States. In these particular areas, the military was to create two boards, a hearing board to recommend release, parole, or internment and a review board to assess the recommendation.

Robert P. Patterson, acting secretary of war, and Francis Biddle, acting attorney general, signed the two-part agreement in July 1941. It became the blueprint for the internment of foreign nationals designated as "alien enemies." This agreement, made months before the United States' entry into the ongoing war, shows that the later actions of these two federal departments were not taken in haste or fueled by wartime panic. An internment plan had been considered, discussed, and prepared; it formed the basis for later coordination and cooperation between these two agencies.

POSTAGREEMENT ACTIVITIES OF
THE JUSTICE AND WAR DEPARTMENTS

After settling on the basic plan, subunits of the Justice and War Departments created a joint committee to coordinate particular activities. At a meeting on October 9, 1941, committee members laid out a framework "relative to the delineation of the responsibility of each department for the custody of alien enemies arrested, detained or interned."[53] This group discussed the nuts and bolts of implementing the main agreement, deciding, for example, that the hearing board was to be composed of three members, one of whom would be from the INS.

The members of the joint committee then made recommendations to their superiors. For example, in November 1941, the War Department decided that the estimate of arrests for those of Japanese ancestry was too conservative: "Under Justice's present procedure, it is contemplated that only 958 Japs would be arrested in the west coast areas during the first twelve-months' period of hostilities and that no more than 50% of this number, or approximately 500, would be arrested during the first two-months period. . . . For the sake of complete safety however, I should assume that 1,000 Japs would be apprehended during the first thirty-day period." There is nothing in the memo to indicate how the army and the Justice Department arrived at their numbers and why the army disagreed. On the East Coast, after the Justice Department told the army that only 1,557 Japanese nationals resided in the most populous state, New York, the army estimated that no more than 250 of this group would be arrested.[54]

THE SPECIAL DEFENSE UNIT

An almost unknown unit within the Justice Department played a crucial role in the internment of foreign nationals. In 1939, after Germany invaded Poland, Justice

Department administrators considered forming a new section to study federal statutes on espionage, sabotage, and the Neutrality Act.[55] This new unit would act in an advisory capacity to aid and inform U.S. attorneys charged with the enforcement of these laws. The Justice Department established the unit, initially called the Neutrality Laws Unit, on May 15, 1940, and appointed Lawrence M. C. Smith as director. In the first year, the unit's name was changed to the Special Defense Unit, and it accepted responsibility for the "control of all prosecutive action growing out of violations or charges of violations of laws relating to neutrality, foreign enlistment, treason, sedition, espionage, sabotage or kindred offenses. . . . The Unit will not handle the prosecution of cases by itself, but is primarily for purposes of control of departmental policy and action in cases falling within those classifications."[56]

Statutes of interest included, for example, the 1939 Neutrality Act, which made it unlawful for American vessels to carry materials or passengers to any warring foreign state, and the 1917 Espionage Act, which focused on "espionage, disloyalty, conspiracy, vessels in port, injuring vessels, obstructing commerce, neutrality, seizure of arms, export embargoes, foreign relations, . . . counterfeiting seals, etc." Other statutes dealt with treason, sedition, foreign or hostile connections, the activities of nationals and anarchists, and even "noninterference with homing pigeons," which were used as carriers of information.[57]

Of particular relevance to foreign nationals was the Justice Department's directive to the FBI instructing the agency to turn over control of the Custodial Detention Program to the SDU in April 1941.[58] The SDU Investigation Section, composed initially of three attorneys, started to review and classify the FBI's custodial detention list. By August 1, the SDU had received some 10,000 names and files, and the FBI constantly added more files. This review section, now with a staff of sixty, concentrated on three main groups, in order of priority: Nazis, Communists, and a category made up of Italians, Japanese, and members of other fascist organizations. The SDU initially reviewed some 18,000 persons for their potential "dangerousness" to the security of the United States. The unit specifically looked into "methods of handling those individuals determined to be engaging in activities inimical to the United States."[59]

The FBI did not cease its intelligence-collection activities in this area and maintained its own custodial detention file. Although the agency probably passed on duplicate cards to the SDU, FBI agents in the field offices kept files on persons they viewed as suspect in their jurisdictional areas. And as we will see, when the time came to arrest these people, a number of them were not on the list finalized by the SDU.

The initial breadth and scope of the prewar enemy alien program was limited. During World War I, the United States apprehended 6,300 civilians, predominantly German nationals, plus 2,300 foreign seamen and interned 2,300 of them.[60] The SDU anticipated similar numbers for the upcoming war, since the alien and naturalized German populations in the United States—about 300,000—were similar to those of World War I.

On September 19, 1941, the S D U estimated arrests of about 7,200 Germans, of whom 2,400 would probably be interned and 4,800 paroled. For Italian nationals and naturalized citizens in the United States, the S D U assumed a population of 700,000 and estimated 8,400 arrests resulting in 2,800 interned and 5,600 paroled. For Japanese nationals, the S D U estimated a population of 100,000 and, based on the assumption that their "organization and their nationalism are not unlike those of the Germans," expected to arrest about 2,400 persons with 800 interned and 1,600 paroled.[61]

As discussed in chapter 6, the actual numbers of Issei and some Nisei who were arrested exceeded the S D U's estimate. Moreover, the origin of this aggregate 100,000 number is not reported. The 1940 census data, to which the Justice Department had access, reports 47,305 Issei in the contiguous United States. There were, however, 69,811 Nisei and a small number of Sansei, making for a total of 126,947 persons. Perhaps the count included both Issei and Nisei up to this point because government agencies failed to make distinctions between nationals and so-called hyphenated Americans.

THE S D U'S CLASSIFICATION SYSTEM

In order to determine the supposed dangerousness of an organization, and thus of its membership, the S D U established a three-tiered alphabetical classification of A, B, and C. Beginning on September 23, 1940, the S D U decided that simply being a member of an A-1 organization after January 1, 1940, "should be sufficient" to warrant classification as dangerous. An A-2 designation was given when "membership alone after January 1, 1940, must be accompanied by actual activities within the organization."[62] The B category, also divided into levels 1 and 2, was for organizations or individuals considered "less dangerous" than those labeled A, while C was used to denote the "least dangerous" organizations and individuals.[63]

The S D U Investigation Section had processed and assigned a "tentative dangerous classification" to 2,000 names by September 8, 1941. This section screened the F B I files to search out the "most serious prima facie case for preferential consideration and for priority of investigation."[64] Ten Nazi organizations were rated A-1, including the German American Bund, Friends of New Germany, and the American National Socialist League. The Communist Party, U.S.A., and the Young Communist League were also placed in this category, as were five fascist organizations, among them, the Circolo Mario Morgantini, the American Fascist Party, and the Black Shirts.

What is surprising is that the S D U included no Japanese organizations in the early classifications, either at this time or even into late 1941. Even though the F B I had names of German and Italian organizations, Gary Okihiro reports that

J. Edgar Hoover admitted in a June 18, 1940, meeting with the army's MID and navy's ONI that the FBI could not estimate the number of Japanese scheduled for internment in a "national emergency ... [because] no provision had been made in the Bureau's estimate for a war involving the Japanese."[65] Since its primary source of data derived from the FBI, the lack of Japanese names from the SDU is understandable. The first Japanese names given by the SDU came in a September 8, 1941, list of 210 people associated with the Japanese consul from the territory of Hawaii.[66] No other Japanese organization or individual name appears on the SDU's list until after the United States entered the war.

A-Category Japanese Groups

In February 1942, the SDU highlighted "suspect" Japanese organizations. Its roster begins with the A category, without the 1- and 2-level distinctions:

> The following Japanese organizations appear to be subject to the direct control of radical nationalist elements in the Japanese Army, Navy or government and therefore to possess a high degree of dangerousness. It is our view that an enemy alien who has been a member of any of these organizations *even without active participation in their activities* may for that reason alone be properly interned and should be interned in his particular case.[67]

The SDU listed twelve Japanese organizations or affiliations, including the Black Dragon Society (Kokuryu Kai), the Fatherland Society (Sokoku Kai), and the Japanese Overseas Convention of 1940.[68]

Before examining particular organizations, we should address the question of where the SDU obtained these names, since it was an evaluative unit, not a primarily information-gathering one. The striking similarity between the SDU's and the ONI's list of suspect Japanese organizations is not surprising. Because the navy was collecting information in Hawaii and on the West Coast years before the Justice Department issued its list, there is reason to believe that the ONI cooperated with the SDU in producing the roster. An FBI teletype from the San Francisco field office to headquarters on December 12, 1941, offers one piece of evidence. Five days after the attack on Pearl Harbor, an FBI agent wrote that the Military Conscription Association (Heimusha Kai), a B-category group, was "promoted and developed for the purpose of rendering aid to military forces of Japan. *A list of members as of nineteen thirty eight was obtained from ONI.*"[69] This teletype indicates that the ONI had a roster of at least one organization and its members dating from 1938. In July 1940, Hoover recognized the prominent role played by the ONI in tracking persons of Japanese ancestry and requested that it share its information with the FBI.[70]

Of the Japanese organizations on the A list, the Black Dragon Society is probably the one that epitomizes the essence of Japanese menace to the American public. According to the s D U, this group was dedicated to committing espionage and sabotage, disseminating propaganda, and recruiting agents in America. Its name alone evokes a sinister image befitting the anti-Japanese stereotypes popular in America from the early 1900s. A 1942 anti-Japanese book claimed that this organization had 7,200 members in subsidiary groups called the Comradeship League and the Military Servicemen's League, which "served as schools of espionage and sabotage." Proof of their illegal activities, the authors claimed, came after the attack on Pearl Harbor: "When the F B I agents made a series of raids on these Japanese communities [in California], they uncovered caches of guns, ammunition, explosives, maps, charts, highpower cameras, signaling devices, short-wave radios, and other equipment of spies and saboteurs."[71]

The authors failed to state that when the F B I and other federal agencies investigated the suspicious activities of the resident Japanese, not a single arrest was made for spying or espionage. Rather, in the instance mentioned, the F B I found that a Japanese American did indeed possess rifles and ammunition because he owned a hardware store; the items were part of a legitimate business endeavor. Furthermore, reported shore-to-submarine signaling was found to be Japanese farmers carrying lanterns to light their way to outhouses. As for the Black Dragon Society, I could find no evidence that resident Issei or Nisei members ever joined this organization for the purpose of acquiring skills in "espionage and sabotage." There is also little to indicate that it even existed as a viable organization. One source, however, states that the F B I reported Satohata Takahashi, mentioned earlier in this chapter, as having entered the United States to "promote the aims" of the Black Dragon Society, but his efforts centered around recruiting African American nationalists in the eastern United States for the imperialist Japanese cause.[72] Takahashi was from Japan, his ties were to the Japanese government, and the F B I carefully monitored his actions through the 1930s.

Another organization on the A list was the Fatherland Society, or Sokoku Kai. There is some doubt as to whether it, too, ever operated in the United States. No other information about the association is found in the government files. However, a Japanese magazine titled *Sokoku* was published before the war, and some Issei did subscribe to it. Since the names of the magazine and organization were similar, the s D U perhaps saw a subscription as evidence of membership in the organization; one Issei internee's wife offered this explanation for her husband's arrest. No interviewed Issei internee confirmed the existence of the organization in this country.

The Japanese Overseas Convention was held in Tokyo in 1940 to celebrate Japan's 2,600th anniversary as a nation. The Japanese government invited representative Japanese emigrants from various countries, and those invited from the United States were the leaders of their communities. The F B I and the O N I investigated any Issei attending the commemoration. Receiving an invitation was a singular honor for the Issei, since it meant recognition by the homeland of their achievements in the Japanese American community. The F B I believed, however, that any recipient of an invitation was going to contribute monetarily to Japan's wartime endeavors in Asia, which would constitute an anti-America position. The agency did not necessarily assume these people would commit espionage or sabotage, but an invitation to the event was sufficient reason for placement onto an A-level suspects list.

B- and C-Category Japanese Groups

The s D U saw the B-category organizations—considered "less dangerous" than those on the A list—as being "directly or indirectly" under the control of the Japanese government with the fundamental purpose of helping Japan in its war effort. If an Issei had been an officer or had participated in any of the organization's "significant" activities, then he or she would be a likely candidate for internment.

The s D U designated nine B-category organizations, including the Current Affairs Association (Jokyoku Iin Kai), the Great Fujii Theater (Nichibei Kogyo Kaisha) in Los Angeles, the Japanese Association of America, and the Military Conscription Association (Heimusha Kai).[73]

The C category contained organizations with some ties to the Japanese homeland. Examples were various Japanese groups doing business in America or cultural organizations such as judo clubs and Japanese flower-arranging associations.

German and Italian Organizations

When the s D U evaluated individual German and Italian nationals in 1942, it used "most dangerous" and "dangerous" designations rather than alphabetical categories. Officers and members participating in the "significant" activities of organizations would be arrested if there were no extenuating circumstances.

The s D U identified three German American organizations as most dangerous, for they were viewed as being under the control of the German government: the Association of German Nationals (Reichsdeutsche Vereinigung), the German-American Bund (Amerikadeutscher Volksbund) and its branches, and Friends of New Germany (Freunde von Neuen Deutschland). It placed four other organizations in the dangerous class because the evidence against them was less conclusive: the central organization (as opposed to the member organizations) of the German American National Alliance (Deutsche-Amerikanische Eiheitsfront), the German-American Vocational League (Deutsche-Amerikanische Berufsgemeinschaft), the Kyffhaeuser League (Kyffhaeuser Bund), and the Kyffhaeuser War Relief (Kyffhaeuser Kriegshilfswerk).

Of the Italian organizations, the s D U marked only one as most dangerous—the Federation of Italian War Veterans in the U.S.A., Inc.—composed of the Associazione Nazionale Combattenti Italiani and the Federazione degli Stati Uniti d'America. Three others were listed as dangerous with qualifications: the Dante Alighieri Society, Italian Black Shirts (Lictor Society), and Mario Morgantini Circle (Circolo Mario Morgantini).[74]

REVIEW OF THE CLASSIFICATION SYSTEM

In July 1943, or nineteen months after the United States entered the war, the Justice Department conducted an internal review of its classification system *as it applied to citizens*. It found the rating system to be without merit and concluded that the process used to classify the organizations ultimately harmed individuals. It also described the manner of assigning ranked designations as being based on "wholly inadequate evidence gathered and analyzed by persons suffering from serious misconceptions as to what evidence should be sought. . . . [It was based on] the use of patently unreliable hearsay and other varieties of dubious information."[75] Moreover, the report continued, the classification system attempted to "determine danger in vacuo," without specifying the nature, type, temporal, or theoretical definition of the danger. The memo then recommended that the "dangerous" classification be expunged for citizens on the custodial detention list.

The review recommendations probably did not include the enemy alien category because of the differences in status. That is, the arrest and internment of enemy nationals came under the authority of the Alien Enemies Act. Yet, there is little doubt that the same conclusion concerning the bases for the arrests for citizens could have been reached in regard to alien enemies.

INTRADEPARTMENTAL DISPUTES

Numerous instances of conflicts and turf wars among units responsible for civilian internees continued at all levels of the government throughout the war years. For instance, two months before the United States entered the war, the s d u sent a memorandum to the attorney general about the proposed alien enemies program. The s d u recognized the f b i as the primary agency responsible for apprehending designated enemy nationals but asserted that i n s agents or U.S. marshals might also make such arrests. Next, the s d u recommended that the i n s be the agency to detain foreign nationals after they were arrested. It suggested that the hearing boards that were to determine the final disposition of internees should consist of a U.S. attorney, a civilian, and an i n s inspector. If the hearing board recommended internment, the s d u proposed that the i n s be responsible for authorizing any later parole.[76]

The f b i was not pleased with these recommendations. It stated that the memorandum "appears to indicate that an effort is being made by or on behalf of the i n s to obtain for that Service complete control of the enemy alien program in the event of war. While it is not so stated, it is apparent that officials of the s d u and the INS must have conferred at length." The FBI opposed all the recommendations, since "it would have a decided effect on the Bureau's custodial detention program." The FBI argued against INS entry into the program, recommending instead that the Bureau of Prisons or local jails handle temporary detention, that the War Department furnish facilities for permanent internment, and that the federal probation system take charge of the parole process. Furthermore, the FBI argued, there was little justification for an INS presence on the hearing boards or for its participation in arresting designated persons. The latter duties, continued the FBI, should rest solely in the hands of the U.S. marshals as supplementary to FBI efforts.[77]

The Justice Department did not agree with all the FBI's recommendations but neither did it reject those of the SDU outright. Arrested enemy aliens were held mostly in INS-run immigration stations or detention camps, while others were held in local jails and even hotels prior to receiving their hearings. INS agents were not authorized to make arrests, and the composition of the hearing boards did not follow SDU suggestions. One can only speculate about the reasons, but in essence, many SDU recommendations did *not* agree with the accord that had been adopted earlier by the War and Justice Departments.

Once war was declared, the SDU's work was ostensibly finished. At that time, however, the unit's director argued that it should continue to evaluate suspect citizens and ethnic newspapers. The Justice Department renamed the unit the Special War Policies Unit and placed it in the department's newly formed War Division on May 19, 1942.[78]

OTHER JUSTICE DEPARTMENT UNITS

Besides the FBI and the SDU, three other Justice Department components were working in different areas of internal security before the country entered the war. The Criminal Division handled a few defense matters referred by other units. It did not play a large role in matters dealing with the internment of foreign nationals but instead limited itself to violations of criminal laws. A few staff members in the Justice Department's Trial Section also worked in the foreign nationals area, handling special prosecutions under particular defense laws.

Within the INS, some national defense matters arose over cases concerning internment, deportation, and denaturalization. INS control of foreign admissions and departures resulted in the maintenance of a large file from which information could be obtained to supplement the cases of those individuals on the "suspect" list.[79]

THE WAR AND NAVY DEPARTMENTS

The War Department's Military Intelligence Division and the Department of the Navy's Office of Naval Intelligence were also active in the prewar internment process. At least as early as October 1938, the War Department began to gather information on Japanese located on the West Coast. A classified memorandum from the San Francisco FBI office reported: "Colonel H. R. Oldfield in charge of Military Intelligence for the Ninth Corps Area [headquartered in San Francisco] confidentially related to [FBI] Agent J. H. Rice that he was compiling data reflecting the Japanese population and determining those areas where the majority of the Japanese reside in California. The purpose of this information is in case at a future date it might be necessary to establish concentration camps for Japanese in case of emergency."[80] Although the memo does not specify the particular nature of the investigation, two points are salient: first, the failure to differentiate between the Issei and the Nisei, and second, the use of the term "concentration camp." Both points indicate that the army's later actions against the Issei and Nisei on the West Coast were not necessarily the result of hysteria or pressure.

In another relevant memorandum, John L. Burling, chief of the Special Projects Section of the Alien Enemy Control Unit, testified in 1943 that the Nisei, and especially the Kibei, were more dangerous than the Issei:

In the United States there are approximately 125,000 Japanese of whom one-third were aliens and two-thirds citizens. . . . The loyalty or disposition of the Jap could not be determined with the speed and promptness that the military situation required. Even citizens of Japanese ancestry had never been assimilated. . . . Our inability to accurately judge the loyalty of these people must be emphasized. At first it was thought that Japanese aliens only would be excluded from certain military areas . . . but this was deemed to be insufficient for the reason that it affected only the alien Japanese and it was feared that the real danger might come from the Japanese citizen group, especially from approximately 10,000 of them who had received their education in Japan.[81]

These sentiments, this time from a Justice Department official, were in agreement with the West Coast military's views of the Nisei.

In addition, the commanding general of the Ninth Corps Area, located in San Francisco, and the commandant of the Thirteenth Naval District, headquartered in Seattle, established a joint army and navy local planning committee. This committee met in Seattle on October 31, 1940, to discuss the military's role in the event of large-scale internment.

By January 13, 1941, the War Department estimated that fewer than 15,000 foreign nationals would have to be moved and interned. The army's corps commanders would have primary responsibility for the temporary detention and internment of these nationals. The army then ordered each corps commander to prepare contingency plans for detaining such persons for about three months. On the Pacific coast, for example, the War Department ordered the Ninth Corps commanding general to prepare plans for the temporary custody of 4,000 people.[82]

The Ninth Corps commanding general responded on April 14 that his corps could detain foreign nationals at six army bases along the Pacific coast and in Utah. The general also included a construction budget asserting that "since a large number of aliens will probably be picked up immediately upon a declaration of war, it is recommended that authority and funds be made available for construction of camps as early as practicable."[83]

In its overall plan, the War Department specified the construction of a number of permanent internment sites "to establish one prisoner of war barracks in the Fourth Corps Area and two prisoner of war barracks in the Eighth Corps Area, each with the capacity of 6,000, to be constructed as required, for the permanent internment of alien enemies forwarded from the various corps areas."[84] Once the United States went into battle, the War Department altered these plans, since these estimates were overly conservative.

THE OFFICE OF NAVAL INTELLIGENCE

For decades, the Department of the Navy had been interested in the security of its installations on the West Coast and in the Pacific Ocean. As early as the 1920s, the ONI conducted sporadic intelligence gathering, for example, against Japan, to learn what the Japanese military was doing on various Pacific islands. It monitored Japanese radio messages and even stole papers from Japanese officials in the United States to see whether they were collecting America's military secrets.[85] Moreover, as we have seen, there was continual interest during that decade concerning the activities of persons of Japanese ancestry. The ONI was particularly interested in Japanese immigrants and their children on the West Coast, since the navy believed that many had purposely located themselves near naval bases: for example, in San Diego, Long Beach, and San Francisco, in California, and in Bremerton, in Washington. Nothing inimical to the interests of the United States was found in these investigations. In addition, as noted earlier, since at least 1938, the ONI had compiled a list of suspect organizations and their members.

In July 1940, the ONI assigned an officer with a unique capability to investigate the "Japanese situation" in the Southern California area. Lieutenant Commander Kenneth Duval Ringle was apparently one of only a few persons in the entire navy who was qualified in the Japanese language. A 1923 Annapolis graduate, Ringle in 1927 served a three-year special assignment in Tokyo during which he learned Japanese and became familiar with the culture. With seventy-five men under his new command, his area of responsibility stretched from Mexico to Sacramento and from the Pacific Ocean to Nevada. From his investigations, Ringle reported two significant observations: "First, the West Coast Japanese were . . . increasingly Americanized and, like most immigrant groups, believed intensely in the United States and its vision of a better life. Second, in spite of their eagerness to be identified as Americans and their record of industry and responsibility, the Japanese on the West Coast were continually subjected to every sort of discrimination—discrimination as brutal and mindless as anything the South ever inflicted on the Negro."[86] Ringle submitted his report and assessment of the loyalty of the Nikkei population to the Navy Department and Secretary of the Navy William Franklin Knox.

Lieutenant Commander Ringle's conclusion was clear: there was no reason to doubt the loyalty of almost all the resident Japanese nationals and their Nisei offspring. This conclusion was probably shaped in part by a burglary that he conducted—with the assistance of the navy, the FBI, and the local police—at the offices of the Japanese consulate in Los Angeles. The names of the authorizing official (or officials) and the exact date remain unknown, although the burglary probably occurred in March 1941, but as Ken Ringle, Lieutenant Commander Ringle's son, first quotes his father and then describes the incident:

> "We had police outside watching. We had the FBI. We even had our own safecracker. We checked him out of prison for the job." The actual break-in, he said, involved only a few men, one of whom guarded the elevator downstairs. They entered the consulate offices with skeleton keys and made their way to a safe in the back which they opened. . . . They removed and photographed everything in the safe, he said, then replaced each item as it had been. Then they left, undetected. The processed films, he said, yielded lists of agents, codes and contact points for Japan's entire West Cost spy network—a network headed by a Japanese naval officer named Itaru Tachibana.[87]

This burglary resulted in an important piece of information. A frequently raised issue concerns the Japanese government's view of its country's immigrants to America and those immigrants' citizen children. It would seem logical that Japan might target the Issei and Nisei as possible intelligence agents who might work on its behalf, but there is little evidence that such efforts occurred. The reason is simple. Ken Ringle reports that his father found "repeated evidence that Tachibana and other official agents of Imperial Japan looked upon most American Japanese—both resident aliens (issei) and American-born (nisei)—not as potential allies but as cultural traitors not to be trusted."[88] Ironically, neither Japan nor America trusted the Issei or their citizen children.[89]

THE ONI CLASSIFICATION SYSTEM

The ONI divided Japanese organizations into three categories: A, B, and Semi-Official and Subversive Japanese Firms in the United States.

The A list contained eighty-eight names of organizations. But on the ONI roster, each organization and its translated name were listed separately, while the s d u's list included the corresponding translated name under the name of the organization. For example, the o n i named and counted separately the Fatherland Society and the Sokoku Kai, while the s d u listed the society and its translated name as one organization.[90]

As stated earlier, there is a close correspondence between the s d u's and the o n i's lists; what is on one list is on the other. On both rosters, the Black Dragon Society is highlighted as the most dangerous Japanese organization. The o n i characterized its A-classed organizations as constituting "an actual threat" to the United States and recommended that all officers and members be given "serious consideration" before they were placed in positions of trust or responsibility.[91]

In the B category, 176 organizations are named, again with their translated titles treated as separate entities. The o n i maintained that these organizations were "potential threats to the national security" and that their officers and members should be "investigated" before being given a position of trust or responsibility with the government.[92] The Japanese Association was listed by the s d u with only four entries for the organization's regional headquarters. In contrast, the o n i specified each regional association along with its numerous local chapters as individual entries.

Those in the third category, Semi-Official and Subversive Japanese Firms in the United States, are described as organizations in which "all executive and key personnel in the Japanese firms listed herein may possibly be engaged in activities inimical to the interests of the United States. Such persons should be thoroughly investigated before admission to a position of confidence or trust in this country."[93] Included were steamship companies, banks with Japanese names, travel agencies, Japanese-language newspapers, and a few businesses with Japanese names.

The o n i acted as the navy's eyes on the West Coast and in Hawaii. Unfortunately for the Nikkei, Ringle's major conclusions do not appear to have had much influence on the secretary of the navy and other military officials.

THE MAGIC CABLES

American cryptoanalysts had successfully decoded one of the highest-level Japanese foreign office diplomatic codes by fall 1940. This project, named Magic, was so sensitive that only a handful of people in the U.S. government knew of its existence, and fewer still were privy to the information derived from it. The distribution of the information was limited to nine: the secretary of war, the army chief of staff, the director of military intelligence, the secretary of the navy, the chief of naval operations, the chief of the navy's war plans division, the director of naval operations, the secretary of state, and President Roosevelt.[94]

A few of these messages dealt with intelligence agents. Few Japanese names are mentioned: one is "Iwasaki," who "had been in touch with William Dudley Pelley, leader of the Silver Shirts, a fascist organization in the United States."[95] Iwasaki was apparently an agent sent by Japan who returned home prior to December 7; he was not a permanent resident Issei.

There is no indication among all the messages of any plan to organize sabotage activities. The messages emphasize the gathering of information from available sources such as publications and journals. Of the nineteen suspects convicted of committing acts of espionage in the United States in the years before and during World War II, none had a recognizably Japanese name.[96]

THE SPECIAL WAR PROBLEMS DIVISION

Although the State Department was not involved as directly as was the Justice Department in operating the World War II imprisonment camps, it nevertheless played an important role in the prewar and wartime processes. In World War I, the State Department assisted American citizens trapped in Europe through the Welfare and Whereabouts Section within the Consular Bureau. During World War II, this section was resurrected as the Special War Problems Division, also known as the Special Division, on September 1, 1939.[97]

As has been established, the State Department was interested in collecting intelligence in the pre–World War II period. By June 1940, although President Roosevelt gave the FBI primary responsibility for foreign intelligence in the Western Hemisphere, the State Department retained some authority for intelligence matters south of the border. Here, diplomats from Germany, Italy, and Japan and thousands of persons of Japanese ancestry, including citizens of South American countries whose parents or grandparents were from Japan, initially came under the administrative lens of the Special War Problems Division.

As soon as the United States was at war, the Special Division became actively involved in maintaining communications with enemy countries and in effecting the repatriation of American citizens trapped in those countries. A while later, the Special Division worked with designated protecting powers to look after enemy nationals who had been brought from Central and South American countries and interned in the Justice Department's camps. For the Japanese on the mainland, the Spanish government served as a protecting power; the Swedish government fulfilled this role for the Japanese in Hawaii, since Spain had no representative there. In addition, the Special Division arranged inspection tours of Justice Department and War Relocation Authority camps for the International Red Cross; these tours were deemed vital for the United States because they allowed for reciprocal inspections of camps in Axis countries that were holding American prisoners. Special Division personnel were ever mindful that the type of treatment meted out to German, Italian, and Japanese nationals in the United States could have consequences for Americans interned in Axis countries. For that reason, the Special Division tried to ensure decent and humane treatment for prisoners under its authority and urged other State Department units to do likewise.[98]

PRESIDENTIAL AIDE

President Roosevelt augmented investigations conducted by federal and military units by employing his own agents to assess the dangers posed by the Issei and Nisei. From February 1941, using secret State Department and, later, presidential emergency funds, John Franklin Carter created a network of agents for Roosevelt. Carter hired Curtis Burton Munson, a wealthy Chicago businessman, who had written earlier reports to the president, including "Investigation into German Interests of Anaconda and General Motors" and "Attitude of French-Canadians toward the European War."[99]

In late 1941, with a cover appointment as special representative of the U.S. Department of Agriculture, Munson's task was to look into the Japanese situation on the Pacific coast. He carried out the investigation with the cooperation of the FBI, the MID, and the ONI.[100] Munson submitted two reports to the president in October and November 1941 that assessed the dangers presented by Japanese agents and by Japanese immigrants and their citizen children. He wrote:

> There is no Japanese "problem" on the [West] Coast. There will be no armed uprising of Japanese. There will undoubtedly be some sabotage financed by Japan and executed largely by imported agents or agents already imported. There will be the odd case of fanatical sabotage by some Japanese "crackpot." . . . For the most part the local Japanese are loyal to the United States or, at worst, hope that by remaining quiet they can avoid concentration camps or irresponsible mobs. We do not believe that they would be at least any more disloyal than any other racial group in the United States with whom we are at war. . . . We do not suspect the local Japanese above anyone else or as much as the Communists or the Nazis.[101]

Munson's conclusions, given to President Roosevelt, were probably read by other top-level cabinet officers. As for the presence of actual or potential Japanese espionage agents, Munson states:

> In each Naval District [three on the West Coast] there are about 250 to 300 suspects *under surveillance.* It is easy to get on the suspect list, merely a speech in favor of Japan at some banquet being sufficient to land one there. The Intelligence Services are generous with the title of suspect and are taking no chances. Privately, they believe that only 50 or 60 in each district can be classed as really dangerous. The Japanese are hampered as saboteurs because of their easily recognized physical appearance. It will be hard for them to get near anything to blow it up if it is guarded. There is far more danger from Communists and people of the [Harry] Bridges [International Longshoreman Workers Union] type on the Coast than there is from Japanese. The Japanese here is almost exclusively a farmer, a fisherman or a small businessman. He has no entree to plants or intricate machinery.[102]

Munson's assertion that only fifty to sixty "really dangerous" Japanese resided in each of the three West Coast naval districts stands in sharp contrast to the thousands of Issei interned and the later mass incarceration of almost all West Coast Japanese Americans. Moreover, they were all under surveillance prior to December 7.

Munson summarized his findings thus: "Japan will commit some sabotage largely depending on imported Japanese as they are afraid of and do not trust the Nesei [sic]. There will be no wholehearted response from [the] Japanese in the United States." Then, after reporting on the sad state of unpreparedness evidenced by unprotected "dams, bridges, harbors, power stations, etc.," Munson stated, "The Japanese are loyal on the whole, but we are wide open to sabotage." He argued that until the situation was rectified, "I cannot unqualifiedly state that there is no danger from the Japanese living in the United States which otherwise I would be willing to state."[103]

Anyone writing reports for the government is virtually certain to hedge his or her bets. Unqualified statements are rare in intelligence reports, since the writers cannot foresee all possible outcomes. Nevertheless, Munson's report is overwhelmingly positive toward the Issei and Nisei on the West Coast.

The president and his cabinet thus had reports on the "Japanese situation" from a trained navy intelligence officer and a trusted civilian investigator months before war was declared. Both Ringle's and Munson's reports exonerated the majority of the Japanese American population of constituting a threat to national security. Yet, this had little effect in sparing them the onus of being labeled a suspect group. President Roosevelt made no such effort to keep watch on Americans of German and Italian ancestry. Greg Robinson argues convincingly that Roosevelt's anti-Japanese views from the early 1930s carried over to persons of Japanese ancestry in the United States and resulted in his making no distinction between the Issei and Nisei. For this reason, "during the prewar years the President consistently regarded Japanese Americans as adjuncts of Japan and therefore as potential enemies, despite their American birth or decades-long residence in the United States."[104]

CONCLUSION

By late 1941, the clouds of war had crossed both oceans and were hovering near the United States. Axis espionage agents sprouted up, but the United States was by then preparing for the upcoming storm. A few federal agencies had entered the scene and tested their powers. They engaged in interagency skirmishes while staking out their respective jurisdictional territories. The two largest departments involved in the internment process, the War and Justice Departments, agreed on a division of territory with regard to jurisdictional authority.

Various agencies compiled lists of organizations and individuals, which included names of suspect nationals of enemy countries, naturalized American citizens, and citizens born in the United States. Others attempted to uncover suspicious activities. As we have seen, written assessments and reports from other sources detailing the security situation before the attack on Pearl Harbor were sent to President Roosevelt or to members of his cabinet; these reports concluded that resident Japanese nationals and their citizen children were basically law-abiding, loyal Americans. Other agencies, however, continued to hold discussions and make preparations to intern "dangerous" persons once war was declared.

We see, then, that in the period before December 7, 1941, the procedures used later to imprison people on the basis of their ethnoracial ancestry and perceived dangerousness were coldly, rationally, and methodically prepared. Once war was declared, these plans needed only to be implemented.

3

The Internment Process
of the Justice and War Departments

No one knew when the United States would enter the war, but many in the government believed the country was inevitably going to join in the fighting. By 1940, even though the administration of President Franklin D. Roosevelt had begun to aid its potential European allies, full-scale assistance efforts were constrained by the nation's isolationist sentiments.[1] No one could foresee the particular events that might effect a change of heart among those Americans who opposed American involvement in the war. The attack on Pearl Harbor, and arguably President Roosevelt's oratory and charisma, proved sufficient for that reversal.

The previous chapter described the process by which the United States identified individuals and organizations for removal when the country finally entered the hostilities. Since different groups of foreign nationals on the mainland were arrested and removed from various locations and by an assortment of agencies, the following schematic overview may be of help to the reader. Figure 3.1 outlines the process by which the Justice and the War Department interned designated enemy aliens.

Briefly put, the Federal Bureau of Investigation delivered those arrested to the Justice Department's Immigration and Naturalization Service, which acted as the custodial agency, except in territorial areas controlled by the military. The INS usually kept the internees in temporary facilities, sometimes called "detention stations," until there were sufficient numbers assembled to transfer to detention camps. Immigration stations such as the ones in Seattle and San Francisco served as initial temporary facilities. Depending on the situation and locale, however, the INS also used city and county jails, hotels—such as the Hotel Franklin in Little Rock, Arkansas, and the Jung Hotel in New Orleans—and even places like the Up and Up Cafe in Havre, Montana. The INS transported internees with physical illnesses to hospitals and those few already in federal facilities to places such as the federal penitentiary at Leavenworth, Kansas.[2] At the detention camp, Issei internees were given a hearing, after which they were released, paroled, or kept for permanent internment. The army operated the initial internment camps; later, the internees were returned to the Department of Justice, which retained authority

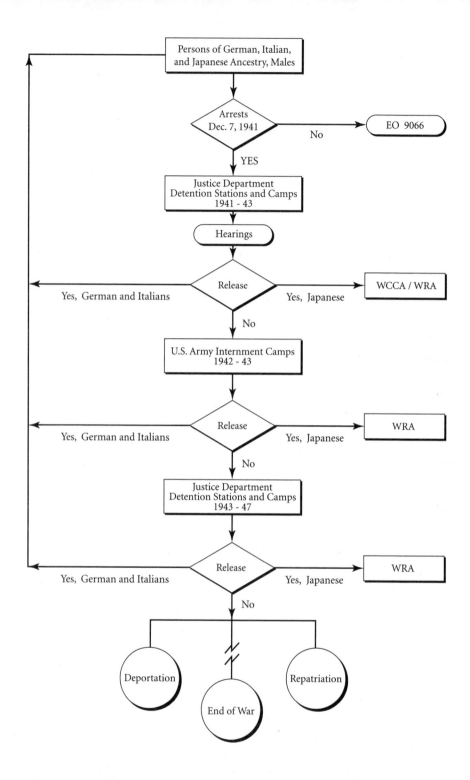

FIG. 3.1. Arrested German, Italian, and Japanese Male Nationals after December 7, 1941

over them until they were released, repatriated, deported, or expatriated (for some Nisei), or held until the war ended.

This chapter highlights the imprisonment process that followed the attack on Pearl Harbor; that is, it covers the stages of arrest, detention, hearing, and transfer to an internment camp. My emphasis here is on the institutional features of the early internment process as the imprisonment organization undertook its preplanned actions. In addition, we will learn about the difficulties experienced by the Issei in dealing with the Justice Department hearings and by some Nisei who were caught in the imprisonment web.

Let us start with one person's experience. On December 7, 1941, just after sundown, Saburo Muraoka of Chula Vista, California, which is about ten miles south of San Diego, had finished Sunday dinner with his family when there was a knock at the front door. His visitors entered, said they were from the FBI, showed their badges, and told him he was under arrest. They offered no reason nor did they show him any warrant. Perusal of the FBI files on Muraoka now reveal that they could not have presented a warrant for his arrest because he had not yet been given a classification and was not on the FBI's custodial detention list.[3] Muraoka, however, had no way of knowing this at the time.

Although Muraoka had heard radio reports of the Japanese navy's attack on the U.S. military bases and fleet in Hawaii, he and his family had no idea that the incident would affect them in any way. He thought the attack would bring America into the war in Asia and Europe, but since he was a permanent resident and his wife and their children were American citizens, he saw no reason to be concerned about events that had happened half an ocean away.

The FBI agents took Muraoka with them and deposited him in the San Diego County Jail. The local police put him in a cell with other Issei and kept them there for thirteen days. Muraoka was a law-abiding person, had lived in the United States for twenty-five years, and had worked as a truck farmer for most of that time. He could not fathom the reason for his arrest, and his attempts to obtain answers proved futile. No official came to talk to any of the Issei.

The prisoners faced difficult conditions at this jail. The police placed Muraoka and the others in cells without cots, blankets, or pillows and forced them to sleep on the bare floor. After nearly two weeks of this treatment, they were put on a train for Los Angeles. More Issei boarded there, and the train proceeded to Missoula, Montana, where the INS had a detention camp. For the next three years, Muraoka and others were shifted from one center to another. After leaving San Diego, he had no opportunity to see his wife and family. When the Justice Department finally released him in 1945, he was reunited with his family, but in another barbed-wire enclosure. By this time, they, too, were imprisoned, by the War Relocation Authority. In Muraoka's mind, these problems reflected the attitude of American officials toward the Issei.

Muraoka's background is significant because it is similar to that of many Issei who were *not* arrested by the Justice Department. There were no unusual events in his history. He was born in Yokohama, emigrated to the United States in November 1916, and settled in Chula Vista, where he worked as a vegetable farmer. He became a leader in the Japanese community, a member of the Japanese Association (Nihonjinkai), the local Buddhist temple, and the Chula Vista Celery Growers Association, a group composed mostly of Japanese farmers. On the day of his arrest, his celery crop was unharvested, and all the subsequent work was left to his wife, Haruko, and their young children. She visited her husband in jail a few times before he was taken away, and their conversations centered on the family, the disposition of the vegetable crop, and a new house nearing completion. Haruko worked to keep the farm going despite her husband's uncertain status, but she and her children were soon faced with forcible exclusion. Several Caucasian celery buyers offered ridiculously low prices for the ripening crop. Finally, not knowing what the future held for herself and her family, she sold the unharvested produce at a price well below market value.

Family and friends tried to obtain Muraoka's release, but their efforts proved futile. Attempts to learn the reasons for the men's imprisonment were also unproductive. Muraoka believes now that the FBI received his name, along with others from the Celery Growers Association, from another Issei member of the association. He also believes that this informant provided the FBI with false and derogatory information about him. Muraoka was never told the identity of this informant, nor was he allowed to refute any of the information presented at his hearing.[4] Although he might have dismissed it as irrelevant, his membership in the Japanese Association could have been a factor. The Japanese Association was listed as a B-category security risk by the Justice Department's Special Defense Unit. Muraoka stated that he was never told the reason for either his arrest or his continued internment, and he was never charged with the commission of a crime.

As other Issei fathers were arrested by the Justice Department, Muraoka's anxiety about his wife and children and their uncertain future was multiplied many times over. These men had done nothing to harm their adopted country, yet their collective feeling of innocence could not protect them from the government's desire to keep "dangerous" persons such as themselves out of the way.

EVENTS OF DECEMBER 7, 1941

The Japanese attack on the U.S. naval fleet at Pearl Harbor and the army's air bases on Oahu lasted from 7:55 to 9:45 A.M. Hawaii standard time. At 4:00 P.M. Eastern time, Japanese Imperial Headquarters declared a state of war with the United States and the British Empire.[5] U.S. Attorney General Francis Biddle was in Detroit when he first heard of the attack, and although he quickly returned to Washington, D.C., he did not meet with President Roosevelt at an emergency cabinet session until 8:30 P.M. The president then consulted with congressional leaders at 9:45 the same evening.

Within hours of the attack, however, the FBI sent the following telegram to all FBI offices: "Urgent. Immediately take into custody all Japanese who have been classified in the A, B, and C categories in material previously transmitted to you. Take immediate action and advise Bureau frequently by Teletype as to exact identity of persons arrested. . . . [signed] Hoover."[6] Using this telegram as authorization, FBI agents began arresting all persons of Japanese ancestry on the lists, regardless of their custodial detention classifications, and delivered them to the INS.[7]

In retrospect, FBI director John Edgar Hoover took a seemingly prescient action two days before the attack when he alerted his agents to prepare for "the immediate apprehension of Japanese aliens in your district who have been recommended for custodial detention."[8] Prescience, however, is not the reason behind the timing of this telegram. Hoover and other agency heads had earlier received messages that, if read correctly, predicted the place and almost the exact date of the attack.[9] On November 27, 1941, the army chief of staff and the chief of naval operations warned their military commanders in Hawaii that "Japanese future action [is] unpredictable but hostile action possible at any moment. . . . You are directed to undertake such reconnaissance and other measures as you deem necessary . . . an aggressive move by Japan is expected within the next few days."[10] Hoover's message alerting his agents to the possibility of apprehending those Japanese on the custodial detention list appears to be a reasonable precautionary measure rather than an indication that he had foreknowledge of the attack.

Even while the attack was still in progress at Pearl Harbor, the U.S. Army wired the four commanding generals and the nine corps commanders to work with the FBI to "round up" all persons on their detention lists:

Japan opened hostilities in Hawaii at eight o'clock Hawaiian time by air attack apparently from carrier involving approximately fifty Japanese planes period *attack still in progress* period hangars at Hickam Field and Wheeler field are in flames and Japanese planes reported as machine gunning over Hickam Field period . . . in cooperation with F.B.I. round up all suspicious characters on your lists period.[11]

If the air attack started at 7:55 A.M. and continued until 9:45 A.M. Hawaii time, the time in Washington, D.C., would have been 12:55 to 2:45 P.M. Presidential press secretary Stephan T. Early did not officially announce the attack to the three major press associations until 2:22 P.M.

By the end of the day, the FBI had arrested and detained 736 mainland Japanese nationals and some German and Italian nationals as well. The primary responsibility for coordinating these arrests within a given jurisdiction rested officially with the regional U.S. attorney for that district.[12] The U.S. attorney, the FBI, and the INS were all under the authority of the Justice Department, however, and they usually achieved a coordinated effort.

The specific timing of these arrests is important to our understanding of the imprisonment procedure: the arrests began before the United States proclaimed itself at war or specified with which country it was at war. Without a declaration of war approved by Congress, and without a formal proclamation by the president, the legitimacy of these early arrests is in serious doubt.

In fact, the numerous arrests carried out under Justice Department authority took place without any warrants at all. As Attorney General Biddle stated: "But on that Sunday night [December 7] Hoover was authorized [by the Justice Department] to pick up several hundred without warrants, and this procedure was followed for a short time until the more dangerous had been apprehended."[13] Biddle fails to mention any contact on December 7 between the Justice Department and the president, at which time Roosevelt could have signed the authorization for these arrests. For example, at 6:25 P.M., only after thirteen Issei and two Nisei had been taken into custody, did the San Diego field agent forward custodial detention cards to the FBI headquarters in Washington, D.C. The government officially arrested at least thirty-one Nisei on the West Coast throughout the war years. On many other reported occasions as well, Issei were not shown any authorization for their arrests.[14]

INITIAL SEARCHES AND ARRESTS

The Justice Department also conducted searches and seizures in homes or other places frequented by supposedly suspicious individuals. The department argued that once an individual was arrested, his or her premises could be searched for prohibited articles, even though the arrest was based solely on an administrative warrant from the Justice Department. However, standard procedure requires a Special Warrant for the Apprehension of an Alien Enemy and Seizure of Prohibited Articles before the Justice Department may enter premises and search for or seize items contained therein.[15] Yet, such legal safeguards were not applied, according to some eyewitness accounts. Various reports describe the flavor of the incidents. One such case occurred in Loomis, Placer County, California:

> December 7 was quite a shock . . . while we were eating, a car pulled up and people got out and identified themselves as being from the FBI. They started talking to us and my father. Then we went into the house. And that's when one of the most amazing things happened: a person who had never been in our house before knew just where to go to look for things. He pulled out correspondence that my father had from Japan. Some old papers from way back, twenty, thirty years before. So, he gathered some things up and he said, "You come with me," and he took my father. My fa-

ther never had a chance to pack his clothing, or his suitcase, or anything. He went in the car, and that's the last we saw of him until he joined the family in Tule Lake.[16]

Later, after the formal declaration of war, the F B I continued to make hundreds of arrests without legitimating warrants.[17] The agents entered Issei's homes, initiated physical searches, and took the individuals into custody, without offering any reason or justification for their actions.

On the East Coast, due to the different demographics, the F B I apprehended fewer Japanese and more German and Italian nationals. The Japanese arrested in New York found themselves at Ellis Island. As one Issei reported:

> Shortly before midnight on December 7, 1941, F B I, led by local detectives, took me to the local police station. There were a dozen or more Japanese gathered there, and the F B I took us to the Federal Court at Foley Square in his Buick limousine. We were arraigned, fingerprinted, and photographed with a number hanging from our neck. I was one of the first 20 Japanese who were shipped to Ellis Island on a small government boat. . . . At Ellis Island, I felt the food was adequate, rooms were comfortably heated, but the living conditions were overcrowded. Hundreds of bunks of Army/Navy type were squeezed into an immensely large hall where 150 to 200 people were confined.[18]

He returned later to Manhattan for his appearance before a Justice Department hearing board.

PRESIDENTIAL PROCLAMATIONS AND A DECLARATION OF WAR

President Roosevelt asked Congress for a declaration of war with Japan on December 8, 1941, and then signed Public Proclamation 2525, predated to December 7. This proclamation invoked the Alien Enemies Act of 1798 (codified as Section 21, Title 50, of the United States Code, April 16, 1918). As explained previously, this act states that, upon a declaration of war or when a "predatory incursion is perpetrated or attempted or threatened" and "the President makes a public proclamation of the event, all natives, citizens, denizens, or subjects of the hostile national or government [fourteen years and older], who shall be within the United States and not actually naturalized, shall be liable to be apprehended, restrained, secured and removed as alien enemies."[19] Various words are key in this section. A threatened rather than an actual incursion is enough to trigger the act. However, the stipulation that the president publicly proclaim the event becomes vital. In other words, an attack need not occur as long as the president makes a public statement that such an incursion is possible; this alone is sufficient to invoke the Alien Enemies Act.

In Proclamation 2525, President Roosevelt announced that "an invasion had been perpetrated upon the territory of the United States by the Empire of Japan." Therefore, nationals of Japan were designated "enemy aliens" and became subject to appropriate regulations. The later proclamations, 2526 for German nationals and 2527 for Italian nationals, both dated December 8, 1941, gave the identical rationale—that "an invasion or predatory incursion is threatened upon the territory of the United States" by Germany and Italy.[20]

The significant questions regarding the different reports concern the dates and the persons who obtained this authorization from the president. Norman M. Littell, assistant attorney general at the time, gives credit to U.S. Solicitor General Charles Fahy: "Charlie, himself, was called on the telephone on Sunday, December 7th by President Roosevelt, in the absence of Attorney General Biddle, to discuss the apprehension of enemy aliens who had been investigated by the FBI. Plans were ready, proclamations were ready, and the FBI was ready. Charlie took the proclamation, 2525, and the necessary orders to the White House."[21] Littell wrote this diary entry after talking with Fahy on March 26, 1942; however, he does not specify whether Roosevelt signed the proclamation on that day or that night, or at a later date.

Another source indicates Edward J. Ennis, later director of the Alien Enemy Control (AEC) Unit, as the responsible person: "Ennis had been working on these internment plans when he received word of the Pearl Harbor attack. Quickly drafting an emergency proclamation that authorized the 'summary apprehension' of any Japanese alien by the Justice Department, Ennis rushed this document to the White House. President Roosevelt signed the proclamation that evening."[22] However, Ennis's superior, Attorney General Francis B. Biddle, does not seem to confirm this action.

Biddle stated that Proclamation 2525 was signed by President Roosevelt on December 8: "That afternoon, I took the proclamation authorizing the Attorney General to intern Japanese enemy aliens to the President to sign. Most of the first group scheduled for detention had already been arrested." And exactly who made up this first group? People whose names appeared on the custodial detention list were certainly included, but various American citizens were taken as well. Then, Biddle continued, "Three days later Germany and Italy declared war against us; and again I brought appropriate proclamations [Proclamations 2526 and 2527] to the White House."[23] That would make December 11 the date of the second and third proclamations.

On December 8, Biddle directed FBI director Hoover to arrest German and Italian nationals and deliver them to the INS. Hoover stated that "there were over 1,200 [persons of German ancestry] yet to be classified and that some of these were citizens. I advised [Assistant Attorney General Francis M.] Shea that last night we arrested those persons on the list he had sent us who we thought were aliens; that we may have arrested a few citizens along with the rest."[24] The FBI arrested 497 German and 83 Italian nationals on December 9.[25] By December 10, the INS reported a total of 1,291 Japanese nationals in custody, including 367 taken in Hawaii; 857 Germans and 147 Italians were also being held.[26] The F B I continued to search West Coast homes from December 10, 1941, through February 15, 1942, arresting individuals on the basis of tips or allegations that they were members of subversive or dangerous organizations. The number of arrests increased and by November 1942 included 5,534 persons of Japanese ancestry, 4,769 of German, and 2,262 of Italian.[27]

In early June 1942, the United States declared war against Bulgaria, Romania, and Hungary. It then placed foreign nationals from these countries in the category of enemy aliens.[28]

ADMINISTRATIVE VERSUS PRESIDENTIAL WARRANTS

The date and time of the signing of Proclamation 2525 are important. One could argue that, to be legal, the arrests of the Issei should have occurred on December 8, after the president made the requisite public proclamation of a declared war, invasion, or perpetrated, attempted, or threatened predatory incursion. Roosevelt's famous "Day of Infamy" speech was such a public proclamation, and he then asked Congress to pass a declaration of war between Japan and the United States. Roosevelt signed the declaration of war at 4:10 P.M.[29] Action taken on behalf of a presidential warrant without a public proclamation and the necessary authorization could be considered questionable. Yet, Hoover telegraphed his field agents on December 7 to start making arrests, especially of the Issei but also of some German and Italian nationals. The military as well ordered the arrest of all "suspicious characters" even while the bombs were falling on Pearl Harbor. However, according to Biddle, Proclamations 2526 and 2527, which authorized the arrests of German and Italian aliens, were not signed until December 11.

Hoover probably would not have initiated the arrest procedures without some authorization. One supposition is that he went to Ennis, soon to become the director of the Justice Department's A E C Unit, to obtain permission. Ennis was interviewed in 1985 concerning his role in obtaining President Roosevelt's authorization and the date and time of that meeting. He did not take credit for obtaining, nor did he address the issue of who obtained, Roosevelt's signature authorizing the arrest of the Japanese nationals. His basic justification was that he saw no distinction between an administrative and a presidential warrant:

> Isn't this just nomenclature? They were all presidential warrants because the whole enemy alien program is triggered under the statute by a proclamation of the President that an enemy alien control is going under effect. But it was never suggested that the warrants be anything other than an authorization from an official in the Department of Justice. We wouldn't let the F B I, an investigative unit, have the authorization. We try to keep a line between an investigative unit and a decisional unit. The F B I was not entitled to pick up anybody unless they had their name and a warrant

for it. But the distinction between presidential and administrative warrants, I think is meaningless. I think the only distinction that means anything is between a judicial warrant, under the constitution signed by a judge, and an administrative warrant of the executive department under a proclamation of the President setting up the program under which a warrant can be issued in the name of the President or the name of the attorney general or under the name of any executive department official authorized by the chain of command to issue such a warrant.[30]

Ennis appears to argue here that since the Justice Department is part of the executive branch of government, the president is responsible for, and sanctions, all its actions. Any warrant except a judicial warrant could be considered a type of presidential warrant.

Yet, the Alien Enemies Act can only be invoked after the president makes a public proclamation. Any act, belligerent or not, against the United States must be recognized as such, and the only person authorized to do this is the president. Assuming that President Roosevelt actually signed Presidential Proclamation 2525 on December 8 and then predated it to December 7, hundreds of people were arrested without warrants or under administrative warrants of questionable authority.

The arrests of German and Italian resident nationals on and just after December 7 occurred under similar conditions. There appears to be little to justify the arrests made on December 7, either by Justice Department officials or the military, since the proclamations authorizing the invocation of the Alien Enemies Act against German and Italian nationals were dated December 8. Moreover, such nationals taken into custody in the three subsequent days might have been victims of questionable arrest procedures, since the proclamations were not actually signed until December 11.

Kept administratively separate from the INS, the Justice Department's Alien Enemy Control Unit became the agency responsible for handling the arrested persons. This unit also oversaw the Alien Enemy Hearing Boards and the Alien Enemy Parole Division; it remained in existence until 1946. Edward Ennis, director of the unit, was formally appointed on December 22, 1941.[31] He stated, however, that the Justice Department's program went into effect on December 7: "You must understand that in time of war, you might argue that there wasn't any declared war with Japan until December 8th or 9th whenever it was declared, but of course there was war from the moment of attack, the country was at war."[32] For Ennis then, a predatory incursion was equivalent to a declaration of war; however, the Constitution states that the authority to declare war resides with the Congress.

PUBLIC OPINION AND PUBLIC FEARS

The military used national security and military necessity as the basic arguments for the imprisonment of enemy foreign nationals and their children. In addition, the various agencies involved enunciated the following two justifications: to appease public opinion and assuage public fears.

In the 1985 interview, Ennis talked about his personal views on the internment episode and maintained that Attorney General Biddle had also taken this perspective. Ennis claimed that both he and Biddle were reluctant to pursue the internment policy but justified their actions on the basis of what he felt was prevailing public sentiment. He asserted that some measures had to be taken against the Japanese and Germans in America. The rationale for the arrests and internment is a significant part of his statement—not such earlier claims as the individual's alleged dangerousness or the prevention of espionage and sabotage, but rather public relations:

> You see, you must understand that Attorney General Biddle and I didn't feel that either the Germans or the Japanese who had been living in this country very long were very strong supporters of these foreign governments in wartime. But you know, a security program is partly a public relations program. You can't just get on the TV and say "Look, you don't have to do anything about anybody, everything here is fine and you just fight the war in Japan and against the Germans in Europe. Everything here is fine and you don't have to worry about any kind of espionage and sabotage." That won't go down. You have to have a program. And so, what you do if you are a liberal like Biddle and I, you make the program as light as you can. You don't get tough with them. And that is part of it, part of it is a public relations business.

After implementing this program, the Justice Department could assure concerned Americans that it had interned some dangerous persons and hope that everyone would feel more secure. In addition, Ennis explained in the same interview, the action was necessary to assuage public fears:

> Oh, my view and I suppose not many people would hold it, is that public relations in a time when the general population is very upset because of an actual war and what they conceive as threats to their lives, that dealing with the persons in the community of enemy nationalities is substantially a public relations matter and something has to be done with them. . . . Sure all security steps have a public relations aspect to it. And it is arguable how big the public relations aspect is and how real the security problem is. . . . I would say that, done at the time it was, at the beginning of the war, with the fear that had been aroused by the Japanese attack and the success of the first months of the Japanese war in the east, that it was about as minimal a program as the public would stand. If I were doing it all over again, I don't think I could've made a lesser program. I couldn't have just said, "Don't worry about the aliens of Japanese nationality, they are not interested in hurting the country they live in." I couldn't have gotten the public to buy that.

Ennis is not the only official who justified his actions on these grounds. In a May 1942 memo, one army general stressed the relationship between public opinion and the detention of foreign nationals. He argued for a higher priority for materials needed to construct the army's internment camps: "Existing [internment] facilities will be most inadequate in the event of an emergency. In this connection, particular attention is invited to the relationship between public opinion and the number of enemy aliens ordered interned. Public opinion would force the internment of a large number of persons in the event of invasion, organized sabotage, or some similar incident."[33] The actual number of saboteurs was not the issue. The general was concerned about the need to intern people before an emergency might inflame public opinion.

DIFFERING VIEWS ON FOREIGN NATIONALS

One of my assertions is that there were differing degrees of animosity toward the people from the three major enemy groups and that this difference affected the general tenor of the treatment they received. President Roosevelt, for example, is on record as holding such multiple views. As Attorney General Biddle brought Proclamations 2526 and 2527, which related to German and Italian aliens, to President Roosevelt for his signature, he recalls the conversation: "'How many Germans are there in the country,' [the President] asked. 'Oh, about 600,000,' I told him. 'And you're going to intern all of them?' he said. . . . 'Well, not quite all,' I answered. 'I don't care so much about the Italians,' he continued. 'They are a lot of opera singers, but the Germans are different, they might be dangerous.'"[34]

Ennis did not expect a public outcry about the far fewer number of Italian nationals interned compared to the Japanese and Germans, regardless of population. As he related:

> Well, you can tell by the fact that how few Italians were devoted to the Il Duche [Benito Mussolini], how few of them we interned. The public didn't require us to do more than that. The public understood the Italians. But don't forget the Italians were able to be naturalized and [were] not cut off from the political life. We couldn't deal like we dealt with the Japanese by race; we couldn't deal with the Germans and the Italians that way because of their political strength.[35]

Thus, for Columbus Day 1942, President Roosevelt signed an order removing Italian nationals from the list of enemy aliens.

Yet, did the American people see the Japanese as a more dangerous group than the Germans or Italians? Arnold Krammer notes that in April 1942, American fears differed: "While the East Coast generally feared the Germans most and the West Coast the Japanese, when people were asked which group of enemy aliens in America were secretly loyal to a foreign government, 82 percent said the Germans were,

29 percent pointed to the Italians, and only 24 percent said the Japanese were."[36] However, there is no doubt that many Italian and German Americans were more familiar, accepted, and active in all walks of life on the East and West Coasts. They were treated with more consideration than were the Issei or Nisei.[37]

TYPES OF JUSTICE DEPARTMENT ARRESTS

After December 11, 1941, the FBI arrested, without warrants, more individuals with A, B, or C classifications and numerous others as well. The latter group was made up of people arrested for violating regulations concerning curfew, travel restrictions, possession of contraband articles, and entrance into prohibited areas. Their number also included Japanese religious leaders, fishermen, and teachers and principals of Japanese-language schools.

Although the FBI made most of the arrests, the Justice Department authorized the regional U.S. attorney to call on the INS or U.S. marshals to capture particular individuals.[38] The INS, for example, apprehended without warrants eighty-seven Issei fishermen living or working at Terminal Island, Wilmington, and San Pedro, California, by January 1, 1942. The INS charged them with "unspecified irregularities in their Immigration Status" and for being "members of the Army or Naval reserve of Japan." The INS transferred this information to the FBI and then asked the Justice Department to issue presidential warrants to justify the arrests.[39]

On the basis of its suspicions, the INS also confined 100 foreign nationals, mostly Issei, in San Diego and 403 people in Los Angeles and then requested presidential warrants to hold them. Its justification was that "if these individuals are permitted to move about at will, they may proceed to lower California and cause considerable trouble at that point where it has been alleged enemy submarine bases are located."[40] The FBI agreed to assist the INS and passed along the names of these Japanese nationals to the AEC Unit so that presidential warrants could be issued. Again, the arrests were made first; legitimating warrants were executed later.

Those arrested without presidential warrants were turned over to the INS for safekeeping while the regional U.S. attorney's office examined their cases. The federal attorneys reviewed the files and determined whether to issue a presidential warrant or recommend a less severe action.

Ennis stated that arrests were made regardless of an internee's personal record. What mattered, he said, was whether the person's affiliations appeared suspicious to the Justice Department: "I might say for your information that a large number of Japanese were apprehended not because there was any indication that the individual himself was suspected of subversive activity but because the occupation group or association to which he made a contribution was suspect, for example, fishermen and Heimusha Kai [Military Conscription Association]."[41]

Thus, a major difficulty for "a large number of Japanese," in Ennis's words, was guilt by association. After an organization was evaluated as dangerous, an individual who was somehow linked to it could be subject to arrest. The connection might be as slight as a mere perceived degree of association—for example, being an officer or attending a meeting. This form of guilt by association was not conditioned on any action deemed to be illegal but rather on chance factors such as choice of friends or having free time to attend a meeting. Such casual occurrences could later result in arrest and internment.

ARREST PROCEDURES

Once the internees were delivered to the INS detention stations, the agency sent information such as name, nationality, gender, address, and other particulars to the INS headquarters, regardless of which agency had actually made the arrests. As basic protocol, internees filled out an alien enemy questionnaire, which asked for, among other particulars, details on nationality, personal data, activities, organizational memberships, family size, and number and dates of visits to Japan. The INS checked the responses against information already collected by the FBI.

At the detention stations, the internees were given their hearings, after which the agency recommended release, parole, or internment. The INS sent its recommendation to the Justice Department in Washington, D.C., for final adjudication. The collected information, with any changes, was transmitted to the AEC Unit, the INS, the Alien Enemy Information Bureau of the War Department's Office of the Provost Marshal, and the Special Division of the State Department.[42] This was the usual procedure for arresting and detaining selected enemy aliens in the early phase of the war.

Arrests of Issei along the Pacific coast were generally similar, but there were some notable differences.[43] Take, for example, the case of Genji Mihara. In the early evening of December 7, Mihara, an Issei and owner and manager of a small restaurant in Seattle, was at home with his family. Four men from unknown agencies came and told him he was under arrest. When he requested a reason, they asked if he knew that Pearl Harbor had been attacked. The visitors went on to say they had been told only that it was their duty to take him to jail. After giving Mihara time to pack a bag, they escorted him to the Seattle INS station, where he stayed until December 22. The INS then transported him to the Missoula Detention Station in Montana, where he received his hearing, after which he was sent to other U.S. Army and Justice Department camps. It would be years before he was reunited with his wife and family.[44]

What were the grounds for Mihara's arrest? The government's file contains four allegations. First, he had a father, mother, and sister living in Japan. Second, he was an officer and council member of the Japanese Chamber of Commerce, the Northwest Federation, and the Northwest Japanese Association. As such, he allegedly raised money through the association for Japanese war-relief efforts. Third, as a representative of the Japanese Association, he was invited to attend the celebration of the founding of the Empire of Japan and received an award from the Japanese consulate in Seattle. Fourth, he was vice president of the Seattle Japanese-language school's Parents-Teachers Association.

All these assertions were true, but the issue is whether they were incriminating enough to warrant Mihara's arrest and internment. In regard to the first point about his family, although his parents and sister did reside in Japan, Mihara had come to the United States in 1907 and lived in the country continuously for thirty-four years, returning to Japan only once, in 1923. His wife emigrated in 1909, and the couple raised three boys, all U.S. citizens. All three sons volunteered for active duty in the U.S. military. As to the remaining three points, which pertain to his affiliations and activities, because Mihara owned a restaurant in Seattle, he belonged to the Japanese Chamber of Commerce. He probably contributed to the Japanese relief effort to help the widows and orphans of soldiers who had died in the Sino-Japanese War. Yet, other Issei who contributed to this charity were not arrested. The Japanese Associations in California and the Pacific Northwest were active in lobbying against anti-Japanese legislation such as the Alien Land Laws, which probably explains the organization's presence on the Justice Department's Special Defense Unit list of suspect organizations. Receiving an invitation from Japan and serving on the board of a Japanese-language school were also activities that qualified a person for the suspects list.

Despite the suspicions that led to Mihara's arrest, the Justice Department's report after his internment stated there was no evidence of any subversive activity. He was "active in the Japanese community, but there is indication he was a leader in Americanization [sic]. Behavior report at Lordsburg [New Mexico internment camp]: all items triple-checked as outstandingly favorable."[45] Despite the positive report, the government did not release Mihara until November 16, 1943, and then, as with almost all Issei, he was paroled to a WRA center. His long stay resulted in no small part from his inability to successfully challenge the government's suspicions; he was forced to remain imprisoned, at the whim of the authorities.

Mihara's background is similar in many respects to that of Issei internees whom we have already discussed—Hibi, Koide, and Muraoka. These men all had relatives living in Japan, contributed to the Japanese-language school, and were members of the Japanese Association, the Japanese Chamber of Commerce, or other suspect organizations. Yet, although many other Issei had similar histories, these four were arrested and later interned. When the government eventually incarcerated the remaining West Coast Issei and Nisei under the authority of an executive order, it asserted that both groups constituted a danger to the nation. In this way, even though the authority to imprison those taken under the Alien Enemies Act and Executive Order 9066 was initially different, the public rationale for their imprisonment was the same—persons of Japanese ancestry, nationals and citizens alike, represented a threat to national security.

AEC UNIT HEARINGS

The AEC Unit in Washington, D.C., was responsible for determining the disposition of foreign nationals. The unit could recommend parole, release, further investigation, or permanent internment. If the foreign national was to be interned, he or she was transferred into the control of the army and placed in one of its camps.

The hearing board was the primary method of determining a person's final disposition. According to the prewar agreement between the War and Justice Departments, internees were to be "accorded the privilege of having a hearing before the Alien Enemy Hearing Board."[46] In theory, the Justice Department was to assemble the hearing boards within ten days of arrest. In reality, the situation became more complicated for the Issei. Lieutenant General John L. DeWitt, Commanding General of the Western Defense Command, headquartered in San Francisco, sent a telegram to the attorney general on December 12, 1941, stating his desire to move all arrested foreign nationals from the Pacific Coast into the interior United States. The provost marshal general concurred in the request, and the Justice Department waited until the West Coast Issei were moved before forming hearing boards.[47]

Because of this delay, the Justice Department authorized a temporary procedure for particular persons. It instructed various U.S. attorneys to hold hearings for those individuals who were considered "least likely of those apprehended to be dangerous to the safety of the United States."[48] These hearings were conducted informally, with only a "friend or adviser," to assist the arrested person. In Southern California, the department held hearings for only five individuals, none with a recognizably Japanese name. Although not explicitly stated, the early hearings were apparently for those who were not of Japanese ancestry.[49]

Once the Japanese nationals had been removed to interior regions, the Justice Department established ninety-three hearing boards in eighty-six judicial districts. Most hearings took place in the INS camps themselves. Each board was composed of three civilian members, usually from the same region as the foreign national and representing a variety of backgrounds. One member was usually an attorney. An interpreter who helped Japanese nationals from Nevada reported, "Our hearings were in charge of a very fine Department of Justice gentleman and watched over by an FBI man. Then there were three judges. Dr. Johnson, a professor of Philosophy from the University of Nevada, Mr. Smith, editor of the Fallon [Nevada] newspaper and a Reno lawyer. There was a secretary taking everything down verbatim."[50] The regional U.S. attorney usually presented the government's case against the internee and recommended a disposition. INS and FBI officers were also present to assist the attorney.

The hearing board members reviewed the evidence and the U.S. attorney's recommendation. According to Ennis, "The purpose of the hearing was to see if any evidence could be produced which showed that the FBI report might be erroneous or any evidence that might be overcome. For example, a person might be charged with being a member of some organization and [he could] just come in and say it was a mistake and say, 'I wasn't' and he would go out. We had a file on each case that was sent to us with all the evidence that was presented plus a recommendation by the Hearing Board. That was the whole thing."[51] The charges, however, were viewed from the start as valid and true, and it was up to the internee to show their inaccuracy or falsity. Internees were asked similar questions, such as, "Whom do you want to win in this war—the United States or Japan?" Based on the answers and on the evidence in their custodial detention files, if available, the hearing board members made their recommendations.

The Justice Department told the hearing board members that their recommendations must be based solely on the presented information, which was limited to the alien enemy questionnaire and the FBI file as supplemented by the INS, Office of Naval Intelligence, the army's Military Intelligence Division, and other governmental units.[52] The recommendations were then forwarded to Washington, D.C., where AEC Unit officials determined the internee's future.

Clearly, a crucial element was missing for the internees: legal counsel. The Justice Department defined the hearing as an administrative proceeding and a privilege granted to the internee. Because it was not a trial, the Justice Department reasoned, there was no need for counsel. The Issei were already interned; the questions raised at the hearings related to their ultimate status and the duration of their stay. A friend or relative of the internee could attend the hearing but was not allowed to object to points made or question any argument presented and could make a statement only as long as he or she was not acting as the internee's attorney.[53]

By denying the internee legal counsel, by interpreting the hearings as a privilege, and by defining the foreign national as an enemy, the Justice Department fostered a situation in which guilt was, in fact, presumed and needed only to be ratified. The internee's task was to prove innocence; failure to do so resulted in long-term internment. With or without counsel, however, proving innocence was virtually impossible. In most instances, the accused person's participation in a B- or C-rated religious, social, or community organization was a fact. And the government's evaluation of the organization's supposed dangerousness could not be questioned. No illegal act such as espionage or sabotage was necessary to bring about a recommendation for permanent internment.

In certain cases, internees remained in confinement even after a hearing board had determined that they were not dangerous. Herbert Nicholson, a missionary returned from Japan, acted as an unofficial interpreter at the Santa Fe, New Mexico, INS detention station for fifty-two Issei who had been picked up in Nevada. He related:

> The hearing would start by the Department of Justice man asking the Japanese if he knew why he was there. Of course he didn't and things were not cleared up when he

was told that it was because he was potentially dangerous! Then the judges and the FBI man would ask him questions such as, "What do you think about Pearl Harbor?" "If the Japanese were landing on the coast of California, and the American army were in the hills and you stood on the beach with a gun, which way would you fire?" Fifty of the fifty-two men tried were uneducated, whiskey-drinking day laborers in a copper mine. The questions meant nothing to them. However, we did find out that the real reason they were picked up was because the foreman took fifty cents from their pay each month to be sent to Japan for relief of widows and children of soldiers who had been killed in the [Sino-Japanese] war. When asked why they did this, most of them did not even know that it was done! After four days of this absurd attempt at justice, the judges agreed that these men were not dangerous.⁵⁴

The committee's final recommendation reveals the importance of the public relations rationale and the government's interest in assuaging public fears: "In spite of the unanimous decision of the judges and the identical nature of the cases, half of them were sent to Japanese relocation centers and half were kept in detention 'to satisfy public opinion.'"⁵⁵

Nicholson did not say which half was kept in detention and which was placed into WRA relocation centers. He stated that there was no evidentiary basis for the outcome: "The whole business was a farce. Absolutely crazy!"

Many Issei internees believed that the real purpose of the hearing boards was to help justify their internment. They saw little chance that they would be allowed to walk out of the detention station, regardless of what they said in their own defense. Release was apparently a more likely outcome for the few Italian and female internees—not for males of Japanese ancestry. Masao Yasui, an Issei farmer from Hood River, Oregon, for example, had his hearing at the INS camp at Fort Missoula, Montana, in February 1942. His son, an eyewitness to the hearing, related, "The proceedings were a complete farce. The official for the [Alien] Enemy Control Unit pointed out that my father was an influential leader in the Japanese community in Hood River, Oregon; that he had extensive property interests; that he had visited Japan for a summer vacation for three months in 1925; that he had been awarded a medal by the Emperor of Japan for promoting U.S.-Japan relations; and that he had been instrumental in obtaining a position with [the] consulate general of Japan in Chicago for [his son]."⁵⁶

The hearing board member then produced drawings made by Yasui's children, showing how the locks of the Panama Canal worked:

The hearing officer took these out and asked, "Mr. Yasui, what are these?" Dad looked at the drawings and diagrams and said, "They look like drawings of the Panama Canal." They were so labeled, with names of the children. Then the officer asked my father to explain why they were in our home. "If they were in my home," my father replied, "it seems to me that they were drawings done by my children for their schoolwork." The officer then asked, "Didn't you have these maps and diagrams so you could direct the blowing up of the canal locks?" My father said, "Oh no! These are just schoolwork of my children." The officer said, "No, we think you've cleverly disguised your nefarious intent and are using your children merely as a cover. We believe you had intent to damage the Panama Canal." To which my father vehemently replied, "No, no, no!" And then the officer said pointedly, *"Prove that you didn't intend to blow up the Panama Canal!"*[57]

Yasui pointed out the inherent foolishness of asking a farmer living in Oregon, 3,000 miles from the Panama Canal, to prove that he had no intention of blowing it up. Yet the A E C Unit had the final say in the matter. They kept Yasui interned for four years, until spring 1946.

Eyewitnesses state that the hearing was not a fair one. Nicholson gave his assessment in no uncertain words:

> Then when it came my time to talk—this was the last hearing—I really let off what I thought about the whole situation. I told a lot of things that I heard from F B I men and from [Edward] Ennis. I finally said, "You've had four thousand five hundred hearings, and you haven't found a single case of espionage or sabotage, and still you're keeping these people here. It just doesn't make sense." The F B I man present said, "That's a lie!" I said, "If it's a lie, I'm through!" and I got up and walked out. Well, the F B I man followed me out and he said, "Say, Nicholson, where did you get all this information you're giving here." I said, "I got it from you fellows." He said, "But we're not supposed to talk." I was always getting in contact with these F B I men. I said, "Well, I know, but you let out a lot to me." I didn't tell him about Ennis—he gave me most of it. But anyway, he never apologized but he did admit it. He said, "What you said is true." I said, "Why did you call me a liar then?" And he walked off in a huff.[58]

Nicholson was correct in stating that not a single case of espionage or sabotage on the part of Japanese nationals was discovered in the course of these hearings.

The public relations rationale suggested by Ennis may be an important unstated basis for these hearings. To allay widespread fears about national security, one early ploy was simply to intern any and all suspect persons. If public relations played a role, then the government could show it was keeping a vigilant eye out for public safety by jailing such untrustworthy people—the arrested foreigner's actual dangerousness might not matter. If this motive is plausible, then the reason for the hearings becomes clearer—they were conducted for the purpose of deniability. By offering a hearing, the U.S. government could tell belligerent governments and the American public that the internment of these civilians was handled fairly and equitably and could counter any argument that the United States had arbitrarily jailed its enemy aliens.

Nicholson reinforced the idea that public relations was a more important factor than the commission of any overtly dangerous act:

> Well, then they began collecting more people because public opinion brought more pressure, "Take these Japs out of here." And the stories that were told the FBI: "This fellow has a short-wave radio. He's in touch with a ship out in the ocean." And every time the FBI heard these stories they had to investigate them. Oh, they were kept busy investigating stories that weren't anything at all. The bomb in the house was a tin pan. It was absolutely absurd, but more and more people were picked up all the time.[59]

The AEC Unit reviewed the hearing boards' conclusions and sent its recommendations to the attorney general for final judgment. According to AEC Unit director Ennis, "All we got were a decision of the Hearing Board and a summary of the hearing and the FBI reports on which the person was apprehended."[60] Ennis said he did not necessarily believe the information or interpretations of subversive activities that he received from the FBI and other sources. The material his office received was

> just whether [the Issei's] social activities indicated a strong tie to the mother country, the Black Dragon Society and all that. My office, we didn't think very much of this kind of thing. And really to us, despite all these associations, the attitude of the Japanese alien in this country on the question of loyalty to Japan or this country was a complete mystery. My own feelings were, and the people who directly worked for me, was that these people would have all been, 90 percent would have been, citizens of the United States if they could have been naturalized. So that we were pursuing a phantom because [the reports were saying] that people whom we refused citizenship and who had some association with Japanese organizations were therefore pro-Japanese enough to do something in favor of their theoretical sovereign against us. We saw that it was just a tissue of smoke.[61]

However, real people continued to spend real time in the internment enclosures.

The internees' problems were compounded by their inability to find out what was going to happen to them. Protracted delays between initial arrest and appearance before a hearing board were common. The long months of waiting underscored the internees' powerless position—they could do nothing for their families and friends. Their wives and families also waited anxiously for months, not knowing the fate of their loved ones.

In some instances, the Justice Department misplaced the files of arrested individuals.[62] This oversight apparently occurred when an arrest took place outside the originating jurisdiction. In such cases, the AEC Unit had to recover the internee's paperwork before starting the administrative process. Only after consultations between the Justice Department agencies and possibly the army could a hearing board be constituted to legitimate the internment. This took time, and meanwhile the internee languished in a detention station, unaware of the reason for his or her unresolved status.

AEC Unit officials in Washington, D.C., had little additional information other than the hearing boards' recommendations upon which to base their final decisions. They could neither question nor invalidate information presented at the hearing. Therefore, in many cases, AEC Unit personnel simply affirmed recommendations for permanent internment. In other instances, when the recommendation was for parole, other agencies objected. According to Ennis, "In all the cases I proposed [that we parole], Hoover sent a memorandum, for the file, as a great bureaucrat, that he was opposed to it, that he was opposed to our recommendations."[63]

Female foreign nationals, internees under the age of fourteen, and married couples were detained separately from male internees. Because the army would not accept responsibility for these internees, the INS retained authority over them. Most were initially taken to the INS-run internment center at Seagoville, Texas, and later to the Crystal City family reunification internment camp, also in Texas.[64] The stranded German and Italian seamen kept in the Justice Department camps from before December 7, 1941, were treated separately. The department retained control over them throughout the war years.

PAROLES AND EARLY RELEASES

The Justice Department placed an information lid on all those taken under the alien enemy program. In April 1942, the department decided that whatever the final decision for a particular internee—whether for release, parole, or internment—the outcome would not be made public.[65] German and Italian nationals who were released or paroled could return to their homes or go anyplace in the United States except to a militarily designated exclusion area.

This policy of information suppression became painfully relevant for many Issei internees paroled into WRA camps. Not allowed to alert their families about their return, these Issei were sometimes dumped unceremoniously into the camps. Never told why they were arrested, they also were not told why they were released while other Issei remained in INS camps. Their early release into WRA camps often raised questions and unfounded suspicions among the other inmates. Why, some argued, would the government have taken these Issei in the first place, unless they were guilty of something? On the other hand, because they were released before other Issei internees, and lacking any exonerating statements from the Justice Department, many of these Issei became the subjects of ill-founded rumors. One common accusation was that some had bought their freedom by becoming informants for the government. Ironically then, release from INS detention complicated an already difficult situation, since the only agency able to set the record straight had a formal policy of not doing so.

This social pressure could become quite extreme, especially because it was up to the released Issei to prove to other WRA inmates that he had done nothing wrong, either before his arrest or later in the Justice Department camp. An Issei in this predicament could defend himself only with negatives—that is, he could say only that he had done nothing to cause his arrest or his later release. According to some stories, this pressure led to mental anguish and even a few suicides among former internees.

The AEC Unit and the hearing boards sent all their recommendations to the attorney general. An internee who was recommended for parole fell under the administration of the Alien Enemy Parole Division. The INS required the parolee to report to a person selected by the hearing board and/or an INS officer at periodic intervals.[66] The parole division worked almost exclusively with German and Italian aliens, since keeping track of the Issei was simple—for this latter group, parole usually meant incarceration in a WRA camp.

ARRESTS AND INTERNMENT OF NISEIS

The Justice Department also arrested and interned American citizens in the early days of the war. Soon after December 7, before the mass exclusion authorized by Executive Order 9066, the FBI arrested two Nisei in the vicinity of San Diego, California. One Nisei was paroled; the fate of the other is unknown.[67] In the Pacific Coast region, thirty-one Nisei had been arrested by the end of the war; some were presumably interned in the Justice Department camps. Further details about these cases are difficult to uncover.[68]

The story of Yoshiju Kimura, born in Long Beach, California, highlights a particular Nisei's plight:

My store was visited in the early morning hours of January 20 [1942] by Immigration Bureau officials. They wanted me to accompany them for just a little while to ask about my birth certificate and draft card. . . . I had to take [my wife] to a doctor. The officials then left, saying they would be back at 8:00 A.M. the following morning, and that I was to be prepared to go with them. At 8 o'clock the next morning, the same official came and took me to the Federal Building. He said the questioning would take about fifteen minutes, but how was I to know that I was to be locked up for ten long months! I was questioned continuously by the Immigration officers from 9:00 A.M. to 12:00 midnight without lunch or supper based on charges by the FBI that I was suspected of engaging in spy activities. They claimed that I was born in Japan and had illegally entered the United States with a birth certificate taken from a deceased U.S.-born American citizen of Japanese ancestry. After hours of cruel interrogation, the FBI then questioned the reason why I moved close to San Diego [a military port] just prior to the outbreak of war after having lived in Arizona for many years. They had made up their minds that my sole purpose was none other than to conduct spy activities. I refused to answer the questioning of the Immigration FBI officers saying only that, "I don't know." I was not charged with any specific act and late at night was thrown into the San Diego County Jail as a U.S. HOLD.[69]

Kimura's wife, his friends, and a lawyer tried unsuccessfully to obtain his release. He remained in the county jail for three months, and as other Japanese Americans were taken to assembly centers operated by the army's Wartime Civil Control Administration, he eventually became the lone Japanese American in the county. On October 15, after nine months of imprisonment, two city detectives arrived and told him he was free to leave the county jail, but because he would still be in a restricted area, they recommended that he go with them to the San Diego city jail, where he could wait for the military to transfer him to an assembly center. Kimura agreed. He then discovered that bureaucratic incompetence was the real reason for his extended stay in the county jail: "Before leaving the county jail, the county security bureau chief gave me a ten-feet [*sic*] long Teletype message from the Federal Government Attorney General Biddle. It stated, 'The country being at war, I had no knowledge of your having been placed in confinement in San Diego. I heard about you in a dispatch from the Spanish Ambassador . . . and deeply regret the circumstances. You must have suffered a great deal and I extend to you my sincerest apology for the injustices.'"[70]

At the city jail, Kimura was fingerprinted and imprisoned. The next day, without explanation, the jailers placed him in solitary confinement. Kimura protested this treatment and asked for an interview with the FBI, in the hope of clearing up his situation. Two days later, an army corporal appeared with orders to take him to an assembly center. The soldier explained that he had experienced some difficulties in finding Kimura. He had arrived in the morning from the Santa Anita Assembly Center, gone to the county jail, and after learning he was not there, looked in various hospitals before checking at the city jail. When Kimura arrived at the Santa Anita center, he found only a few hundred people remaining; the army had shipped most of the inmates to the WRA camps. The army then took Kimura to the WRA camp at Gila River, Arizona. Only in mid-January 1943 did he finally join his wife at yet another WRA camp.

The AEC Unit's official policy stated that holding Nisei was improper because they were American citizens and the unit's authority did not extend to this group. Ennis stated, "It was just a mistake. It was very clear that we had no authority whatever, and not only did we not have authority, we did not want any. Because as we have said to the War Department we had no power over citizens, and we don't want it. We don't exercise it. We won't propose any laws for it because it is unconstitutional. Citizens can only be dealt with on the basis of an individual charge of a crime."[71]

Yet, a relatively small number of Nisei continued to be arrested by the Justice Department and the army, both on the mainland and in Hawaii, and kept for varying lengths of time. For example, as part of the October 21, 1941, raid on the Los Angeles Japanese Chamber of Commerce and the Central Japanese Association, Eiju E. Tanabe was interrogated because he was the executive secretary of the latter organization. He was arrested shortly after December 7 and is identified as "Tanabe, Eiju, alias Eiju (Eddie) Tanabe, United States Citizen with Japanese Tendencies."[72] What happened to Tanabe is not known. Mention of a different case comes from a Japanese-language source, which tells of a young Nisei voluntarily accompanying his physically ill father into a Justice Department camp. Nisei with dual citizenship could be said to be eligible for internment as aliens, but the Justice Department apparently never made this argument. Instead, their American citizenship was given precedence and allowed them protection from the label of "enemy alien."[73] They nonetheless experienced an internment as real as that endured by other groups of people who were designated permanent internees.

CONCLUSION

After December 7, 1941, preplanned steps developed through interagency cooperation led to the arrests of German, Italian, Japanese, and other foreign nationals whose names may or may not have been on the Justice Department's custodial detention list. Some American citizens were arrested as well. Although neither resident Japanese nationals nor their children committed any acts of sabotage or espionage, scores of Issei were detained and subjected to summary hearings that changed the course of their lives.

Let us return to Saburo Muraoka, with whose story we opened this chapter. After going back to California at the war's end, Muraoka, his wife, and family worked assiduously to rebuild their lives. Although they had suffered tremendous personal and financial losses, they still had control of their land, unlike many Issei farmers, because legal ownership rested with Mrs. Muraoka, a Hawaii-born Nisei. Benefiting from an expanding postwar civilian market for produce crops such as celery and tomatoes, they were among the few lucky families to find financial success in agriculture. If farm production had not been interrupted for five years during the war, Muraoka and his family might have become wealthy people.

4

The Territory of Hawaii

The number of Japanese Americans living outside the contiguous forty-eight states, within the territory of Hawaii, was slightly larger than the population residing on the mainland. The very dissimilar treatment accorded these Issei and Nisei stands in stark contrast to the wartime experiences of the similar mainland population. This chapter focuses on Hawaii and the many reasons why imprisonment procedures there diverged so radically from those in the United States. The differences are very important, for collectively they show that alternative procedures not only were possible but were implemented with regard to this American racial minority.

The divergence in treatment between mainland and island groups arose from the social and historical conditions in Hawaii before the start of World War II. For one, persons of Japanese ancestry constituted a numerically important portion of the territory's population from the early 1900s, and they played a significant role in its economy and social history.[1] By the 1940s, 37.3 percent of Hawaii's total population of 423,330—or 157,905 people—were of Japanese ancestry. The majority of this group, 73 percent, were American citizens, mostly Nisei and some Sansei.

In contrast, on the mainland, the Nikkei always constituted a comparatively small population. Moreover, they figured prominently as an unwelcome immigrant group and were the target of West Coast anti-Asian discrimination from the start of the century. As a result of earlier prejudicial actions against them, members of this group led relatively isolated lives in ethnic enclaves. By the 1930s, the entire mainland group occupied a nearly powerless position within the body politic. Its physical and cultural presence was almost totally ignored in the general society, a situation vastly different from that in Hawaii.

MILITARY AND POLITICAL BACKGROUND

Throughout World War II, there was no mass incarceration of persons of Japanese ancestry from Hawaii. Why was this so? The general historical background is important, but the actions of Hawaii's military and political leaders in the years before and after 1942 command special attention. Specifically, for a number of years the military in Hawaii was concerned about the islands' Nikkei population. From

1935 to 1937, Lieutenant Colonel George S. Patton Jr., then a senior U.S. Army intelligence officer in Hawaii, drafted a plan to arrest designated Japanese residents and hold them as hostages if hostilities broke out between the United States and Japan. This plan "called for the arrest of 128 hostages, the closing of 60 amateur radio stations, and the confiscation of 23 businesses under a martial law regime."[2] Modest in scope as these ideas now appear, Patton's words indicate that the army recognized the importance of this island population and thought to include them in a military contingency plan.

Along with the army, the Federal Bureau of Investigation (FBI) also gathered data on the islands' Nikkei residents. In August 1939, the FBI sent Agent Robert L. Shivers to Hawaii to compile names and addresses of potentially "dangerous" persons. Shivers's self-stated goal was to identify the Issei leadership, as he believed that arresting them "of itself, will break the backbone of any Japanese alien resistance or organized attempt of interference." He created a custodial detention list and placed on it names of businesspeople, Japanese consular officials, Japanese-language school teachers and principals, Buddhist and Shinto priests, and "others of no particular affiliation but who by reason of their extreme nationalistic sentiments would be a danger to our security as well as others who have seen Japanese military service."[3]

It was not a long list. From 1939 to the beginning of the war, the FBI designated only 338 Issei and 9 Nisei in Hawaii as candidates for custodial detention.[4] These numbers represent less than 0.1 percent of Hawaii's Issei population. The FBI's Hawaii list also included the names of a few American citizens of Japanese ancestry.

The U.S. military was also preparing its intelligence units for an expected upcoming action. In early 1940, the FBI in Hawaii met with the U.S. Navy's Office of Naval Intelligence (ONI) and the army's Military Intelligence Division (MID). On March 13, 1941, the War Department ordered its Hawaiian department commanding general to prepare for the internment of enemy foreign nationals and crews of foreign vessels, "should the international situation become more critical."[5]

Using military intelligence lists, the army in Hawaii estimated that 1,500 Issei and Nisei would have to be interned. Of this number, approximately 500 were Issei; the remaining 1,000 might be arrested if and when they gave cause for alarm. Relative to the total Nikkei population, these numbers are quite small. The army also assumed that the advent of war and possibly martial law, which eliminated recourse to civilian judicial procedures, would enable the military to arrest these civilians. This expectation was in accord with the early prewar agreement between the Justice and War Departments concerning enemy aliens in the territories outside the United States. The military made no estimate of the number of enemy seamen subject to internment, since that figure would depend on the quantity and type of ships in the harbor at the time. Despite this uncertainty, however, the military assumed this number would also be rather limited.[6]

As mentioned earlier, perceptions of the Japanese held by various territorial leaders and officials were an important factor. In mid-August 1941, Assistant Attorney General Norman M. Littell visited Hawaii and wrote that local leading figures were not worried about the Japanese population, regardless of whether the United States went to war with Japan: "The head of the F B I, military authorities, lawyers, judges and others confirmed that the great mass of the Japanese would not go back to Japan if they could; are fearful of possible Japanese intervention; and that only a small minority of them, who are being watched and are allegedly detectable, would be Japanese fifth columnists or representatives."[7] He then noted that quick action taken against this "small minority" would alleviate any problem. This conclusion is strikingly similar to those reached by Curtis Munson and Lieutenant Commander Kenneth Ringle regarding West Coast Japanese Americans. Yet, even with similar assessments on the West Coast and in Hawaii, two different courses of actions ensued.

INVOCATION OF MARTIAL LAW

On December 7, 1941, at 4:25 P.M., after the attack on Pearl Harbor was over, Territorial Governor Joseph B. Poindexter placed Hawaii under martial law. In doing so, the governor abdicated his civilian powers and transferred them to General Walter C. Short, head of the Hawaii command. This transfer of power apparently was not a purely voluntary act by the civilian governor. Littell reports that Poindexter reluctantly signed the proclamation only after he had refused two or three times. General Short even threatened Governor Poindexter by saying that he would be held responsible for any loss of life from a Japanese invasion unless he signed the martial law proclamation.[8]

There was an alternative available to the governor; the Hawaii Territorial Senate had on September 23, 1941, approved a plan to give Poindexter broad powers in the event of an emergency. Once the martial law proclamation was signed, however, Hawaii's course for the war years was set.[9] The next day, the military closed the civilian courts and established its own courts with authority over civilians.[10] On December 9, President Franklin D. Roosevelt formally approved the imposition of martial law and the suspension of habeas corpus.

Figure 4.1 provides a schematic overview of the process that took place in Hawaii from December 7 until the end of the war. The remainder of this chapter will refer to the points illustrated here.

ARRESTS OF JAPANESE RESIDENTS

On December 7, even while the attack on Pearl Harbor was still in progress, the War Department ordered the internment of everyone on the F B I custodial detention list.[11] The F B I and the army, assisted by the local police, carried out the arrest plan that had been approved by F B I headquarters only six days earlier.[12] In

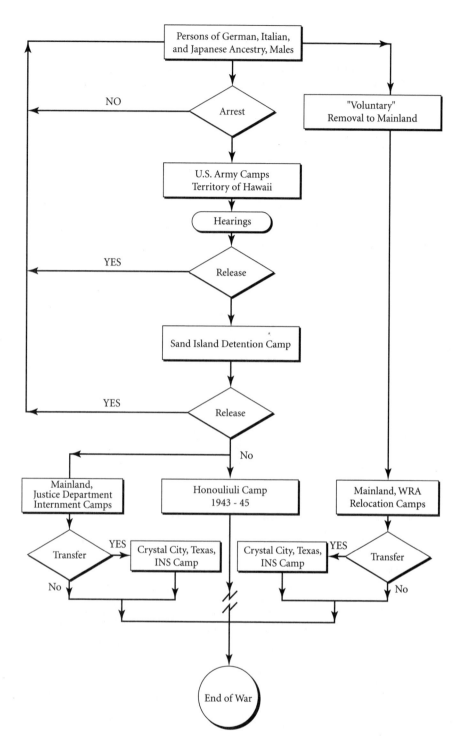

FIG. 4.1. Arrested German, Italian, and Japanese Male Nationals
in the Territory of Hawaii after December 7, 1941

Honolulu and the outlying areas of Oahu, thirteen squads, consisting typically of three men—one from the F B I, another from the army's M I D–Intelligence Branch, and the last from the military police—went to make the arrests. The procedures were somewhat different from those used on the mainland because of the agreement between the War and Justice Departments as to the handling of civilian aliens. After making the arrests, the F B I in Honolulu handed its prisoners over to the military police at the Honolulu I N S building, which was then used as the temporary detention station.

As on the mainland, however, officials seldom told the prisoners on whose authority or for what reason they had been arrested. The procedure was simple:

> Three by five cards had been prepared previously on every custodial detention subject who was to be picked up, showing his name, address, and citizenship status. It was therefore only necessary to give to each squad the cards on the subjects to be picked up in the districts to which they were assigned. These cards had been stamped on the back with the statement, "Received custody of the person named on the reverse side." As the individuals were picked up by the various squads, they were taken to the Immigration Station where they were receipted for on the reverse side of the card by the Military Police.[13]

On the other islands, except on Kauai, where there were only two F B I agents, the F B I telephoned the army's military intelligence personnel and made the arrests, working with local police.

The first people picked up were on the December 4, 1941, list of 347 Japanese named in custodial detention memorandums:

TABLE 4.1
F B I Custodial Detention List of Japanese, December 4, 1941

Location	1st Stage/Plan I			2nd Stage/Plan I		Plan II	
	Consular Agents	Priests	Other	Priests	Other	Priests	Other
Hawaii	67	0	1	2	2	1	9
Kauai	38	1	0	1	0	1	0
Lanai	2	0	0	0	0	0	1
Maui	45	2	0	2	3	0	6
Molokai	4	0	0	0	0	0	0
Oahu	56	9	6	22	26	12	18
TOTAL	212	12	7	27	31	14	34

N O T E : Compiled from File 4, December 1941, F B I, F.N. 100-2-20-23, Washington, D.C.

The largest group of the 347 total includes 212 Japanese identified as "consular agents," and most of these individuals constitute a unique category. On islands other than Oahu, where the Japanese consulate did not or could not afford to place a permanent staff member, the consul asked for unpaid volunteers to assist other Japanese in filling out reports of birth, marriage, and death. These reports were sent through the consul's office to Japan for entry into the Issei's village records (*koseki*). The FBI took note of this activity and concluded that these volunteers were working as agents and/or spies for the Japanese government.[14] It is difficult to specify the exact threat to national security posed by this group, since most were longtime residents of Hawaii. None in this group was ever charged with a criminal offense involving espionage or sabotage.

The December 4 list also included a "priest" category, covering those from Japanese religious organizations. Those so identified were mainly Konkokyo or Buddhist priests. The "other" category refers to, among others, Japanese community leaders such as noted businessmen and Japanese-language school principals. Although most of the 347 persons were Issei, 9 are identified as Nisei. The Hawaii FBI's plan was to apprehend these 347 persons of Japanese ancestry, plus 80 German and 29 Italian nationals, for a total of 456, even though an FBI report stated "it is true that investigative reports have not been submitted in every case but such reports are being prepared."[15]

From December 8, the FBI and the military also arrested people who were not on the custodial detention list. These were Nisei taken "as a result of our investigative efforts and investigations conducted by the corps of intelligence police under G-2 [military intelligence, often at the army level]."[16] The FBI and the army also arrested additional individuals of German and Italian descent under authority of martial law, even though President Roosevelt did not officially authorize it until December 9.[17] By that date, the number arrested totaled 473: 345 Issei, 22 Nisei, 74 German nationals, 11 Italian nationals, 19 citizens of German ancestry, and 2 citizens of Italian ancestry.[18]

As was true for arrests on the mainland, three questions can be raised about the legitimacy of the early arrests conducted in Hawaii between December 7 and 8 and possibly up to December 9. First, it could be asserted that the arrests conducted on and just after December 7 were justified under martial law. However, President Roosevelt did not formally recognize this edict until December 9.

Second, from the time military control was established in Hawaii and for three days afterward, the military and FBI arrested citizens and foreign nationals alike—in many cases apparently without showing arrest warrants. As if aware that this might pose a potential legal problem, the Justice Department told the War Department on December 9 that in certain cases their warrants should be resubmitted for the secretary of war's signature:

I think this is desirable in order that there may be no question raised as to the validity of the arrests. You will note that the warrant with respect to the Japanese is dated December 7 and the other warrant is dated December 8. This is because the arrest of the Japanese began on Sunday night. . . . If you agree with me in this, I suggest you have these warrants properly prepared on the Secretary of War's stationery and have them executed and returned to me so that I can refile them with the FBI.[19]

The secretary of war apparently heeded the Justice Department's advice and issued appropriate orders on December 10.

Third, these orders stated in part that, based on presidential proclamations regarding the classification of German, Italian, and Japanese nationals as "enemy aliens" (Proclamations 2525, 2526, and 2527), the commanding general of the Hawaiian department should assume responsibility for their arrest, detention, and internment. Arresting persons on the custodial detention lists assumes that they are enemy aliens or otherwise "dangerous" persons. As stated in an earlier chapter, the declaration of the change of status for the Japanese from nationals to enemy aliens likely did not occur until President Roosevelt signed Proclamation 2525, on December 8, and the relevant proclamations for German and Italian aliens, probably on December 11. Some of these early arrests thus relied on redated warrants issued by the commanding general on authority of the secretary of war. By these means, the Hawaii command attempted to preclude any legal challenge from those whom it arrested in the two days following the Pearl Harbor attack.

HEARING BOARDS

The Hawaii command then established hearing boards similar to those formed on the mainland by the Justice Department. One major difference was that those arrested in Hawaii were allowed to testify on their own behalf and could be represented by counsel.[20] However, no records were found of any person asking for or receiving such representation.

Other important differences were specified in the prewar agreement between the War and Justice Departments. For example, the hearing boards' recommendations were sent to the secretary of war rather than to the attorney general, and final disposition or appeal of the cases remained with the commanding general of the Hawaii department. There is no indication that those arrested were informed of this appeal process, nor is there any evidence that anyone ever formally appealed a decision. Unlike on the mainland, those arrested in Hawaii went through a two-stage hearing process, as detailed in the prewar agreement between the Justice and War Departments. The first hearing was conducted in front of a military intelligence board with members drawn from the ONI, the MID–Intelligence Branch, and the FBI. If the board recommended indefinite internment, the internee's case proceeded to the second tier, a review board composed of three civilians and two army officers. The internee was then paroled, released, or held for permanent internment. After completion of the initial process, the army recommended permanent internment for about 100 persons and "estimated that there will be approximately 400 more of such internees."[21] These permanent internees were ordered shipped to army internment camps on the mainland.

INTERNMENT FACILITIES

Meanwhile, the military established temporary facilities on each of the major islands for prisoners whose cases had not yet been decided.[22] The internees were shipped to Oahu soon afterward for their hearings and the final disposition of their cases. The island with the largest Nikkei population, Oahu became the center for internment and the final point before transfer to the mainland. Kumaji Furuya, an Issei living in Kalihi, Oahu, recalls the initial visit by the FBI:

> [He] heard a knock on his front door on the evening of December 7. The FBI had come to pick him up. Although he was certain that he would be questioned and released that night, his wife insisted he take a coat. Furuya went into his bedroom and pulled open the top dresser drawer. Suddenly, he felt the cold, hard barrel of a handgun pressed against his back. The MP withdrew the weapon only when he saw that the drawer held handkerchiefs and socks. . . . Furuya did not return that night. For the next four years, he was held without any formal charge in crowded prison cells and barren internment camps.[23]

The army took those it had arrested on Oahu to Honolulu's immigration station. Prisoners arrested after their initial questioning were ferried westward across Honolulu Bay to the Sand Island Detention Station. It was here, from December 1941 to February 20, 1942, that the military confined about 300 Issei and Nisei, mostly men but also some women, along with others from European countries: Austrians, Finns, Germans, Italians, and a few Norwegians. Although specific information about those of European ancestry was not found, the assumption is that the FBI used the same criteria in Hawaii as on the mainland for collecting the names of people suspected of having ties to or sympathies with Nazi, Communist, or Fascist organizations.

The Sand Island Detention Station encompassed an area of about five acres and was ringed by a fifteen-foot-high double fence topped with barbed wire: "There was a long cement sidewalk that connected the headquarters to an open air pavilion which was also surrounded by tough meshed wire. This pavilion served as a dining hall. A kitchen with oil stove was under this roof in an adjoining room. There were two latrines, one at each end of the enclosure."[24] The original sleeping quarters were small tents without floorboards until the army constructed regular barracks about six months later. Prisoners were not permitted newspapers, pencils, pens, or writing paper. As on the mainland, these internees were considered civilian prisoners of war and were treated accordingly.

After each meal, the army counted the eating utensils in order to prevent their use in an escape attempt.[25] When two spoons and a knife appeared to be missing in January 1942, detention station personnel summoned the 164 male Issei internees and ordered them to line up and remove their clothing. During this afternoon inspection, the internees stood almost nude as army personnel examined their bodies and their discarded clothing.[26] The missing utensils were not discovered during the search; instead, after recounting the silverware, the army realized that the knife was not missing after all, while the spoons were found on top of a kitchen cupboard.

DELOS C. EMMONS AND THE POLICY OF INTERNMENT

In Washington, D.C., at the War and Navy Departments, larger issues were brewing. Following the official inquiry into the attack on Pearl Harbor, the military installed new army and navy commanders in Hawaii. On December 18, 1941, Air Corps Lieutenant General Delos C. Emmons replaced Lieutenant General Walter C. Short, and Admiral Chester W. Nimitz took the place of Admiral Husband E. Kimmel.

A few days later, in a report dated December 22, Lieutenant General Emmons made clear his concern about the civilian Japanese population and those interned at Sand Island. He acknowledged the particular and peculiar status of those individuals and assured their families that the internees would not be mistreated: "Additional investigation and apprehensions will be made and possibly additional suspects will be placed in custodial detention, but their friends and relatives need have no fear that they are mistreated. These people are not prisoners of war and will not be treated as such. . . . There is no intention or desire on the part of the Federal authorities to operate mass concentration camps."[27] For Emmons, the interned foreign nationals were not to be viewed or treated as prisoners of war— quite a different attitude from that of John L. DeWitt, commanding general on the West Coast.

Another development was the visit of Secretary of the Navy William Franklin (Frank) Knox to examine the losses at Pearl Harbor. On December 15, 1941, Knox commented in a now oft-quoted press conference, "I think the most effective 'fifth column' work of the entire war was done in Hawaii, with the possible exception of Norway," a remark directed at Hawaii residents of Japanese ancestry.[28] This statement contradicted the findings of FBI, army, and naval intelligence investigations that there was no evidence of Hawaii Japanese or their citizen children participating in this kind of activity. Unfortunately, the public remarks of such a high-level official created considerable anxiety within the American populace regarding the loyalty of Issei and Nisei in the territory of Hawaii and, by extension, on the mainland.

On December 18, President Roosevelt's cabinet discussed the necessity of re-moving Hawaii's Issei population and interning them on a less populated island for the duration of the war. Secretary Knox argued strongly that such action be taken not only with the Issei but with all citizens of Japanese ancestry in Hawaii.[29] Those opposed to the measure pointed out the constitutional issue raised by forcibly removing American citizens from their homes without cause. Rather than press the issue, Knox, along with Secretary of War Henry L. Stimson, recom-mended that enemy aliens be removed and placed on an island other than Oahu. President Roosevelt accepted this recommendation.[30]

This decision resulted in some confusion. The Justice Department thought that only designated Issei were to be removed and eventually brought to the mainland. When the FBI checked this assumption, Stimson's assistant, Harvey Bundy, replied that President Roosevelt's view was that all Issei should be interned.

Then there were questions about where to keep the internees. On January 10, 1942, Stimson, in a classified radiogram, requested information from Lieutenant General Emmons about the "practicability" of removing and concentrating all the Issei and placing them on an island other than Oahu. The radiogram indicated that the secretary of the navy was the originator of the request, thus distancing the War Department from its implications.[31] In response, Emmons argued that whole-sale removal and displacement was dangerous and impractical. His argument was unique: "All outlying Hawaiian Islands are potential air bases for attack on Oahu. Concentration of Japanese nationals on any other island would greatly increase hazard of attack on that island including possibility of dropping weapons and am-munition into concentration camp."[32]

It is difficult to imagine that Emmons considered the Issei a military risk to the islands, and even more difficult to think that he seriously believed Japan could or would parachute weapons to a group of elderly men and women with no military training and then expect them to capture the island and launch assaults on Oahu. A more plausible explanation for Emmons's statements is that he needed a rea-son, far-fetched or not, to counteract or reject Secretary Knox's suggestion. Em-mons's earlier message of reassurance to the relatives of the internees at the Sand Island camp favors this interpretation. It was clear to him that the secretaries of war and the navy as well as the president were asking him to consider doing what he had said he would not do—create a concentration camp.

In this reply, Emmons also stressed the tremendous logistical problems such a move would create. The army would have to furnish adequate housing, food, san-itation facilities, water, and other supplies and utilities if the internees were placed on a separate island. Further, additional manpower would be needed to guard them. As his superiors continued to insist on removing the Issei from the islands of Oahu and Hawaii, Emmons's recommendation was to transport them to the mainland using returning freighters and transport ships.[33]

The War Department granted permission for Emmons to send those Issei he deemed dangerous to the mainland.[34] However, he moved quite slowly and deliberately in sending any Japanese to the mainland. Because of the militarily strategic location and importance of the Hawaiian command, Emmons seemingly assigned a lower priority to this order so that other issues continually intervened before the project could be completed.

Emmons's primary concern in this matter might have been the immediate needs of his command. He did not institute the order to remove all the Issei, nor did he recommend discharging all soldiers of Japanese ancestry from the service. The probable reason for his resistance was that the Issei and Nisei supplied needed labor. He told the War Department that any plan to "evacuate" the Japanese would require sufficient personnel to serve as replacements.

By January 16, FBI Agent Shivers reported that Lieutenant General Emmons had decided against implementing President Roosevelt's and the War Department's wishes to intern the Issei and their citizen children. Emmons's plan was to maintain the "present policy of picking up those where information and facts justify this action."[35] The War Department, however, continued to make preparations even into late January to remove various Issei and other citizens: "In anticipation of the possible evacuation of large numbers of persons from Hawaii and the Western Defense Command, the Provost Marshall General has instituted a survey to determine concentration camps or areas for resettlement or internment of those persons."[36] The War Department notified its Hawaiian department to move any Issei it desired to the mainland and readied three Pacific Coast areas as initial receiving places: Fort Lewis in Washington, Fort McDowell at Angel Island, California, and Griffith Park in Los Angeles. It also prepared three inland facilities: Fort Bliss and Fort Sam Houston in Texas and Fort Sill in Oklahoma.[37] On February 4, Emmons reported that approximately 200 internees were ready for transport to the mainland.

On February 9, Emmons declared that a serious labor shortage existed and that all available Japanese hands were needed on the islands. In the event that the War Department ordered an extensive evacuation, he placed a high price on compliance—he argued that it would be necessary to send a large group to the mainland since it was difficult to separate loyal from disloyal Japanese: "Every effort [has been] made to uncover the disloyal group but there [is] little hope of being able to distinguish between the loyal and disloyal until too late. In order to get the disloyal it will probably be necessary to evacuate approximately 100,000."[38] The implication was clear. If this large a labor force was compelled to leave the islands, the War Department's order would hamper military efforts at this Pacific outpost.

Since this statement appears to contradict an earlier remark made by Emmons in which he maintained that persons of Japanese ancestry did not constitute a military threat, it needs further explanation. Loyalty and the commission of espionage and sabotage are two different issues. Emmons could declare that this group did not present a military threat and be confident that no evidence had been offered to contradict him. But the positive loyalty of various Japanese subgroups toward the United States might still be an open question—especially given the imprisonment organization's views of the Issei and Kibei.

TRANSFER OF HAWAII RESIDENTS TO THE MAINLAND

From December 7, 1941, to March 30, 1942, the total number of people arrested as part of Hawaii's custodial detention program came to 733. Of that number, 650 were still interned, and the majority of this group—482, or 74 percent—was composed of Issei males. The number of arrested or interned Nisei males, 92, totaled more than all German and Italian nationals combined.

Given the makeup of Hawaii's population, it is not surprising that the largest percentage of those interned were of Japanese ancestry.[39]

At this time, the army began transporting some of these internees to the mainland. On February 21, an initial group of 199 prisoners—156 Issei, 16 Nisei, 10 German nationals, 14 citizens of German ancestry, 1 Norwegian, 2 citizens of Italian ancestry, and 1 Japanese prisoner of war (Sub-lieutenant Kazuo Sakamaki, Imperial Japanese Navy)—left Oahu on the U.S. army transport ship *Grant,* bound for Fort McDowell, on Angel Island, in San Francisco Bay.[40] The army transported additional prisoners on five occasions in 1942 and three times in 1943.[41]

Removing American citizens from Hawaii and sending them to the mainland

TABLE 4.2

Persons Interned or Released in Hawaii, December 7, 1941–March 30, 1942

| | Japanese | | | | German | | | | Italian | | | | |
| | Nat'l | | Citizen | | Nat'l | | Citizen | | Nat'l | | Citizen | | |
	M	F	M	F	M	F	M	F	M	F	M	F	Total
Interned in Hawaii	159	7	54	1	20	9	13	12	6	1	0	0	282
Transported to mainland (2/21 & 3/21/42)	323	0	17	0	12	0	14	0	0	0	2	0	368
TOTAL	482	7	71	1	32	9	27	12	6	1	2	0	650
Released (12/7/41–3/30/42)	26	0	21	0	10	17	0	1	5	3	0	0	83
TOTAL	508	7	92	1	42	26	27	13	11	4	2	0	733

NOTE: Compiled from FBI Memo, R. L. Shivers to J. E. Hoover, 30 March 1942, 100-2-20-155 raised an alarm in the Justice Department. When the War Department discovered the Justice Department's concern, it wrote to the Hawaii command: "It is believed advisable that hereafter no U.S. citizens be transferred to the mainland. . . . Legality of detention of citizens under internment order issued in Hawaii questionable when internees transferred to mainland."[42] The army then returned citizen internees and other foreign nationals to Hawaii. By November 3, the total of persons returned included 19 Nisei, 1 German national, 13 citizens of German ancestry, and 2 citizens of Italian ancestry. The army placed these prisoners in the Sand Island Detention Station. Excluding the returned prisoners, the army eventually shipped to the mainland a total of 616 persons—576 Issei, 21 Nisei, 18 German nationals, and 1 citizen of German ancestry—in 1942. Arrests and internment continued throughout the islands, and by December 1, 1942, the army held in Hawaii 52 Issei, 347 Nisei, 3 German nationals, 30 citizens of German ancestry, and 2 citizens of Italian ancestry.[43] A local person offers this example of an arrest allegedly made at the whim of the authorities:

> I [Isao Okada] was a food peddler, and certain foods were scarce right after Pearl Harbor. So I used to save them—things like cucumber and celery—for my regular customers. One day I sold some celery I had hidden in my truck to a regular customer. The FBI agent's wife saw me do that. The next day the agent came and asked to buy some celery. When I told him that I didn't have any, I was told to report to the Immigration Office for interrogation. I got called in seven times. Finally, I got tired and told them that they should put me in if they thought I was dangerous.[44]

The FBI arrested and interned Okada.

Internees shipped to the mainland did not find the trip a pleasure cruise. They were herded onto the transport ship, where the army crowded seven to ten of them into a small cabin. The doors were secured, creating a shipboard jail cell. The military police unlocked the doors at three-hour intervals to escort people to the latrine. Going to the latrine outside this strict time schedule, even for an emergency, was not allowed.[45]

The internees' usual port of arrival was Fort McDowell, California, and afterward the army transferred them to several camps. One group went to Camp McCoy, Wisconsin, where they stayed for seventy days, then to Tillahoma, Tennessee, and later to Fort Livingston, Louisiana. They remained there until June 1943, at which time the army moved them to Santa Fe, New Mexico. Their stay in Santa Fe lasted until April 1944, when the Justice Department gave the internees to the WRA or placed them in other areas of the interior states.[46]

In Washington, D.C., on February 23, 1942, Secretary of the Navy Knox began pressing for the removal to a separate island of all persons of Japanese ancestry under the authority of Executive Order 9066. His memo to President Roosevelt stated:

You will recall that on several occasions at Cabinet meetings, I have urged the policy of removing the 140,000 people of Japanese blood from Oahu to one of the other islands in the group. Each time the question has become bogged down because it dealt with the matter of interfering with the constitutional rights of American citizens of Japanese descent. Is not this difficulty now cleared up by your recent order covering exactly this question on the mainland?[47]

President Roosevelt replied to Secretary Knox on February 26 that he wanted the entire 140,000 evacuated and had no qualms about the legality of the move: "I do not worry about the constitutional question—first, because of my recent order [Executive Order 9066] and second because Hawaii is under martial law."[48]

On March 18, the Joint Chiefs of Staff sent Lieutenant General Emmons a classified memorandum ordering "That such Japanese residents of the Hawaiian Islands (either U.S. citizens or nationals) as are considered by appropriate authority in the Hawaiian Islands to constitute a source of danger be transported to the U.S. mainland and placed under guard in concentration camps."[49] No specifications were made as to whether the concentration camps would be the responsibility of the Department of Justice or the military, or both.

On March 21, the attorney general informed the provost marshal general's office that he was aware that naturalized citizens had earlier been removed from Hawaii and sent to Camp McCoy in army custody. He asked for information on the internment of all such Americans now in the army's mainland internment camps. The War Department agreed to furnish the names and apprised the attorney general of the recent secret recommendations by the Joint Chiefs of Staff and the president for the removal of such persons from Hawaii.[50] This particular inquiry should have reminded the army that the Justice Department questioned the legality of putting citizens into mainland internment camps. When the adjutant general asked Emmons about the transported citizens, he replied that two of the three—Harold L. Deponte and Tadashi Neil Morimoto—could return, but he excepted Mignon Charney since she "has for years been a resident of enemy countries and her presence here is not desired."[51] Emmons apparently did not initiate any additional action to comply with the March 18 memorandum authorizing the removal of more Issei and Nisei from the islands.

On June 27, 1942, the War Department chief of staff resolved the problem of removing Hawaii Nikkei to the mainland. He sent a classified policy statement to the Hawaiian department and canceled the order to intern and transport all Japanese in Hawaii. What the War Department proposed instead was a selective removal of up to 15,000 people who are "believed to be dangerous, or are most likely to become so during any period of invasion or immediate threat of invasion." Those removed were subject to transportation to the mainland and were to be given to the WRA for placement into "resettlement areas with housing facilities and opportunities to work provided by the government."[52] It was further stipulated that these resettlement areas were not to be called "internment camps." Hereafter, selected arrests and internment or incarceration of some Issei and Nisei continued into mid-1942.

INVESTIGATION OF KIBEI POPULATION

In July 1942, a Honolulu FBI agent ordered Iwao Kosaka to report to the agency's office in the Dillingham Transportation Building on Bishop Street. Kosaka was a Kibei, and in his interview he stated that he had done nothing wrong and had even taken a physical examination in 1940 to prepare for induction into the U.S. Army. Kosaka believes that his prewar job of teaching at a Japanese-language school and the fact that his parents had sent him to Japan when he was younger were prime factors in attracting the FBI's attention:

> Kosaka remembers well the questions posed by the FBI. "Can you shoot your father if your father came to attack Hawaii?" they asked. Kosaka turned the tables on them. "I wonder if I can shoot him. How about you? Can you shoot your father?" he asked the agents. . . . "Maybe I should have said, 'Sure, I'm going to shoot my father.' But it's not an honest answer." They also asked him why he had gone to Japan as a child. "I don't know why. My parents took me when I was a baby," he replied. They asked him why he had taken military training in high school in Japan, which was then compulsory for any student enrolled in a Japanese high school. The questioning continued for about an hour, after which Kosaka had expected to be released.[53]

Instead, the FBI detained Kosaka and took him to the Honolulu immigration station. He stayed there for a few days, unable to inform his family and friends of his whereabouts. Later, the FBI transported him to the Sand Island Internment Camp on Oahu and kept him there for almost a year before shipping him to the mainland on March 2, 1943. Since he was a citizen, the Justice Department would not accept him as an internee. Kosaka was placed in various WRA camps—first at Topaz, Utah, and later at Tule Lake, California. The WRA finally released him in March 1946, after he had spent more than three and a half years in confinement.[54] It is significant that Kosaka's case again shows an instance of interagency cooperation, this time between the WRA and the Hawaii command. The WRA administrators accepted the custody of a prisoner, taken by the army under martial law, whom the Justice Department was unwilling to accept.

In late 1942, the Hawaii department's military intelligence units investigated all Kibei who had not already been arrested in the islands. The Kibei were American citizens but were considered untrustworthy by some army intelligence officials. An army official reasoned: "Their presence in this country and their possible relationship with certain Japanese authorities before returning to this country, make them necessarily suspicious. The mission of the Kibei in the United States, therefore, is not clear and must be regarded with suspicion."[55] This perception caused the military to question the motives of all Kibei, resulting in searches of their homes for incriminating evidence; apparently none was ever found.

From October 21 to 26, 1942, army military intelligence agents questioned or tried to account for all the Kibei on the island of Maui, as they had done previously on the islands of Oahu and Hawaii. Nothing suspicious arose as a result of this inquiry: "The search of homes and personal belongings brought to light no article of extreme pro-Japanese or anti-American nature," and "The Kibei investigated were found to be very much similar to those interrogated on the island of Oahu." Ironically, the military intelligence agent who signed this memo was named Kanazawa, perhaps also of Japanese heritage.[56]

The army spent considerable time interrogating the arrested Kibei. The questions were similar to those posed at the mainland hearing boards. Hajime Takemoto, a Kibei living in the town of Ewa on Oahu, vividly recalled two particular questions from his interview, even after more than four decades had elapsed: "If you were in an American bomber and you were told to bomb the Imperial Palace with the Emperor there, would you do so?" Takemoto recalls thinking that if he answered yes, the interrogators probably would not believe him, so he responded, "No, I don't think so! The Japanese people consider the Emperor to be a living God, so I don't think I could do that." The other question was, "If you are standing on the beach and the Japanese soldiers were coming in and the American soldiers were defending the beach, which way would you shoot?" He replied, "Since I am an American, I would shoot toward the Japanese side." Takemoto was married to a Nisei and had one child when the war started. He was allowed to go home, while a fellow Kibei with essentially the same personal history was given long-term internment. Takemoto found this decision inexplicable.[57]

The military in Hawaii appeared to use fluctuating standards for releasing or interning this subgroup of Japanese Americans. It appears that even without any accusation of involvement in questionable or unlawful actions, merely being a Kibei could result in internment. On Maui, for example, army military intelligence identified sixty-three Kibei among all the Japanese Americans residing there. Unable to reach thirty-six of them—twelve were on another island, five were in the U.S. Army, and six were already interned—the army investigated and released nine and recommended that the remaining eighteen be interned. None in the latter group had engaged in any acts against the United States; rather, this judgment appears to have been based on highly subjective grounds. For example, the army described the "adverse factors" of one twenty-eight-year-old Kibei recommended for internment: "a) subject is a Kibei with all the characteristics of the type, b) subject spent 21 formative years in Japan, c) subject's education was exclusively in Japan and he speaks no English, d) subject will inherit property in Japan at the death of his mother." Two factors considered favorable were given: "a) subject has one U.S. Defense Bond, b) subject donated to the Blood Bank."[58] On these grounds, the military intelligence board unanimously recommended internment for this Kibei. The meaning of the first adverse factor, "all the characteristics of the type," was not clarified.

Another case involved Mr. K., a twenty-nine-year-old Kibei who had lived in Japan for twenty years and whose "family ties are predominantly in Japan." Favorable factors included the following: "a) subject speaks fair English, b) subject has substantial financial interests in the United States."[59] The board unanimously recommended Mr. K. for internment.

In a contrasting case in Maui, the military intelligence board recommended the release of a twenty-four-year-old Kibei. His profile included "Adverse Factors: a) subject is a borderline Kibei, b) subject was educated in Japan, with no education in America." There was no explanation of what constituted a "borderline" Kibei. The favorable factors were "a) subject has a substantial account in Maui Pineapple Company's Credit Union, b) subject has no interests in Japan, c) subject's family ties are divided and are not centered in Japan, d) subject has one $25.00 War Bond, e) subject's broken English is better than that of the average Kibei, f) subject donated blood to the Blood Bank, g) when asked questions by the interpreter in Japanese, subject tried to answer in English, h) subject seems to be assimilated." A significant part of the army's assessment, however, is the remark that the "subject's intelligence is not sufficiently high to enable him to be dangerous."[60] The Hawaii command recommended release, and the FBI agreed.

In the Kibei cases, we see that for some ten months after the outbreak of the war, the army and the FBI continued to arrest these individuals on the basis of their generational identity, interned some without evidence, and considered them to be inherently dangerous. In hindsight, there appears to be little to differentiate the Kibei who were permanently interned from those who were released. While these investigations were ongoing, a memorandum on the Kibei from the officer in charge of military intelligence on Maui admitted that this group of Japanese Americans had done nothing to cause alarm: "In spite of the potentially dangerous appearance of this type, it is noteworthy that, insofar as is known, no case of subversive action by Kibei has been brought to the attention of authorities."[61] Yet, the distrust, arrests, and confinement continued for some Kibei.

On March 2, 1943, the army shipped 175 Kibei (among them, Iwao Kosaka, whose case is described above) to the WRA Relocation Camp at Topaz, Utah. Although the army apparently reviewed their cases in 1944, it continued to question the Kibei's loyalty to the United States. Even a Kibei's proclaimed allegiance to the United States was suspect, according to one Hawaii military authority:

Based on the findings of Hearing Boards and intelligence reports, it is my opinion that despite the fact that so many have made statements of loyalty to the United States, that they are dangerous to the security of the United States and that their utterances of loyalty are inconsistent with their backgrounds and training in Japan. If any of them should institute habeas corpus proceedings in the local United States District Court, we might not be able to present a strong case against them. I therefore propose to evacuate from Hawaii for resettlement in war relocation centers on the United States mainland those Kibei who have professed loyalty to the United States. Request your approval of this proposal.[62]

To this officer, it did not matter what the Kibei said. Regardless of their avowed loyalty and without any facts to justify suspicion, he believed that Kibei were likely to be disloyal and were therefore dangerous.

HONOULIULI GULCH CAMP

The situation for prisoners who were not shipped to the mainland was also fraught with anxiety and uncertainty. Throughout the early part of the war, as we have seen, a few internees who were transported to the mainland were rejected by the Justice Department and returned to Hawaii. In the meantime, other Issei and Nisei continued to be arrested and charged with a variety of offenses such as violations of the army's curfew rules or the blackout regulations. After sending most of the Issei to the mainland, the army closed the Sand Island Internment Station on March 1, 1943.

The next day, the army took the remaining prisoners to a newly erected camp northwest of Honolulu near the town of Ewa, in Honouliuli Gulch. The camp was intended to hold mainly American citizens of Japanese ancestry, both male and female, but it soon held some Issei, non-Japanese internees, and various prisoners of war from the Pacific theater.[63]

The Honouliuli Gulch Internment Camp was nestled in sugarcane fields and covered nearly 160 acres. With armed guards patrolling a dual barbed-wire fence and watchtowers positioned at strategic spots along the perimeter, this camp was a grim, primitive prison. The civilian internees were housed in fifteen wooden army-type barracks and in tarpaulin tents that held six to eight people.[64] Military prisoners of war were kept in a separate area.[65] The army configured Honouliuli to hold 3,000 internees, but its peak population at any one time was only 320. Some prisoners stayed for a few months, while others remained for more than two years.

There are reports that the army required the internees to construct elements of their own prison. First, the army forced them to build a part of the internment camps: "[Nishikawa] said . . . guard towers were built later by the internees."[66] Second, and more important, the internees found it impossible to question the legitimacy of their internment if they wished to be released:

Before being released, each parolee was required to sign a promise that he would not bring a damage suit against the U.S. government as a result of the internment. Sakakihara, [a Nisei, aged] 76, recalls that he signed a statement after he returned to Hilo.

"I was coerced—intimidated—into signing that statement," he said. "I was told that if I didn't sign I would again lose my freedom. I could have taken it to any court and had it nullified. But it's all pau [finished] now."[67]

If a person wished to leave the camp and was eligible to do so, the only choice was to sign the statement. Failure to sign resulted in continued imprisonment. By precluding the possibility that an internee might contest his or her status in a court of law, the army, in effect, created the conditions under which an individual's status was affirmed as guilty and blocked the internee from obtaining legal redress for unlawful imprisonment.

Honouliuli Gulch differed in at least two significant ways from army internment camps on the mainland. First, internees reported that many of the army guards from Hawaii were unlike those from the mainland. For example, one soldier from the islands, a Sergeant Loveless, reportedly lost his stripes for allowing some internees to go outside the gate to collect seashells and coral—he accompanied them without his weapon. In contrast, the guards from the mainland were feared after an incident in which an internee who was hard-of-hearing approached a guard and failed to heed his order to halt. The guard fired several shots at the internee's feet.[68] Second, the families of internees in the Hawaiian camps could visit the prisoners twice a month in a relaxed atmosphere in the mess hall. At the Tuna Canyon Detention Station in California, the INS used a barbed-wire fence to separate family members from Issei internees and allowed only English as the medium of communication.

Another Nisei describes the effect of his internment on a personal relationship. In January 1942, the FBI arrested Henry Tanaka of Kauai. Although the agency made no specific charges, the FBI kept him interned for two years and three months—first at Wailua County Jail, then at Sand Island, and finally at Honouliuli Gulch. In 1944, Tanaka finally demanded that the army make specific charges against him, and two weeks later he was paroled on condition that he release the government from future damage claims. He agreed under duress. Along with monetary losses, he states that a more profound hurt occurred: "During my parole, my Caucasian benefactress who helped me financially during my high school became critically ill. I went to her home with a bouquet of flowers but she refused to see me, sending word that she was extremely disappointed in me because I had been disloyal to my country. This was one of the saddest moments of my life. Shortly thereafter, she passed away." Tanaka carried this burden with him, saying, "This has left an everlasting scar in my heart."[69]

A final aspect of the Hawaii experience is the secrecy imposed and maintained by the military. Many Japanese Americans in Hawaii are still unaware of the full story of the forced detention and removal of island persons to the mainland and the existence of the two camps. Martial law and use of the military-security classification restricted information about the entire wartime episode.

The army closed Honouliuli Gulch in 1945. Nothing remains of this camp or the one at Sand Island. Honouliuli is now unkempt land owned by the Oahu Sugar Company, which leases it out to hold wrecked autos. Sand Island became a state park, and on weekends, families picnic on the sparse lawn growing over the red volcanic sand.

SELECTIVE REMOVAL POLICY

The army also sent other Hawaii residents to the mainland throughout World War II. To recapitulate, during the war years, the army shipped a total of 875 Issei to the mainland Justice Department camps, along with 100 Germans and 4 others of European descent.[70] The Issei were kept in a number of places including Bismarck, North Dakota; Lordsburg, New Mexico; and Crystal City, Texas. From 1943 to 1944, the largest single Hawaii contingent of about 350 Issei males resided at the Santa Fe Internment Camp in New Mexico.[71]

In response to the push by the War Department and President Roosevelt to bring Japanese Americans to the mainland, Lieutenant General Emmons instituted a selective removal policy. He established two categories: (1) "primarily for the purpose of removing nonproductive and undesirable Japanese and their families from the Islands," and (2) "largely [as] a token evacuation to satisfy certain interests which have advocated movement of Japanese from the Hawaiian Islands."[72] The Hawaiian department's response indicates Emmons's compliance with political and public relations pressures but is consonant with his public statement that in general the Japanese in Hawaii did not constitute a serious threat or danger. A reasoned guess might be that it was the removal of some numbers of the Kibei population that constituted the "token evacuation to satisfy certain interests."

Under this selective policy, an additional 1,217 persons eventually were shipped to WRA relocation camps from November 23, 1942, to July 1945. The largest group, numbering 1,037, arrived between November 1942 and March 14, 1943, and were primarily family members of husbands and fathers previously taken to the Justice Department camps. In this group, 40 percent were under seventeen years of age.[73] This total includes the 176 Kibei males who were recommended for internment but could not be placed into a Justice Department camp. The army put all these Hawaii residents in WRA camps; most of them went to Jerome, Arkansas, or Topaz, Utah, but some ended up at Minidoka, Idaho, and Tule Lake, California. After the war, 806 of these 1,217 prisoners returned to Hawaii, 125 stayed on the mainland, 136 went to Japan, 115 were interned by the Justice Department, 25 voluntarily joined family at the Crystal City INS camp in Texas, and 10 died.

Adding this count of 1,217 to the 875 predominantly male Issei produces a total of 2,092 persons brought to the mainland. Along with the estimated 300 persons who remained in Hawaii, the total number of Hawaii residents of Japanese ancestry who were detained in permanent imprisonment facilities comes to 2,392. Compared to the prisoner population of Nikkei on the mainland, this is a very small number. The contrast in treatment between these two groups is stark and revealing.

CONCLUSION

The differences in the treatment of Nikkei on the mainland and in Hawaii should not obscure the similarities. The vast majority of those arrested and interned in the islands were removed as a result of prior contemplation and later cooperation and coercion. There is no evidence that any of them had committed espionage or sabotage or had in any way hindered the war efforts of the United States. Yet, except for those who applied to accompany their spouses or fathers, these people were involuntarily removed from their homes and communities under the same rationale used by the Western Defense Command. In some cases, people were removed for explicitly political considerations—they were innocent victims of military and political forces in the United States.

At the same time, contrasts with the mainland experience are dramatic. Hawaii's early history and relations with this large minority population were the most obvious mitigating factors, but it is also true that Nikkei labor was of vital importance in sustaining both the territory's economy and the war effort. Thus, it can be argued that economic and military needs prevented mass internment and incarceration of Hawaii's Japanese-ancestry population. Yet, despite the generational distinctions, no one of Japanese descent in Hawaii could ignore the possibility of immediate arrest.

5

The Territory of Alaska
and Latin America

The wartime imprisonment process also affected people of Japanese descent in places far from the U.S. mainland, although it did so in different forms. This chapter will explore two of these areas.

The first is in the extreme north—the territory of Alaska, where after the declaration of war, the U.S. Army quickly took command of the inhabitants. The discussion here addresses the rationalization and justification by which almost all persons of Japanese ancestry were removed from the territory and shipped to lower mainland states. It will become apparent that when the military first took control, the process in Alaska was similar to that in Hawaii. Later, however, the situation changed, and arrests of Issei and removal of all persons of Japanese ancestry became identical to procedures on the West Coast.

A second area discussed in this chapter is south of the U.S. border, in certain Latin American countries. There, designated persons were arrested, brought against their will to the United States, and interned in Justice Department camps. This intriguing segment of a broader American story demonstrates the pervasiveness of the U.S. government's political influence and power, which enabled it to become involved in the affairs of foreign governments in this hemisphere.

THE TERRITORY OF ALASKA

Only a few people of Japanese descent lived in the territory of Alaska in 1940. There were about 240 foreign nationals and citizens of Japanese ancestry living there, out of a total population of 72,524. Their presence was almost unnoticed by other residents, since Alaska encompasses a large land area and its population has always been sparse and widely dispersed, yet this minority was not entirely ignored. The eventual exclusion of Japanese nationals from Alaska was part of the prewar plan of March 11, 1941—the same plan that affected Nikkei in the contiguous states.[1] In prewar meetings, representatives of the War and Justice Departments discussed Alaska's "dangerous" persons. Soon after, agents for the FBI in Juneau began to compile a custodial detention list, and by May 5, they had a roster of sixty foreign nationals of unspecified designations ready for possible arrest. Within this group, the FBI identified only eight individuals as dangerous; the remainder were placed in the "potentially dangerous" category.[2] On December 5, F B I director John Edgar Hoover instructed the Juneau agents to hold discussions with representatives of the Office of Naval Intelligence and the army's Military Intelligence Division to formulate plans for the "immediate apprehension of Japanese aliens . . . who have been recommended [for] custodial detention."[3]

Two days later, on December 7, 1941, the commanding general of the Alaska Defense Command, Lieutenant General Simon Bolivar Buckner Jr., received a priority telegram from the provost marshal general in Washington, D.C., instructing him to contact the U.S. attorney in Juneau. He was to provide facilities for the internment of eleven supposedly dangerous foreign nationals as specified by the Justice Department.[4] The F B I arrested the eleven men and handed them over to the I N S, which in turn sent the internees to Fort Richardson, nine miles north of Anchorage, for detention.[5] Although their ethnicity is not specified, the eleven were most likely nine Japanese nationals and two German nationals.[6] On December 8, another telegram ordered the commander to place German and Italian nationals in an enemy alien category.[7]

From December 10, however, it was not clear which government agency was responsible for the enemy aliens, and weeks elapsed before the issue was resolved. On December 10, F B I director Hoover told his Juneau agents that the army had instructed the Alaska Defense commanding general to assume responsibility for all matters concerning foreign nationals. Hoover interpreted this instruction to mean that "all arrests and detention of such persons will be handled by them." Moreover, the F B I would "have no responsibility or duty to perform incident to the foreign national enemy arrest administration and internment" except to give the army whatever information it had on file concerning the enemy aliens.[8] The next day, the Juneau agents reported to the F B I that seven foreign nationals, all Issei, were in custody.

The army then told the F B I that it wanted only partial jurisdiction over the territory—namely, the Alaska Peninsula and the adjoining Aleutian, Pribilof, and Kodiak Islands.[9] Hoover certainly knew of the prewar agreement between the Justice and War Departments establishing their spheres of influence; according to the agreement, Alaska was to fall under the army's jurisdiction. The F B I director thus instructed his agents: "Get this matter straightened out. It is my understanding that the War Department is to assume complete control of alien enemy matters in Alaska and I don't want to have any divided authority. It is either their job and their whole job, or not."[10] Although Hoover seemingly relinquished authority to the army, he did not tell his agents to assist the military unconditionally. The F B I agents in Juneau were never, in any instance, to go beyond limited cooperation: "Bureau instructions of December ten should be followed. Decision as to persons to be taken into custody now rests with Army authorities there. You should furnish them only names of German, Japanese and Italian nationals. Names of citizens and of communists and communist supporters should not be furnished."[11] Thus, as in the lower forty-eight states, the FBI had already compiled a list of suspect persons and of enemy aliens.

Because of the prewar agreement, however, Hoover had little basis on which to protest the War Department's action. But he instilled an attitude of tepid cooperation in his agents, and the Alaska Defense Command probably became aware that it was essentially on its own. The army might have been reluctant to take full responsibility for even the small number of enemy aliens because it had limited personnel in the isolated Alaskan villages who were capable of investigating a civilian population. Nevertheless, on December 17, the army accepted complete control of the program and started to formulate plans for the arrest and detention of the foreign nationals.

Hoover then instructed the Juneau FBI agents to turn over available information on foreign nationals to the army, "and, thereafter, take absolutely no action in connection with the apprehension or detention of alien enemies."[12] Although the FBI then had no jurisdiction over the enemy alien program, Hoover's interest in a related area continued. On December 18, he ordered Juneau FBI agents to furnish his office with names and data on "persons of American citizenship of Japanese, Italian, German, Hungarian, Bulgarian, or Rumanian nationality who should be considered for custodial detention, if and when the [Justice] Department decides such action is necessary." The reply from Juneau was that there were no persons of Bulgarian, Hungarian, Italian, or Romanian ancestry identified for detention. It did list twelve people of German ancestry—two foreign nationals and ten citizens—but none of Japanese descent. The slate was clean here: "There are no persons of Japanese nationality who are citizens of the United States who are being considered for custodial detention."[13]

The significance of this last memorandum is clear. The FBI field office had already completed its investigations and concluded that no Japanese—resident national or American citizen—in Alaska constituted a threat to the security of the United States. There is nothing in the records to show that this information was shared with the Alaska Defense commander, but as a group, persons of Japanese ancestry had also been investigated by military intelligence agencies and none was arrested throughout the war years. Subsequent events overshadowed this internal intelligence information, however, and other pressures led to the later arrest and removal of all Nikkei. A significant deciding factor was probably the War Department's December 12 order placing the Alaska Defense Command under the Western Defense Command (WDC) and Lieutenant General John L. DeWitt. From that point, per the army's chain of command, the orders of the WDC superseded any local authority.

In Washington, D.C., on December 29, President Franklin D. Roosevelt signed an executive order officially transferring responsibility for foreign nationals in Alaska to the commanding general of the Alaska Defense Command. It was then time for the FBI to make amends. That same day, Hoover instructed his Juneau agents to cooperate fully with the Alaska alien enemy program. In a letter to the army's judge advocate general, Hoover stated that the bureau offered its full cooperation.[14] Even so, for some twenty-one days after the attack on Pearl Harbor, these Issei were apparently considered such a threat that they had to be held even though the agency imprisoning them had no clear assignment to do so.

By February 14, the army had fifty-five resident foreign nationals interned in Alaska: seventeen were kept at Fort Richardson, five at Chilkoot Barracks, thirty-one at Annettee Island Landing Field, and two at Nome.[15] The Alaska Defense Command later transported these internees to Fort Lewis, Washington, where the army established hearing boards. It recommended that all the Issei, except four very elderly Japanese, be permanently interned. The army then transported the Issei to the camp at Fort Sam Houston, Texas, and then to Lordsburg, New Mexico.[16]

Foreign nationals taken into custody by the Alaska Defense Command under the alien enemy program came to 104 persons—92 Japanese males, 2 Japanese females, 9 German males, and 1 Italian male. The army arrested and then paroled or released 9 additional Germans and 5 Italians.[17]

Mike Hagiwara, a Nisei internee from Ketchikan, wrote to the Alaska territorial governor, Ernest Gruening, on behalf of families separated from fathers taken to camps in the contiguous states. The governor brought Hagiwara's concern to Abe Fortas, then undersecretary of the Interior Department, who in turn passed it on to WRA director Dillon Myer. Myer replied that although he was willing to cooperate and help the families, the Issei men were not in the custody of the WRA but were the responsibility of the Justice Department. As one author points out, "It was a classic bureaucratic maneuver of passing responsibility from one agency to the other in order to avoid taking any action, and there the matter rested."[18]

In February 1942, after this first group of Issei were taken, the army widened its net and proposed to incarcerate all persons of Japanese ancestry. On February 25, the army informed the FBI that it had a list of all Japanese resident nationals and American citizens of Japanese ancestry in Alaska. It further stated that these Nikkei would be moved to Fort Richardson in Anchorage and then transported into the Alaskan interior. One potential relocation site mentioned by the army was Matanuska Valley, near Anchorage.[19] Using Executive Order 9066 as his authority, the commanding general of the Alaska Defense Command determined to remove all known "Japanese at large in Alaska, either alien or native born."[20] On March 5, the army issued the first arrest orders for all male Japanese, sixteen years and older, excluding those with families.

In early April, the Alaska Defense commanding general declared the territory a military area that required protection of national defense premises and materials against espionage and sabotage. With this declaration, he ordered the removal of all residents of Japanese descent. They were to report on April 20 to the nearest army post for eventual transportation—not to the interior of Alaska but to the lower forty-eight states. In late April and early May, the army sent four separate groups of

Alaska Japanese, mainly women and children, to the army's wcca assembly center in Puyallup, Washington, not to the Justice Department internment camps where some heads of families had been taken earlier. For most of them, the final destination would be the wra relocation camp in Minidoka, Idaho.[21]

One unverified case serves as an example of the dilemmas raised by this expulsion order. The Alaskan military command arrested the Native wife of an Issei male already interned in a Justice Department camp and sent her and her children to the Puyallup Assembly Center. The mother approached the camp director and asked about the fate of her children: "As an Eskimo, I am under the responsibility of the Bureau of Indian Affairs and my husband is now held by the Justice Department," she said. "Do my children come under the Bureau of Indian Affairs, the Justice Department, or the army?" The camp director couldn't respond immediately but promised an answer shortly. For days, the mother sat on the front steps of the administration building, awaiting the government's response. Finally, the camp director emerged and told her that the Bureau of Indian Affairs and the U.S. Army had equal authority because the children were half Eskimo and half Japanese, and although she fell under the jurisdiction of the BIA and could leave, her children would have to stay. She remained with her children.[22]

In addition to a few late-comers, 145 persons from Alaska were finally taken to Puyallup. Within this group, 121 were American citizens, of whom 50 were under eighteen years of age; many of their fathers were Japanese fishermen or cannery workers who were married to Indian or Eskimo women.[23]

The military's unwillingness to deviate from its rules is exemplified by a story of one of the incarcerated children (pseudonyms are used):

Peter Ogata was born at Taka Harbor in 1915. His Indian mother had become pregnant by an Indian man. To salvage her respectability, she married Hajime Ogata while Peter was still in her womb. She and Hajime had two boys of their own before Hajime deserted the family. The boys were brought up by missionaries among other Indians. They had never been to a city, much less around Japanese Americans . . . but the government took them anyway because they had a Japanese last name. At the same time, they left free full-blooded Japanese Alaskans who had taken Indian names.[24]

Removal from their homes created considerable hardships for Alaska's incarcerated population. Consider the case of Henry Hope, a seventeen-year-old boy:

Lucie and Sammy Hope, the former an Athabaskan Indian and the latter an Eskimo, had adopted Henry, whose father had been a Japanese, as a baby. Henry helped support his adoptive parents but was evacuated nonetheless. [An appeal was made to the Alaska Governor who] regretfully reported that his request [to the wdc] had been denied and that "no exception can be made."[25]

As stated earlier, the w d c wielded authority over the Alaska Defense Command.

Alaska's residents thus were imprisoned like thousands of others of Japanese ancestry in the internment and incarceration centers.[26] For wives of Eskimo ancestry, the situation was undoubtedly quite strange—especially the sudden, extreme change in climate and the overwhelming presence of an unfamiliar ethnic group.

Bureaucratic rules were a fact of life for this group of Alaska exiles. Even after they were no longer seen as a threat to the territory of Alaska, their return was hampered by a tedious and protracted exit process. After the Alaska Defense Command rescinded its exclusion order, just for the Nisei, on January 3, 1945, those who were willing and able to return had to gain leave clearance from the w r a camps. Inmates next had to obtain and complete a State Department Permit to Depart.[27] The State Department required them to submit five copies of the form to Alaska's territorial governor for approval. Then, returning Alaska residents were required to notify the ports where they were planning to land and arrange for transportation to their final destinations. This cumbersome process took time—obtaining the forms, assembling the necessary information, mailing the forms to the appropriate agencies, waiting for the agencies to respond, and finally traveling home.

The Issei were allowed to return in March 1945. Before doing so, however, they also needed exit permits from the State Department and concurrent approval from the Justice Department. For those under w r a control, the provost marshal general's office in Washington, D.C., and the commanding general in Alaska both had to grant approval. After this, returnees had to find relocation officers to arrange for their actual transportation back to Alaska. Finding an Alaska-bound ship that was willing to take passengers was not an easy task in 1945, because all nonmilitary spaces were reserved for cannery workers. Only in June 1945 did space finally became available for returning Issei.[28] Yet, even after arriving in Alaska, if commercial transportation was unavailable, Issei had to request further assistance from the army. Essentially, from December 1941 to June 1945 at the earliest, these Issei had little choice but to remain imprisoned thousands of miles from their homes.

It was not until September 4, 1945, that the army removed these complicated travel restrictions, allowing the Alaska Nikkei residents to return freely. But upon arriving home, they found themselves placed under parole status until the Alaska Defense Command determined the status of each returnee. This situation lasted until November 1945, when the army removed all restrictions.[29]

In this way, people of Japanese ancestry, and sometimes those connected with them by choice or circumstance, were removed from Alaska. For more than three years, they were unwilling pawns of the Justice Department, the Western Defense Command, the Alaska Defense Command, and the War Department. These people were forcibly moved from place to place for no reason other than their actual or perceived ethnoracial ancestry and the bureaucratic inflexibility of government agencies and officials.

JAPANESE LATIN AMERICA

During World War II, the U.S. government was instrumental in transporting and interning in its camps numerous foreign nationals from areas outside the forty-eight states and U.S. territories. A meeting of the ministers of foreign affairs from various Pan-American republics was held in Rio de Janeiro, in January 1942, and played an important role in this process. At the meeting, the ministers reached an overall agreement to control "potentially dangerous aliens, to intern Axis nationals, to restrict the naturalization of enemy aliens, and to cancel the naturalization of Axis supporters."[30] Such individuals, provided they were enemy aliens of the United States, were to be transported summarily to this country. The United States also agreed to pay all costs related to the internment process. Arrangements were then finalized for an inter-American plan to remove enemy nationals from fifteen countries, including Bolivia, Ecuador, Panama, Peru, and even Haiti.[31]

This inter-American removal process, however, had its beginning prior to the United States' entry into the war. In 1940, the FBI's Special Intelligence Service (SIS), newly established by Hoover, posted about 360 agents in various Latin American countries to identify and compile lists of "dangerous" persons of German, Italian, and Japanese ancestry.[32] The people named on these lists, and others identified by the countries involved—a total of 2,253 persons of Japanese ancestry—were shipped northward for internment in the United States beginning on April 4, 1942, and continuing through 1944.[33] The purpose of this inter-American effort was to create a pool of people who could be exchanged for U.S. citizens trapped in Axis countries.[34] Although a few exchanges were made, primarily of diplomatic personnel, the procedure did not affect most persons of Japanese ancestry who had been brought up from these countries.

Not all the internees transported to the United States for this reason were actually designated as dangerous persons. The State Department, for example, discovered that Panama had sent all its Japanese nationals, based on the assumption that the United States was going to determine which ones should be permanently interned.[35]

One INS official commented later on a bizarre aspect of the inter-American program:

> The rationale for the international form of kidnapping was that by immobilizing influential German and Japanese nationals who might aid and abet the Axis war effort in the Latin American countries where they lived, the United States was preventing the spread of Nazism throughout the hemisphere and thereby strengthening its own security. However, the project turned out to be something of a farce for as the internment camp commanders became better acquainted with their Latin-American charges, they learned that a number of them were not the "potentially dangerous" Germans and Japanese originally arrested but impoverished peasants who had been paid to act as substitutes for them.[36]

Although these proxies arrived as part of the foreign enemy alien group, there was nothing in the files to show that the State Department recognized or addressed their improper internment. Not only were proxies used, but certain administrators of the Latin American countries could be bribed: "The more affluent Japanese were finding that a well placed monetary contribution would bring immunity from deportation."[37]

Not all Latin American countries agreed with the provisions of the Pan-American conference. Brazil, with 170,165 persons of Japanese ancestry in 1938, sent none of its permanent residents to the United States. Instead, it assured the United States that its Japanese population was under surveillance; later, the Brazilian government moved them farther inland, away from the Atlantic Ocean. However, Brazil did repatriate some Japanese and German diplomatic personnel, and it sent one male German national to a U.S. INS camp. No details are available about this individual or what became of him after the war.[38]

Mexico

Mexico also refused to send its resident Japanese population to the United States; this country's treatment of the ethnic group is similar to that of Brazil. In 1940, Mexico had a population of nearly 4,700 persons of Japanese ancestry. Between December 7 and 9, 1941, Mexico ended diplomatic relations with Japan, and fifty-four members of the Japanese legation with its staff and dependents were repatriated through the United States on February 18, 1942.

On December 9, 1941, all bank deposits of the Japanese in Mexico were frozen, and in Mexico City, where 602 Japanese nationals and their families lived, nighttime travel and meetings of more than ten people were banned. In Baja California, just north of Ensenada, Mexico, and south of San Diego, California, on December 12, 1941, the government confiscated two Japanese-owned fishing boats and ordered their crews and nine other persons, previously identified by the United States, to move to Mexico City. These specific incidents occurred while a more general policy concerning their country's Nikkei population was being considered by Mexican government officials.

Mexico then defined a ribbon of land (125 miles along the Pacific coast and 62 miles along the Mexico-U.S. border) from which all Japanese would be excluded.[39] The first removal orders arrived in Baja California and Baja California Sur on January 2, 1942, and the Japanese were notified that they had five days to leave the area:

> The Baja California evacuation was by far the most massive, hasty, and strictly enforced in Mexico. In other states, the orders came later and the application of the order was more flexible, depending on the decisions of the individual state and local administrations. The order was negotiable to a certain extent, as is seen in the case of

a farmer in Navajoa, Sonora, who had the enforcement of evacuation postponed until he harvested his crop in June, 1942.[40]

One author reports that 235 Japanese residents inside this exclusion area, mostly from Tijuana, Ensenada, and Mexicali, were removed from their homes in early 1942.[41]

Those residing in the excluded zone could choose between relocation to two sites—Mexico City or Guadalajara. The government reasoned that concentrating the group in two areas would allow for more efficient control and surveillance. There were no other restrictions imposed on the relocated persons, except that they must report their arrival.

After May 28, 1942, when Mexico declared war on the Axis countries, foreign nationals of these countries became enemy aliens, and the Mexican government announced additional decrees. All Japanese immigrants were required to move to one of the two cities, and exit permits were necessary in order to leave. However, the Japanese in Mexico were free to engage in any work and activity that they could find.

Not everyone was willing to be expelled. Antonio Kisaburo Yamane, born in Japan in 1888, arrived in Mexico when he was nineteen. He learned Spanish, worked at odd jobs until he enlisted in Mexico's revolutionary army in 1911, fought in the war, and rose to the rank of major. Yamane recalled that in 1942, "Japanese immigrants were required to live in Mexico City or Guadalajara. I was called to report to the city authority, so I took with me my record of service in the Revolution, including the *Legion de Honor Mexicana*. I was exempted from the relocation order and nobody bothered me ever since."[42] It probably did not hurt Yamane's case that he was, by that time, a naturalized Mexican citizen, was married to a Mexican woman, and had two Japanese Mexican children.

It is difficult to ascertain the number of Japanese who actually obeyed the exclusion order. One source estimates "that about 80 percent of the Japanese scattered over Mexico were relocated to either of the cities."[43] Most of them chose Mexico City over Guadalajara because there were more Japanese already there. A larger population obviously meant more hope of finding friends and help through mutual aid systems. They were also closer to the central government in the event they required assistance in expediting decisions. The government permitted the Japanese to construct and operate a Japanese-language school in Mexico City, while various government officials and agencies also gave jobs to incoming Japanese nationals.

Life in Mexico City was not necessarily easy for the Japanese. Some were suspect because of their ancestry, and other Mexicans boycotted their stores at different times during the war. Further difficulties included the government's refusal to give them contracts or orders, the scarcity of apartments and rooms, and government confiscation of businesses owned by some Japanese. Not all the rules were enforced stringently, however; for example, although the Japanese officially were not allowed to leave Mexico City or Guadalajara until 1945, many returned much earlier to their prewar communities.

Mexico established three internment sites, the first at Perote, Vera Cruz, to hold stranded German and Italian seamen. From February 8, 1942, some 500 such sailors were taken from their ships in Tampico and kept there throughout the war years. As for those of Japanese ancestry, no more than sixteen were ever interned at Perote; four of them were moved there because they had been mining in Sonora and fled into the mountains rather than relocate to central Mexico. They were caught and spent six months in the camp. The Mexican government placed one Issei at Perote for twenty-two months for unspecified reasons. He describes his internment as being "in a pleasant environment in the suburbs of Perote City" and providing him the opportunity for "having a good time with German, Italian, and Japanese friends."[44] The second site was a maximum-security prison on Isla Maria Madre, about sixty miles off the coast of Nayarit, Mexico. A harsher prison than Perote, it housed four Japanese residents, for unknown reasons. Two others were arrested "subsequent to censorship of their letters" and held for two years. The third site was a converted hacienda in the state of Mexico, an area different and separate from Mexico City. No further information is presently available on this last location.[45]

Some writers have asserted that the Mexican government protected its Japanese residents. Prior to December 1941, the FBI had some 200 agents in Mexico City, working out of the Hotel Maria Cristina on Reforma 31 to identify German, Italian, and Japanese nationals and Mexican citizens for arrest and internment when the war started. The United States tried to arrest nine suspected spies in Baja California by sending an army patrol into Mexico. Former president Lazaro Cardenas, who had been recalled from retirement and appointed commandant of the Pacific Military Zone, refused to allow them to enter the country. Instead, the designated "spies" were evacuated to Mexico City and set free.[46] In addition, when President Roosevelt met with Mexican president Manuel A. Camacho in Monterrey, Nuevo Leon, on April 20, 1943, one item on the agenda was a request to arrest and transport northward various Japanese nationals identified by the United States. Hearing of this request, some resident Japanese successfully argued to President Camacho through their contacts that acceding to the request would be tantamount to allowing the United States to interfere in Mexico's internal affairs.[47] President Roosevelt did not receive his requested Japanese nationals.

Cuba

The Cuban government began surveilling all of the country's 796 resident Japanese nationals and Japanese Cubans and its approximately 600 German nationals. With the approval of the United States, the Cubans then interned all adult Japanese males, some 345 of them, and German nationals on the Isle of Pines, which was used as a prison during the war. The United States offered $400,000 to offset the expense of holding these internees. The conditions there can best be described as difficult; the internees complained about the inferior food and their unjust separation from their wives and families.[48] Edward Ennis, director of the Alien Enemy Control Unit, spoke about the Cuban program to intern dangerous persons:

> Early in the war, you know like early '42, the German submarines were very successful off the Atlantic Coast. You could stand on the beach in Miami and see ships going down. And we had information that they were being refueled by Germans in Cuba. And so I went down to Havana and talked to the foreign minister there, with our ambassador, and we arranged a program with the Cubans. That, if they would pick up the Germans which we designated, on which we had the information, and intern them, they have a prison island in the south of Cuba, then we would pick up the cost, about 5 dollars a day, I think at that time.[49]

The FBI later told Ennis that the Cuban government was picking up not only "dangerous" Germans but others including German Jews and then confiscating their property. After conferring with the attorney general, the United States terminated the program.

Peru

The inter-American internment program produced extreme uncertainty and anxiety among the Japanese in Peru. The Japanese had been in that country since 1899, and a period of increased immigration occurred in the 1920s. By 1940, there were nearly 26,000 persons of Japanese ancestry living in Peru, composed of 17,000 Issei and 8,500 Nisei or Peruvian citizens. Relations between the Japanese and the Peruvians had ranged between friendliness and social hostility over the years. As wartime approached, various clashes took place, including a riot caused by racial tensions in 1940.[50]

Given the hostile social background, it is not surprising that Peruvian officials agreed to the arrest of selected Japanese nationals. In Lima, the authorities arrived without warning, sometimes in the middle of the night or very early in the morning, bundled the Issei into waiting cars, drove them to the harbor, and placed them on U.S. Navy ships for transport to the United States. The arrest criteria were not clear to those being taken and seemingly not even to those making the arrests.

For Peru, this removal program was a way to rid itself of individuals who were undesirable for economic or social reasons. As one American eyewitness stated: "Peru never revealed the criteria it employed for designating individuals as potentially dangerous. Given the emotionalism, irrationality, prejudice, envy, and other subjective factors nurturing anti-Japanese sentiment in Peru, the whim of enforcing officials played a major part in the designation of the undesirables."[51] The Peruvian detention list included men and women who were leaders in their Japanese associations, schools, and businesses and those who had earned the enmity of Peruvian officials.

In one situation, Lima's chief of police tried to send all "miscellaneous vagrants and petty miscreants with Japanese faces" to the United States.[52] In another instance, Peruvian authorities deported entire families, including many infant citizens of Peru.[53] Of all the Latin American countries, Peru deported the largest number of people of Japanese descent—1,771, or 79 percent of the total 2,253 shipped to the United States under the Pan-American agreement during the war years.

The Japanese Peruvian experience might be best understood through the plight of one family. In June 1942, unidentified officials came to Kakuaki Kaneko's house in Lima at 2:00 A.M., rousted him out of bed, and rushed him to the dock, where a U.S. Navy ship, the SS *Shawnee,* was waiting. On this trip, the *Shawnee* carried 342 Japanese, 196 Germans, and 10 Italians.[54] Before Kaneko's unexpected expulsion from Lima, he headed a family-owned import mirror company and was a prominent member of the local Japanese community. The problems of the Japanese Peruvians were compounded on board the ship, because they spoke only Spanish and Japanese and the crew and officers spoke only English. Food was an issue: the navy prepared rice for the Issei but allotted only one bowl per person and dumped the remainder overboard. The Japanese thought this wasteful practice was a shame, but their requests for more rice were either misunderstood or ignored. Another problem was the stress induced by their condition: one Issei, apparently suffering from depression over his treatment, tried to commit suicide. Attempts to obtain medical assistance for him were unsuccessful because of the language barrier.

Mr. Kaneko could not inform his family of his whereabouts until the ship landed in Panama and the navy placed him and the others in an internment camp constructed by the U.S. Army's Caribbean Defense Command. According to official policy, the United States was supposed to relinquish control of this camp to the Panamanian government; in fact, the United States maintained its control throughout the war.[55] The camp became the temporary detention station for internees brought from various Central and South American countries until they could be shipped to the United States for permanent internment. Even then, Mr. Kaneko could tell his family very little, since the navy gave him no information about his final destination. After departing from Panama, the ship headed into the Gulf of Mexico and then to Texas, where the INS split the men into two groups bound for either Kenedy, Texas, or Santa Fe, New Mexico.[56]

The navy brought 1,024 Japanese Peruvians to the United States between April 1942 and July 1943. Three categories of people were involved in this early period: 25 diplomats (13 men, 5 women, 7 children), 687 deportees like Kaneko (483 men, 63 women, 141 children), and 312 volunteers (129 men, 57 women, 126 children). Most of the prisoners from Peru originated in Lima—643 of them—while the remainder came from twenty-seven other cities.[57]

John K. Emmerson, then third secretary of the U.S. embassy in Peru, who assisted in the Peruvian internment process, questioned the wisdom of the program:

> As I look back on the Peruvian experience I am not proud to have been part of the Japanese operation. . . . It is hard to justify our pulling them from their homes of years and herding them, whether born in Japan or in Peru, onto ships bound for a strange land, where they would live in concentration camps under conditions which at best were difficult, in spite of chicken on Sunday. . . . During my period of service in the [American] embassy, we found no reliable evidence of planned or contemplated acts of sabotage, subversion, or espionage. . . . The forcible detention of Japanese from Peru, arising out of a wartime collaboration among the governments of Peru, the United States, and the American republics, was clearly a violation of human rights and was not justified by any plausible threat to the security of the Western Hemisphere.[58]

EXPERIENCE IN THE UNITED STATES

The INS took custody of the Peruvian deportees upon their arrival in the United States. These individuals then entered their own Kafkaesque situation. The U.S. Navy had confiscated their Japanese, Peruvian, or other South American passports aboard the ship, and in their initial intake interviews, the INS informed them that they were illegally entering the United States because they did not possess valid passports or entry visas.[59] In this way, the INS could expedite its later deportation proceedings. It also defined the deportees as enemy aliens of the United States, although some of them—in particular, the minor children—were actually citizens of friendly Central and South American countries.

After the men were taken to INS internment facilities at Kenedy, Texas, or Santa Fe, New Mexico, women and children were moved to the INS internment center at Seagoville, Texas. The families were later united at the INS facility at Crystal City, Texas. Certain Pan-American Japanese, especially the diplomats, were rushed to an exchange ship for repatriation to Japan on June 18, 1942.

From late 1942, some U.S. officials raised doubts about the legality of transporting Japanese nationals and citizens of Central and South American countries to this nation. The War Department adamantly defended the program, but some in the State and Justice Departments asked whether the War Department was behaving properly. Ennis stated in 1942:

> The [Justice] Department has already accepted the custody of a large number of allegedly dangerous alien enemies from Latin American countries pending their repatriation which now seems not likely to be consummated. After custody of these persons was accepted, this Department discovered that a number of them apparently

were not dangerous but refugees who were included in the group for some unknown reasons and that a few of them were not even of enemy nationality. It is hoped that efforts will be made to accept for transmission here only dangerous aliens of enemy nationality.[60]

However, even with such a high-level official raising doubts about the efficacy of the procedure, the inter-American effort did not end.

The State Department's Special War Problems Division, for one, continued to insist that more Japanese nationals and their wives and children be brought up from Latin American countries whether or not they had been classified as dangerous. The Justice Department apparently continued to question this practice, and in January 1943, both departments agreed to send a Justice Department representative to Peru specifically to determine that those detained warranted internment. The Justice Department also won the authorization to review any case once the United States agreed to accept Latin American internees.[61] Regardless of this procedure, the number of incoming internees did not slacken through 1943 and 1944. For example, on January 29, 1944, 9 persons arrived from El Salvador and Guatemala, and the United States expected an additional 502 others of unspecified nationality and place of origin. Sixty-eight Japanese were also expected from Peru on March 11, 1944, and others were scheduled to arrive through May 16.[62]

As of June 30, 1945, the INS had in custody 1,213 persons of Japanese ancestry from Peru, 49 from Bolivia, 1 from the Dominican Republic, 1 from Haiti, 9 from Honduras, and 1 from Panama. In addition, Japanese Peruvians gave birth in the United States to 55 children who were born American citizens.[63]

With so many able-bodied Americans fighting in Europe and Asia, there was an acute labor shortage in the United States. Certain agricultural businesses decided to use prisoners from the WRA camps to harvest ripening sugar beets and fruit crops. In 1945, the largest employer was Seabrook Farms Company, Inc., a large frozen-food processing plant in Bridgton, New Jersey. One Seabrook Farms superintendent said that he "was not partial to people of Japanese extraction, but that one Japanese was worth six Puerto Ricans to him."[64]

Eventually the Justice Department was also asked if its internees could be so employed. While the legal status of the Japanese Peruvians remained uncertain, the INS established a new category for those from Latin American countries. The Justice Department permitted the internees to leave the Crystal City Internment Center with a new status it called "relaxed internment" or "restricted parole." In either case, internees remained under Justice Department control.

The number of Japanese Peruvians who worked at Seabrook Farms is unclear. One author posits that 1,688 persons of Japanese ancestry, many from the WRA camps, were there in late 1945. The numbers peaked in January 1947 at 2,300–2,700 workers of Japanese ancestry out of a total workforce of 5,000.[65]

Toward the end of the war, the United States tried to return all these prisoners to their respective countries. Although some Latin American countries did accept them, Peru in particular refused to do so. The United States then attempted to deport the Japanese Peruvians to Japan under the preplanned rationale of their "illegal" immigration. Although some 1,200 elected to accept the trip to Japan, many others refused to go.

POSTWAR DEPORTATIONS

In 1946, two attorneys from San Francisco, Wayne M. Collins and Theodore Tamba, were in the Justice Department internment camp at Crystal City, Texas, on other business. By this time, almost all the Japanese Peruvians were concentrated in this particular camp. A group of them approached the two lawyers and asked for assistance. The Justice Department had recently notified ninety internees of their imminent transfer to Terminal Island, California, for deportation to Japan. After listening to their case, "Mr. Collins reached for the telephone and called Mr. Tom Cooley in Washington D.C., who represented the Department of Justice in the Japanese cases. We heard [Mr. Cooley] say, 'Oh my God, have you got those cases too?' Collins replied, 'We just got them ten minutes ago and we will be at Terminal Island with writs of habeas corpus before they arrive there.' The incident created much embarrassment for the government. Literally speaking, it had been caught with its hands in the cookie jar."[66]

As for the Kaneko family, the situation became more difficult. After being forcibly removed from Peru in 1942, Kakuaki Kaneko did not see his wife, Otari, or his four children until they met at the Justice Department camp at Crystal City on March 1, 1944. When the war ended, the family felt it had few options. Peru wanted to exclude its former immigrants, the United States saw them as undesirable, illegal foreign nationals, and Japan was a war-ravaged country. With the assistance of their attorney, Collins, they decided to fight to stay in the United States. They were also bereft of any financial resources, since they had lost their glass company in Peru. The Kanekos heard later that their business was vandalized during the war, and there would be no compensation forthcoming for their losses. They went to work at Seabrook Farms, but Kakuaki Kaneko found the conditions there akin to working as a slave. Under the sponsorship of a Buddhist priest in San Diego, California, the family moved to that city in July 1946. More children had been born to the Kanekos in the United States, and there were now four boys and three girls. Collins argued in their 1952 case that the Kaneko family included children who were U.S. citizens. He asserted that the three youngest children were U.S. citizens through no choice of their parents, but since the children could not be deported, the parents and their siblings should be allowed to stay to care for these Americans. The Kanekos family won their stay of deportation ten years after they were forced to enter the United States, having spent the first four of those years languishing in a primitive prison.

Most Latin American Japanese lost their means of livelihood when they arrived in the United States. It was difficult for almost all of them to earn a living, and it was especially difficult for those helped by Collins to pay his attorney's fees. Collins recognized their financial straits and asked only for what his clients could afford. He served many on a pro bono basis, and one client apparently made frequent partial payments in chickens that he raised for his livelihood. Many, like the Kaneko family, arranged for long-term monthly payment plans. Kakuaki Kaneko said that he and his wife felt a sense of pride when they eventually paid their debt while feeding and caring for seven children on his wages as a landscape gardener. He said, however, that they could never repay their personal obligation to Wayne Collins.[67]

The legal status of these Latin American internees remained ambiguous for years as Collins and Tamba fought for their stays of deportation. In the end, the courts made a final disposition in their favor. According to Tamba, "The actions filed in San Francisco [where Collins filed the test cases] were never tried on their merits. After ten years, the government eventually conceded that all efforts to deport them to Japan would fail, since it would be difficult to prove that Peruvian nationals were enemies of the United States."[68] Even into the mid-1950s, Peru allowed only 34 of the internees to return there, and the United States permitted only 364 to stay. The remaining 1,373 either went or were sent to Japan.

CONCLUSION

All the people of Japanese ancestry who were brought by the U.S. government from places outside the contiguous forty-eight states were held under duress for an indeterminate period without accusation, evidence, or due process. Their only crime was the accident of nationality or parentage. Reviewing the unintended consequences of the inter-American cooperation program decades later, Ennis, the director of the Alien Enemy Control Unit, said: "I think that whole program was a disaster, an unnecessary disaster. After all, so was our own [program of] exclusion from the Pacific coast a disaster, it was just another wartime foolishness."[69] But deeming it "wartime foolishness" to commit individuals and families to years in crude prisons is hardly a comfort for those who suffered personal injuries.

6

Justice Department
and Army Camps

The Tuna Canyon Detention Station in Southern California, formerly an old Civilian Conservation Corps camp, was used as a temporary center to hold enemy aliens by the Immigration and Naturalization Service, a division of the U.S. Department of Justice. The INS brought Yasutaro Hibi and Taju Koide (the two Issei fishermen introduced in chapter 1) from the immigration station at San Pedro, California, to this camp, which was located near Pasadena on Tujunga Canyon Boulevard. It was also here that Reverend Daisho Tana arrived after his arrest on March 13, 1942, and a short stay at the Santa Barbara County Jail. Reverend Tana was born in 1901 and came to the United States in 1928 to serve as a priest with the Buddhist Churches of America; at the time of his arrest, he also worked as a Japanese-language teacher in Lompoc, California.[1] He described his first full day at Tuna Canyon:

> Today [Sunday, March 15] is the dawn of the C.C.C. camp of Tujunga which is outside of Los Angeles. . . . I got up at 6 o'clock in the morning and they called our names, lunch at noon, they called our names at 4:15, and dinner was at 5:00. At 8:30 they called our names and at 10 P.M. they turned off the lights. And this kind of regulated and group life makes me think of a soldier's routine. We are prohibited to go within ten feet of the fence, and it is most painful to be cut off from the outside world. At 1 P.M. some visitors came; today and Wednesday are visiting days and especially because today is the first Sunday after being put into camp so many families were excited and came here. . . . After thirty minutes of the visit, I can see people's eyes filled with tears—of those internees who are waving their hands good-bye as the visitors go to the distant parking area. What can they talk about for thirty minutes through the iron fence? And those who cannot speak English must talk through someone who can understand Japanese.[2]

After Lieutenant General John L. DeWitt, commanding general of the Western Defense Command (WDC), ordered those arrested under the Alien Enemies Act removed into the interior of the United States, the INS assembled groups of internees and trucked them to the Los Angeles train depot for shipment eastward to other INS camps.[3] Reverend Tana stayed at Tuna Canyon for eleven days and was then taken with 208 other prisoners on the long train trip inland. Their destination was an INS facility at Santa Fe, New Mexico; other internees were transported to the INS camp at Fort Abraham Lincoln, North Dakota. Along the way, the northbound trains usually stopped at Sacramento, California, to collect Issei taken in the San Francisco Bay Area, and then at Portland, Oregon, to pick up those from the Pacific Northwest.[4]

In this chapter, we continue the story of the imprisonment process used by the Justice and War Departments. But first, we must step back and look at the different centers in which enemy nationals were interned immediately after their arrests. Although the process itself was straightforward, the many types of camps create a seemingly complex picture. Instead of detailed descriptions of each type, brief overviews are offered, followed by sections on particular camps that were typical, held mainly Issei internees, or were the sites of important events.

This portion of the imprisonment experience can be divided into three main parts. First, as described in chapter 3, beginning with their arrests in early December 1941, people designated as enemy aliens were kept in Justice Department holding centers until they appeared before a hearing board. Second, if the hearing board recommended permanent internment, male internees were placed under the jurisdiction of the U.S. Army. And third, from early 1943, the army returned these internees to the control of the Justice Department, where many remained until—and sometimes even after—the end the war.

JUSTICE DEPARTMENT CAMPS

Before the United States entered the war, the INS had only a few facilities designated for holding enemy aliens. Especially important were seven permanent INS stations and three prewar internment camps that already housed stranded German and Italian seamen.[5] Several points about the early internment centers are noteworthy.

First, the War and Justice Departments used different types of centers with distinct designations for holding their internees. Camps usually differed in the ethnoracial type of internee, the particular categories of internee, physical size, geographic location, and administrative personnel. Treating each camp individually is beyond the scope of this presentation, so we will take a selective approach.

Second, particular camps operated for varying lengths of time. Some were open for a few months, while others operated for years. The last camp at Crystal City, Texas, for example, remained open administratively until 1948, years after the Axis powers had capitulated.

Third, the number of internees changed constantly between 1941 and 1948. There was a continual flow of entering, departing, and transferring internees; some died while imprisoned, and others saw their children born in confinement. Moreover, while the total number of internees was not large when compared to those in the War Relocation Authority (wRA) camps, it still represents a considerable number.

Fourth, the Justice Department was not consistent in its own terminology. For example, the designations "station" and "camp" were generally but not always given to different types of centers. A camp could be called by different names at any given time, depending on the type of internee it held. In many cases, the words "temporary" or "permanent" preceding "detention" or "internment" indicated a temporal mode. However, certain centers might be called "temporary detention stations" for years before the *temporary* was dropped and the place became known as a permanent detention station. The names and changes are significant because they usually reflect the category of internee. The designation "permanent detention station," for example, was usually reserved for a long-standing INS immigration station, while a detention camp might hold the same category of internee but operate on a comparatively short-term basis.

A fifth and final point: although the internees were mainly Issei males, Justice Department camps also held females, American citizens, and nationals from allied nations, such as children born in Latin American countries.[6]

Internment Camps

Between 1941 and 1943, the Justice Department, working through the INS, operated at least sixty-five facilities in which to intern enemy nationals. Most of these sites were established soon after the United States entered the war, and forty-nine sites were in operation by July 1942. By September 1942, this number was reduced substantially as internees were paroled, released, or transferred to the army's jurisdiction for permanent internment.[7] At least nineteen of the facilities held Japanese nationals and their families.

Twelve Issei females under INS control were placed in the army's assembly center at Santa Anita, California, on July 14, 1942.[8] The housing of these women represents more than just an instance of interagency cooperation between the Justice and War Departments. This assembly center held 18,719 persons of Japanese ancestry from March to October 1942 by authority of a presidential executive order. Nothing in the Justice Department records tells why these INS female internees, who were arrested under the Alien Enemies Act, were kept there. Most similar internees were transported to the INS internment camp at Seagoville, Texas. The internment of these twelve females at this assembly center calls into question the rationale by which the Justice Department and the wRA normally separated their internees from each other. The INS must have considered these twelve to be sufficiently different from the general Nikkei population to have arrested them as enemy aliens. Yet, although the category might have been different, the INS decided that the assembly center could safely hold them.

One possible conclusion is that the INS detention camps and the War Department's assembly centers were no different in their capacity to hold both sets of supposedly dangerous internees. Both places were, in fact, primitive prisons. Or one could assert that the two agencies saw no real variance in the degree of threat between these Justice Department internees and the War Department's inmates. If there were significant differences between this group and the rest of the assembly camp population, the two departments might be expected not to combine the two types there, and yet they did. The possibility exists that the only difference between an internment camp internee and an assembly center inmate was a difference in who had authorized the arrests rather than any qualitative distinction between the two populations.

Permanent and Temporary Detention Stations

As stated earlier, the INS initially used seven regular INS immigration stations to hold arrested enemy aliens in the continental United States. Five of these were officially permanent detention stations: Gloucester City, New Jersey; Detroit; East Boston; Ellis Island, New York; and Seattle. Three of these—East Boston, Ellis Island, and Seattle—at one time held from a few to hundreds of Issei. The Justice Department used the five stations to confine what it called "detainees" until these people were moved to temporary detention stations or detention and internment camps. The Miami station was initially designated a permanent detention station but was later downgraded to temporary status.[9] Two California INS stations that also held numerous Issei—San Pedro and San Francisco—were never labeled "permanent detention stations."[10]

By September 1942, the INS had reduced the number of its temporary detention stations from twenty-one to eleven. (Despite the name, some stations stayed in existence for years.) The locations of the initial twenty-one sites ranged from California to New York and included community centers, unused state armories, a former fire station, and even a private residence.[11] These were transitional facilities that held or detained enemy aliens until a sufficient number were assembled for transportation to detention camps for their hearings. After the hearings, the enemy aliens were released, paroled, or kept for permanent internment by the Justice Department after it had assessed the recommendations of the hearing boards. If the decision was for permanent internment, these nationals were then transferred into the custody of the army.

The largest number of internees of Japanese ancestry on the West Coast were kept at Sharp Park and Tuna Canyon, California, and, on the East Coast, at Ellis Island, New York.

Sharp Park Temporary Detention Station. In Northern California, the San Francisco immigration station on Silver Avenue was soon filled to capacity with enemy aliens. In order to relieve the congestion, the INS opened a former state relief camp located twelve miles south of the city and renamed it the Sharp Park

Temporary Detention Station. The INS increased the camp's original capacity of 450 to 1,200 by adding ten barracks and also built a ten-foot-high fence.

The station's early population, from March 30, 1942, was made up of German, Italian, and Japanese nationals; the Japanese were held only until they could be transported to an inland detention camp. The INS did not send all of them inland, however, and even as late as July 14, 1942, the station held 83 Germans, 105 Italians, and 191 Japanese.

The INS used Sharp Park as the main holding center for those arrested in the Northern California area. On July 15, 1943, the station also held 119 Peruvian Japanese, but they were soon transported to Fort Missoula, Montana.

There were also some Chinese internees at Sharp Park. The INS probably kept them there while it considered their applications for admission into the United States, based on claims of their birth here or their status as sons or daughters of U.S. citizens.[12] One intriguing incident narrated by C. Harvey Gardiner occurred between the Chinese, Japanese American, and Peruvian Japanese groups in summer 1943, "when trouble flared up with the Chinese, who were divided into pro-Kuomintang and pro-Communist groups. The fracas featured a Chinese flag which, once it was raised, was lowered and seized by the Japanese, the Japanese Americans and Peruvian Japanese joining forces in the melee."[13] The presence of Japanese Americans is unusual, since by this date all others in California were already in the WRA relocation camps. If Gardiner's account of the incident is accurate, the Japanese Americans he mentions were perhaps Nisei arrested by the Federal Bureau of Investigation (FBI) and held by the Justice Department for some reason. Publicly, the INS claimed responsibility for Japanese nationals only during 1942 and 1943.[14]

Detention and Internment Camps

The INS usually took internees from its immigration and temporary detention stations to detention and internment camps. In these were found the stranded German and Italian seamen plus those who were awaiting their hearings. INS designations for these camps were inconsistent, and the agency listed from seven to eleven facilities between 1942 and 1948. In September 1942, when it was turning over many internees to the army, the INS listed five such facilities: Fort Stanton, New Mexico, which held mainly stranded German seamen; Kenedy, Texas, used to hold Japanese and German nationals from Latin American countries;[15] Santa Fe, New Mexico, for an almost exclusively Issei population; Missoula, Montana, which held a large Issei population and stranded Italian seamen; and Fort Abraham Lincoln (Bismarck Camp), North Dakota, used for German and Japanese nationals and stranded German seamen.[16]

In addition to these camps, three others require notice. The Old Raton Ranch Camp in New Mexico was a unique but short-lived internment camp. It held both Issei and Japanese Americans from New Mexico and is rarely listed among the INS camps. The Seagoville camp in Texas housed women and children, some of whom were paroled to WRA camps. A number of women and families arriving from Latin American countries added to the total of internees there; later, all were moved to the INS internment center at Crystal City, Texas, where families were reunited. Highlighted here will be those camps holding Japanese internees in 1942.

Fort Missoula Detention Camp. Fort Missoula is located in Montana, on the southwest outskirts of the city of Missoula. The INS took over the facility on April 13, 1941, and increased its capacity from 525 to 2,100. By October 14, 1941, it held 1,182 stranded Italian seamen. The first Issei taken there, on December 18, were 25 men from Salt Lake City, and by the end of the year, 633 Issei were being held at the camp. Beginning on about April 1, 1942, the INS sent Issei males from other temporary detention stations to Fort Missoula, and the camp soon held a total population of 2,003, comprising 985 Issei, 28 Italian nationals, and 990 Italian seamen. The average age of the Issei was apparently about sixty. Hearing boards for the Japanese were held from June to August 1942, and Issei recommended for permanent internment were sent to Camp Livingston, a U.S. Army internment camp in Alexandria, Louisiana. By August, there were 109 Issei left at Fort Missoula.

The Japanese and Italian internees lived in different barracks and ate in separate mess halls, but they occasionally played softball together. In October 1942, only 29 Issei remained, while the Italian population had increased to more than 1,200. On March 30, 1943, however, the army started to send back its internees, and by February 1944, this camp held 258 Issei and 347 Italian internees. The next month, the INS transferred the remaining Issei to Santa Fe, New Mexico, and the Italians to Ellis Island, New York, leaving a population of 550 Italian seamen. The INS then shut down operations and on July 1, 1944, relinquished control of the camp to the army, which planned to use the site to hold European prisoners of war.[17]

Fort Abraham Lincoln Detention Camp. Fort Abraham Lincoln, also called Bismarck Camp, originated as an army post in 1873. It is located in Morton County, North Dakota, some four miles southwest of Bismarck. Initially, 800 stranded Italian seamen arrived in April 1939 but were soon moved to Fort Missoula, Montana, while 284 German seamen were also detained there before hostilities commenced. Anticipating more arrivals, the INS enlarged the camp's capacity to 1,700 persons.

After December 7, 1941, Fort Lincoln became a detention station, intended for German aliens and Issei. By February 1942, 1,129 Issei, 282 German seamen, and 107 German nationals were confined there. One Issei described his life at Fort Lincoln as being "like that of birds in a cage. We were surrounded by barbed wire fences, and we had no freedom. The food in the camp was no good, but we had enough even under wartime conditions."[18] The Justice Department convened hearing boards beginning on July 14, and by the time they were completed on October 14, only 7 German nationals, 269 German seamen, and 21 Japanese remained. In the meantime, two Issei died at Fort Lincoln, and a few sick and disabled prisoners were repatriated to Japan.

Once its Issei internees were transferred to the authority of the army in 1942, the camp held only German nationals; it became a permanent INS internment camp in early 1943. On February 14, 1945, as a result of the citizenship renunciation campaign (discussed in chapter 8), nearly 650 Nisei and Kibei arrived from the WRA's Tule Lake Segregation Center in California, and another 100 followed in July. The Germans and Nisei reportedly mingled socially, although they lived in separate barracks. In the mess hall, a partition at first divided the two groups, but this was later removed, and a line painted on the floor was the only division.

On December 26, 1945, the INS deported 360 Nisei to Japan, while others recanted their renunciation of citizenship. The officer in charge wanted to empty Fort Lincoln of the remaining 200 Germans and 239 Japanese internees, and by March 1, 1946, the INS had sent 150 Germans to Ellis Island and returned the other 50 to Germany. Of the Nikkei population, the INS sent 39 to Japan and shipped the remainder to the Santa Fe Internment Camp in New Mexico. The camp at Fort Lincoln was closed on March 6, 1946.[19]

Santa Fe Detention Camp. The INS detention camp at Santa Fe, New Mexico, was located two and a half miles west of the city center and occupied an area of approximately eighty square acres. In 1933, the site served as a CCC camp and consisted of tarpaper-covered wooden buildings with a capacity of 450. In February 1942, the INS obtained permission from the New Mexico State Penitentiary to use this facility and quickly renovated the buildings, built new structures, erected a twelve-foot-high barbed-wire fence around a twenty-eight-acre compound area, and placed eleven guard towers at strategic places along the spotlighted enclosure.[20]

Then able to hold 1,400 internees, the camp received a group of 425 Issei from Los Angeles on March 14. During its first year, it held 826 Issei, all from California.[21] Only 50 internees underwent hearings before coming to Santa Fe, and between April and June, the remainder met with five separately constituted hearing boards. Of the initial 826 persons, the INS later paroled 523 internees to the WRA and kept 302 for permanent internment. One Issei died in confinement. The army ordered those slated for permanent internment to its own camps; the first group of 73 Issei went to Fort Bliss, Texas, on May 24, while others went later to a newly constructed army center at Lordsburg, New Mexico.

One INS official reports a probably apocryphal confrontation in August 1942 between the Santa Fe camp officer in charge and DeWitt, the commanding general of the WDC. The anecdote is important for its expression of interagency conflict and differing perceptions of the Issei internees on the part of the two groups:

In August 1942, shortly after [Ivan] Williams had assumed charge of the Santa Fe camp, he was informed that the General [DeWitt, WDC] was arriving at the railroad station with more than one thousand Japanese aliens who, having been judged "too dangerous" to be interned in the War Relocation centers, were to be transferred to his custody. So obsessed was the General with the dangerous character of the aliens that he had ordered an armed escort of one thousand soldiers with fixed bayonets, almost one guard for every prisoner. When Williams arrived at the Santa Fe railroad station with his contingent of sixteen border patrol guards, who were to escort the one thousand aliens to the camp, DeWitt began to admonish him for not providing a larger guard, shouting that with so few patrolmen the Japanese could easily break away. "What kind of a fool are you?" he stormed. Without raising his voice, Williams stood up to the general. "Suppose the Japanese do try to run, what would you and your thousand guards do about it?" he asked. "Fire at them and endanger the lives of innocent bystanders? With all that shooting somebody would be bound to get hurt and it might not be the Japanese. No, General, I'm not a fool. You are the fool," and with that Williams ordered his sixteen patrolmen to march the Japanese to the camp.[22]

Various details make it difficult to accept this colorful story at face value. For example, there is no other report about DeWitt accompanying a group of Issei internees to New Mexico and no confirmation that such a large contingent of Issei traveled to Santa Fe in August 1942. In fact, INS files record a decrease in the Santa Fe population during that time—from ninety internees on August 7 to thirty-four on August 29.[23]

From April to September 24, 1942, groups of Issei were turned over to either the WRA or the army. The last group of twenty-seven Issei departed for the army's camp at Lordsburg, and the Santa Fe camp was nearly closed. The INS posted three guards to maintain minimal custodial services and kept it ready for immediate reoccupancy if the need arose.[24]

Old Raton Ranch Internment Camp. A significant, short-lived, and little-known installation, the Old Raton Ranch Camp, was created and run by the Justice Department in New Mexico. Issei and Nisei men, women, and children were confined there for almost a year after the United States entered the war until they were taken eventually to WRA camps. Old Raton Ranch reveals the level of cooperation between the two agencies that were dealing with an unusual internee population.

The story of this camp begins with the social history of Clovis, New Mexico, which is situated some 220 miles east of Albuquerque. On December 7, 1941, Clovis's Nikkei population stood at thirty-two. Ten Issei men had lived in Clovis from before 1922, and five of them were married. Their wives were also Issei, and the families had a total of seventeen children. The town of Clovis was an important western terminal point for the Santa Fe Railroad; in fact, it was a company town, and all the Issei men had come there for work.

After the attack on Pearl Harbor, suspicion and resentment grew against the Japanese in New Mexico, and the Santa Fe Railroad instructed the Issei men to stop working and stay close to their homes. With the increasing fear and anxiety about the war in the Pacific, the town's thirty-two Nikkei residents attracted more and more attention. New Mexico's U.S. attorney announced that the only agency authorized to arrest and detain enemy aliens was the FBI, and on January 23, he sent four INS officers to Clovis to take all thirty-two into custody.

They were trucked to Old Raton Ranch Camp, an isolated and abandoned CCC camp (F-17-N) located within the Baca Ranch Camp site in Lincoln National Forest.[25] Old Raton Ranch was thirteen miles east of the INS's Fort Stanton camp, which was responsible for Old Raton Ranch's administration. The Justice Department categorized these Issei as enemy aliens who were accompanied voluntarily by their citizen children.

John Culley asserts that Clovis residents were predisposed to treat their Nikkei neighbors in this fashion for a number of reasons: a prewar prejudicial attitude, resentment over some Issei men occupying supervisory positions with the railroad, and bitterness over the deaths of New Mexican soldiers who had fought the Japanese in the Pacific arena. He then concludes that "in the face of public hostility, the indifference of the railroad, and the inimical bureaucracy of the Justice Department, the Japanese were helpless. Internment was the simplest policy for all concerned, except for the Japanese."[26]

Conditions at Old Raton Ranch were bleak; the place was remote and without amenities. With no schooling available for the children and no work for the adults, it was difficult to keep active and alert. These conditions lasted until November 1942, when the WRA agreed to accept the Old Raton Ranch internees. By December, most had been taken to WRA centers at Poston and Gila River in Arizona or at Topaz, Utah. And by December 18 , all the internees were gone, and the camp was closed.

The Justice Department's imprisonment of American citizens along with enemy aliens was unusual, yet it continued for almost a year. What explains this phenomenon? Why weren't the internees sent earlier to the Justice Department's camp at Seagoville, Texas, where other women and children were kept? No answers were available in the files, and only conjectures can be offered here. Enemy aliens at the INS Seagoville camp had previously been identified as such by the FBI or other governmental agencies. The people from Clovis were neither suspects nor considered dangerous, yet they were apparently brought before a hearing board after January 4, 1942.[27] Further, they could not be treated like the later West Coast prisoners, since their removal in January 1942 preceded Executive Order 9066, which was issued in February 1942. Another question involves why they were not immediately transferred to WRA camps after the executive order was passed and the camps were constructed. One plausible reason is that Clovis is outside the WDC's military exclusion area, and a change in status from internee to inmate had not been authorized. However, the WCCA did hold twelve INS females at the Santa Anita Assembly Center, in California, in July 1942. The precedence for such cooperation was therefore available to the imprisonment organization. Regardless of the reasons, these Japanese immigrants and their families suffered for many months in a bureaucratic limbo from which there was no deliverance. After the war, none of the thirty-two internees returned to live or work in Clovis.

Seagoville Internment Camp. In its prewar agreement with the army, the Justice Department retained responsibility for female internees. Other than Old Raton Ranch and the WCCA assembly center at Santa Anita, California, where the twelve Issei women were interned, the Justice Department kept the women primarily in two places: Seagoville, Texas, and, later, Crystal City, Texas.

The Seagoville camp was located southeast of Dallas and had been constructed by the Bureau of Prisons as a minimum-security federal reformatory for women in 1940. The INS was granted control of the camp on April 12, 1942. Small contingents of foreign nationals brought to the United States from Latin American countries under State Department custody were also held there. For some, it was the last U.S. stop before repatriation to their homelands. On July 14, 1942, the initial internee population consisted of 23 German females, 15 Japanese females, and 4 German males.[28]

Camp accommodations were luxurious in comparison to those for male internees in other INS camps. As one observer stated: "Mrs. Wada took me to her room, which had wall to wall carpet, a lovely twin bed, writing desk and wash stand, as good as any hotel room. . . . Then she took me to . . . lunch in a beautiful dining room with four at a table with linen cloth and napkins and dainty china and silverware. I was told that this establishment had been built for women who had entered the States illegally. They wished to make a good impression on them!"[29] Mrs. Wada, a Christian pastor's wife from Los Angeles, had been arrested for being a teacher in a Japanese-language school along with her Issei husband. However, the INS separated her from her husband, who was in a Justice Department camp for men, and from her two daughters, who were incarcerated in a WRA camp at Granada, Colorado. During 1942, the Seagoville camp held 722 internees; half of this group was later repatriated to Germany and Japan, while the others were kept for permanent internment. After 1942, most internees were sent to the Crystal City Internment Camp. However, approximately 250 Japanese in family groups were brought to Seagoville in September 1943 and later sent to Japan. On August 1, 1944, 380 persons were interned there—372 Germans, 6 Italians, and 2 of other nationalities. The INS expected to keep this camp open until June 30, 1945, after which the remaining internees were to go to Crystal City.

ARMY CAMPS

After the male enemy aliens underwent their initial detention and hearings, the INS handed them over to the army for permanent internment. Issei recommended for parole or release were shipped to WCCA assembly centers or WRA incarceration camps.

While the army was waiting for the construction or completion of camps for permanent internees, it used parts of existing military bases for this purpose. By May 2, 1942, it had firm plans or sites for ten permanent and fourteen temporary internment camps in the United States.[30]

Temporary and Permanent Internment Camps

Due to shortages of basic supplies, the proposed camps were not yet being built, and the army needed to show cause for making their construction a priority.

The army's provost marshal general used three reasons to justify the immediate construction of the internment camps. The first was obvious need: the total prisoner capacity for all army internment camps, including those under construction in May 1942, came to only 30,700, and the army "estimated 51,000 internees and Prisoners of War will be received by the War Department by the end of this year." A second rationale was public relations: the provost marshal general's office stated that "particular attention is invited to the relationship between public opinion and the number of enemy nationals ordered interned. Public opinion would force the internment of a large number of persons in the event of invasion, organized sabotage, or some similar incident." Because the War Department had little substantive reason by this time to fear acts of sabotage from the Nikkei population, since most on the mainland were in WCCA or Justice Department camps, the provost marshal general's invocation of public opinion is disingenuous. The third rationale played on the fear of retribution by enemy countries on imprisoned Americans. In a form of bureaucratic blackmail, the army tried to distance itself should such action occur: "Any violation of the provisions of the Geneva Convention, 1929, which govern the War Department in its treatment of interned foreign nationals and Prisoners of War, will probably be met with retaliation by enemy countries. The PM General desires that such possibilities be obviated by the immediate construction of all internment camps presently under construction."[31] The Corps of Engineers complied with the construction requests and completed most of the camps. By March 12, 1943, the army had available twenty-three different sites for imprisoning enemy aliens.[32]

Throughout the war years, the army transferred its internees from one camp to another, seemingly without reason. According to army policy, a camp commander could transfer internees anywhere within a camp but needed the provost marshal general's approval to move them from camp to camp. Official reasons for transfer were vague: "Such transfer may be made to preserve the health of the internees, to maintain discipline, and to make better use of an internee's talents."[33] One probable unofficial reason for the transfers may have been the army's desire to keep internees occupied with moving and adjusting to new environments and situations, which allowed them less time to think about or plan escapes. Frequent transfers also made it difficult for internees to socialize or form attachments with guards or other army personnel. Administrative reasons likely also played a part. As camps became too crowded or were closed, internees were forced to move.

The army often placed German, Italian, and Japanese internees in the same temporary internment camp and usually separated them with fences. Temporary camps noted for holding Issei males were Camp McCoy, Wisconsin; Fort Sill, Oklahoma; Fort McDowell, Angel Island, California;[34] Fort Mead, Maryland; Fort Bliss, Texas; Fort Sam Houston, Texas; and even Griffith Park, California.[35] Although permanent internment camps were known to contain a preponderance of one nationality group, enemy aliens of different nationalities might occasionally be mixed in as well. A few permanent internment camps stand out as places noted for holding Issei and some Nisei: Lordsburg, New Mexico; Camp Livingston, Louisiana; Camp Forrest, Tennessee; Stringtown, Oklahoma; and Florence, Arizona.[36]

Lordsburg Permanent Internment Camp. The Lordsburg camp held the army's largest number of Issei internees. Located two and a half miles from that city, it consisted of 1,300 acres of sprawling New Mexico land. Starting from January 30, 1942, plans were that it would hold 3,000 internees in ninety-six barracks, but the army completed a smaller camp by June 6.[37] It was reportedly the only army camp built specifically to intern the Issei but later became a POW camp especially for German soldiers. The first group of 80 Issei arrived on June 15 from the INS camp at Missoula, Montana; thereafter, hundreds of other Japanese and a few German nationals arrived from various places, so that by July 27, Lordsburg reached its reduced holding capacity. By September 19, it held a total of 1,289 Issei, and its peak population eventually came to 2,500.[38]

Each internee wore clothing with an identification number printed on the back.[39] At first, there were two daily bed checks—in the morning and at night—but by June 27, 1942, the routine was reduced to a Saturday head count.[40] The army constructed athletic fields where the internees could play softball, tennis, volleyball, and a short golf game. Internees started a garden patch and grew vegetables to supplement their diet. Outside the double-fenced, barbed-wire enclosure, guards patrolled the perimeter in jeeps with mounted machine guns.

At Lordsburg, as at most of the large camps, the army organized the internees into a battalion-type configuration of 1,000 men. There were three battalion-size compounds. From the start, the First Battalion was empty and existed in name only, the Second Battalion consisted of the Fifth to Eighth Companies, and the Third Battalion held the Ninth to Twelfth. This particular configuration will prove relevant in an upcoming conflict situation between the army and the internees, which is discussed in chapter 9.

Internees were ordered to elect their own leaders—usually a governor, vice-governor, chief secretary, chief welfare officer, chief mail officer, and chief accountant. These leaders were allotted office space and the use of intracamp telephones by which to communicate with administrative personnel. Each battalion was subdivided into four companies of 250 internees, with each company having a separate dining hall. The company elected its own mayor, vice-mayor, and chief secretary, and each barrack within a company elected a dormitory chief and vice-chief. Holders of all major positions down to the company level were paid 10 cents per hour, as were doctors, orderlies, cooks, barbers, and canteen staff.

The army returned the Issei internees to the INS in 1943 along with certain Italian POWs and closed the camp in mid-1944. Then, on December 1, 1944, it reopened the facility for German military POWs.[41]

Camp Livingston Permanent Internment Camp. The army constructed Camp Livingston in Louisiana in mid-1942 to accommodate 5,000 people. The first contingent of Issei came from the INS camp at Missoula, Montana, in the hot and humid summer months. To gain some relief from the 130-degree temperature, internees dug shallow depressions in the dirt under the barracks. There, in the shaded area, they sat, rested, chatted, or read during the hottest times of the day.[42] At night, poisonous reptiles and insects appeared, making a midnight excursion to the latrines potentially hazardous.

Herbert Nicholson, who visited the camp, relates his experience with the officer in charge when he asked to meet with certain Issei of his acquaintance. The colonel's negative reply reflects a common perception of the internees:

> "Oh, you can't! These are dangerous men!" I said, "Now, just wait a minute, Colonel. There's not a single dangerous man there. They're all loyal Americans. They would be citizens if they were allowed to be. They picked the cream of the Japanese, the leaders of the Japanese community, and they're wonderful people. Have you noticed— haven't they organized already? Don't they have a mayor? Don't they have a city council?" "Sure," he said, "they're well organized. They got together on their own, and they have a little town of their own inside." [Eventually] I saw all I wanted to see. Before we got through, he shook my hand and said, "Nicholson, I'm so glad you came. I realize these are decent people. They're not dangerous."[43]

Internees were told that they could volunteer for work unrelated to the maintenance of the camp and would receive 10 cents per hour. Other internees were ordered to the nearby forest to cut pine trees with which to construct an airport. The army informed these internees that they would not be paid since the purpose of some of their labor was to provide firewood for the camps. The internees balked and insisted that helping to build an army airport constituted military labor. The camp administration took immediate action to prohibit the internees' movements inside the camp and threatened to close the canteen. The internees met and decided that they would cut and carry only those trees needed for their camp and that other prisoners who wished to volunteer their timber-cutting efforts to the army could do so.[44] Camp Livingston soon held as many as 1,200 Issei internees.

INTERNEES TRANSFERRED TO THE JUSTICE DEPARTMENT

In March 1942, the Justice, State, and War Departments held a series of meetings concerning the military's forecast that more Axis prisoners of war from Europe were going to be sent to the United States. The army told the Justice Department that these new prisoners required custodial care and facilities, and since it was unable to care for both internees and military prisoners, it asked the Justice Department to take back the civilian internees. The Department of Justice agreed to accept the civilians, and the army relinquished its responsibility for the enemy aliens after transmitting reports of their condition to the belligerent nations, as stipulated by the 1929 Geneva Convention.[45] During the early months of 1943, before the transfers, the army kept records of civilian foreign nationals as if they were in the same category as military POWs. It is therefore difficult to trace the army's civilian internees during these last few months. After foreign civilians were transferred back to the Justice Department's INS, the army camp population was composed wholly of military POWs.[46]

From June to July 10, 1943, 9,341 people of mainly Japanese and German ancestries were returned to INS control. A year later, despite receiving 2,425 more prisoners during that time, the total internee population was reduced through various means including parole of numerous Issei to WRA camps, which resulted in a population of 6,238: 3,126 Japanese, 2,971 Germans, 86 Italians, 5 Hungarians, 3 Romanians, 1 Bulgarian, and 36 others.[47]

INS Internment Camps

It is difficult to compile a definitive list of the places where the INS kept these internees, since the agency shunted them to various camps and their numbers continued to fluctuate. From November 1, 1943, for example, the INS listed seven and then ten places as temporary detention stations. Six others were immigration stations, and sites for holding internees included eight permanent internment camps, four jails, seven hospitals, seven "hotels/homes," six railroad projects, eleven Forest Service projects, and five army posts.[48] Issei men and women and their children continued to be transferred among agencies and various types of camps.[49] Meanwhile, still other internees left for WRA centers.

In 1943, a new category of foreign national came under the control of the INS. Through the State Department and the FBI's Special Intelligence Service, as discussed in chapter 5, thousands of nationals and other voluntary internees began to arrive from Latin America for permanent internment. They, along with spouses and dependent children who arrived later, were given to the INS for internment and control. This new internee group created demand for more holding areas and caused the expansion of existing facilities, such as those at Kenedy and Crystal City,

Texas. Then, in 1944, the INS added an additional category of internee—Nisei and Kibei transferred from WRA camps.

The INS quickly accommodated the civilian internees it received from the army. The following discussion centers on three INS camps: Santa Fe and Fort Stanton, New Mexico, and Crystal City, Texas.

Santa Fe Internment Camp. The INS reopened its camp at Santa Fe, New Mexico, in February 1943, and the first contingent of 375 men arrived on March 23 or 24 from the army's camp in Lordsburg, New Mexico. After additional barracks were erected, Santa Fe held 2,144 Japanese internees.[50] A U.S. Public Health Service official described the 1943 conditions: "The camp is composed entirely of Japanese civilians. . . . The internees supply the cooks, scullery help, laundry help and in fact, do all sorts of work. In this respect the camp is practically self-sustaining. The 'key' workers are paid up to $.80 per day. . . . The average age of the internees is about 55, and most of them prefer recreation which requires less physical exertion, such as cards, reading, and a game somewhat similar to checkers."[51]

An incident in March 1944 provides some insight into the camp. Tensions between camp administrators and internees flared when the men accused the INS of deliberately impeding the process of the reunification program by which they could join their families at the INS internment camp at Crystal City, Texas. The program had been in place since June 1943. The atmosphere became so heated that authorities segregated 360 internees in the stockade. The internees called in the Spanish consul, the representative of their protecting power, and the State Department's Special Division to assist with the situation, but camp officials considered none of the segregated internees to be "trustworthy" or acceptable as legitimate spokespersons.[52] Eventually, the INS removed the most difficult internees and sent them to WRA camps.

This incident is revealing in four ways. First, it again shows two governmental agencies cooperating in order to control the prisoner population. Usually, the WRA ejected its Issei "troublemakers" by sending them to Justice Department camps; in this particular case, the opposite occurred. Second, the incident demonstrates that the government did not always follow its own guidelines for imprisoning different types of prisoners in various types of camps run by separate agencies. Third, it confirms that Issei internees were willing to protest INS-instituted actions when they believed there was just cause. The protests were peaceful and, unlike some handled by other officials and agencies, did not result in physical degradation or harm to the internees. Fourth, when the Justice Department was unable or unwilling to send internees it defined as troublemakers to the WRA, it created its own version of an even higher security center, which it called a "segregation camp."

On August 1, 1944, 1,076 Issei internees were held at Santa Fe—587 from the continental United States, 484 from Hawaii and Alaska, and 5 from Latin American countries. The decrease in the camp population between 1943 and 1944 was the result of parole to the WRA, transfer to the Justice Department's internment camp at Crystal City, or repatriation to Japan.[53] Then, from January 13, 1945, the Issei population increased, to 1,409. It would grow again as 866 Nisei "renunciants" plus 184 Issei were sent from WRA camps between January and July. While others were arriving from Crystal City and Fort Lincoln, North Dakota, 1,224 internees were repatriated or deported to Japan and some were sent to other camps.

The social conditions at Santa Fe were difficult. In particular, internees resented the censorship of their mail. As one Issei complained to his friend, "I am interned at Santa Fe. Rights and freedom are restricted so I am having an awful time. All the Caucasian officials in here are big and seem strong, but they are good for nothing. They are good for nothing. They are useless. Also the censors in here are all dam [sic] fools. Our desire is to see those dam fool censors to be destroyed. We are the people of great imperial Japan, from the beginning to the end we are all faithful to our nation."[54] The writer was called in and asked about this letter. The Santa Fe camp officer in charge reported that "The internee states his main reason [for writing the letter] was that he was angry due to the mail situation at this camp. . . . Further questioning did not develop the main purpose behind the stress and throughout the balance of the hearing the subject maintained an attitude so belligerent, we were unable to definitely establish his reason for writing such a letter. From reports of the Internal Security Office and the Japanese spokesman we learned the subject was more-or-less an agitator within the camp." The INS punished the writing of such a letter with "twenty days in the small stockade outside the main detention area."[55] The lesson was clear. Whatever the activity and even if the reason was not well defined, the Justice Department could impose almost any penalty it desired.

On January 3, 1946, the Santa Fe camp held only 477 internees: 304 male Issei and 173 Nisei. Of this figure, 199 had come from the continental United States, 88 from Latin America, 14 from Alaska, and 3 from Hawaii.[56] During the next few months, the INS continued to import hundreds of internees from WRA and other Justice Department camps while it repatriated or deported many others to Japan. Finally, on May 13, 1946, the INS sent the last 12 Issei to the Crystal City camp. It ceased those operations related to holding Japanese internees in September 1946.

Crystal City Family Internment Camp. The Crystal City camp in Texas was unique among INS camps.[57] The INS opened this 290-acre facility on November 2, 1942, and intended it to hold Japanese aliens and their children; however, the first internees were thirty-five German aliens and their families, who arrived in December 1942. They along with a family of Italian ancestry were to be interned there on a temporary basis. Although the INS camp at Seagoville, Texas, could and did hold men, women, and children, it had limited facilities and was not able to accommodate the population increase expected under the INS family reunification program. Since relatively few women were arrested under the Alien Enemies Act, there was initially room enough for them at the Seagoville camp. However, many married Issei male internees who were not released or paroled wished to have their families join them. Since their wives and children were already incarcerated in w r a camps, the plan was to create one camp where this could be accomplished.

The first Nikkei families came to Crystal City in March 1943, but the fathers, who were in other i n s camps, were unable to join them until June 11, 1943. The initial Japanese internee group came from the Seagoville camp, but Crystal City soon held families from w r a camps and individuals and family members from Latin American countries. Rather than remove the families of German and Italian descent, the i n s divided the camp into distinct ethnic sections. The internee population eventually included American citizens, Issei, German and Italian enemy aliens, and others from Latin American countries.[58]

The Crystal City camp was located in the south Texas county of Zavala, next to its namesake town, and was originally built to house migratory farm laborers under the Farm Security Administration. The camp was surrounded by a ten-foot-high barbed-wire fence with strategically placed floodlights illuminating the perimeter. Armed guards patrolled the fence. Internee families lived in three-room cottages and apartment-type buildings of one to three rooms with shared bathrooms. The internees did their own cooking, used cash vouchers to buy food, published their own newspapers, and ran services such as a canteen, barbershop, and beauty parlor. Before allowing family members from w r a centers to enter the Crystal City camp, the i n s was forthright in stating its position and expectations. New arrivals were told that they were expected to work "at such other labor as may be assigned [since] the idea was that reuniting families is a rather special privilege and that persons who are not willing to cooperate wholeheartedly should not be expected to be reunited."[59]

Proper jurisdiction and authority were not an issue when families came from Justice Department control, as did internees from Latin American countries, and the State Department had transferred its responsibility for them. For others, however—such as family members initially incarcerated under Executive Order 9066 and then released by the w r a—entering Crystal City placed them under a different authority. w r a inmates coming under the authority of the i n s were told they must accept the same status as their parents or spouses. That is, they would be subject to rules set by the Articles of the 1929 Geneva Convention rather than those created by the w r a. The changes included, for example, stringent mail censorship and inspection, confiscation of personal funds, and a personal search of any visitors.

By August 1, 1944, Crystal City held 2,104 people of Japanese ancestry and 804 of German descent.[60] Within the Nikkei group, 48 percent, or 1,006 persons, came from Latin America and 44 percent were from the continental United States. A significant number were minor children—52.4 percent, or 1,106 individuals—most of them citizens of the United States or born in a Latin American nation.

By June 1945, Crystal City i n s officials expected more internees and built additional units to accommodate them; some 3,374 internees in all—2,371 Japanese, 997

Germans, and 6 Italians—were held there by the end of that year. With the war's end, the Justice Department started to transfer more of the Nikkei internees and their families to the WRA or allowed them to work at the frozen-food processing plant in Seabrook, New Jersey, under a new status known as "relaxed internment." Because of the stay of deportation orders for various Japanese Peruvians, Crystal City became the largest INS facility to hold internees after the conflict ended.

As late as 1947, Crystal City still held 86 Japanese nationals and their families, many of whom were from Peru. Other families originated in the United States. For example, Reverend Yoshiaki Fukuda of the Konkokyo Church was from San Francisco; he and his family were kept at Crystal City while the Justice Department tried to deport him to Japan. On September 29, 1947, after spending five years and ten months behind barbed wire, he and his family were paroled to San Francisco. He was still required to report periodically to a federal agency.[61] The INS finally closed the Crystal City camp on February 27, 1948.

Fort Stanton Segregation Camp. Located in Lincoln County, New Mexico, five miles southeast of Capitan, Fort Stanton was the first INS internment camp. As mentioned in chapter 2, from January 1941, the Border Patrol Service of the INS brought the officers and crew of the scuttled German liner SS *Columbus* to Fort Stanton and kept them there. For a number of years, this camp housed German seamen and nationals almost exclusively.

Fort Stanton never held a large number of Nikkei internees, and those it did hold arrived late in the war, in March 1945. These internees were markedly different from all others in the INS camps. Years earlier, in February 1943, the INS decided it needed a place to house German internees who were designated as "troublemakers," "instigators," or "potentially troublesome" along with those it wanted to segregate from other INS internees. Fort Stanton was chosen.

Only a portion of the entire camp was assigned to this new purpose; the larger section of Fort Stanton was kept separate from the segregation camp and continued its original role of holding German seamen. The INS placed a total of thirty-one German internees and seamen, referred to as "segregants," into this segregation camp, with some men going to and coming from the larger seamen's enclosure. By the end of December 1944, many of these segregants had been repatriated to Germany or administratively dispersed back into other INS internment camps.

Starting in March 1945, the INS sent seventeen Nisei and Issei internees to the Fort Stanton Segregation Camp. Interestingly, of the seventeen men, only seven were Issei; the larger number were Kibei or Nisei. A case in point is Tsutomu Higashi, a forty-four-year-old Kibei who was born in San Pedro, California. His transfer from the INS camp at Santa Fe, New Mexico, resulted from his so-called insubordination:

Herewith is the record of an investigation conducted by Officer in Charge Ivan Williams, Santa Fe Internment Camp, of an incident involving insubordination on the part of [Tsutomu Higashi] who was recently transferred to that facility from the Tule Lake Relocation Center. It is noted that you also found this individual to be one of the most troublesome at the Tule Lake Relocation Center, where he had been a leader of the Hokoku Seinen Dan [identified by the WRA as a pro-Japan organization] for a period of one month. Following the hearing, internee Higashi was sentenced to the guardhouse for a period of twenty days. Consideration is being given to his further segregation at Fort Stanton. It is interesting to note the discipline which was (and doubtless continues to be) maintained over the members of the Hokoku Seinen Dan, discipline which admittedly is so strict that at least one subordinate member would feel obligated to carry out any order of its leader, including an order to commit murder![62]

That Fort Stanton was the facility for holding Japanese American "troublemakers" was not public knowledge. It was a secret camp at a hidden locale. The INS especially did not want its existence known to any Nikkei prisoners held in WRA or other Justice Department camps and ordered that it be called simply Japanese Segregation Camp No. 1. The INS officially referred to Nikkei internees at Fort Stanton as "segregants," rather than by the standard term "internees," denoting their change in status.

A classified INS memo authorizing the removal of Higashi to this camp underscores the furtive method used by the INS to effect the transfer:

The transfer of the above-named Japanese from the Santa Fe Internment Camp to the segregation camp at Fort Stanton, New Mexico, is authorized to be effected at your convenience after making proper arrangements with the Officer in Charge at Fort Stanton. It is desired that all necessary precautions be made to prevent other Japanese from knowing where Higashi is being sent. This applies particularly to those Japanese held at our Santa Fe and Fort Lincoln camps and to those remaining in War Relocation Centers. In order to keep secret the whereabouts of this internee, his mail should be sent to the official post office box at Santa Fe and his location shown on Form M-35 should be "Japanese Segregation Camp No. 1" without further address.[63]

The INS planned to run this camp as a tougher version of its other internment camps—with more guards and greater restrictions on the internees. All of the seventeen Issei and Nisei came to the Justice Department camp as a result of the turmoil at the WRA segregation camp at Tule Lake, California. Their stay at Fort Stanton was relatively brief, and these Issei and Nisei segregants were transported to the INS immigration station at Terminal Island, California, on October 10, 1945. The Terminal Island station was then redesignated "Segregation Camp No. 1" for Japanese and was used as a holding station while the INS prepared to deport them to Japan.

The shortness of the internees' stays does not lessen the importance of this camp in the imprisonment process. This step represents the culmination of the Justice Department's program to rid itself of American citizens it deemed suspicious or disloyal. Nothing in the records of these Nikkei segregants indicates that they were enemy agents or dangerous persons. Had there been evidence, they would have been charged, tried in criminal court, and if found guilty, placed in federal penitentiaries. Instead, by creating the conditions under which Americans found their loyalty in question and were then helped or even encouraged to renounce their citizenship, the government laid the tracks for expelling them smoothly from their country of birth.[64] (The process by which some Nisei came to renounce their citizenship will be explored in chapter 8.)

THE CLOSING OF THE INS CAMPS

Allied forces celebrated V-E Day on May 8, 1945. On June 30, the INS still held 7,364 internees, 5,211 of whom were of Japanese ancestry. With its captive population diminishing, the INS began closing some camps. One unusual project, the Kooskia Road Construction Project Camp, in Idaho, where Issei men had labored to help build the Lewis and Clark Highway from May 1943, was closed in May 1945.[65] The Seagoville, Texas, women's camp was closed in June. After the surrender of Japan, in August 1945, most of the other camps ceased operations: the camp at Kenedy, Texas, shut down in September, followed later that same year by those at Tuna Canyon, California; Santa Fe, New Mexico; Fort Lincoln, North Dakota; and Missoula, Montana. In early 1946, the INS closed down the Sharp Park camp in California and portions of the Fort Stanton Internment Camp in New Mexico. The INS then held foreign nationals with dependent American-citizen children mainly at Crystal City, Texas, and the Ellis Island immigration station in New York. Nikkei internees were still in the former camp until at least September 29, 1947, or more than two years after the end of World War II. During 1947, except for Crystal City, the INS moved the remaining foreign nationals to regular immigration stations for detention or disposition of their cases. The Crystal City family internment camp officially closed in January 1948.

NUMBER OF INTERNED PERSONS

One vital issue concerns the actual number of internees held by the Justice Department during World War II. Different sources give varying numbers, and it would be instructive to point out probable reasons for the inconsistencies.

First, the enumerators reported different categories and definitions. In some cases, internees were arrested and released relatively quickly, while others were arrested, kept for some time, and then released. In other cases, internees came "voluntarily" over time from many places, usually with their children, to be with their spouses. Statistics for these so-called volunteers vary depending on the particular agency or camp destination. And the Justice Department considered internees who had not been given hearings but might have been held for more than a year under detention or arrest status to be categorically different from those it sent promptly to the army for permanent internment.

Second, a number of agencies might have been responsible for the internees as they went from one center to another. For example, an internee might be arrested by the army, interned by the Justice Department, released to the WRA, and then brought back to the Justice Department. The number of internees affected in this way fluctuated constantly from one day to the next.

Third, internees originated from widespread locales—the continental United States and its territories, Latin America, and various military theaters of war. Some Justice Department statistics do not appear to include internees from outside the boundaries of the United States, while others did count them. As a result, multiple agencies were responsible for the prisoners' arrest and adjudication, although they might ultimately be brought to the Justice Department. For example, some Justice Department administrators included in these statistics German and Italian seamen captured before December 7, 1941, while others did not.

As to the numbers themselves, Attorney General Francis Biddle, in discussing the Justice Department's Alien Enemy Control Program, placed the total number arrested at 16,000. Of these, he said, "Only about one third were interned, nearly half of them Germans, and the rest were paroled, released, or (in a few instances) repatriated."[66] His numbers equate to about 5,300 interned, of whom 2,600 were of German ancestry. Other officials give divergent statistics. Ugo Carusi, then commissioner of the INS, reported on August 24, 1945, that a total of 24,886 enemy nationals had been arrested and interned. This total consisted of German, Italian, and Japanese nationals, those brought up from Latin American countries, and seamen captured before the start of the war.[67] And finally, W. F. Kelly, then assistant commissioner for the Alien Enemy Control Program, reports that the Justice Department arrested and interned 31,275 nationals during the war. He specified that 16,853 internees were persons of Japanese ancestry.[68] Kelly gave a figure of 11,507 for those of German ancestry, which includes 402 seamen captured before the start of the war. The number of Italians came to 2,730—1,518 from the continental United States, 78 from Latin American countries, 1 from Alaska, and 1,133 seamen captured before the war. A nonspecific others category comprises 185 resident Bulgarian, Hungarian, and Romanian nationals.[69]

Based on the Justice Department's Alien Enemy Control Program files, Kelly's numbers appear to be the most accurate. Although almost complete, they still seem to undercount persons of Japanese ancestry. Based on additional information, an updated number would be 31,899: 17,477 of Japanese ancestry (54.8 percent), 11,507 of German ancestry (36.1 percent), 2,730 of Italian ancestry (8.5 percent), and 185 of other ancestry (0.6 percent).

TABLE 6.1

Persons of Japanese Ancestry Interned or Placed
under the Jurisdiction of the Justice Department during World War II

Place of Origin	Classification	Number
Continental U.S.	Interned	6,978
Continental U.S.	Interned-Voluntary	1,026
Continental U.S.	Interned-Renunciant	5,589
Continental U.S.	Renunciant-Voluntary	26
Alaska	Interned	94
Alaska	Interned-Voluntary	2
Alaska	Interned-Renunciant	1
Hawaii	Interned	875
Hawaii	Interned-Voluntary	230
Hawaii	Interned-Renunciant	383
Hawaii	Renunciant-Voluntary	5
Latin America	Interned or Interned-Voluntary	2,253
Marshall Islands	Interned	15
TOTAL		17,477

NOTE: Calculated from memorandum, Willard F. Kelly to D. Schedler, 24 May 1948, INS, RG 85, F.N. 56125/Gen., N.A., and other references from relevant chapters.

Table 6.1 shows a total of 17,477 interned persons of Japanese ancestry. This count includes individuals in some unusual categories. For example, the Interned-Renunciant category represents Nisei who renounced their American citizenship after July 1944 and who then came under the jurisdiction of the Justice Department. Although many of them were transported out of WRA camps to Justice Department centers, about half of them remained where they were while theoretically under Justice Department jurisdiction. Another group consists of internees from the territory of Hawaii. Here, as discussed in chapter 4, the army sent "voluntary" and Kibei internees to the mainland. These were family members wishing to be reunited with spouses or parents held by the Justice Department. Upon their arrival on the mainland, they were placed in WRA camps, and after the reunification program started, many entered the INS internment camp at Crystal City, Texas, for family reunification. They were then counted by the Justice Department.

In World War II, then, 17,477 persons of Japanese ancestry, nationals and citizens alike, were interned or came under the jurisdiction of the Justice Department. They formed the largest portion of those interned or controlled by the department. The total number, including German, Italian, Japanese, and other nationals interned for some period of time during and after World War II by the Justice Department, comes to 31,899 persons.

CONCLUSION

As prewar agreements between the Justice and War Departments unfolded, more than a hundred facilities held thousands of civilian internees who entered, left, and moved from camp to camp. Unplanned measures were also taken, such as the creation of a Justice Department segregation camp and the interning of American citizens who were not covered in the earlier plans. Although the two agencies used their own terminologies and criteria to assess the behavior of internees, they employed the same methods to control those they defined as troublemakers.

The closing words of this chapter, like the opening remarks, come from Reverend Tana. At his hearing in April 1942, he said: "If you would allow me to speak freely, I think I would like America to grant American citizenship to those who live in the United States even after the war. If America had given [the Issei] citizenship up to now, I guess the people who are put in these camps would be one-tenth the present number; however, since it didn't give us the citizenship, it happens that their children as well as their parents are evacuated equally as enemy aliens. I think this is a sad thing for a liberal country like the United States."[70]

7

The Arbitrary Process of Control

The internment of the Issei, some Nisei, and other foreign nationals by the U.S. Department of Justice described in the previous chapters did not physically affect the vast majority of Nikkei in the continental United States.[1] Then, early in 1942, the Western Defense Command (WDC), through its Wartime Civil Control Administration (WCCA), herded almost all remaining residents of Japanese ancestry in most of the Pacific Coast states into fifteen temporary assembly centers. Later, a civilian agency, the War Relocation Authority (WRA), took custody of the inmates and placed them in ten hastily constructed relocation camps for permanent incarceration. Numerous sources are available on the WCCA and WRA camps themselves. Chapters 7 and 8 therefore focus on the process used to control the inmates and examine particular camps that have been given little attention.

To begin with, all inmates were not treated alike. Some were seen as members of socially distinct groups and received disparate treatment. Inmates whom the WRA defined as "troublemakers," "instigators," "pro-Japan," and "anti-WRA" were treated in one way, while others who were considered "pro-administration" and "pro-American" were treated in yet another way. We will see that rules were created and enforced, often haphazardly, and that supposedly troublesome persons were subject to swift reprisals for their failure to obey camp rules. Punishment included incarceration in special centers created to isolate these inmates from the rest of the prisoner population. The WRA and the U.S. Army used fear and terror, and even condoned homicide, in order to control the inmates.

In contrast, prisoners of German and Italian descent received markedly different treatment. Using the same executive order that resulted in the mass incarceration of resident Japanese nationals and their citizen children, the War Department created the Individual Exclusion Program, which differed procedurally from policies affecting Issei and Nisei inmates. A schematic outline is provided here to clarify the many components of this imprisonment process.

Figure 7.1 displays the actions taken by the WRA and the army after the signing of Executive Order (EO) 9066. Through this executive order, all remaining persons of Japanese ancestry on the West Coast were forced into WCCA assembly centers and WRA relocation camps. From December 1942, the WRA reacted to the

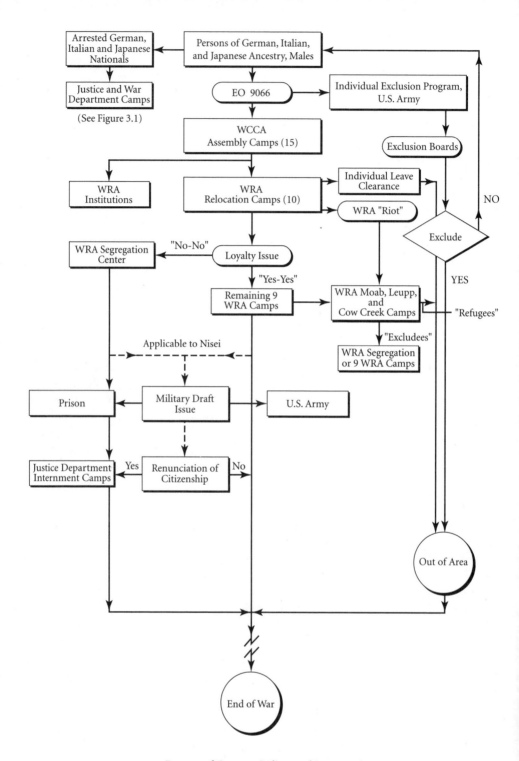

FIG. 7.1. Persons of German, Italian, and Japanese Ancestry
on the Mainland after February 19, 1942

struggles, resistance, and other actions of inmates within its camps by instituting extreme measures to control individuals and their families. The W R A created other types of camps, such as isolation centers, to hold those American citizens it designated troublemakers and dissidents. The agency transferred various categories of citizens from the camp at Manzanar, California, to isolation centers. Later, individuals labeled as troublemakers by the directors of other W R A camps were also sent to these centers. The isolation camps deserve special attention because they constitute an important part of the W R A control process. Concurrently, the W R A created another camp at Cow Creek, California, where individuals and families who were viewed as cooperative were placed for short stays. This chapter examines the first half of the imprisonment process depicted in figure 7.1, and the following chapter explores the second half.

FROM VOLUNTARY RESETTLEMENT TO MASS REMOVAL

Let us start with the actions taken against the Nikkei immediately after the attack on Pearl Harbor. From December 7, 1941, through early 1942, all Japanese Americans still residing on the Pacific coast after the Issei and some Nisei had been arrested by the Justice and War Departments were involved in numerous and diverse events. From early December, those who were designated as enemy aliens but had not been arrested were encouraged to leave the three West Coast states voluntarily and move inland. From February 1942, anyone with family links to an enemy nation was encouraged to move. In all, 4,889 Issei and Nisei resettled until the W D C prohibited further movement on March 27, 1942. On March 24, the W D C instituted a nighttime curfew, between 8:00 P.M. and 6:00 A.M., which was enforced against Japanese nationals and their citizen children. The curfew was applicable only to German and Italian nationals, however; citizens of German and Italian ancestry were unaffected.

From mid-December 1941, newspaper columnists, editorialists, radio commentators, and other spokespersons expressed anti-Japanese sentiments. Many agitated for some action against Japanese Americans, and not a few called for the removal of the entire group from the West Coast. However, John Edgar Hoover, director of the Federal Bureau of Investigation (F B I), privately held a different view: "The necessity for mass evacuation is based primarily upon public and political pressures rather than factual data. Public hysteria and in some instances, the comments of the press and radio announcers have resulted in a tremendous amount of pressure being brought to bear on [California's] Governor Olson and Earl Warren, Attorney General of the state, and the military authorities."[2] Although Hoover mentions "public hysteria," he narrows the focus to California's elected officials.

Other officials publicly or privately arguing for a mass evacuation program included army officers (Lieutenant General John L. DeWitt, W D C Commander;

Major General Allen W. Gullion, Provost Marshal General; Captain and later Colonel Karl R. Bendetsen)[3] and War Department officials (Secretary Henry L. Stimson, Undersecretary Robert P. Patterson, and Assistant Secretary John L. Mc-Cloy). Military necessity, they claimed, was the fundamental reason for the exclusion. Certain Justice Department officials, including Attorney General Francis Biddle, Alien Control Coordinator Tom C. Clark, Assistant to the Attorney General James H. Rowe Jr., and Alien Enemy Control Unit Director Edward J. Ennis, initially opposed the mass removal of American citizens of Japanese ancestry. On February 7, the attorney general told President Franklin D. Roosevelt that "mass evacuation at this time [was] inadvisable, that the FBI was not staffed to perform it; that this was an Army job, not in our opinion advisable; [and] that there were no reasons for mass evacuation."[4] The president, however, sided with the WDC. On February 11, "the President in effect turned the Japanese problem over to the Army. Thereafter the question was how and when measures would be taken."[5]

The mass incarceration of Japanese Americans demanded by these and other army officials and media spokespersons could be seen as a form of war-generated frenzy. Another interpretation, however, is perhaps more plausible. As we have seen, high-level army and navy officials on the West Coast had for decades before 1941 anticipated and prepared for war with Japan. Part of these prewar preparations included discussions and incipient plans to intern the immigrant Issei and their American-citizen children, the Nisei. Once the Issei were interned by the Justice Department, similar actions could then be implemented to remove the Nisei.

Deep and long-standing racial animosity against the Japanese was a salient feature of prewar West Coast attitudes. Such racial antipathy, as discussed earlier, was acknowledged by Curtis B. Munson and Lieutenant Commander Kenneth Ringle. At the national level, even President Roosevelt and Secretary of the Navy William Franklin Knox, in their private correspondence and actions, argued for or certainly did not block the imprisonment of Japanese Americans on the mainland and in Hawaii.[6] No commensurate animosity was evident against people of Italian heritage as a whole and was directed only against selected persons of German ancestry.

Thus, the mass incarceration of Japanese Americans on the mainland might more properly be viewed as an action based on an existing plan to remove an undesirable ethnoracial group from the West Coast rather than as a sudden and confused reaction to the war. The removal of the Issei supplied a blueprint, and the later mass exclusion was undertaken without fear of public condemnation or political consequences.[7]

MILITARY NECESSITY AND EO 9066

On February 17, the Justice Department capitulated to the War Department. At a meeting between the two, Justice officials agreed to the removal of West Coast Japanese nationals and American citizens of Japanese ancestry. The War Department used three arguments to support the actions. First, because the Justice Department had refused to undertake the logistics necessary for a mass incarceration, the army said it was willing to do so. Second, the army argued that mass incarceration was a military necessity; it was difficult for the Justice Department to challenge this contention since military matters were outside its area of expertise. Third, the War Department countered Justice's concerns regarding the unconstitutionality of the incarceration by asserting the authority of an executive order.[8]

The Justice Department bowed to the army's pressure, stating: "The stakes were too high and the emergency too great. Therefore, the Attorney General let the Army have its way."[9] Attorney General Biddle later wrote, "The program was ill-advised, unnecessary and unnecessarily cruel, taking Japanese who were not suspect, and Japanese Americans whose rights were disregarded, from their homes and from their businesses to sit idly in the lonely misery of barracks while the war was being fought in the world beyond."[10]

On February 19, 1942, President Roosevelt signed EO 9066, which constituted the authority for mass incarceration. It used military necessity as the prime justification—"Whereas, the successful prosecution of the war requires every possible protection against espionage and against sabotage to national-defense materials, national-defense premises and national-defense utilities"—and authorized the secretary of war "or any military commander he so designated to prescribe military areas ... from which any or all persons may be excluded, and with respect to which, the right of any person to enter, remain in, or leave shall be subject to whatever restriction [he] may impose in his discretion." The order did not specify any particular person or group for exclusion, but the intended target was clearly understood from discussions preceding the signing. In the WDC, the order was written for and applied to all persons of Japanese ancestry—nationals and citizens alike—who were in the designated military exclusion area and were not already interned. The resulting action led to the incarceration of anyone of at least one-sixteenth Japanese parentage.[11]

There is some similarity between the actions permitted under EO 9066 to accomplish the mass incarceration and those sanctioned by the Alien Enemies Act to effect the earlier internment of the Issei. While EO 9066 asserts the right to exclude persons from designated areas and restricts the "right of any person to enter, remain in, or leave," the Alien Enemies Act likewise allows for an enemy alien to be "apprehended, restrained, secured and removed." Both permit the restraint of movement and/or the imprisonment of individuals who fit their definitions of relevant persons. There are important differences as well. The historic roots of the Alien Enemies Act are centuries old and cover an internationally recognized legal category. In contrast, the executive order was crafted to affect one ethnoracial group (although the group went unmentioned), and it offered military necessity as the prime reason despite there being no evidence at that time to justify this reason and the justification itself is no longer considered of much merit.[12]

All of these factors—the long-standing racial animosity against the Japanese on the West Coast, the prewar meetings about creating concentration camps in which to imprison the Issei once war broke out, and the doubts raised at those meetings about the security threat presented by citizens of Japanese ancestry—argue that EO 9066 was more than a spontaneous wartime measure. The wholesale incarceration of the remainder of the Nikkei population was an action to which all relevant agencies of the executive as well as the legislative and judicial branches of the government agreed.

A blueprint is a template for action, and one such blueprint had been created before the war for the internment of "dangerous" or "suspicious" individuals who were members of various ethnoracial groups. The commanding general of the WDC and crucial members of his staff, as well as high-ranking officers in Washington, D.C., were also unwilling to distinguish the Issei from their citizen children. The prewar action carried out on selected Issei after December 7, 1941, was also desired for anyone deemed dangerous or suspicious. What was missing was the particular means to override the constitutional objection raised by the Justice Department, which sought to exclude American citizens who had not been accused of any wrongdoing. President Roosevelt finessed this legal objection through EO 9066, giving the military the power to remove "any or all persons" it desired.

MILITARY EXCLUSION ZONES

Lieutenant General DeWitt, commanding general of the WDC, announced under Public Proclamation Number 1 (7 F.R. 2320) on March 2, 1942, that Washington, Oregon, California, and Arizona were military areas. Declared as a military exclusion zone were the western halves of the first three states, including the entire portion of California southward from the Los Angeles area and the southern half of Arizona. On March 16, Public Proclamation Number 2 (7 F.R. 2405) designated the others areas under the WDC—Idaho, Montana, Nevada, and Utah—as military but not exclusion areas. Then, with the concurrence of the War Department, the WDC issued the first of 108 civilian exclusion orders on March 24 by which all persons of Japanese ancestry, citizens and resident nationals, were to be removed from the designated areas.

Congress then passed a Public Law (PL 77-503 [18 U.S.C. 1383]), usually referred to as PL 503, and President Roosevelt signed it on March 31. PL 503 became the enforcement legislation for EO 9066 and stipulated that failure to comply with the exclusion orders was a misdemeanor subject to maximum penalties of $5,000 and one year in prison.

On March 30, DeWitt announced that certain classes of people would be exempt from the exclusion order and the travel and curfew regulations. These people included German and Italian nationals seventy years or older; German and Italian nationals who were parents, wives, husbands, or children of members of the U.S. armed forces; orphans; and those unable to see, hear, and speak.[13]

Comparable persons of Japanese ancestry were not exempted. As commanding general of the WDC, DeWitt was viewed unfavorably by not a few fellow officers. His actions on December 8 and 11, 1941, include vilifying San Francisco's mayor Angelo Rossi and 200 civic and business leaders for failing to "black-out" the lights of the city during what turned out to be a false air attack. Yet, he is reported to have said, "Last night [December 8] there were planes over this community. They were enemy planes. I mean Japanese planes. And they were tracked out to sea. You think it was a hoax? It is a dammed nonsense for sensible people to think that the Army and Navy would practice such a hoax on San Francisco."[14]

Two days later, on December 11, DeWitt and his staff heard that an "armed uprising of twenty-thousand Nisei" was in the works and made plans to place all of them under military arrest. The plan was never implemented when the FBI told the army that the information source was noted for his "wild imaginings." On the next day, on the strength of a report that "an enemy attack on Los Angeles was imminent," DeWitt's staff drafted a general alarm advising all civilians to leave the city. The order was never broadcast, but Major General Joseph Stilwell, then a DeWitt subordinate, "wrote in his notebook that General DeWitt was a 'jackass.'"[15]

The WDC contained within its area the vast majority of Issei and Nisei residing on the mainland. DeWitt's later actions, which adversely affected this entire group, were most likely motivated in no small part by his personal opinions. In a press statement given a year later, he stated: "I don't want any Jap back on the Coast. . . . There is no way to determine their loyalty. . . . I don't care what they do with the Japs as long as they don't send them back here. A Jap is a Jap."[16] DeWitt's sentiments at that time were not unique to him. Many West Coast residents shared his desire to exclude all people of Japanese descent. DeWitt and others seemed incapable of distinguishing Americans of Japanese ancestry and their permanent-resident parents from subjects of the Empire of Japan, yet they did not confuse German and Italian immigrants and their children with residents of Axis nations.

With Japanese Americans, the WDC took actions apparently not mandated by EO 9066 or PL 503. The executive order allows for the *removal* of persons from designated military exclusion areas and for arrangements to be made for "transportation, food, shelter and other accommodations as may be necessary." There is nothing in the order justifying the incarceration of such persons without their consent after they were so removed. That is, the presidential directive authorized the creation and operation of incarceration camps, but it did not specify whether an individual could be placed there and then held for any length of time.[17] The army justified its actions by a broad reading of the order. From March 1942, the army's WCCA was the agency that removed resident Japanese aliens and Japanese Americans from their homes and placed them in holding areas it called "assembly centers," which were located *within* designated military exclusion zones. That is, those who had been removed were then detained in exclusion areas, where the army had authority to prevent them from leaving. As a result, persons of Japanese ancestry residing in the WDC were ousted from their homes and placed in the army's prisonlike assembly centers.

WCCA ASSEMBLY CENTERS

Fifteen fairgrounds, racetracks, and livestock exhibition buildings were redesignated army WCCA assembly centers, with one site serving as a reception center. In these places, from March 31 until June 6, 1942, the WCCA incarcerated 93,574 persons after forcibly removing them from their homes and communities. It circumscribed these fifteen camps with barbed wire, patrolled the perimeter with armed military guards, and erected observation towers manned by sentries equipped with rifles or machine guns. The inmates occupied horse stalls or hastily constructed barracks in which living areas were frequently separated by nothing more than a sheet. They ate in communal mess halls, slept on mattresses filled with often flea-infested straw, and made do with communal-style restrooms. Theirs were lives of deprivation, and they were completely subject to the rules of their army captors. Although these centers were supposedly temporary collection points, most inmates were incarcerated for months. The government described these assembly centers in benign terms: "A convenient gathering point, within the military area, where evacuees live temporarily while awaiting the opportunity for orderly, planned movement to a Relocation Center outside the military area."

WRA CAMPS

On March 18, 1942, President Roosevelt established a civilian agency, the War Relocation Authority, through Executive Order 9102. He appointed Milton S. Eisenhower its first director, and the WRA selected ten sites in isolated and mostly bleak desert areas within the WDC area and in Arkansas, Colorado, and Wyoming.[18] These relocation centers were also primitive prisons. Like assembly centers, relocation centers were encompassed by a barbed-wire fence and boasted armed guards, observation towers, and barrack-style environments. The WRA described the centers as "a pioneer community, with basic housing and protective services provided by the Federal Government, for occupancy by evacuees for the duration of the war."[19] There is no mention of the inmates' forced exile from their homes under armed guard, or the coerced nature of their stay in the centers. Neither is there mention of the anxiety and fear they felt. The length of stay was not stated more specifically than "the duration of the war," and inmates probably came up with terms other than "pioneer community" to describe the conditions. The quality of "protective services" provided by the government, as we will see, also became an issue at most WRA camps, since many inmates felt more like victims than recipients of such services.

The army and the WRA proceeded to develop legal justification for incarcerating Japanese Americans *outside* the WDC's military exclusion area. The government's approach was simple: it categorized all WRA relocation centers as proscribed military areas under the authority of EO 9066. Thus, the military had the power to prevent any person brought there from leaving. The government issued Public Proclamation WD 1 (7 F.R. 6593, August 13, 1942), designating four relocation camps outside the WDC as military areas: Rohwer and Jerome in Arkansas; Granada (also called Amache), Colorado; and Heart Mountain, Wyoming. The order prohibited any movement outside these areas without express permission from the authorities.[20]

The army and the WRA presented a different face to the wider American public. Twenty months after the start of the war, the WRA said that the removal and incarceration of Japanese Americans were meant to be temporary measures and that it had established procedures enabling "loyal citizens and law-abiding aliens" to leave the centers. There was no reference to the earlier rationale of military necessity or the need to create separate military areas in which to hold the inmates. The WRA implied that removal and incarceration were for the inmates' benefit: "The decision to provide relocation centers for the evacuees was not made until some 6 weeks after evacuation was decided upon, and was made largely because of the recognition of the danger that the hasty and unplanned resettlement of 112,000 people might create civil disorder."[21] The agency neglected to mention that the idea of separating and removing persons of Japanese ancestry from the West Coast was discussed years before World War II began.

EO 9066 cast a wide net for persons of Japanese ancestry. Dewitt, the WDC's commanding general, intended to include any person of Japanese origin, regardless of whether the individual was aware of his or her ancestry. As stated earlier, according to DeWitt's *Final Report,* persons with "as little as one-sixteenth Japanese blood" were seized, and, as in Alaska, even individuals who were not of Japanese ancestry but whose adoptive parents had Japanese surnames.

This represents a social construction of a racial category, since the criteria for qualifying as a person of Japanese ancestry applied to those with little or no actual blood ties to the enemy in Japan. Out of the entire population, the WDC allowed only one exception of a "full-blooded" Japanese American.[22] The WDC wanted to ensnare the entire group.

An issue arose over whether to incarcerate a person who was not of Japanese ancestry but had married someone of that background. The WCCA initially held 1,479 people with non-Japanese spouses (among them, 816 Issei and 376 Nisei) and about 700 to 900 others who were in a "mixed" ancestry category.[23] The WDC instituted the Mixed-Marriage Program with five categories of people who might or

might not be incarcerated, or who might or might not be allowed to return to a restricted area. For example, in a family with an Issei or Nisei mother married to a
citizen husband who was not of Japanese ancestry, he and their minor children
were allowed to return to an exclusion zone. The children in this case would be
considered one-half Japanese. Families consisting of a Nikkei husband married to
a non-Nikkei mother, with or without minor children, could not return unless the
husband was deceased or the couple was separated.[24] And in a bizarre ruling in
1942, even when both the mothers and fathers were absent, the WDC decreed that
"nineteen orphans of mixed parentage and eighty-two youngsters of pure Japanese descent" living in the Los Angeles Japanese Children's Home should be taken to
the Manzanar WRA camp.[25]

On April 17, 1942, the War Department and the WRA met and agreed that a
minimum of 5,000 inmates was necessary before the WRA would designate a center as a relocation camp. The army could then station a military police escort company at the camp for the purpose of guarding the inmates.[26] Between May and October, the WRA eventually assumed control of 120,313 persons, almost all of whom
were of Japanese ancestry—permanent residents and citizens alike. Of this number, 118,803 eventually found themselves in WRA camps.[27] Not until May 1944 did
Secretary of War Stimson recommend termination of the exclusion order to President Roosevelt. Even then, Roosevelt did not move to do so until November of
that year. There is some reason to believe that the public relations aspect of the incarceration had something to do with the delay. If Roosevelt terminated the order
before he was reelected and allowed the "dangerous" Japanese Americans to return, his critics might raise embarrassing questions concerning the reasons for
their release. Instead, he waited until the matter became politically irrelevant.

THE INDIVIDUAL EXCLUSION PROGRAM

Many people believe that only Japanese nationals and Japanese Americans were
forcibly moved during World War II under EO 9066. In fact, there was another
army program in place to remove selected German and Italian aliens and American citizens. But in contrast to events among the Nikkei population, no large-scale
arrest or exclusion program was enacted under EO 9066.

On the West Coast, the WDC pressed for a program to exclude some nationals
and American citizens of German and Italian ancestry in addition to those already
removed under the Alien Enemies Act. The War Department had not granted this
WDC request as of March 24, 1942. One probable reason for the inaction was the
noticeable lack of public concern over these groups. As stated before, on Columbus Day in October 1942, President Roosevelt proclaimed that Italian nationals
would henceforth not be considered "aliens of enemy nationality."[28] Another
probable reason was that, unlike the Japanese group, the Italian and German population had politically influential supporters; many of their sons and daughters

were conspicuous in American public life—for example, in the government and military.

Although German and Italian nationals could be and were placed in the Justice Department's internment camps, there was little the War Department could do to remove American citizens who had not committed an unlawful act. However, on August 19, six months after EO 9066 was signed, the War Department announced the Individual Exclusion Program (IEP), which would enable the removal from a military exclusion area of those "whose presence was considered dangerous to national security." The authorities invoked were EO 9066 and PL 503.[29] There was no incarceration; an individual was simply unable to remain within the particular area. The IEP was initially aimed at the eight states within the WDC, but on September 10, the War Department announced that the sixteen states of the Eastern Defense Command would be included in the program. The War Department also gave leave to the Southern and Central Defense Commands to implement this program if they so desired.

From late August 1942 to July 1943, the WDC arrested individuals with alleged ties to German or Italian organizations in the United States or those who had expressed sympathy or loyalty to Axis policies or officials. These people, according to FBI information, were "not already interned or being prosecuted under some criminal statute" and were considered "potentially dangerous." Among them were alleged members of fascist groups such as the Silver Shirts or individuals, mainly of German ancestry, who were believed to have acquired war materiel or armaments information.[30]

Several critical elements distinguish the IEP from the incarceration practices applied to Japanese Americans. Scrutiny of individuals rather than judgment of a group constitutes the central difference. The IEP quickly established individual exclusion boards consisting of three field-grade officers that convened after the individual's arrest. A quite important point was that arrested persons could be represented by legal counsel. At the individual exclusion board hearings, the military presented its case, but the defendant could call or challenge witnesses and question the facts presented. Finally, whatever the regional commander recommended, a defendant could appeal the decision through military and then civilian channels.

Few people were actually arrested under the IEP. In the WDC, 335 persons were taken, and the individual exclusion boards recommended 174 for expulsion from the area. After a review of the cases by the U.S. attorney and the military's civil affairs unit, agreement was reached for 141 cases. The commanding general of the WDC then ruled on the 33 cases without unanimous recommendations and decided to exclude all the individuals. In the Eastern Defense Command, the commanding general ordered the exclusion of 59 persons, while the Southern Defense Command removed 21 people.[31] The total taken under the IEP in the United States came to 563 persons, of which 254 were excluded from the particular military command area.[32]

Once a person was ordered excluded, the F B I processed the individual by taking his or her photograph and fingerprints. On the West Coast, the W R A was given responsibility for handling personal property, transportation, and funds for food and other necessities.[33] In certain cases, a military commander tried to extend the order to include other command areas. If a person refused the exclusion order, the military initially asked the Justice Department to prosecute the case. In early 1943, however, Attorney General Biddle told Lieutenant General DeWitt that the prosecution procedure was unconstitutional and refused to take the cases to court.

Unable to convince the Justice Department, the W D C resorted to force. After the attorney general agreed that the W D C could evict persons as part of its wartime powers, the W D C started to remove designated persons from military zones on its own. The attorney general warned the W D C that this procedure could be found illegal if tested in court. For some time then, if an arrested individual even threatened a lawsuit, the W D C immediately reviewed the case, and "the tendency was to rescind the order in order to avoid the litigation."[34]

Because of the differences in opinion as to the legality of the IEP, some antagonism apparently arose between the W D C and the Justice Department. For example, the W D C believed that a Sylvester Andriano from San Francisco had connections with Benito Mussolini and the Italian Fascist government. DeWitt recommended exclusion. The U.S. attorney disagreed with the recommendation, but DeWitt ignored the Justice Department and ordered Andriano excluded not only from the W D C but from Washington, D.C., as well. The Justice Department decided to counter this action: "It soon came to the attention of the CG [DeWitt] that Andriano had violated his order by going to Washington, D.C., from which he was excluded, and, in fact had held conferences with the Attorney General on that trip." Andriano apparently made other trips, and the attorney general refused the War Department's request to prosecute him for violating the exclusion order. Moreover, whenever the military learned that Andriano was in the Washington, D.C., area and went to remove him, they found that Andriano had just left. Army officials suspected that the attorney general's office kept Andriano informed of the military's actions.[35] And yet, the Justice Department did not overtly embarrass the military by making public such questionable behavior.

Months later, in 1943, some persons who had been excluded under the IEP raised legal challenges. One naturalized German citizen in Philadelphia refused to leave the command area as ordered, and the case went to trial. The federal judge hearing the case upheld his refusal, saying the "Army lacked the right to exclude persons arbitrarily from coastal defense areas under present circumstances."[36]

In another case, the W D C commanding general ordered the exclusion of Karl Labedz because of his alleged connection with the German Bund chapter in Portland, Oregon. On October 1, 1943, Labedz, a naturalized citizen, brought suit stating that the individual exclusion order was unconstitutional and sought an injunction against the forced removal. Labedz's attorney questioned whether his client was really a "potentially dangerous person." The court found in January 1944 "that the action of the military authorities was not arbitrary or capricious and that there was a racial basis for this action, but the main ground of decision was that Labedz had brought his action prematurely in that the question of the illegality of the order could not be noticed before either Labedz submitted to the Exclusion Order or until he was found prosecuted for violation of Public Law 503."[37] In finding against the defendant, the court sidestepped the question of whether or not the exclusion order was legal.

Lieutenant General Delos C. Emmons, past commanding general of the Hawaii Command, replaced Lieutenant General DeWitt at the WDC in September 1943.[38] Emmons initiated an examination of the 174 individual exclusion cases, and by June 1944, he had rescinded 155 of them, suspended 2, and left 16 cases intact; one person had died in the interim.[39] The IEP orders ceased before the end of the war. While German and Italian American citizens were receiving individual attention, more than 100,000 Nisei and Issei remained sequestered in WRA camps, unable to return to their prewar homes and communities.

"ANTI-WAR" AND "PRO-WRA" CENTERS

The WRA's creation of three virtually unknown incarceration sites in 1943 is of notable significance. The WRA called two of them—Leupp and Moab—"isolation centers" and used them to hold American citizens labeled "persistent troublemakers." Another center, Cow Creek, although short lived, was created for a group of inmates who were viewed as pro-WRA. Besides their relative anonymity, these camps represent important facets of the control process. The ad hoc regulations for removing individuals to the new centers were replete with procedural omissions and errors. The creation and use of these facilities exemplify not only the extent to which the WRA would go to achieve an appearance of tranquillity in its centers but also the brashness of the authorities in their willingness to use any power at their disposal in order to control inmates.

The spark that ignited the creation of the new centers was struck at the WRA camp at Manzanar, California. The incident did not occur in a vacuum: for months, the inmates had been prodded and moved, from their homes to WCCA and then WRA centers, producing a group whose frustrations were very near the surface and needed only a slight stimulus to combust. There are many available sources on what has come to be known as the WRA Manzanar "riot" of December 1942, although very few concentrate on what transpired *after* this incident.[40]

Examination of prior events is vital to understanding the process by which the new centers were created. Beginning in early August 1942, officers of the Army Language School went to WRA camps to recruit Nisei volunteers to serve as Japanese linguists. At the Manzanar camp, from late November, a few mainly Nisei inmates attempted to dissuade and intimidate other Nisei who expressed interest in joining the military. This event exacerbated existing tensions, and the WRA administrators began to identify certain inmates as being either "pro-Japan" or "pro-American," judging by their words and actions.[41]

On December 5, six masked men assaulted Fred Tayama, a Nisei who publicly espoused a pro-WRA viewpoint and who was reputedly an FBI informant. Tayama was hospitalized for his injuries, and Manzanar's internal security police arrested three inmates who they believed had instigated the attack. Camp police placed two persons in the camp jail and spirited the third, Harry Ueno, to the Inyo County Jail, six miles away, in Independence, California.[42]

The next day, at about noon, 200 to 400 inmates gathered near the front gate to demand Ueno's return to Manzanar.[43] The demonstrators later formed a five-member negotiation committee to talk with Manzanar's project director, Ralph P. Merritt, and his chief of internal security. Merritt called the officer in charge of the Manzanar military police (MP) battalion with the warning that a crowd problem might occur. Twelve armed military policemen entered the camp, ready for crowd control, and posted themselves in a line in front of the center's jail. The negotiation committee and a crowd, now numbering nearly a thousand, came to the administration building to demand Ueno's release. Merritt at first refused to talk to the committee with the crowd present and ordered it to disperse. The crowd refused the order, and Merritt met with the committee. He consented to Ueno's imminent return to face trial at Manzanar if the crowd agreed to leave and hold no further unauthorized mass meetings. In addition, the committee was to find Tayama's real assailant. The crowd disbanded, and Merritt had Ueno returned to Manzanar at about half past three.

That evening, at about six, another large crowd gathered to listen to inmate speakers discuss three topics: Ueno's arrest, the rampant corruption some inmates saw within the Manzanar WRA staff, and the presence of administration or FBI informants, or *inu* (dog), as the inmates called them. The inmate informants were a particular grievance.[44] The MP detachment stationed in front of the center jail had increased to thirty and become another inmate concern. At about nine, the crowd divided into two parts: one group of 100–200 people left for the hospital to "fix" Fred Tayama, while another, approximately 500 strong, started for the camp jail to demand Ueno's release.[45]

Accounts of subsequent events differ in emphasis and detail. The WRA's version is that the larger crowd rushed and entered the police station, but Ueno refused to leave unless the Manzanar project director released him. According to the army, "the Committee and a portion of the mob entered the police station, whereupon, the Director called the MP headquarters and asked that the military come in and take over the camp."[46] Ueno himself recalled, "A lot of people came in, and we shake hands. Nobody carry any stick or any rock or anything."[47]

After another call to the MP commander, thirty-five more MPs entered the camp, secured the police station, and pushed the inmates away from the building.

The WRA's version is that with the arrival of the additional MPs, shouting arose from the crowd and a mob atmosphere developed. Forming a rank in front of the station, the MPs donned gas masks and faced the crowd with shotguns, submachine guns, and rifles. They also deployed two heavy machine guns, one at each end of the line of soldiers, and pointed them at the crowd. The MP ranking officer, Captain Martyn L. Hall, ordered the crowd to disperse. When the inmates refused to do so, the military threw at least six tear-gas and vomit-gas grenades into the gathering. Unfortunately for the army, a thirty-five-mile-per-hour wind blew the cloud back toward the soldiers, nullifying the effects of the gas. However, the lobbed canisters raised the fear level in the crowd; when the grenades hit the ground, many people panicked and started to run. In the pell-mell rush, some inmates ran toward the soldiers. Ueno recalls one MP sergeant yelling, "Remember Pearl Harbor, hold your line."[48]

Some soldiers, without an order, then opened fire into the crowd: "The best information available is that there were three short bursts of submachine gun fire and three shotgun shots."[49] The crowd re-formed, but after the military police threw two more tear-gas grenades into their midst, the inmates finally fled from the soldiers. James Ito, a seventeen-year-old Nisei, was shot and killed, and Katsuji James Kanegawa, a twenty-one-year-old Kibei, was mortally wounded. Nine others (seven Nisei and two Issei) suffered gunshot wounds.[50]

After the second set of thrown grenades, the army reports that an inmate started the Manzanar fire chief's car, which was parked nearby, and aimed it at the guards and the police station. Once it was rolling toward the target, the driver jumped out: "The MP CO [commanding officer] ordered that the car be fired upon in an attempt to stop it. Shots were directed at the tires, one of which was hit, whereupon the car veered sharply and struck the police station tearing off the corner, and then careened into a truck parked nearby."[51] No fatalities occurred during this second episode.

Dr. Goto, Manzanar's chief surgeon and chief of the medical staff, examined the killed and wounded. According to one Nisei eyewitness, the army board of inquiry that convened later wanted to whitewash the shooting incident: "They tried to get the evacuee doctors and nurses and all the other witnesses to say that the evacuees who died or were injured were threatening or were in the process of attacking the military police and, therefore, it was justified for the military police to fire upon the evacuees. However, the medical examination, the records, and the trajectory of the bullets showed that the victims had been either shot in the side or in the back."[52] According to this witness, the army board asked Dr. Goto to alter the records and change his testimony to show that the bullets entered the victims from the front. He refused to do so, and the next day he was relieved of his position as chief of the medical staff. The WRA later transferred him to another WRA center. If this account is true, and there is nothing in the WRA files from that time to state otherwise, the WRA and the army demonstrated that it had few qualms about shooting into a crowd to quell a difficult situation and distorting facts or falsifying records to protect its image.

Meanwhile, the Manzanar military police rearrested Ueno, the five members of the negotiation committee, and two others and took them into custody at Bishop, California, for three days.[53] This group was then trucked to the jail at Lone Pine, California, with eight others from Manzanar. They stayed there until January 9, 1943. The WRA identified these sixteen inmates as troublemakers and provided them with accommodations befitting their new status:

> They only had four bunkers for sixteen people to sleep in. You could hardly walk around. And one light hanging from the ceiling and the ceiling was pretty high— about ten or twelve feet, and one small light in the corner there. They had an oil stove but no oil in it. They didn't feed us for almost twenty-four hours. Mr. Arataka had diabetes and he needed insulin every day. They didn't give it to him for two, three days, and finally WRA sent a man to check him out. That's when we complain. We only have one cup for sixteen people to drink the coffee. We had no oil to burn; it was cold out there.[54]

From Lone Pine, the WRA shipped the prisoners by bus, train, and then truck to a deserted Civilian Conservation Corps (CCC) campsite at Dalton Wells, Utah (DG-32 [CO 234]). Located nearly ten miles north of the city of Moab, Dalton Wells is just outside the beautiful natural rock formations of Arches National Monument, yet the site itself is flat, drab, and desolate. The CCC planted some trees in the early days, but most of the vegetation is desert sagebrush and tumbleweed. The only remnants of the center today are a small commemorative plaque, a few forlorn concrete building foundations, and an unused water-storage structure. For no discernible reason, the WRA referred to the Dalton Wells site as the "Moab Camp"; in order to preclude misunderstandings, this WRA isolation camp will be called Moab here as well. Arriving at the center on January 11, 1943, Joe Y. Kurihara described his sense of isolation:

> To the sixteen of us there were sixteen soldiers guarding us day and night throughout the length of the route from Lone Pine, California to Moab, Utah, an approximate distance of 1,100 miles. . . . We alighted at Thompson [railroad spur] from whence we were taken to the present Moab Relocation Center on an open truck. The morning was freezingly cold. We felt the cold penetrating to the very core of our bones. The top of my head felt as if it was going to crack open, and the ears stung with cold. Thank heavens, the ride wasn't very long. We soon found ourselves within the confines of the camp, a former C. C. C. camp of the size of single block of Manzanar. Here we made ourselves at home with the forlorn thought of having been cast on a barren isle.[55]

The camp at Moab opened up a new chapter in WRA operations. Later inmates would originate from almost all the WRA relocation camps. Before entering fully into this episode, let us consider the fate of another group that was treated quite differently—those seen as pro-administration. The WRA defined the two groups—the Moab and the pro-administration group—as dissimilar from other inmates and treated them quite differently from the rest of the inmate population.

COW CREEK CAMP

Not understanding that the vocal inmates at Manzanar were responding to the stresses they had undergone since their initial incarceration, the WRA portrayed them as either pro-Americans or troublemakers. Those identified as pro-American were clearly favored by the WRA. As the WRA saw the situation: "The pro-Americans took the position that, if Japanese Americans were to be accepted in the future of this country on equal terms with other citizens and earn their respect, they must go the extra mile to prove themselves loyal to their native land."[56] After the gunfire and deaths at Manzanar, the WRA heard rumors that nine or ten people suspected of being administration informants, or *inu,* were targeted for assault. Their names were on a death list. Friends and families of the named parties heard the rumors as well and asked for protection. The WRA and the army sent the military police to gather these individuals and their immediate families and trucked them to the MP barracks a half-mile south of Manzanar.

Some 40 individuals and their families, or a total of about 150, were affected.[57] By day, they remained at the MP barracks; the women and children stayed in the small infirmary. At night, a truck transported them back to the Manzanar administration building where they slept on cots while the MPs guarded the building. This went on for three days as Manzanar WRA officials searched for a site to which these people could be removed for a longer period. The military finally transported sixty-six of these inmates, thirty-two of whom were wives or children, plus an additional ten WRA staff members and twelve guards to Cow Creek, California, on December 10, 1942. This site was an abandoned CCC camp in Death Valley National Monument Park, "adjacent to the old National Monument headquarters near the Park Service Residential area."[58]

In an interesting twist of terminology, Manzanar WRA administrators referred to these inmates as "refugees" instead of by the usual designation "relocatees," perhaps because they could not return to Manzanar and no one knew where they were going.[59] The WRA saw the creation of the Cow Creek camp as a humanitarian gesture that saved the so-called pro-Americans from other elements at Manzanar. Were these inmates the victims of ill-founded rumors, or were they actual informants for the WRA? An FBI memorandum specifically credits two removed persons with being valued informants and alludes in a like but general way to certain others brought to Cow Creek.[60]

When the inmates arrived, they found the camp needed renovation before it would be habitable. They organized themselves into work groups for cooking, carpentering, setting up heating and electricity, and so on and did the work themselves. After providing for their basic needs, they still had time for leisure activities such as swimming and playing poker. Unlike at Manzanar, there were no guard towers or sentries. Here, camp officials and guards shared the showers and latrines and ate with the inmates. A cordial relationship existed among them: "Camp Director [Albert] Chamberlain who also supervised the soldiers, informed the mess hall gathering that to the outside visitors such as the press, it would not look well if the soldiers were found intermingling with the Japanese at meals, and requested that from then on, the soldiers should eat at one table reserved for them."[61]

While there, many of the men worked as volunteers with the National Park Service. Within two weeks, the WRA was allowing some refugees to leave and resettle outside the WDC area. But two people—Karl Yoneda's wife, Elaine, who was not of Japanese ancestry, and her son—left for Los Angeles on December 19.[62] If the provisions of the mixed-marriage program had been followed, she would not have been allowed to return to a military exclusion area: her Nikkei husband was still alive, and they were not separated or divorced. In Los Angeles, she was required to "report monthly to the military on the behavior of her Japanese son—now almost four."[63] Thus, in at least one instance, the WDC reinterpreted its own rule when it suited its purposes.

The American Friends Service Committee (Quakers) came and interviewed various refugees for jobs and housing in Chicago and later helped them resettle. In mid-January 1943, six more men and their families left for Boulder, Colorado, to become Japanese-language instructors at the Navy Language School.[64] Others departed for distant points eastward. In this way, the WRA emptied the Cow Creek camp on February 15, 1943, two months after it opened.[65] Half a month later, it returned the site to the U.S. Park Service.

The creation and operation of the Cow Creek camp show the Janus-faced nature of the WRA. The agency smiled on those in its favor and allowed them the luxury of returning to the West Coast or granted them indefinite release to the East Coast, but those who were out of favor saw the stern face of the WRA. Harsh treatment was in store for the inmates at Moab.

MOAB ISOLATION CENTER

On December 30, 1942, WRA director Dillon S. Myer wrote that the Moab camp in Utah would henceforth be known as the Moab Relocation Center.[66] This designation was later changed to "isolation center," most likely because of the nature of its inmates and because it fell short of the 5,000 minimum population the military required to justify the stationing of a large MP contingent.

Simply put, as a result of the so-called riot at Manzanar, the WRA wanted a place where it could summarily imprison any inmate for whatever purpose it wished. The camp was meant for isolating selected inmates, regardless of evidence or cause. As the WRA put it: "In many instances, it has not been possible to secure evidence on which court action would seem justified, and an isolation center at Leupp, Arizona, is maintained, to which instigators, chronic troublemakers, and inciters are sent on the recommendation of the project director and after review of the evidence by a Review Board here in Washington."[67] The WRA created this camp and could then banish anyone it desired to "facilitate the maintenance of law and order within the relocation centers."[68]

The operational definition of "law and order" was a product solely of and for the WRA. From the inmates' perspective, the law was forever changing, depending on the circumstances and the whims of WRA officials. It could never be explained to them, since the WRA could define any situation as a disturbance and punish or arrest anyone it thought was involved. The WRA never charged the sixteen original occupants of the Moab Camp, the men from Manzanar, with the commission of any offense. Ultimately, there were few safeguards for the inmates of the two camps established by the WRA in order to ensure their docility.

Manzanar Inmates Transferred to Moab

Moab was a miniature high-security prison. Like all the camps, it had barbed-wire fences, but Moab maintained a large ratio of armed guards to inmates and a more intensely security-conscious stance. One inmate, Harry Ueno, gives a vivid picture of the situation:

We ended up in Moab. We stayed together, most of the group. For a while MPs were controlling everything. They had a sentry on the front of the barracks so nobody came in or out. We were cooped up in one building. If you wanted to go to the bathroom, you had to tell the MP; he had to come with us. That is isolated place, Moab, thirty miles away from a small mining town, dinky old town. We were way out nowhere. All around, nothing but sagebrush, not even trees. About seven or eight Civilian Conservation Corps (CCC) camp buildings left standing there. No place to go.

MPs cooked for us, and every day at lunchtime we line up, and they had an MP guarding us at both ends. We marched to the mess hall and ate. First two or three weeks, no mail came in, and you can't write nobody. We were completely shut off from outside. Then after that every bit of mail is opened up, I mean, it came in with a seal. Then we protest, "We put the three-cent stamp on them, and you got no right to open up our mail, not with a stamp on it." "Well," they said, "next time don't put the stamp on it." And then they say not to seal the letter because they going to open it up anyway. So everything's opened.[69]

Myer, the WRA director in Washington, D.C., formed a board of review on December 26, 1942, to evaluate the cases of the Manzanar sixteen. Its three members were WRA deputy director Elmer M. Rowalt, WRA solicitor Philip M. Glick, and WRA chief of community services John Provinse. In its initial report of February 12, the board recommended that the four Issei be transferred to the Justice Department; this was done on March 14. For the twelve Nisei—ten of whom were Kibei—the recommendation was that eleven be kept for an indefinite period, or, in the WRA's words, "for the time being."[70]

Various WRA administrators had different opinions on the efficacy of this new policy. The security officer at Moab, for example, admitted that certain inmates taken from Manzanar were not necessarily more anti-WRA than other inmates. He reported that a certain Mr. B. was removed from Manzanar and shipped to Moab based on information provided by another Manzanar inmate, Mr. A. The WRA's own investigation later questioned the value of Mr. A's testimony and noted that Mr. A was an avowed communist "whose reputation among the Japanese people is that he is a liar who has, on more than one occasion, distorted facts to further his own ends."[71] This security officer states:

[Later, Mr. A] publicly retracted his accusation against [Mr. B] at a meeting of the Block Leader's Council in the Town Hall at Manzanar saying they were untrue and that he would give [Mr. B] a written apology for having falsely accused him. . . . Further investigation revealed that Mr. B actually did receive written apologies from [Mr. A and three others], and from the leader of Block 27 which should change materially the evidential value of their statements as indicated on page two of Segregation Docket #12.[72]

Yet, Mr. B suffered the consequences. The WRA separated him from his family and friends for six months and, upon his release, refused to return him to the Manzanar camp.

Other WRA officials raised questions about the rationale for sending certain Nisei and Kibei to Moab. For example, one Nisei from the first Manzanar group was born in Hawaii and had no problems with the administration. According to the WRA's own files, he "does not like to associate with any California Japanese. In fact [he] says that he does not like any Japanese not born in Hawaii. He is very much Pro-American and it is believed that if he can relocate to a center where many residents are from Hawaii, he would not cause much trouble."[73] Although this particular Nisei did not create disturbances at Moab, the WRA kept him there for seven months until he was finally transferred to the WRA camp at Topaz, Utah. The power was in the WRA's hands—it accepted the information it desired, including the testimony of informers who were known to be less than reliable.

The Dual Image of Isolation

The WRA presented the American public with a different justification for the Moab camp. It became a "rehabilitation" center:

> [The] primary purpose of the isolation procedure was preventative rather than punitive—to skim off the known sources of aggravated agitation and community disruption, and allow the healing processes of time, adjustment to center life, crystallizing community organization, and improved methods of liaison between WRA and the evacuees to operate. The isolation center functioned as a rehabilitation center, and its inhabitants were gradually retransferred to other centers.[74]

In fact, no rehabilitation was taking place. The WRA frightened the inmates of all the other camps with demonstrations of its power and its readiness to use punitive measures as means of eliminating intractable behavior. It refused to tolerate conduct it construed as disruptive and removed any vocal opposition in order to ensure a calm atmosphere in the camps.

The isolation center project director correctly saw the program's resemblance to a jail and thought to mitigate the image. He wrote to Myer that the center should be seen not as a penal colony but as a place where inmates would stay for "no specific period of time, but when they have had a chance to think over their past activities and are ready to live in peace and harmony with their fellow men, they may be transferred to another Relocation Center. This procedure I believe, is better adapted to rehabilitation than one of trial and sentence."[75] No explanation of the words "think over their past activities," "ready to live in peace and harmony" or "rehabilitation" was offered. It was true, however, that inmates would spend "no specific period of time" in this new center and could not leave it without the WRA's permission. In reality, then, the isolation camp was a prison like the other WRA centers, but one with an even tougher attitude toward controlling its inmates.

Many inmates believed that being removed from a WRA camp was a form of administrative retaliation. Merely being defined as troublemakers by the WRA—which could mean they had openly questioned camp rules or procedures—was sufficient for their removal. Others attributed their transfer to Moab to their public statements that certain WRA officials were behaving like thieves or participating in black-market operations and profiting from the outside sale of sugar and pork intended for the inmates.[76]

The WRA's claim that removing these inmates assisted in "healing processes" and helped them in their "adjustment to center life" is a time-honored rationale of jailers. The removals did bring about the desired result of intimidating and pacifying the remaining inmates of the camps. The show of force and the killings by the WRA and the army resulted in outward calm at Manzanar. Those remaining then knew that raising questions or taking action of any sort could lead to immediate arrest and transfer.

Transfers from Other Camps

The number of Moab inmates quickly increased. Added to the first sixteen from Manzanar were sixty-seven from various WRA camps, for a total of eighty-three inmates—seventy-nine Nisei or Kibei and four Issei.[77] As with the Manzanar group, these additional inmates were identified as "aggravated troublemakers" and, according to the WRA, were responsible for "fomenting disorders or threatening the security of center residents, [and were] addicted to troublemaking, and beyond the capacity of regular processes within the relocation centers to keep under control."[78]

Nisei and Kibei who were sent to the isolation center tended to stay there. For example, the four Manzanar Issei who came in December 1942, remained at Moab until March of the next year, when the FBI removed them to a Justice Department camp. At around this time, for whatever reason, one of the Issei had proclaimed himself ready to be an informant, and the WRA suggested that he might be sent to Tule Lake and used for that purpose.[79]

As time went by, even some Moab and Leupp WRA administrators came to question the basis on which certain inmates were brought there. Especially expressive was the chief of internal security, F. S. Frederick, who expressed doubt as to whether the WRA should have taken a particular Kibei from Manzanar simply for allegedly making a telephone call and for his pro-Japanese attitude. Frederick's report states:

> The telephone conversation factor appears to have been based upon the testimony of one Joe Blamey who was, according to his own statements, hiding under the desk in the dispatcher's office when the alleged conversation took place. . . . Hysteria of this type is hardly conducive to accurate testimony. . . . Regarding [the inmate's] loyalty, it is true that he stated he wanted Japan to win the war, etc. but one must consider the circumstances under which he made these statements. As described in his Legal History, he was angry at the time and gave vent to his feelings by uttering such statements. The fact that he had much conflict with his stepmother and his unhappy home life in Japan predicating his coming to this country, should be considered regarding his interest in Japan.[80]

After nine months in the isolation center, the WRA released this inmate to its Heart Mountain Relocation Camp.

Frederick also mentioned an interesting method of circumventing the need to justify an inmate's transfer to Moab, a technique he called the "typewriter strategy." Frederick stated, "Under the Suggested Findings of Fact included in the Segregation Docket, it appears that an effort was made to build a case against [inmates] by the space-filling technique of itemizing non-essential facts such as where he was born, that he was block leader of block 2, etc."[81] This ploy worked for one simple reason. There were initially no accountability measures in place that required justification for transferring an inmate to an isolation center.

A WRA internal review board existed in Washington, D.C., but in some instances, its actions were less than effective. For example, the board had difficulties with the reasons for transferring ten Manzanar Kibei to Moab on February 24, 1943, a little more than a month after the first arrivals from Manzanar. The board stated, "There is little evidence that the ten evacuees have engaged in serious trouble-making at Manzanar. However, it appears that dockets are incomplete."[82] Once at Moab, seven of the ten inmates wrote to the project director, asking him about the charges for which they had been transferred to the isolation center. They also wanted to know about a hearing promised them before they left Manzanar. The Moab director asked Myer for assistance in this matter, stating, "I do not have any information on each individual case."[83] It seems the Manzanar project director felt that they were all "in varying degrees pro-Japan in their sympathies" after five of the ten asked for expatriation to Japan.[84] For this reason, the Moab director accepted them and kept eight of the ten inmates until the isolation center closed. The two other inmates went to a different WRA camp in June and September, from four to seven months after their initial arrival. These cases illustrate that any qualms felt by the review board seemed to have little result. This situation continued for some time until the weight of such questionable actions became impossible to ignore, even for those within the WRA administration.

After his own investigation of these latter ten Manzanar inmates, Frederick wrote, "Part of the Ind[ependent] group from Manzanar all arrested on suspicion. Finger put on them by the Peace Committee. It appears that it might have been better if the Peace Committee had been pinched instead of these guys."[85] On August 11, 1943, the isolation center project director seconded the idea that the ten individuals did not deserve to be there. In a letter to WRA director Myer, he observed, "While I have no complaint against the boys forwarded to us from Manzanar, it occurs to me [that] they were transferred to the Isolation Center as a result of information received from informers, and not because they are known to have a record as constant trouble makers."[86]

Yet, the men were kept at Moab and at Leupp. In the interest of quieting the voices of dissent at Manzanar, the WRA gave more credence to the words of those it defined as pro-American and pro-WRA. For the Manzanar inmates, the situation was more complex. Even before the mass exclusion of the Nikkei from their homes and communities, some individuals—especially the leadership of the Japanese American Citizens League (JACL)—advocated a show of support and obedience regarding the government's orders. All the inmates did not unanimously agree with this stance, but faced with the reality of military reprisals for refusal to obey the exclusion orders, almost all those on the West Coast allowed themselves to be taken into the assembly and relocation centers. Differences of opinion on persons espousing pro-JACL and pro-WRA positions became evident as part of the Manzanar calamity. Not a few Manzanar inmates felt that the JACL was interested in advancing its organizational self-interests over the interests of Japanese Americans as a whole. The Manzanar JACL leadership was seen not as working with the Manzanar protesters but as assisting the WRA in popularizing the idea that the protesters were anti-American and therefore dangerous to the well-being of the center. For months after the pro-WRA people were taken to Cow Creek and the "disrupters" to Moab and Leupp, Manzanar was quiet. The lesson had been learned: protest and you would be treated harshly and taken from family and friends.

Inmate Resistance

The Moab Isolation Center administration viewed its inmates with a wary eye. As many as 150 MPs were initially detailed for guard duty there. Yet, despite a small inmate population and large guard contingent, the center experienced its own resistance incident.

On April 13, 1943, the Moab internal security office heard rumors that seven inmates in Barrack 2, from Manzanar, entered Barrack 7, threatened other inmates, and planned to disrupt the camp. In order to control the reputed actions, the next day the Moab administration drafted and announced an intracamp general order forbidding inmates of one barrack from visiting another barrack without express permission from the administration. Moreover, any inmate allowed to visit another barrack had to be escorted by a Caucasian and communicate in English. That same day, twenty-one inmates engaged in civil disobedience by marching to the administration building. Upon their arrival, the WRA arrested them and charged them with unlawful assembly, a violation defined under WRA Administrative Instruction Number 85.

The administrative instructions, which had been written by the WRA, gave the agency broad powers over inmates. Number 85 in particular dealt with unacceptable actions by the prisoners. For example, the WRA defined an unlawful assembly as "any two or more persons who assemble together to do an unlawful act, and separate without doing or advancing toward it, or who assemble together to do an unlawful act in a violent, boisterous or tumultuous manner, shall be deemed guilty of unlawful assembly." Thus, talking to another person could be construed as violating Number 85. Similar actions could also be treated as "offenses against the peace and security of the relocation center." A precise definition of "offenses against the peace and security" was never specified, but inmates could be found guilty of committing them. The project director could mete out punishment at his discretion for an "act of an evacuee that he considers inimical to the orderly administration of the center or that violates any regulation applicable to the center."[87]

A "trial" was held for the seven protesters on April 14 at 3:00 P.M. Frederick, the center's internal security officer, acted as the presiding judge. Another trial was held the next day for the remaining fourteen inmates. Two inmates pleaded not guilty, and nineteen entered guilty pleas, stating that they had acted to test the new rule.

The maximum punishment allowable, according to WRA Administrative Instructions, was a three-month jail term and suspension of various privileges—such as clothing allowance and welfare grants—for up to the same period. If the inmates were found guilty and the sentence was for separate incarceration, the project directors could place them in a city or county jail. Frederick judged eighteen to be guilty and three not guilty. Seven inmates were sent to the Grand County Jail in the town of Moab, ten miles to the south, to serve a three-month sentence. Eleven others were sentenced to one to three months in the center stockade plus suspension of other privileges.[88] These Moab convictions exemplify another aspect of WRA-style administration: disobey or protest a rule and the reprisals could be swift and harsh. Frederick wrote about his complete power over the inmates:

> I enjoyed the unique position of passing a law—by the powers vested in me as Acting Project Director—directing the arrest of twenty-one evacuees, presiding as judge in their individual trials, sentencing eight leaders to three months in jail and placing the others on probation. Besides being in charge of the jail, I was probation and parole officer. It has been said that the law mentioned in the foregoing was a deliberate design to goad the leaders into doing something for which they could be arrested. While I do not choose to enter into a discussion on this point at this time, I do recall having rescinded the same law within six hours after it was passed. Where else but WRA could one gain such extraordinary experience?[89]

That Frederick knowingly created an intolerable situation in order to force a reaction is one way of understanding the last three sentences. The episode also reveals his arrogance and willingness to wield his power as acting director against the inmates of the Moab camp.

According to WRA policy, sending an Issei to a Justice Department internment camp required only that an allegation be filed against the individual. After March 4, 1943, however, even this simple procedure became a formality. When the WRA wished to send an Issei to the Justice Department, it required simply that a project director relay his desire to remove the inmate: "In the interest of promoting the success of a difficult task in administering the War Relocation Camps involving the detention of citizens and aliens together, it was agreed that a limited number of trouble-some Japanese aliens would be taken and interned *even though their conduct did not establish subversive activity* under the standards heretofore applied."[90] The Justice Department cooperated willingly with the WRA and accepted any Issei the latter agency sent.

Moab WRA administrators also discussed the possibility of transferring some

Nisei inmates to Justice Department camps. Certain Justice Department officials seriously considered allowing such transfers. In order to do so, the WRA needed to provide only those facts that were available about the "undesirable Japanese aliens or nonaliens located in Relocation Centers, and the Attorney General [would] then order the removal of these individuals to another camp."[91] As stated earlier, "nonalien" was a convenient euphemism used by the WRA to avoid calling a Nisei an American citizen. This policy change concerning the Nisei was not instituted, and Myer informed the Moab project director on March 10 that the Nisei, at this time, could not be so transferred.[92] The inability to remove the Nisei, coupled with the concern that more citizen inmates would be forthcoming, was probably the impetus behind the move to a larger site. The WRA closed Moab on April 27, 1943, and transferred all remaining inmates to the isolation center at Leupp, Arizona.

LEUPP ISOLATION CENTER

The Leupp Isolation Center in Arizona was initially slated to be simply a larger and more permanent version of the Moab camp. Located at an abandoned Indian school in the Painted Desert near Winslow, the facility belonged to the U.S. Department of the Interior. The WRA was granted control of the site on March 24, 1943, and moved the forty-five inmates that were then at Moab on April 27 of that year.[93] Since the Leupp center could be expanded to hold 2,000 inmates, the WRA had more freedom to accommodate all those whom it wished to isolate.

Again, a troublemaker or a dangerous person was not necessarily a person who posed a military threat to the United States, as stipulated in EO 9066; the WRA defined the terms to serve its purposes. As Myer stated in an internal memorandum, Leupp was to be viewed "as an isolation center for trouble-makers residing in Relocation Centers. Persons who cannot be sent to internment camps—i.e. American citizens—or who cannot adequately be dealt with in the civil courts are sent there when it is discovered that they are responsible for dissension and interference with the Government's program, or in case they are carrying on pro-Japanese propaganda."[94]

As at Moab, imprisonment at Leupp meant an indeterminate stay and separation from family and friends. Writing of the inmates, WRA director Myer stated that "if their behavior at the center justifies it, they may be released to return to a relocation center."[95] With no explicit criteria as to exactly what behavior might secure the inmates' release, their length of stay was subject to the judgment or whim of WRA administrators. Even at that, if isolated inmates were released, the WRA's intent was to preclude their return to the WRA camp from which they originated. Thus, for reasons never explained to released inmates, they were no closer to their families and friends than if they had remained at Leupp.

At least for some inmates, the move from Moab to Leupp was a degrading and torturous ordeal. By one account: "[Harry Ueno] and four other inmates [were] locked in a coffinlike box on the back of a flatbed truck for the transfer. . . . Wedged together in a five-by-six foot space with only one small hole in back for air, the five men nearly suffocated and [according to Ueno] 'the 11 hour long drive never seemed to end. In 36 years of my life this was the first time that I had ever experienced such a painful, agonizing and helpless feeling.'"[96]

Questionable Reasons for Transfer

The isolation center operations can be better understood through the experiences of particular inmates who were brought there. For example, some inmates at the w r a relocation center at Gila River, Arizona, had formed an organization called the Gila Young People's Association (GYPA). On February 18, 1943, the w r a sent thirteen people to Moab because they were officers and members of the GYPA. Although the w r a had come to see the GYPA as pro-Japanese, it had earlier formally approved of and recognized its existence.

Leupp's security chief reported of one thirty-one-year-old Nisei inmate: "[Mr. X] was a treasurer [of the GYPA] and has been in the Isolation Center of Moab and Leupp for over five months. His transfer to Moab and separation from his family was apparently brought about administratively rather than as a result of arrest, fair trial and conviction. There was no sentence, he was merely transferred. Since the GYPA enjoyed official sanction of the authorities at Gila, and in the absence of other evidence, it does not appear that [Mr. X] committed a crime by being treasurer of an authorized organization."[97] In effect, the w r a arrested, isolated, and incarcerated Mr. X without telling him that being an officer of the GYPA was sufficient to warrant imprisonment and separation from his family and friends for an indefinite time period.

Another Gila River inmate, Mr. Y, was apparently isolated because of a bureaucratic bungle. This mistake was recognized even while Mr. Y was being brought to Moab:

What some of the [w r a] guys call dangerous is certainly questionable! Johnston picked up one guy by the name of [Mr. Y] who had the misfortune of having the same last name as his cousin and lived in the same house as the latter. The cousin's first name was something like "Y," something similar and thus the wrong guy was grabbed. Understand that friends of this kid protested to [Gila River w r a project director] Bennett and he is alleged to have said that it didn't make any difference if it was a mistake; he was staying there. Johnston also knew it about half way up here and I asked him why he didn't call from here about bringing him back but he wouldn't nor would he bring him back. . . . Rather disappointed in Johnston.[98]

In this case, although the w r a Gila River project director, the Moab project director, and two Moab security officers knew of the identification error, they did nothing to help the inmate—"[Mr. Y] has spent over five months in the Isolation Center and was still at Leupp."[99] Then, after keeping Mr. Y there for five more months, the W R A finally sent him to its Tule Lake Segregation Camp in California and placed him in the newly constructed stockade. Reports exist that other inmates were also taken to Moab and Leupp Isolation Camps as a result of administrative errors or on the basis of information from questionable sources.[100]

The W R A administration in Washington, D.C., knew about the erroneous transfers of inmates to isolation centers. For example, as late as August 11, 1943, the Leupp project director reported to W R A director Myer that the paperwork for the new inmates from Gila River, who had been transferred on April 15, had not arrived.[101] Some higher-level W R A administrators had also written about this situation. On August 14, the W R A assistant solicitor, Lewis Sigler, stated, "We still don't have dockets on many of the men sent to Leupp from Gila." Although Sigler did not report which particular files were missing, he did mention that the Leupp filing system "is still woefully inadequate," and "many of the dockets are still incomplete."[102]

There was probably a very good reason why the W R A never tried to correct this situation. The agency desired to create a placid inmate population in its other ten camps by excising difficult individuals. For example, the removal of the first thirteen inmates from Gila River had an enormous effect on those who remained. Even the W R A overtly acknowledged the results of its policy: "A few were removed to Moab. The consequence was that for a long time, the people [at Gila River] were afraid that any anti-Administration word or deed would lead to summary removal; this fear continued well into 1944."[103]

The W R A administrators in Washington, D.C., were also aware that project directors were offhandedly transferring individuals to Moab or Leupp. For example, when fifteen Nisei or Kibei came to the Moab camp from Tule Lake on April 2, 1943, the Tule Lake administrators did not send their files to the board of review until May 17. For a month and a half then, these inmates were separated from their families for no reason recognized outside the W R A. On June 22, or three months after their departure from the Tule Lake camp, Myer reported that these fifteen were not "aggravated trouble makers" and there was insufficient evidence to justify their isolation. Still, Myer kept them at the isolation center, stating, "I have noted, however, that these men are all now living at Leupp, and that you [the Tule Lake project director] have stated that you feel that their presence at Tule Lake would be detrimental to the internal security of the Project. I believe therefore, that it is best for these men to remain at Leupp until we can determine whether they should remain indefinitely at Leupp, be transferred to another relocation center, or be transferred to the segregation center on its establishment."[104] The W R A later sent three of the fifteen inmates to different W R A camps; the remaining twelve were transported to the Tule Lake Segregation Camp. No appeal process was offered to the inmates.

From June 1943 onward, many W R A project directors shipped inmates to Leupp. Commenting on two of the three inmates sent from the W R A relocation center at Jerome, Arkansas, the Leupp director wrote: "[Mr. I] and [Mr. T] formerly of Jerome are both thoroughly Japanese, but from reading their dockets I am unable to find any other reason for sending them to Leupp."[105] Nevertheless, the Jerome inmates stayed at Leupp.

In another case, the Tule Lake camp internal security officers arrested five inmates in early March 1943 and charged them with rioting after they splintered doors and broke some windows in Block 42 while looking for another inmate. The WRA brought them before a superior court judge in Modoc County, California. Although no one was injured in the melee, the judge found the five guilty of attempted assault and battery and sentenced them to varying lengths of prison time. One person, for example, received six months' imprisonment with a three-month suspended sentence, and another was sentenced to four months in jail with a two-month suspended sentence.[106] After they served their time at the Modoc County Jail, the WRA sent these inmates to Leupp on May 6. In a confidential memo, Myer stated, "In the case of these men also, I believe that under the circumstances they should remain at Leupp until we decide what further disposition should be made."[107] He gave no reason for this decision, and four out of the five stayed there for the seven months that remained before it closed. Then, the WRA sent them to the internal jail at the Tule Lake Segregation Center. The fifth person was released on August 13 to the WRA camp at Minidoka, Idaho.[108]

After the March 1943 disturbance at Tule Lake, the WRA project director tried to convict fifteen others. Rather than going to trial in civil court, the WRA held its own hearing and sentenced these inmates to spend from sixty to ninety days in the Tule Lake stockade. The WRA prosecuted them for participating in the fracas, refusing to register for the draft with the Selective Service, and interfering with an internal registration process.[109]

An Attempt at Reform

Six months after establishing the isolation centers, the WRA tried to amend some of its incarceration procedures. Myer finally admitted to his project directors that transfer to an isolation camp did constitute a form of punishment and issued an order instructing all WRA project directors to give each individual a hearing before removing him to Leupp. These hearings, the WRA clarified, did not have to be public, nor was it necessary to permit the inmate to confront his accusers. The WRA need only supply minimal information, "with as much evidence as the Project Director may present without revealing the identity of informants or other confidential sources of information."[110] In effect, this memo put WRA project directors on notice that they must assemble a case file, complete or not, before removing an inmate. Various project directors still never bothered to justify the removal of certain inmates, apparently lost or misplaced other inmates' files, or never sent files to Leupp with their transferred inmates. WRA investigators later found incomplete and missing files on inmates who had been at Leupp for more than six months. Moreover, the "typewriter strategy," in which noticeably unimportant information was used to justify a transfer, was still a method of completing some removal orders. Myer said nothing in his memo about what constituted a defensible case for removal, only that a file was needed for each transfer.

Myer did instruct his project directors to avoid sending an inmate to the isolation center solely for criticizing w r a policies or the administration. In the next sentence, however, he qualified this position by saying: "I know that it may be difficult to determine when an evacuee is merely voicing criticism or attempting sincerely to accomplish reforms and when he is using criticism and related tactics as a method of creating disorder as an end in itself. The Project Director must conscientiously probe as deeply into the evidence as possible in order to make this determination; any doubt should be resolved in favor of the evacuee."[111] Again, the decision was left to the discretion of each project director, and the w r a apparently never contemplated offering inmates a formal or separate appeals process.

The overpowering authority structure that confronted w r a inmates was a frightening reality. And it was not just the w r a. Other agencies such as the Alien Enemy Control Unit, the army, and the f b i could and did make recommendations that resulted in transfers to isolation centers or the Justice Department's internment camps.

At times, even the participating agencies saw through their own abuse of power. In one case, the camp at Topaz, Utah, shipped twelve inmates to Leupp on July 3 and 10, 1943, accused by the f b i of signing a statement "that they would commit sabotage to this country in the event that they were asked to do so from the Emperor of Japan or a representative."[112] The chief security officer at Leupp characterized this transfer as "based on idiotic interviews of the f b i."[113] The Leupp project director reported, "The Topaz group all seem to be at Leupp not because they are trouble makers, but because they are pro-Japanese. . . . The majority of the boys speak and understand very little English. However, the ones who do, stated that the line of questioning was so ridiculous that from disgust and contempt they answered 'Yes' to nearly all of the [f b i] agents' questions."[114] The f b i recommended their transfer to Leupp, and it was done.

Some inmates came to Leupp as a result of negative responses to portions of a 1943 "loyalty questionnaire," which the army and the w r a required them to answer. And yet, thousands of other Nisei also gave negative responses and were not brought to the isolation center. Thus, there was often seemingly little to differentiate those who were transferred to Leupp from those who were not.

Review and Closure

On August 11, 1943, a new Leupp project director, Paul G. Robertson, reported to w r a director Myer about administrative irregularities in the inmate-transfer process. According to him, sixty-seven men were presently incarcerated, and "of the evacuees now at Leupp, at least according to their dockets, I fail to find but two cases involving other than a first offense and no indication of attempted correction." Robertson pointed out that according to recent WRA regulations, "persons should not be considered for Leupp who do not persistently interfere with effective administration or engage constantly in threats or beatings and then only when the administration attempts to control it, punish it and prevent it."[115] Despite this, the inmates remained.

Robertson went on to say that the inmates obviously viewed the process as flawed, since "in nearly every case where an evacuee is transferred to Leupp, he has been told that he would be given a fair and speedy hearing. . . . No formal charges have ever been made against these evacuees, and no hearing has ever been held. Few if any of them with whom I have talked have ever been interviewed prior to transfer, but have been told they would be given a hearing after they reached Leupp."[116] Robertson was telling the WRA administrators that certain WRA officials either did not follow their own regulations or chose to ignore them.

Eight months after the WRA established the isolation centers, the agency's assistant solicitor questioned their continued existence. On August 14, 1943, after pointing out problems with the handling of inmates' files and administration of the inmates, he likened Leupp to a Nazi camp: "Finally, I should like to see a reexamination made of the advisability of continuing the Leupp Center. I think it is an un-American institution, and is premised on Gestapo methods. I don't like the idea of individuals being sent to Leupp without being told why they are being sent."[117] Although there is no evidence to show that this particular recommendation was responsible, Leupp operations soon slowed.

In late August, the Leupp project director met with the WRA review committee in Washington, D.C., to discuss problems with forty-nine inmates. WRA director Myer accepted the committee's recommendation that most of the inmates be sent to the newly created WRA segregation center at Tule Lake. In all cases, Robertson said, these inmates would cause no trouble there.

On October 12, the review committee wrote to Myer recommending that Leupp be closed no later than the first day of 1944. They also proposed that future troublemakers be handled through normal judicial action or by transfer to the segregation center. The committee also recommended that the Tule Lake project director review the cases of Leupp inmates with regard to the advisability of transferring them to the segregation camp.[118]

By this time, even Leupp's project director believed his isolation center should be closed. In a confidential memo to Myer on October 23, after expressing serious doubts about Leupp's continued operation, Robertson pointed out that of the fifty-seven inmates who were still there, thirty-nine were slated to go to Tule Lake and two others to another WRA center. Of the remainder, he recommended transferring thirteen to Tule Lake, sending one to the FBI, and giving the last two indefinite leave from the camp.[119]

The WRA notified Robertson on November 29 that the isolation center at Leupp would be officially closed on December 2, 1943. The WRA administration transferred Leupp's fifty-two inmates to the Tule Lake Segregation Center on December 4 and suspended all inmate operations.

This transfer did not end the stringent conditions of the inmates' incarceration. The Tule Lake project director received the men and immediately placed them in an internal stockade. After another investigation of the group by the army, the FBI, and the WRA, the WRA finally released forty-two to the general camp and kept ten in the stockade.[120] The WRA did not dismantle the Leupp campsite but elected to keep it running with minimal maintenance in case it was needed again.[121]

On April 11, 1944, Myer proposed to reactivate Leupp as "a division of the Tule Lake Center in order to isolate from the segregation center those evacuees who have been trouble-makers."[122] The WRA initially planned to send 175 Nisei then held in the Tule Lake stockade as well as an unspecified number of other inmates to Leupp. The War Department and the WRA also discussed reopening the camp with military guards under the command of the Tule Lake military police.[123]

The WRA received its requested approval, and on April 26, Secretary of the Interior Harold L. Ickes announced in a press release that the WRA planned to reopen the Leupp center on or about May 15 to hold designated agitators and troublemakers from the Tule Lake Segregation Center.[124] In fact, Leupp never reopened, and the WRA found another way to remove and control Nisei whom it viewed as suspect, anti-WRA, or anti-American (discussed in the next chapter). Instead, the WRA closed Leupp and returned it to the Interior Department on September 20, 1944.[125]

CONCLUSION

The arbitrary, unpredictable, and sometimes self-serving actions of the WRA and the army, under the authority of EO 9066, have been examined here. The government freely discriminated among supposedly suspect people. The army's Individual Exclusion Program removed persons of German and Italian descent and treated them in a fashion that differed markedly from the approach taken with West Coast persons of Japanese ancestry. In the first case, individuals were selected for possible punitive treatment; in the second, an entire ethnoracial group was incarcerated.

The WRA's power to reward or punish inmates at will is strikingly illustrated by its establishment of a pro-WRA center and two isolation centers. The relative anonymity of the isolation centers belies their importance. The WRA preferred to downplay these centers and disguise their true purpose by referring to them publicly as rehabilitation centers. However, their existence calls into question the agency's pronouncements of fairness, humaneness, and concern for its inmates. The isolation centers represent the W R A's ability and willingness to inflict harsh and unwarranted punishment on those in its care. The centers became the equivalent of maximum-security prisons in which to hold American citizens. The W R A had absolute power over the inmates, which it both used and abused.

Almost all earlier writings on the World War II incarceration story have neglected the important role these camps played in the imprisonment process.[126] The isolation centers undercut the benevolent self-image the W R A projected to the wider American public. Some W R A officials later recognized the damaging impact of the isolation centers. In recommending the closing of the camp, the Leupp review committee stressed: "The Leupp Center is not to be explained as a mistake, despite the fact that it was unfortunate that such a center had to be established."[127] To this day, W R A official pronouncements have not deviated from that position.

8

Segregation Centers
and Other Camps

The War Relocation Authority (WRA) not only played a central role in incarcerating most of the Nikkei on the mainland but was responsible for
imprisoning other types of inmates in separate centers as well. This chapter continues the discussion started in the previous chapter and begins with the
government's attempt to identify and segregate "loyal" from "disloyal" Japanese
Americans. After ordering the inmates to respond to a flawed questionnaire, the
U.S. Army and the WRA selected those who had allegedly revealed themselves to
be of suspect loyalty or who were seen as definitely disloyal and transferred them
to the WRA segregation camp. In its attempt to rid itself of unwanted American
citizens, the government then established a process by which it could turn these
people into noncitizens and thereby subject them to deportation proceedings. The
government also instituted a plan to draft eligible Nisei into the armed services;
those men who protested the draft were charged and often jailed for violating Selective Service statutes. In addition, the WRA's fingers were quite nimble in reaching other groups of inmates: those in sanatoriums and penitentiaries as well as certain European refugees. The U.S. Department of State also created its own
temporary internment hotels in which to hold Axis diplomatic persons during the
first part of the war.

Although these camps held different types of inmates, the incarcerators' paramount concern was the need to control their prisoners. Regardless of WRA public
relations statements to the effect that the agency's actions arose from a benign and
fair attitude toward the inmate population, this larger purpose becomes evident.

THE LOYALTY QUESTIONNAIRE

In 1943, the WRA designated the Tule Lake Relocation Camp, in California, as a
segregation center for housing inmates of questionable loyalty to the United States
and those requesting repatriation or expatriation to Japan. Although the complete
story of this segregation center is beyond the scope of this presentation, a brief discussion is in order.[1]

The story of the WRA segregation centers begins in 1943, after the army expressed its need for volunteers and the WRA wished to determine the loyalty of

Japanese Americans. The army's desire was clear. It needed Japanese-language interpreters and translators in the Pacific to assist in gathering military intelligence from Japanese prisoners of war and their documents. As pointed out earlier, the inmates' differences of opinion on whether to volunteer for the military while in a wra camp played a role in the Manzanar "riots" of December 1942. The army also wanted volunteers for a segregated all-Nisei military unit to join the many Nisei volunteers from the territory of Hawaii. As for the wra, the agency sought to differentiate its inmates for two reasons. Farmers and industrialists were suffering from a wartime labor shortage. Large numbers of potential workers were available in the camps, and the inmates, on the whole, welcomed the opportunity to leave, even temporarily, to tend and harvest sugar beets or fruit crops. Another Nisei group found that its labor was needed in distant cities, necessitating a more permanent departure from the camps. In places such as Chicago, Cleveland, and other midwestern and East Coast cities, certain Nisei worked from 1943 onward as, for example, domestics, secretaries, and lathe operators. Still other Nisei were accepted into colleges and universities outside the military exclusion areas. The wra and the army developed a release process for these inmates, so that the agencies could assure themselves and the public that those who were leaving the camps were not saboteurs or espionage agents likely to harm the U.S. war effort.

Between February and March 1943, the army and the wra produced their own questionnaires for all wra inmates seventeen years of age and older. The army's version, DSS Form 304A, was for Nisei males. It bore a Selective Service seal at the top and was titled "Statement of United States Citizens of Japanese Ancestry." The wra's questionnaire, Form wra-126, was titled "War Relocation Authority Application for Leave Clearance" and was to be completed by Nisei females and Issei of both sexes.

The two questionnaires were very similar in content; most questions were innocuous, such as requests for name, prior addresses, education, and occupations. However, two questions on both forms, Numbers 27 and 28, became the center of a storm of controversy. Question 27 on the wra form asked: "If the opportunity presents itself and you are found qualified, would you be willing to volunteer for the Army Nurse Corps or the WAAC [Women's Army Auxiliary Corps]?" The army's Question 27 was "Are you willing to serve in the armed forces of the United States on combat duty, wherever ordered?" The wra's Question 28 asked: "Will you swear unqualified allegiance to the United States of America and forswear any form of allegiance or obedience to the Japanese emperor, or any other foreign government, power or organization?" The army's corresponding Question 28 asked: "Will you swear unqualified allegiance to the United States of America and faithfully defend the United States from any or all attack by foreign or domestic forces, and forswear any form of allegiance or obedience to the Japanese emperor, or any other foreign government, power or organization?" With these four questions, the army and the wra created an extraordinarily difficult situation for the inmates.

The WRA thought its questions would be easily answered in the affirmative by loyal Americans. For a variety of reasons, however, affirmative responses were difficult to make. To ask Issei males in Question 27 to volunteer for a women's military unit was absurd, and to ask Issei women to do so was to propose that elderly women separate themselves voluntarily from their husbands and families. Partly because of the ensuing uproar, project directors in some camps did not require the Issei to answer this question.[2] As for the army's Question 27, Nisei males found it difficult to volunteer for military service, since the Selective Service System had in early January 1942 categorized them as 4-C (unqualified for service due to their ancestry) and disallowed their entry into the military. Not a few Nisei men took umbrage at this question. As one Nisei reportedly said, "They rob us of our property, throw us into concentration camps, knock us down and spit on us and then invite us to 'prove' our loyalty by volunteering to go into an all-Nisei suicidal combat team to be thrown into front-line fighting."

The three-part construction of the army's Question 28 complicated an affirmative reply. Nisei males might easily give yes responses to the first and second parts (to swear allegiance to and defend the United States), but indicating yes for the third (to forswear allegiance to Japan) might imply that they had been or still were loyal to a foreign government. Conversely, a negative response would be seen as withholding one's loyalty from the United States and, in addition, might then be construed as allegiance to Japan. For Issei men and women, the WRA's Question 28 represented two questions in one. Answering positively to the second part, forswearing allegiance to their homeland, meant renouncing their country of birth and declaring themselves to be stateless persons, since Japanese immigrants had been ineligible for U.S. naturalization since 1922. The question was later revised for the Issei to read: "Will you swear to abide by the laws of the United States and take no action which would in any way interfere with the war effort of the United States?" This new wording helped Issei to answer affirmatively to Question 28, but the damage had been done.

Many feared that if family members gave different answers, they might be placed in different camps. Discussions about the intent and meaning of these questions and how to answer them were often vehement and acrimonious within families and among friends. Various camp factions tried to influence inmates to answer in certain ways. In addition, the WRA displayed a heavy hand in the process. The WRA administration instructed the project directors at the centers to threaten the inmates with violating the Espionage Act if they prompted others or advised some not to answer the questions: "Dissenters and parents were ordered to promptly desist from 'sabotaging' the drive by advising sons, daughters, and colleagues not to register [or] risk facing a future of twenty years in prison, a $10,000 fine, or both."[3] The WRA told Nisei males that if they did not register, they would be in violation of the Selective Service Act and subject to penalties of up to twenty years in prison.

Moreover, if w r a officials believed that anyone was trying to influence others to resist the registration program, the result could be immediate expulsion to the isolation camp at Moab, Utah, for Nisei or a Justice Department internment camp for Issei. For example, at the w r a's Gila River project in Arizona, "Permission was secured from the Director to remove from the Center a number of citizens, largely Kibei, who had shown most active resistance and hostility to the registration program. On February 26, 1943, agents of f b i and Internal Security with some cooperation from MP units removed 28 persons, half to Moab, half to f b i camps."[4] Between February and April 1943, the w r a sent thirty-eight Nisei or Kibei to the isolation center.

The War Department informed the w r a on February 26 that it was not necessary for draft-age Nisei to register or respond to the so-called loyalty questionnaire.[5] The w r a, however, did not inform Nisei males of this development nor did it remove the threat of penalties. For whatever reason, the w r a continued to make registration mandatory.

Physical tactics were implemented with those who refused to register. A San Francisco newspaper reported an incident in 1943:

> The Army moved in, followed by the f b i. There were mass arrests, and one hundred men were thrown into nearby jails and deserted C.C.C. Camps. When the prisoners were carried off they were surrounded by howling Japanese who yelled, 'Banzai!' . . . "You can't imagine how close we came to machine-gunning the whole bunch of them," one official said. "The only thing that stopped us, I guess, were the effects such a shooting would have had on the Japs holding our boys in Manila and China."[6]

Of the 77,957 inmates eligible for registration—those seventeen years or older—almost 75,000 completed the questionnaires. Although Questions 27 and 28 dealt with separate matters, they were referred to collectively as the Loyalty Questions, and the forms themselves became known as the Loyalty Questionnaires. As for Question 28, the one dealing with allegiance, by September 1943, 68,018, or some 87 percent, of the respondents had answered in the affirmative. Of the 9,939 who had not, approximately 5,300 had answered no, while the rest had not registered, failed to answer this question, or qualified their answers. There were 40,306 persons within the eligible Nisei population (21,047 males seventeen years and older and 19,259 females). Of that number, 1,490 did not respond to the questionnaire, 6,333 responded negatively to Question 28, 585 offered qualified responses, 354 did not respond at all, and 146 gave unknown responses.[7] Answers such as "Yes, if the government restores my rights as a citizen" or "No, not unless the government recognizes my right to live anywhere in the United States" were considered qualified statements and were scored as a negative response.[8] Response rates differed at each w r a camp; for example, at the Tule Lake camp, about 42 percent of all eligible persons did not register or answered no to the loyalty questions.[9]

At the Minidoka, Idaho, and Granada, Colorado, camps, the number was 3 percent or less.

Answering no to the loyalty questions might represent a group decision or a personal protest. As an example of the former category, some Issei believed the false rumors that negative responses would result in their removal to another center but that they would not be deported because the government was going to maintain the center as a permanent community even after the war ended.[10] This group believed that the new center would be closer to their prewar homes and there would be less chance of having to resettle in the East or Midwest after the war. And as mentioned earlier, if even one family member decided to answer in the negative, others in the family believed that giving the same response was the only way to keep the family together. Personal reasons might also lie behind an individual's no response. There was the "'No' of protest against discrimination, the 'No' of protest against a father interned apart from his family, the 'No' of bitter antagonism to subordination in the relocation center, the 'No' of a gang sticking together, the 'No' of thoughtless defiance, the 'No' of family duty, the 'No' of hopeless confusion, the 'No' of fear of military service, and the 'No' of felt loyalty of Japan."[11] A particular response could therefore represent a complex set of issues, to a greater degree than the WRA or the military thought worthwhile to consider. In the heat of the registration process, the attitude of the WRA and the army was single-mindedly purposeful. They saw a black-and-white situation, "loyal" or "disloyal," and ignored any shadings of gray.

The registration process can thus be seen as an application of brute power against the inmates and a concomitant insensitivity on the part of officials. As Allen Bosworth points out: "In retrospect, the entire registration program appears to have been a sophomoric and half-baked idea, if not indeed, a stupid and costly blunder. In the long run, nothing could have been more certain or more simple than this: If there had been any actual Japanese agents or spies in the Relocation Centers, in February 1943, they would have been the very first to profess their loyalty on paper, so that they could carry on their work."[12]

For the thousands of Nisei who answered in the negative or with qualified positive responses, the government had concrete "evidence" of disloyalty. Whereas government officials may initially have entertained suspicions about the loyalty of Japanese Americans, some felt they now had proof that elements of this population were dangerous to the United States. Once a group of inmates was branded as disloyal, the government's actions were swift and dire.

TULE LAKE SEGREGATION CENTER

After the Loyalty Questionnaire proceedings were completed, on July 6, 1943, the U.S. Senate passed a resolution urging the WRA to separate persons on the basis of their loyalty to the United States. On July 15, the WRA designated the Tule Lake Relocation Camp as the site at which to house those persons whose "loyalties lie with

Japan during the present hostilities."[13] Inmates to be transferred to Tule Lake included those who requested repatriation or expatriation to Japan, answered Question 28 in the negative, refused or failed to answer it, or were denied leave clearance from WRA centers. The WRA made provisions allowing family members to accompany those required to move to Tule Lake if they so requested.

The WRA redesignated Tule Lake as a segregation center, and between September 18, 1943, and May 1944, the agency brought in 12,173 persons and dispersed 6,500 others to eight of the nine remaining relocation camps. Tule Lake's capacity was 15,000, but 6,249 original inmates elected to stay rather than be uprooted again, and the camp's population quickly swelled to more than 18,400.

By May 1946, the Tule Lake camp held a heterogeneous population. Those in the "disloyal" or "suspect" category numbered 12,655, while family members of the segregants and others eligible to leave but who chose to remain in Tule Lake numbered 5,767, or 31 percent of the total 18, 422 inmates. Included in the segregant category were those who replied in the affirmative to the loyalty questions, but because they requested repatriation or expatriation to Japan they were placed in the "suspect" group.[14] The stigma of disloyalty continues today for anyone who was at the Tule Lake Segregation Center.

The actions of the army and the WRA reinforced the idea that everyone at the Tule Lake camp was dangerous. The WRA constructed an eight-foot-high double fence, built a new gate to separate the inmates from the administration, increased the number of guards from a few hundred to 930, fingerprinted all arrivals, and parked six army tanks near the fence to intimidate the inmates.[15] The new segregation camp director, Raymond R. Best, had just come from running the Leupp Isolation Center in Arizona. The WRA saw Best as an administrator who was capable of handling difficult situations and taking an uncompromising stance toward inmates.

Crisis and Conflict

After all the inmates had been transferred to Tule Lake, a series of events both minor and major caused a breakdown in confidence between the prisoners and the segregation camp administrators. On October 7, 1943, officials terminated the employment of forty-three inmate coal workers. The other inmates saw this as an unacceptable way to resolve a labor dispute. The administration could find no one willing to replace the fired workers and was forced to reinstate them. In the same month, officials closed the camp office that handled inmate requests to leave Tule Lake for jobs, post–high school education, or other reasons. This action gave rise to the rumor that the closure was part of a WRA plan to detain everyone at Tule Lake before deporting them to Japan.[16]

These two events did not affect the entire camp. But when a major conflict arose, the Tule Lake administration handled it brutally. On October 15, a farm truck overturned, killing one Nisei and injuring five others. The inmates initially protested the lack of W R A safety precautions and used the occasion to voice other dissatisfactions about conditions at the camp. Camp director Best also became an object of animus when it was learned that he had apparently denied permission for a public funeral for the deceased Nisei and balked at sending a condolence note to the widow. In order to discourage open expressions of grief, he ordered that the public address system be made inoperable. Nevertheless, thousands of inmates gathered on October 23 to honor the deceased. They grew angrier when they learned that the W R A's total compensation to the widow and her child was to be two-thirds of the farmworker's $16 monthly salary—$10.66.

Some inmates organized an agricultural work stoppage to bolster their demands for better food, increased safety precautions, and procedures for airing their grievances. Instead of acting to calm the situation, Best fired participants in the stop-work movement after they introduced additional demands on October 28. And he announced that he was importing 150 farmworkers from other W R A camps to replace them. Best promised to pay the prospective workers $1 per hour, a significant increase over the monthly wages of the camp's current workers, and assured candidates that there would not be any labor troubles at Tule Lake. When the Tule Lake farmworkers learned about the difference in wages and that food for the new workers would come from their own kitchen, they grew even more incensed.[17]

On November 4, the situation deteriorated further. The segregation camp internal police found some Nisei in the motor pool area that evening—an area open to all during the day but restricted at night—and an altercation ensued. When Best heard about the fracas, rather than investigating it himself, he called in the army's military police.[18]

The next set of events has been called the "Tule Lake riot." According to the W R A's account, 150 inmates came into the administration area to thwart what they thought was the removal of their food for the volunteer farmworkers. Several internal security police resisted the group's advance, and in the subsequent struggle, one security person "tripped, struck his head on a stone, and was then struck by evacuees. No other persons were injured."[19] This led to the use of coercive power by the military police. The army arrested several hundred inmates for being "troublemakers" or for leading or participating in the protest movement. That night, "eighteen evacuees in the center were escorted forcibly by members of the internal security police to the police squad room where they were severely beaten with clubs. A number of them were beaten into insensibility and all were hospitalized."[20]

One inmate's eyewitness account reports that the segregation camp director called the military police

into the inner camp to suppress a riot which never occurred and was never even threatened. The armed troops drove every resident indoors at the point of bayonets and then forcibly and violently searched every internee, man, woman and child, and every apartment, house and barrack. This generalized search continued daily and nightly until about November 12, 1943. Thereafter, periodically until about March 1, 1944, when the troops were removed altogether from the Center, indiscriminate forcible searches were conducted by the troops of hundreds of internees and their quarters. Hundreds of internees were arrested by the troops and were detained in isolation quarters for days and months without any charges being brought against them and without any hearings being given them on the reasons for their detention. These violent searches and seizures kept the whole camp in a constant state of worry, despair, wild fear and terror of troop violence.[21]

The WRA and the army assumed a menacing position so that they could maintain their power over the inmates. As one WRA official put it, "The plan is to run it [the segregation center] like an Internment Camp—WRA version. The Japs will just eat and sleep—no work. All administration and function would be operated by Caucasian workers which means much recruiting for new employees."[22] The army imposed an inmate curfew from 7:00 P.M. to 6:00 A.M. and forbade any gathering that might resemble a crowd. Any group of inmates that looked like a crowd to the army was subject to being dispersed with tear gas. The directive closed all schools, halted recreational activities, and kept prisoners' work to a minimum.[23]

Arrested "troublemakers" were kept in a newly established enclosed area inside the Tule Lake camp; officials called it Area B or the Surveillance Area. The inmates dubbed it the Stockade. At first, it was a collection of tents enclosed by a barbed-wire fence. Later, it was enlarged to hold six barracks guarded by military policemen stationed in four observation towers. Meanwhile, camp inmates underwent a "forcible 12-day search [resulting] in the lawless seizure of scores of innocent internees who were thrown by the troops into the stockade . . . where many were forced to languish for months without charges being filed against them and without hearings being accorded them."[24] The military curtailed any communication with those in the Stockade by censoring and intercepting mail. They denied the Stockade prisoners medical attention and visitors. Initially, family and friends could at least see and wave to prisoners inside the stockade, but the army quickly erected a twelve-foot-high beaverboard wall to prevent even this slight interaction.

Thousands of forced searches of people and property by internal security police took place throughout the waning months of 1943 and into 1944. The authorities eventually kept more than 450 prisoners in the Stockade without proffering charges against them or giving them hearings. Some were held there for eleven months.[25]

Tule Lake inmates endured a life of terror. As an eyewitness stated, everyone "lived in momentary fear of being seized, jailed and held incommunicado. Life in the Center became one of bewilderment and stark fear. All of us were in the most abnormal state of mind imaginable. Several persons were driven insane."[26] The Justice Department started to investigate those incarcerated in the Stockade, first scrutinizing the arrested Issei. Subsequently, the w r a and the Justice Department removed a number of Issei to Justice Department internment camps. The interagency cooperation was apparent to those at Tule Lake.

Worsening Conditions, Resistance, and Violence

As the inmates were unable to challenge the intimidation techniques, many started a resistance movement based on noncooperation. Some began a hunger strike in January 1944, and the administration quickly retaliated. As Michi Weglyn reports in her book *Years of Infamy,* "The price of non-cooperation began to take its toll on the embattled community. Along with the futility of jobless and hopeless days, young and old suffered acutely from the constant disruption in services: from the sudden cutoffs in the milk supply, shortages in food, hot water, fuel, warm clothes" (p. 167). While inmates continued to suffer, the situation became even worse.

On January 14, 1944, the Selective Service System's local boards, commonly known as draft boards, announced that Japanese Americans were now eligible for the military draft. Not a few Nisei men in the segregation center who had suffered the consequences for answering "no-no" to the Loyalty Questionnaire now feared that they would be taken by the military. Some Nisei who wanted to avoid service thought their earlier efforts to resist might have been for naught.

On May 16, 1944, army sentry Bernard W. Goe fired his rifle and killed a Nisei, Soichi James Okamoto. As one inmate stated, "The shooting of this boy filled the whole camp of internees with an unspeakable horror and a deep fear because of the want of protection accorded the internees against outbursts of violence against them. Panic reigned in the camp."[27]

During this time of uncertainty for all inmates, on July 2, 1944, someone attacked Yaozu Hitomi, manager of the Tule Lake canteen, and slashed his throat. Hitomi was known as a friend of the administration and had openly criticized a dissident anti-administration group. His death had a chilling effect on anyone who wished to oppose the dissidents. The murders of Okamoto and Hitomi increased the nonaligned inmates' fear of physical violence that could come from two directions, the w r a and certain fellow inmates. Neither the army nor camp officials did or could curtail coercive behavior within the camp, and their inaction assured the dissident faction that it could do whatever it wished inside the camp.

Renunciation of Citizenship

Another major government action soon exacerbated the terror felt among all w r a inmates but especially those at the Tule Lake Segregation Center in California. On July 1, 1944, President Franklin D. Roosevelt signed Public Law 405, "Renunciation in Time of War," as an amendment to the Nationality Act of 1940 (58 Stat. 677). The earlier Nationality Act (54 Stat. 1169; 8 U.S.C. 801) detailed eight ways in which a citizen could renounce or lose his or her U.S. citizenship. This amendment, Public Law 405, made it possible to do the same while residing within the United States.[28]

There is a similarity between one provision of this act and Question 28 of the Loyalty Questionnaire. Section (b) of the act states that a person who is a U.S. national, by birth or naturalization, shall lose his or her nationality by "taking an oath or making an affirmation or other formal declaration of allegiance to a foreign state." Question 28 addressed this issue in a roundabout way by asking whether one would "forswear . . . allegiance . . . to any foreign government." Public Law 405 asked for direct action and allowed an American citizen to give up his or her citizenship by making a formal written renunciation. Persons taking such actions became known as "renunciants."

Anyone signing the renunciation form could then be treated in accordance with his or her new status. The United States could treat these former American citizens as if they were enemy aliens and institute deportation proceedings. As Ernest Besig, then executive director of the San Francisco American Civil Liberties Union (ACLU) stated, "Indeed, in my conversation with each of these W.R.A. officials [Tule Lake Segregation Camp director Raymond Best and four others], each of them stated quite frankly that they had gotten rid of some alien Japanese by sending them to the Santa Fe, New Mexico, internment camp, and that they expected to solve their [Tule Lake] Stockade problem by getting the imprisoned men to renounce their citizenship and then send them on to Santa Fe for internment."[29] Given the earlier conflicts at Tule Lake and Best's handling of them, it is not difficult to imagine the type of action he might take to convince the Nisei in the Stockade to sign the form.

Some sources state that renunciation signatures were occasionally obtained through intimidation. A Tule Lake inmate describes the tactics used by the FBI to force one Nisei to sign the renunciation form as "Gestapo-style." Kinzo Wakayama, a Hawaii-born Kibei, World War I veteran, and dissident leader, "was rudely awakened about 3 or 4 in the morning. The FBI came to his quarter[s] with a pistol brandishing, and the officer that accompanied the FBI compelled him to renounce."[30] Wakayama signed the renunciation "under protest"; he was then taken to the Justice Department camp at Santa Fe, New Mexico, and then to Crystal City, Texas.

When asked in 1985 about the renunciation issue, Edward Ennis, past director of the Alien Enemy Control Unit, acknowledged that Public Law 405 was used to remove citizens from WRA camps. Agreeing with Besig some forty years later, he said: "The reason for the renunciation program was to alleviate the problem of militant, active dissident persons in places such as Tule Lake. As citizens they could not be readily sent to alien camps."[31] Moreover, although Ennis does not explicitly so state, the desired end was not simply to solve the problem of maintaining a segregation camp stockade but to deport troublesome individuals.

Three dissident factions arose out of the discord of November 1943 at Tule

Lake. These alliances became highly visible, and the WRA even assisted the groups by sanctioning them. The Issei group, formed out of the earlier Resegregation Committee, changed its name to Sokuji Kikoku Hoshi-dan (Organization to Return Immediately to the Homeland) on October 27, 1944, and declared its allegiance to Japan.[32] The Sokoku Kenkyu Seinen-dan (Young Men's Association for the Study of the Mother Country) was for Nisei men; early meetings began in May 1944, and regular activities commenced on August 9 of that year. The Sokoku Kenkyu Joshi Seinen-dan (Young Women's Association for the Study of the Mother Country) enrolled Nisei women. After the WRA announced the citizenship-renunciation program, the Nisei groups changed their names to Hokoku Seinen-dan (Young Men's Association to Serve the Nation) and Hokoku Joshi Seinen-dan, for the women's group. They displayed a militaristic stance by practicing close-order drills and engaging in early morning calisthenics; the men shaved their heads in a style modeled after the Japanese military.

Very few Nisei initially renounced their citizenship—only 107 such applications trickled in between July and mid-December 1944 from all the WRA camps.[33] Then, on December 17, 1944, the WRA administration announced that the army planned to revoke the 1942 exclusion order. This announcement raised questions that the WRA could not answer. The most troublesome one was "Where would we go?" Others asked whether those who had answered the loyalty questions differently from their parents or children would be separated from them. At the Tule Lake camp, the Hokoku Seinen-dan allegedly preyed on other inmates. The group told neutral Nisei that the WRA's intention was to separate family members from one another and that they could only remain with their parents by renouncing their citizenship and receiving equal treatment.[34]

A rebuttal to the assertion that the organization forced inmates to renounce their citizenship comes from Teruko Kumei's interview of eighteen former Hokoku members now living in Japan. Masaru Hashimoto, then secretary of the central committee, denied the allegation: "It's not true. It's a fabrication after the war. It's a fabrication to restore citizenship. But I tell you, we never threatened anyone. I can assure you of that. The Hokoku Seinen-dan never ever threatened anyone to join, or threatened to punish them if they didn't. We were sincere in our desire to become good Japanese. That is what we wanted. That's all."[35] Opinions on whether forceful techniques were used to convince the Nisei to renounce their citizenship probably depend on one's definition of the word *coercion*. What is indisputable, however, is that not a few inmates have reported that the dissident groups made widespread use of implied force and fear-raising tactics.

The Justice Department tried to alleviate some of the inmates' anxieties by announcing that they could stay together in the segregation camp until January 1, 1946.[36] But whatever the effect of this announcement, it was eclipsed by another set of events. The Justice Department apparently decided secretly to punish the members of the Hokoku Seinen-dan. At 5:00 A.M. on December 27, 1944, it picked up sixty-four Hokoku leaders and members plus six others—mainly the Issei Kikoku Hoshi-dan leaders—and prepared them for shipment to the Santa Fe Internment Center. Before they could be moved, however, other Tule Lake inmates heard about the early morning raid, and many gathered to give the seventy inmates a boisterous farewell. The Justice Department had inadvertently created resistance heroes.

From that time until mid-1945, the authorities conducted a series of raids within the Tule Lake camp to capture more dissident leaders and transport them to Justice Department camps. Beginning with that first group and continuing until March 1945, a total of 1,416 men—1,098 Nisei renunciants and 318 Issei—were eventually removed. The majority were sent to the Santa Fe Internment Camp, while the W R A took a few hundred to the camp at Fort Lincoln, North Dakota.

Many Tule Lake Nisei thought that the W R A and the Justice Department could get away with treating them so callously because their nation cared little about them. The remaining dissident leaders were then able to recruit new group members by pointing to the overt hostility and acts of violence committed by the W R A and the Justice Department. The number of renunciants began to increase. By April 1945, 5,589 Nisei and Kibei had signed away their birthrights, and 2,360 of them were sent to Justice Department camps.[37] Within this latter group, 2,031 Nisei or Kibei were deported to Japan, and the remainder waited for years before their deportation orders were canceled. Almost all the renunciants originated from the Tule Lake Segregation Camp; only 128 came from other W R A centers. During this period, 313 Issei were also shipped from Tule Lake to the Justice Department camp at Santa Fe.

The W R A finally prohibited the cultural activities, marching, and calisthenics of the Hokoku Seinen-dan and the Kikoku Hoshi-dan on March 16, 1945. The very next day, the Justice Department completed its renunciation hearings and left the segregation camp. At that point, the Hokoku Seinen-dan members began to squabble about whether or not to abide by the W R A edicts restricting their activities, and the strife adversely affected renunciation fever. Their membership as well as their influence on other inmates quickly and dramatically decreased.

With the diminished tension at the segregation camp, many Nisei asked to retract their renunciation petitions. The Justice Department and the W R A were not favorably disposed to these requests, and the Nisei had to take their cases to the legal arena. Wayne Collins, who earlier had assisted the Peruvian internees, became the lead attorney of record for all Nisei and Kibei, as far as is known, fighting to restore their U.S. citizenship. With the assistance of fellow attorney Theodore Tamba, Collins worked for years to obtain individual depositions for a rehearing of each case. He argued that the atmosphere of fear, anxiety, and duress within the segregation camp at the time the renunciation forms were signed created a highly unusual and volatile situation. It mattered little, he asserted, that each renunciant had been given a hearing by the Justice Department. The threats and outright incidents of physical harm and the uncertainty of day-to-day events were such that the individual was unable to act in a voluntary manner. The inmates' renunciation statements were obtained, Collins argued, under duress and should be made null and void. He initially requested a single combined case for all his clients. The government objected, and Collins set about pursuing each case on an individual basis.

It took more than a decade of legal struggle before almost all the Nisei won their cases. Of those who remained in the United States, all but eighty-four eventually regained their citizenship by 1959. To this day, a U.S. national may still renounce his or her citizenship on U.S. soil in time of war, but the ability to do so includes an important provision. Any person making a formal written renunciation of nationality "shall be presumed to have done so voluntarily, but such presumption may be rebutted upon a showing by a preponderance of evidence that the act or acts committed or performed were not done voluntarily."[38] This latter clause was perhaps included as a result of the Herculean task undertaken by Collins and Tamba in assisting those thousands of Nisei and Kibei who had been placed under tremendous personal pressure during the dark days of the segregation camp experience.

MILITARY SERVICE AND DRAFT PROTESTERS

In 1944, adult Nisei males faced another difficult situation. Earlier, on June 17, 1942, the War Department had ruled that persons of Japanese ancestry were unacceptable for military service except for unusual cases such as interpreters or Japanese-language instructors. The Selective Service System made this a formal regulation on September 14, 1942, and classified eligible Nisei as 4-C, or "unsuitable for service because of nationality or ancestry."[39]

The army changed its attitude in 1943 and accepted Japanese American volunteers to serve in a segregated unit. The army formed the 100th Infantry Battalion with Nisei from Hawaii in June 1942, brought the soldiers to the mainland for training, and sent them to the European theater of war. Meanwhile, by incorporating the 522nd Field Artillery Battalion and the 232nd Combat Engineers, and utilizing mainland Nisei, the army created the famed 442nd Regimental Combat Team (RCT) in February 1943. In June 1944, the 442nd joined the 100th, which had already left for Europe.

Another unit of more than 6,000 Nisei and Kibei worked in the intelligence and linguistics areas and served in the Pacific theater. Although the forerunner of this latter group, the Military Intelligence Service Language School, started in November 1941 at the Presidio in San Francisco, it was not until May 1942 that the War Department recognized its value and assumed control of its operations. From the very early years of the war, the language instructors and students were mainly Nisei or Kibei volunteer servicemen. On July 28, 1943, the War Department set a quota of 500 Nisei women, which allowed them to serve in the military, often as army nurses or with the Auxiliary Service Corps. Some 139 women applied, and 116 were accepted for service.[40] Altogether, more than 33,000 Japanese Americans served in the military during World War II.

On June 21, 2000, President William Jefferson Clinton awarded twenty Medals of Honor, the nation's highest military award for valor, to Japanese Americans for their actions as members of the 100th Infantry Battalion and 442nd RCT. Decades earlier, this unit had earned, among other honors, 9,846 Purple Hearts, fifty-three Distinguished Service Crosses (DSC), and one Medal of Honor. Many recommendations that deserved Medals of Honor were instead awarded the DSC. Racial considerations were seen to play an instrumental role in the War Department's assessment of the appropriate level of award, and the actions of those who received the DSC were reexamined some fifty later.[41] This account of these valiant soldiers is deliberately brief, since much of their story is well known to many.

Especially important here, however, is another portion of this military story. As stated earlier, on January 14, 1944, the Selective Service System's local boards officially changed their policy and announced a draft call for Nisei males from W R A centers. With the stroke of a pen, the accident of ancestry was no longer an impediment for Nisei who wished to serve their country. Relief from their former status was only partial, however, since the draft call was aimed at providing replacements for a segregated unit and supplying more trained Japanese linguists.

From January 20 to August 26, 1944, draft notices were sent to 2,213 Nisei; 267 initially refused to report for their physical examinations, and 91 others refused to be inducted.[42] Although coordinated draft resistance occurred at two W R A incarceration centers—Heart Mountain, Wyoming, and Tule Lake, California—significant individual and smaller group efforts also took place at Topaz, Utah; Poston, Arizona; and Granada, Colorado.

At the W R A camp at Heart Mountain, one Nisei group called itself the Fair Play Committee and questioned the legality of drafting someone from within a barbed-wire enclosure. In February 1944, the group asked the A C L U to help with its legal challenge to the draft. Roger Baldwin, speaking for the A C L U, responded by saying that these resisters had a strong moral case but not a legal one, and that "men who counsel others to resist military service are not within their rights and must expect severe treatment."[43] Initially, seven Nisei from Heart Mountain were indicted and convicted in November 1944 for conspiracy against the draft. They served a year in prison and were released after an appeal found that the judge had given improper instructions to the jury.[44] Meanwhile, sixty-three other drafted Nisei from Heart Mountain refused their induction notices; the judge found them guilty and sentenced each to serve three years in prison.

At the W R A's Tule Lake Segregation Center, a group of twenty-seven Nisei refused the draft. The U.S. district court judge hearing their case, Louis Goodman, dismissed the indictments in July 1944, stating that "It is shocking to the conscience that an American citizen be confined on the grounds of disloyalty and then, while so under duress and restraint, be compelled to serve in the armed forces or be prosecuted for not yielding to such compulsion."[45] After the war, on December 12, 1947, President Harry Truman granted full pardons to the 267 Japanese Americans convicted of violating the Selective Service Act and restored the full rights and privileges of citizenship.[46]

Through the ensuing decades, many of the reluctant draftees endured disfavor within the Japanese American community. One Sansei, who wished to remain anonymous, noticed that at the traditional New Year's gathering at her house in Seattle, the same group of Nisei men inevitably came to partake of the ceremonial meal. Although they had come for as long as she could remember, she was never introduced to them. When she was twenty-two, she finally asked her mother about her father's friends. "Well," said her mother, "your dad and those men were in prison together during the war." The mother then told her of her father's draft resistance at Heart Mountain and his subsequent sentence. When the daughter asked why her mother had never before mentioned her father's wartime history, the mother replied, "You were too young before, and we didn't want to burden you with what went on in camp."[47]

From 1988, various individuals and a few regional chapters of the Japanese American Citizens League (JACL) tried to reopen the subject of resistance for public discussion. After some debate, in 1990, the JACL commissioned a report on the draft resisters and its own actions during the war. The results of this investigation by Deborah Lim were highly critical of the JACL leadership at the time: "That the JACL urged charges of sedition against the sixty-three men at Heart Mountain who resisted being drafted from inside a concentration camp until their constitutional rights were first restored and their parents released from camp . . . the JACL, through newspaper editorials, attacked not only the actions but the character of the Heart Mountain resisters. One editorial alone brands the resisters as 'slow witted,' 'warped minded,' 'wild eyed,' 'whimpering weaklings.'"[48] The complete Lim Report, as it is called, was never made public by the JACL, and these particular Nisei continue to feel the stigma of their wartime resistance. A few JACL regional chapters now acknowledge that the actions of many of these draft resisters were based on moral and constitutional principles and not on opportunism as charged by the wartime JACL leadership.

CLOSING THE WRA CAMPS

On December 17, 1944, the WRA officially changed its policy from one of mass incarceration to one based on "a system of individual determination and exclusion of those individuals whose presence within sensitive areas of the WDC is deemed a source of potential danger to military security."[49] This change, which came nearly three years after the signing of Executive Order 9066, arose in response to early information of the upcoming Supreme Court decisions on two relevant incarceration cases. On December 18, 1944, the U.S. Supreme Court ruled by a narrow margin that the "evacuation" of Fred Korematsu from the West Coast was constitutional where a situation of military necessity prevailed. In its ruling on Mitsui Endo, however, which was handed down on the same date as the Korematsu decision, the court ruled that an admittedly loyal American could not be held in detention or released conditionally. The WRA, along with the WDC, then started to review the cases of 122,000 Issei and Nisei and quickly cleared 108,545 of them. The remainder, or those whose freedom of movement continued to be restricted, were the Issei and others still in Justice Department camps, internees paroled to the WRA, those denied leave clearance such as WRA segregants and renunciants, plus 1,334 persons who were in a "suspense" category. The latter group was composed of persons "who qualified their answers to the loyalty questions, or had been officers in the suspected Japanese organizations, or had been denied permission by the WRA to leave the center."[50]

The WDC took control of the clearance process within the camps, resurrected the Individual Exclusion Program used earlier with persons of German and Italian ancestry, set up hearings, reviewed files, and assigned a classification to each individual. It issued 5,426 individual exclusion orders against Japanese residents or their citizen children and prohibited them from leaving the WRA centers. The criteria for assigning the classification, according to Edward Barnhart, was arbitrary, not based on facts: "The individual exclusion program for the Japanese Americans appears to have been an ineffective measure based on indefensible and arbitrary placement into groups, which continued for nine months to deprive a large number of American citizens of many of their rights and liberties."[51] In effect, the incarceration program remained in place until September 4, 1945, when imperial Japan surrendered.

OTHER INSTITUTIONS

In addition to the camps discussed previously, the WRA oversaw inmates in hospitals, mental institutions, tuberculosis sanatoriums, penitentiaries, reformatories, and a "recreation area." The two states with the largest inmate populations were California and Washington. On October 19, 1942, the WRA was given custodial powers and financial responsibility for patients and inmates of Japanese ancestry who were physically unable to enter WRA camps. By March 20, 1946, this category represented 1,122 persons in 125 different institutions in sixteen states.[52] In California, for example, the WRA held 123 persons suffering from tuberculosis at Hillcrest Sanitarium in La Crescenta. An armed sheriff was on hand to maintain security if needed; his job was to stand at the gate, allow no one to enter the hospital without a pass, and maintain control over patients, even though they were too ill to move.[53]

Table 8.1 lists the number of Nikkei inmates at other sites and includes a category for penal institutions. Persons of Japanese descent numbered 152 in

TABLE 8.1a

Persons of Japanese Descent and Number of Institutions
under WRA Jurisdiction, March 20, 1946

States	Total Persons	Mental		Tuberculosis	
		Persons	Institutions	Persons	Institutions
Arizona	45	9	1	2	2
Arkansas	11	4	1	4	2
California	781	393	12	244	30
Colorado	9	4	1	–	–
Georgia	1	–	–	–	–
Idaho	11	7	1	–	–
Kansas	30	–	–	–	–
Minnesota	1	–	–	–	–
Nebraska	2	–	–	–	–
Oregon	27	20	4	7	2
Pennsylvania	1	–	–	1	1
Texas	11	–	–	–	–
Utah	17	9	2	–	–
Washington	142	29	3	27	3
West Virginia	3	–	–	–	–
Wyoming	30	4	1	–	–
TOTAL	1,122	479	26	285	40

NOTE: Compiled from WRA, 1946b, pp. 187–89. California had one institution housing mental, TB, and other medical patients, another institution housing both mental and other medical patients, and seven institutions housing both TB and other medical patients. The total number of separate institutions was 125.

penitentiaries and 12 in reformatories. Counted in this number were Nisei who refused the 1944 Selective Service draft order.[54] McNeil Island Federal Penitentiary, in Washington, held the largest group, seventy-seven inmates; Leavenworth Federal Penitentiary in Kansas held thirty others; and the Catalina Federal Honor Camp in Arizona held forty-five convicted Nisei draft resisters plus Gordon Hirabayashi, who served his sentence for violation of the WDC curfew regulations.[55]

One location for which there is only minimal information available was a recreation satellite for youth groups from the WRA camp at Topaz, Utah. Located at Antelope Springs, ninety miles west of Topaz at the foot of Swasey Peak, the unused CCC campsite (DG-29) housed the children in about twenty buildings. It served as a respite center, where the children could camp, swim, and hike in the

TABLE 8.1b

Persons of Japanese Descent and Number of Institutions
under WRA Jurisdiction, March 20, 1946

| States | Other Medical | | Penal | | | |
| | Persons | Insti-tutions | Penitentiary | | Reformatory | |
			Persons	Insti-tutions	Persons	Insti-tutions
Arizona	–	–	34	3	–	–
Arkansas	–	–	3	1	–	–
California	120	32	23	5	1	1
Colorado	–	–	4	1	1	1
Georgia	–	–	1	1	–	–
Idaho	2	2	2	1	–	–
Kansas	–	–	30	1	–	–
Minnesota	1	1	–	–	–	–
Nebraska	2	1	–	–	–	–
Oregon	–	–	–	–	–	–
Pennsylvania	–	–	–	–	–	–
Texas	–	–	–	–	11	2
Utah	5	5	3	2	–	–
Washington	4	2	78	2	4	1
West Virginia	–	–	3	1	–	–
Wyoming	–	–	26	3	–	–
TOTAL	134	43	207	21	17	5

mountains. When this satellite opened, how it was operated and when it closed are open for further research.[56]

FORT ONTARIO CAMP

In 1944, the WRA was given the responsibility to hold a group that was not in its original charter: 982 Europeans, 89 percent of whom were Jewish refugees and the remainder primarily European Catholics. Most of the refugees originated from Yugoslavia, while others came from sixteen different countries including Austria, Czechoslovakia, Germany, and Poland. Nearly 10 percent were survivors of the Nazi camps at Dachau and Buchenwald.

Their journey to the United States started in May 1943, when Allied refugee camps in Egypt began to reach their saturation point. About a thousand refugees were stranded in southern Italy, and on June 1, President Roosevelt agreed to allow them to enter the United States. He designated Fort Ontario, an unused army base near Oswego, New York, as their American sanctuary. The W R A was probably given responsibility for this group because of its immediate experience in incarcerating civilians.

Although they are part of the story of this country's World War II incarceration sites, the W R A 's Fort Ontario camp and State Department internment hotels, discussed next, held a different category of prisoners than those described above. Inmates of the W R A relocation camps were permanent residents or citizens of the United States and internees brought to the United States through the cooperation of Latin American governments. Fort Ontario was a limited humanitarian gesture on the part of the U.S. government to assist refugees who would otherwise face extreme conditions or even death if they stayed in Europe.

The Fort Ontario camp was a solution to a logistical problem. If space had been available in Europe to hold these refugees, it is likely that the United States would have refused them entry. Jewish refugees fleeing Nazi tyranny had tried for years to find sanctuary in more benevolent places, but the United States accepted few of them.[57] This does not mean that the United States did not accept immigrants during the prewar and war years. From 1933 to 1943, some 580,000 people entered the United States, but the vast majority were not Jewish refugees. Rather, they were persons who qualified under ordinary quota status from all countries: "By the [Immigration] Act of 1924, we are permitted to admit approximately 150,000 immigrants each year. During the last fiscal year [1943] only 23,725 came as immigrants. Of these, only 4,750 were Jews fleeing Nazi persecution."[58]

From mid-1943, knowledge of the Nazi extermination of European Jews was more definite and widespread. The U.S. government felt it had to deflect possible criticism about its lack of concern and failure to aid these refugees.[59] On January 22, 1944, President Roosevelt signed Executive Order 9417, creating the War Refuge Board (W R B) "to take all measures within its power to rescue the victims of enemy oppression who are in imminent danger of death."[60] Roosevelt gave the main responsibility for implementing the board's programs to the State, Treasury, and War Departments.

Of the three departments, only Treasury's Henry Morgenthau Jr. worked closely with the W R B. Secretary of War Henry L. Stimson delegated Assistant Secretary John J. McCloy as his liaison, and Secretary of State Cordell Hull had little time for the board. Overt anti-Semitism was not uncommon in the U.S. government during the 1940s. As Ruth Gruber noted in *Haven*, "The time-honored distaste for Jews—if not outright hatred—was still a hallmark of the upper echelon of some government agencies, particularly the Department of State. I knew it firsthand working in Washington" (p. 17).

The W R B did its most spectacular work in Europe, and David Wyman credits it with saving nearly 200,000 lives by the war's end. Through the board's assistance, Jewish refugees were evacuated and protected by a W R B -sponsored underground, and diplomatic pressure for better treatment was brought to bear on relevant countries.[61] In its early days, the WRB tried first to help Jewish refugees find shelter in Europe and Africa. As for the United States, Wyman contends that a "major problem was strong opposition to immigration (especially Jewish immigration) in the Congress, in the State Department, and among the American public" (p. 261). Since there was already a precedent for transporting German, Italian, and Japanese foreign nationals from Latin American countries to the United States, one answer was to create refugee camps here. The working supposition was that the United States could and would repatriate the Jewish refugees to their homelands after the war ended.

This small humanitarian gesture evoked media protests directed at President Roosevelt: "Syndicated columnist Westbrook Pegler used the refugees as a club to attack Roosevelt. He warned that 'many thousands' more would be coming, including Communists and crooks. Later, he wrote that, 'Mr. Roosevelt may admit 500,000.' Promises to send them back after the war, [Pegler] insisted, were worthless. Patriotic organizations took up the cry, fearful that the first thousand might form a precedent for breaking down the immigration laws."[62] Pegler's predicted deluge of Jewish refugees never materialized, and only a trickle was actually allowed to enter the United States.

The Fort Ontario site consisted of army barracks that were partitioned into family-size units. The refugees ate in communal mess halls and cleaned and maintained their own areas. The WRA allowed the refugees to leave the camp for up to six hours at a time, and during the day, they could wander freely in the nearby town of Oswego. Their children, 190 of them, were placed directly into the Oswego public school system.

The WRA designated Fort Ontario as an emergency refugee shelter, telling the residents that they were expected to work to maintain basic camp services. In return, the agency gave them $8.50 each per month for incidentals and up to $9.50 per month for their camp work. By January 1943, some refugees started to show signs of resentment at their confinement and questioned the need to perform what they considered to be menial work at a meager salary.[63] Not a few refugees refused to work, and those who continued to do so performed at a minimal level. Others complained that they were not allowed to leave the camp to visit relatives living in the United States.

After Germany's surrender in May 1945, the U.S. government discussed the possible repatriation of these exiles. Returning to a war-torn Europe where there were millions of other displaced persons was not an attractive option to the refugees. On December 22, a presidential order expedited the admission of displaced persons into the United States and made them eligible for permanent quota immigration visas.[64] The refugees were sponsored by American Jewish, Protestant, and Catholic groups, and the WRA then closed Fort Ontario in January 1946.

Throughout the war, the United States allowed 21,000 Jewish refugees to enter the country. Considered in proportion to its territory and population, other countries did much more for this persecuted group. For example, Sweden allowed some 12,000 Jewish refugees to find asylum between January 1944 and April 1945, while Denmark brought in roughly 8,000 refugees, and Norway about 1,000.[65]

Even allies of Nazi Germany aided some Jewish refugees. In one noted case, some refugees fleeing eastward from Nazi-controlled portions of Europe received assistance from an agent of the Japanese government. From July to August 1940, Vice-Consul Chiune Sugihara at the Japanese consulate in Kovno, Lithuania, issued more than 3,000 transit visas to mostly Polish refugees seeking to escape the Nazis. Sugihara was also able to persuade Russian officials to issue transit visas so that these refugees could travel through Russia to get to Japan. The Japanese transit visas were executed against the express orders of Japan's Ministry of Foreign Affairs, since Japan was "aligned, but not yet allied with Germany through the 1935 Anti-Comintern Pact."[66] The Japanese foreign ministry allowed the refugees to enter Japan for the purpose of crossing the Pacific Ocean, and a number of them sailed for the United States. After December 7, 1941, they stayed in Japan until they were taken to Shanghai, where they remained along with 17,000 other refugees.

The United States' refusal to accept more Jewish refugees is a multifaceted issue. Several factors limited public pressure to assist them: "Among them were anti-Semitism and anti-immigration attitudes, both widespread in American society in that era and both entrenched in Congress; the mass media's failure to publicize Holocaust news . . . the near silence of the Christian churches and almost all of their leadership; the indifference of most of the nation's political and intellectual leaders; and the President's failure to speak out on the issue."[67] The particular brand of prejudice that affected the Jewish refugees was akin to the wartime treatment of resident Japanese nationals and Japanese Americans.

INTERNMENT HOTELS

In addition to the Justice Department and the WRA, the State Department, through its Special War Problems Division (known as the Special Division), established and ran its own internment centers during World War II. These State Department establishments, which are here called *internment hotels,* stood in marked contrast to Justice Department and WRA camps. These facilities were sumptuous resorts at such locations as the Homestead Hotel in Hot Springs, Virginia, the Grove Park Inn in Asheville, North Carolina, and the Greenbrier Hotel in White Sulphur Springs, West Virginia. These hotels and a few others housed not only public agents of enemy countries, such as diplomatic and consular corps staff, but also business and corporate executives from Axis countries.

The State Department did not have a special designation for these internment hotels, since it expected to keep them open for only a short while. They are important to the discussion because their purpose and operation resulted from their internees' status as enemy aliens. More significant, the State Department transferred to these hotels some internees from Justice Department camps and mixed them with diplomatic personnel in later exchanges between nations. Although these internees were the responsibility of the Special Division, the INS was in charge of daily operations, assisted by the FBI and the Border Patrol.

Arrests of these internees began on December 7, 1941, when FBI agents arrived at the Japanese embassy in Washington, D.C. They kept all persons there under house arrest. For days afterward, they also entered homes and placed diplomats and all other occupants under house arrest. Gwen Terasaki, for example, was an American citizen married to a Japanese diplomat, and her mother was visiting when the FBI first came to their house. Her mother found that she could not return to her home in Tennessee until her congressman intervened on her behalf with the State Department.[68]

The State Department's Special Division chief offers his views on the treatment of Japanese diplomats in his diary entry for December 17, 1941: "Have been pretty tough on the Japs. For six days they slept 40 in the Embassy prepared to sleep 10. They had no mattresses, no bedclothes, no clean linen. At the end of that period I allowed emissaries to get laundry, beds, mattresses and four of them to return to their accustomed place of abode where their wives and children were under guard."[69] The Special Division also moved quickly to obtain favorable treatment for captured American personnel trapped in Axis-controlled territory.

The State Department not only held diplomatic persons and family members in the United States but also brought Axis officials from Latin American countries and readied them for exchange for American diplomatic personnel. The State Department treated these prisoners in what can only be called a regal manner. Their international status required that they be accorded above-minimal treatment, as the United States hoped its diplomatic officials would receive similar treatment.[70] One example is the Homestead Hotel in Virginia, which held 335 Japanese, including 75 or 80 children, from December 24, 1941, to June 1942. The Justice Department maintained twenty Border Patrol inspectors and forty INS guards for security purposes. This establishment boasted "a 17,000 acre vacation paradise with golf courses, tennis and badminton courts, bowling alleys, and ballrooms. It had luxurious suites, luxurious single rooms, and a superb cuisine."[71] Those originally brought to Homestead came from Japanese embassies or consulate offices in various cities such as Washington, D.C., Mexico City, and Havana, Cuba. Although the setting was comfortable, the Japanese ambassador, Kichisaburo Nomura, complained to the State Department that they were overcrowded and mistreated, and in April 1942, the State Department moved the inhabitants to the Greenbriar Hotel in West Virginia. The State Department used the Homestead Hotel until June 1942, when its occupants left for New York to board the Swedish exchange ship MS *Gripsholm*.[72]

A substantial number of diplomats and other officials and their dependents were placed in internment hotels. Counting only those persons originating in the United States, the total, including those who were not arrested, came to 785: 363 Japanese, 212 Germans, 113 Italians, 71 Hungarians, 16 Bulgarians, and 10 Romanians. Of this number, 655 diplomats, officials, and dependents actually resided at internment hotels from December 1941 to early September 1942. The State Department repatriated 633 by exchange, while 22 persons petitioned and were allowed to stay in the United States. By September 1942, 130 others—63 Japanese, 19 Italians, 18 Hungarians, 13 Germans, 10 Romanians, and 7 Bulgarians—were being sought and remained at large.[73]

The State Department transported 1,735 diplomatic or other officials to the United States from Latin American countries for the purpose of diplomatic exchange. This group consisted of 1,194 Germans, 493 Japanese, 38 Hungarians, 9 Bulgarians, and 1 Swiss. By September 8, 1942, the department had repatriated all except 131 persons—125 Germans, 5 Japanese, and the Swiss official. State Department officials expected that this latter group, kept at the Grove Park Inn in North Carolina, would eventually be repatriated.[74] The last internment hotel closed on February 15, 1944.[75]

CONCLUSION

The administrative scope and depth of the incarceration process were far reaching, resulting in the designation of a segregation center for the "disloyal" and the creation of "noncitizens" who could be processed for deportation. The reach of the WRA extended to inmates of Japanese ancestry in hospitals, sanatoriums, and prisons and to a thousand European Jewish refugees. Meanwhile, the State Department provided luxurious resort-type environments for diplomatic personnel during the early war years.

The WRA's overall concern was to maintain control of its inmate or internee population, excluding those in the refugee camp. And to the extent that the inmates were perceived as suspect or dangerous, any treatment, harsh or otherwise, could be justified on the grounds that they deserved nothing better. Wayne Collins, attorney for the renunciant plaintiffs at the Tule Lake Segregation Camp, left no doubt as to how he saw the officials and their actions there: "Abnormal times beget abnormal results when abnormal minds are permitted latitude in dealing with citizens they are suffered to command."[76]

9

Abuses, Protests, and the Geneva Convention

n their public relations pronouncements, government officials stressed the benevolence and humaneness of their treatment of World War II internees and inmates. For example, in 1944, the commissioner of the Immigration and Naturalization Service (INS), Earl G. Harrison, said about the alien internment program: "Some day when the full story can be written, it will become known that in the United States that program has been carried out with all the strictness required to protect the country and at the same time with a spirit and understanding that have made new friends for the democratic way. After these years of bitterness and fighting have passed, *no American need have any regret over the manner in which his government's representatives treated alien enemies during their days of internment.*"[1]

A contrasting interpretation exists. This chapter asserts that agents of the government employed a range of measures, from mild to extreme, to control their internees and inmates. This process of control began with the first arrests, as Issei internees suffered psychological abuses and physical assaults. Facing an apparently overwhelming force, the Issei at first felt powerless to resist.

It is not true, however, that the Issei simply acquiesced. In many significant instances, they made their objections known, vocally and through their actions, and protested vehemently when they believed the situation warranted it. In incidents at all levels—from individuals, to small groups, to an entire Issei internee population at one camp—Issei prisoners staunchly objected and demanded fair treatment from their captors. To better their conditions, they were willing to submit to harsh treatment, endure personal deprivation, and risk physical injury. A few prisoners even suffered the ultimate penalty in the camps, the loss of their lives. These two themes—the imprisonment organization's control mechanism and the protests of the internees and inmates—make up the substance of this chapter. The struggles of inmates in the WRA camps have been covered earlier, so this chapter will concentrate mainly on the internment camps operated by the U.S. Department of Justice and the U.S. Army.

It is obviously not true that all government officials acted with ill will toward internees and inmates. Rather, the total context of the imprisonment story reveals that the government created a situation in which it failed to adequately protect the persons for whom it had assumed responsibility. This chapter presents selected incidents; unverifiable events or unpublished examples have been excluded. As a result, the reader may discern a favorable bias toward the government, since much of the information in this chapter comes from government files. With this caveat, let us start with the Issei arrested by the Justice Department.

ABUSES IN INS CAMPS

Issei internees reported physical and social abuses that began with their arrests on December 7, 1941. Some abuses were apparently cases of individual harassment. For example, some internees found their jail food extremely oversalted or heavily peppered, rendering it inedible.[2] In Yakima, Washington, the local police kept Hisashi Tateoka in solitary confinement for eighteen days, and his sole nourishment for the day consisted of half-boiled mush and milk.[3] In other cases, internees were deprived of blankets, cots, or clothing appropriate to the cold of their cells at night. Other internees reported that some were kept in handcuffs and placed in solitary confinement, and that while they were thus restrained or in detention cells, the guards demanded instantaneous compliance with their orders. Failure to respond with alacrity resulted in the brandishing of unsheathed bayonets and threats of bodily harm. Internees also stated that at one camp, physicians administered unwanted medications and questionable injections.[4]

The INS reports a remarkable example of physical assault. On February 15, 1942, the agency detailed an interrogation team of six persons from the Los Angeles district to the Justice Department's internment camp at Fort Missoula, Montana. The team included three immigration inspectors and one senior patrol inspector, each with nearly fifteen years of experience, plus two temporary INS interpreters. Their assignment was to investigate the immigration status of certain Issei then held at the Missoula camp. According to the INS report, the team used extreme methods to obtain answers to its questions. The INS personnel made thirty elderly Issei stand for hours at a time while they questioned them, shouted in a threatening manner (calling them "liars" and "damned liars"), and pushed, slapped, and punched them. Two Issei were hurt so badly that they needed medical attention, and a third required hospitalization. The team placed several internees in solitary confinement for from one to twenty-seven days with the knowledge and approval of the Missoula camp director.[5]

The Issei internees complained to the camp director, but he apparently did not report the incidents to his superiors or initiate an investigation. When he left, presumably through a routine transfer, the next camp director continued the sentences of solitary confinement without monitoring the length of the internees' isolation.

In a specific case, Yoshiaki Fukuda reports that the INS questioned Yaichi Kubota's status as a legal immigrant. Officials at the INS detention camp at Missoula apparently attempted to get the "truth" out of him by striking him in the face until they knocked out several of his front teeth. This torture continued for more than a month, along with solitary confinement. Kubota was not allowed to use the bathroom and was forced to leave his waste on the floor of his small dark cell.[6]

Meanwhile the Justice Department issued its own rules for the treatment of enemy aliens on April 28, 1942.[7] Instruction Number 58, or "The Rules for Detainees," asserted in part that "detainees must at all times be protected against acts of violence, insults and public curiosity. Physical coercion must not be resorted to and, except in self-defense, to prevent escape or for purposes of proper search, no employee of this Service under any pretext shall invade the person of any detainee. No measures calculated to humiliate or degrade shall be undertaken."[8] Rules of conduct toward foreign nationals might have been stated specifically by the organization's upper echelon, but these did not necessarily translate into commensurate behavior by those in the field.

From Fort Missoula, the same INS team, minus one inspector, traveled to the internment camp at Fort Lincoln, North Dakota. Here, beginning on May 8, 1942, it used the same abusive interrogation techniques; three Issei were left in need of medical attention and hospitalization, and others were recommended for isolation and solitary confinement. This time, however, the camp director refused to use the guardhouse for this purpose.[9] The other internees probably catalyzed the INS inquiry by demanding that the Missoula and Fort Lincoln incidents be reported to the Spanish consul, who represented the relevant protecting power.

The internal investigation, which began in June 1942, found that the internees had been subjected to unjust physical abuses, beatings, and solitary confinement. The INS blamed the most serious assaults on the temporary interpreters and subsequently dismissed both of them. Three INS inspectors were found guilty of mistreating the Issei and of failing to report the instances of physical abuse to the camp directors. Their penalty was suspension without pay for ninety days, and one inspector was demoted. In justifying these relatively light penalties, the INS commissioner reasoned that dismissal was too severe, given the inspectors' long service with the INS, and "the penalty in the way of financial loss of salary, when coupled with the mental punishment which the officers undoubtedly already suffered by reason of the uncertainty as to the outcome of the charges, would operate as an effective deterrent to any recurrence of such misconduct in the future."[10] The INS announced the decision on September 17 but restored the inspectors to full employment a month later.

The INS also initiated a review to see if any testimony had been obtained from internees involuntarily or under duress. This process began on January 25, 1943, or more than eleven months after the first incident of abusive interrogation; eight internees claimed to have given testimony as a result of coercion. The INS dismissed two of the eight cases, kept four others for probable dismissal, and held the remaining two internees for deportation.[11]

Another Fort Missoula action occurred in June 1942. The Issei internees complained to the Spanish consul about the lack of meat and vegetables in their diet, a deficiency they believed had resulted in illness and even three deaths. The consul agreed with the internees and further noted to the State Department: "As adequate medicines are not available, there is much suffering around, specially since most of the internees are middle-aged."[12] Government files do not indicate the disposition of this case or any subsequent action taken by the Justice Department.

HOMICIDES

In addition to cases of individual harassment and physical attack, there is evidence of homicides against the Issei and Nisei. During the imprisonment period, at least seven people were killed by gunfire. These homicides are, of course, the severest examples of inhumane treatment meted out to the internee and inmate population.

Army Internment Camps

On July 27, 1942, shortly after 2:00 A.M., 147 Issei arrived at the army's Lordsburg internment camp in New Mexico from the INS's Fort Abraham Lincoln (Bismarck) Internment Center in North Dakota. Among them were two bachelor Issei who did not survive that day. The first was Toshio Kobata, born June 2, 1884, in Hiroshima prefecture, who had worked as a farmer in Brawley, California, before the war. The other was Hirota Isomura, born November 11, 1883, in Shiga prefecture, a fisherman from Terminal Island, California, near San Pedro.

According to friends, Kobata suffered from the aftereffects of tuberculosis contracted some sixteen years earlier. He had difficulty breathing and needed to take frequent breaks from work to catch his breath. From 1939, Kobata was active in the Japanese Association (Nihonjinkai), an organization on the Justice Department's B list of suspect groups; the affiliation is the likely reason for his arrest and internment.[13]

Isomura had badly injured his spinal column after falling from his fishing boat ten years earlier and was permanently stooped. As one acquaintance said, "He could not walk fast any more after that."[14] There is nothing in the records to indicate why the government interned Isomura, although his occupation was the most likely reason, since other fishermen were arrested at Terminal Island, California.

Just before they arrived at the Lordsburg camp after midnight, First Sergeant John A. Beckham of the 309th Military Police Escort Guard Company armed twenty-three soldiers with submachine guns and 12-gauge riot-type shotguns. He told them that "if any Alien tries to escape, you are to holler 'Halt' and if he does not halt, to holler 'Halt' again, and if he does not halt this time, to fire on him."[15]

After the internees arrived, the military police (MPs) ordered the internees to form three columns. The train guards told the MPs that two internees were ill and would not be able to keep up on the march to the camp. The other 145 Issei were quickly put into columns and marched toward the camp entrance. A paved road leads south from the train tracks for 2.1 miles, with a camp guardhouse situated at the halfway point. The road then angles ninety degrees to the east; 400 yards beyond the turn was the front gate of the Lordsburg compound.

Sergeant Truman C. Fambro Jr., Ninth Section Sergeant of the 309th Military Police Escort Guard Company at the Lordsburg Internment Camp, assigned twenty-nine-year-old then Private and later Private First Class (PFC) Clarence A. Burleson to escort the two less mobile men. Fambro's instructions were to let the two internees set their own pace, rest when they wanted, and take as much time as necessary to walk to the compound gate.[16] Burleson was armed with a 12-gauge shotgun.

Fambro testified that he told Isomura and Kobata, in English, to "stay on the pavement and not leave the hard surface at no time."[17] He also testified that his instructions were translated to the two men through the Issei leader, who was acting as interpreter. Senmatsu Ishizaki, the translator for the internee group that morning, testified that he received "no orders" to give to the internees "relative to their march to Camp."[18] Fambro also detailed PFC Joseph F. Kelly to be the rear guard to prevent any cars or traffic behind the group to interfere with the internees' march.

Burleson and Kelly walked down the path at a slow pace with their two internees. When the main body of internees reached the compound gate, the Issei inside the camp shouted words of welcome and recognition to the new arrivals. Meanwhile, down the road, Kelly called out to Burleson that he was going off the road to get a drink of water from the fire hydrant by the nearby engineers' building. Kelly testified that the fire hydrant was located some 75 to 100 feet away from the road and that while he was away from Burleson, he could hear the yelling from the compound, characterizing it as a big celebration. He then heard two shots and related that it took about two minutes before he got back to where Burleson was standing, about thirty-five paces away from Isomura and Kobata, who were lying wounded, off the road, close to the fence. Military witnesses stated that the two Issei were within two to six feet of the fence. There were no Japanese internees who observed where the bodies lay.

When the new internees later asked about the condition of their two compatriots, the Lordsburg camp physician told them that the victims were at the camp hospital receiving medical care.[19] The next morning, when internees again asked the doctor about the two men, he replied that they had been shot trying to escape on the way to the camp but gave no details of the shooting.[20]

Other internees learned about the deaths in a more melodramatic way. The army forced two Issei to dig two holes about the size and dimensions of a human grave. Since the New Mexico earth is hard and is difficult to shovel, the two workers asked for rest time. Their guard told them, in effect, "These graves are for the Japanese who died; if you don't do your work quickly, I will make you dig two more graves."[21]

The internees demanded that the Lordsburg camp commander conduct an investigation and an autopsy. The camp commander, Lieutenant Colonel Clyde A. Lundy, replied that they had already buried the bodies and refused the internees' request. However, the commander ordered a funeral for the two slain men at 4:00 P.M. the day after the shootings and required all internees to attend. The internees refused the order and instead observed individual moments of silence for the deceased. They also composed a telegram to the Spanish consul in New Orleans, requesting an investigation of the incident, and gave it to the commanding officer to mail.[22]

Lieutenant Colonel Lundy appointed three officers to a board investigating the deaths of the two Issei. From 2:30 to 4:00 P.M. on the afternoon of the shootings, the board heard testimony from four people: the accused, PFC Burleson; First Sergeant Beckham (responsible for the guard company that day); First Lieutenant Harold C. Stull, the officer of the day; and PFC Kelly. The board concluded that the two Issei "died as a result of gunshot wounds inflicted at the hands of PFC Clarence A. Burleson, who was acting in the performance of his duty under legal orders of a superior authority." The board recommended that Burleson be tried by a general court-martial "so that his guilt or innocence may be forever established."[23]

The next higher reviewing authority, at Fort Sam Houston, Texas, found that Lundy had charged Burleson with "willfully and lawfully" killing the two men. Since this wording does not allege an offense for which Burleson could be charged, Lundy was ordered to redraw the charge sheet and conduct another investigation. Lundy appointed another Lordsburg officer to investigate the killing. This investigation again found that PFC Burleson did kill Isomura and Kobata, but the killings were not felonious or unlawful. The investigating officer, "believes the accused to be innocent but deems trial advisable in the interest of the service and for the protection of the accused . . . that the specifications and charge be tried by General Court-Martial."[24] Lundy signed his concurrence on August 21, 1942.

At a pretrial hearing held on September 3, the army heard a group of Lordsburg Issei offer character references and affirm the illnesses of the deceased men. For example, Senmatsu Ishizaki testified that Isomura always walked slowly and with a stoop, and that at the previous INS camp he was allowed to leave for the mess hall twenty minutes earlier than the rest of the internees. Ishizaki stated, "They say they were running away, but they couldn't run because of the physical condition one of them was in."[25] Others testified as well: "[Isomura] was always bent and had to take short quick steps. When he stood still his whole body would tremble."[26]

Burleson's general court-martial trial started on September 10 at 8:50 A.M. and ended the same day at 4:50 P.M. The charge was violation of the 93rd Article of War, manslaughter, with two specifications. First, that Clarence A. Burleson "did, at Lordsburg Internment Camp, Lordsburg, New Mexico on or about July 27, 1942, feloniously and unlawfully kill one Hirota Isomura, a human being, by shooting him with a 12 gauge shotgun." The second specification had identical wording except that the deceased was identified as Toshio Kobata.

There was no witness to the shooting. However, Lieutenant Colonel Lundy testified that he was in his quarters (about 150 feet from where the killings took place) at about 3:30 A.M.: "I heard a shout that sounded like 'Halt' to me, a couple of times. I couldn't distinguish it accurately, so I did not say anything about it. There was a shout before the shots were fired." In the cross-examination phase, he was asked whether he had given the following statement in an earlier disposition: "While I was still lying in bed I heard a shout, 'Halt.' I don't recall whether it was one or two but I think it was two." Lundy affirmed, "I did make that remark and I still think the same thing."[27] No one else, such as Kelly or the engineer watchman, who were closer to the shooting, testified about any shout coming from the area where Burleson and the two Issei were standing. These two witnesses did say that the welcoming ruckus made by camp internees as they greeted the new arrivals could be heard for more than 400 yards away from the compound.

Burleson was the sole defense witness. In a previous sworn statement, he testified that "They were able to run fast. After the last time they rested the sentry that was behind me said he was going to step out and get a drink. I believe the prisoners heard him for they started talking to each other and walking fast and the other prisoners that had gone on ahead of us started shouting and these two men started running. I called to them to halt twice; that they did not do. I fired on the first one, the second did not halt, I fired on him. . . . The first man might have reached the fence, I don't believe that he had, though."[28] At the trial, he testified that during the walk near the engineers' building, after PFC Kelly went to get some water, the two Issei started to "walk fast" and then "both men started running for the fence to the right. I called out to them to stop, called to them to 'Halt!' and they didn't. I immediately threw a cartridge into the chamber of the gun and called to them again, and they still ran, and the man in the front apparently, the best I could see at that distance, had gotten over to the fence almost, and had turned down the fence south, evidently to keep from running into the fence. . . . After I called to him the second time, I fired and he fell; the other man then turned in the direction that he fell, straight toward him. The other man was back three or four steps to the rear of him at that time; so I reloaded my gun and fired on him and he fell."[29] During a brief cross-examination, Burleson was unable to say how fast the two men were running but stated that he thought they could hear him shout "Halt!" and refused to do so. All the military witnesses differed in their estimates of the distance between the two deceased men on one side and Burleson and the fence on the other; however, all agreed that the two men were off the road.

In both the earlier Lordsburg internal investigation and the general court-martial, little attempt was made to obtain a clear picture of the incident. That there might have been another reason for Isomura and Kobata to be off the road and nearer the fence was a possibility never raised by the prosecution. An intriguing fact arose during the cross-examination of Burleson. He had previously testified in a deposition on September 2 that the two internees conversed with him during the march: "While we were proceeding up the highway both of these Japanese talked to me freely in English, asking me considerable questions, and we talked about several things." In the court-martial cross-examination phase, he was asked about Isomura's and Kobata's questions. He replied, "Well, sir, the first time they asked me any question, the reason I wouldn't let him stop on the way; there was a car behind us and he said he wanted to stop and relieve himself. Immediately after the car had went around and pulled up towards the head of the column, I suppose of the group that had gone on, he asked me the same question again and I let him do so. After we had gone, I would say, a hundred or a hundred and fifty yards, the other asked me the same question."[30]

Considering the long train ride and the early morning hour, the two men may not have thought that wishing to relieve themselves constituted unreasonable behavior; however, decorum and etiquette proscribe doing so in the middle of the road. Burleson's testimony offers an alternative explanation for the two men's presence off the road and closer to the fence. Private Kelly, who was fifty yards behind them, said nothing about the possible earlier trip of one Issei to relieve himself, nor was he asked whether one of the internees had ever left the road with Burleson's permission.

Also unresolved was the issue of whether or not the internees could actually run. The prosecution raised this topic by attempting to question witnesses about the victims' physical condition. The defense responded by saying the matter was irrelevant to the case. When the camp medical officer was questioned about this issue, he thus could not make a statement about Isomura's and Kobata's ability to march, run, or walk since an autopsy had not been conducted on the bodies. Moreover, there were nine "bullet wounds" on each body, but the doctor did not or could not determine whether they were exit or entrance wounds.[31] The doctor testified that he looked at the two bodies, pronounced them dead, and sent them to the local mortuary.

Although the prosecution could have constructed other possible scenarios, it did not do so. The doctor testified that there were nine bullet wounds in each body, and Burleson testified that his shotgun, a "riot gun," contained nine pellets in each shell. No questions were raised regarding how the nine pellets of each shell hit both men or the diameter of the buckshot pattern on the two bodies, although exploring both of these details might have proved valuable in determining the relative positions of the three parties. There was also no information given about any prior escape attempts from Justice Department camps by one or both internees.

No one questioned the likelihood of two elderly Issei trying to climb a fence and flee into a desolate and isolated field. The defense counsel maintained that the only issues were whether a legitimate military order covering such a situation had been given, whether the defendant was under such an order, and whether, after attempting to prevent an escape by shouting "halt," he was then justified in preventing the escape. If so, by refusing to obey Burleson's command to halt, the deceased men justified his firing on them, and there was no one alive who could contradict his statement.

The court-martial board acquitted Burleson of both counts. Isomura and Kobata were initially buried at the Lordsburg Internment Camp cemetery. On October 4, 1942, Kobata's remains were sent to Brawley, California; Isomura is now buried at the Fort Bliss National Cemetery in Texas.[32]

Two additional points should be noted. According to the Articles of the 1929 Geneva Convention to which these internees were subject, an attempted escape from a camp carries the severest penalty of confinement for up to thirty days. Nothing the internees had done warranted a death sentence. In addition, the prosecution never explored the factor of motivation. If these two men were trying to escape, they had to climb a ten-foot fence, drop to the other side, traverse an open field surrounding the fence, and then escape by fleeing into an area that was completely unknown to them. Why anyone would contemplate an escape attempt in full view of an armed guard, and why the two men could be fired upon for refusing to obey a command to halt, are two questions that remain unanswered.

A third homicide occurred at the army's internment camp at Fort Sill, Oklahoma. Kanesaburo Oshima, age forty-five, a gardener by occupation, lived with his family in Los Angeles when the FBI apprehended him on December 7, 1941. The most likely reason for his arrest was his earlier service in the Japanese military. From the start, other internees noticed that he was very concerned about the safety and well-being of his wife and children. Then, during the train ride to the INS internment camp in Missoula, Montana, he inexplicably tried to bite off his tongue. The other Issei restrained him, placed a piece of wood between his jaws, and watched him until they arrived in Missoula.[33] He seemed to improve slightly but then later tried unsuccessfully to asphyxiate himself.

After the army routinely transferred the internees to the Fort Sill camp, Oshima again showed signs of mental illness, so the army placed him in the camp hospital. On May 13, 1942, at 7:30 A.M., he went to the camp perimeter and, according to the FBI, "climbed the first fence, ran down the runway between the fencing, one hundred feet and started climbing the second [fence], when he was shot and killed by two shots, one entering the base of his spine, the second entering the back of his head. The guard gave him several warnings." There is no mention in the FBI report about the internee's mental condition.[34]

Oshima's death occurred six months after the Japanese attack on Pearl Harbor and after the army had extensive experience with the internment of Issei. During this time, as far as the records show, none of these internees had ever tried to escape or use violence of any kind. Moreover, in this case, Fort Sill military personnel were aware of Oshima's mental problems and attempts at self-destruction. Yet the records indicate that he was shot in the back while attempting to "escape."

WRA *Camps*

In addition to the three deaths in army camps, four inmates died by gunfire in WRA camps. At the WRA center in Manzanar, California, as discussed in chapter 7, James Ito and Katsuji James Kanagawa were killed by MPs during the Manzanar camp upheavals of December 6, 1942.

On April 11, 1943, at the WRA camp in Topaz, Utah, a military sentry shot and killed James Hatsuaki Wakasa, an Issei bachelor. The sixty-three-year-old former cook from San Francisco suffered from impaired hearing. The FBI reports that the killing occurred as Wakasa attempted "to leave the center without a pass. Wakasa had reportedly made two previous attempts to leave the center and had been warned by the guards on each occasion. He was shot while making his third attempt to cross the barbed wire enclosure between sentry stations."[35]

The Topaz WRA administration report states that Wakasa was fatally shot at 7:30 P.M. by an MP sentry "near the west fence . . . from 40 to 65 inches inside the fence."[36] Anyone who has lived in Topaz knows the bleakness of the surrounding area. The nearest settlement was the small town of Delta, some nine miles to the southeast; there was nothing but sagebrush and dust between the camp and the town. If Wakasa had really tried to escape, then his plan was not the product of a rational mind, but he was shot and killed anyway. There is another interpretation.

The State Department's Special War Problems Division and the Spanish embassy sent representatives to investigate the homicide. They reported that the body was lying five feet inside the fence, and in such a way that Wakasa seemingly "had been facing the sentry tower and walking parallel to the fence; and the wind was from Wakasa's back, making it highly improbable that he could have heard [the sentry's] challenge. The official account from the Spanish official concluded that the incident was 'due to the hastiness on the part of the sentry,' who, not receiving an immediate response to his challenge, 'probably fired too quickly.' The Army court-martialed [the sentry], charging him with manslaughter. He was acquitted."[37] A question remains as to what Wakasa was actually doing—trying to escape or simply walking parallel to the fence. Regardless, this action shows that the controlling agencies, the WRA and the army, were quite willing to use the ultimate weapon of control over the inmates.

As mentioned in Chapter 8, a military sentry shot and killed Shoichi James Okamoto on May 24, 1944, at the WRA's Tule Lake Segregation Center in California. Okamoto, a thirty-year-old Nisei, was driving a construction truck back and forth between the camp and a worksite. At the end of one trip, the center-gate sentry confronted him and demanded that he step out of his truck and show his pass. Okamoto stepped out of the cab but refused to show his pass, whereupon the sentry struck him on the shoulder with the butt end of his rifle. The two exchanged words, and the sentry shot Okamoto.

Inmates stated that the sentry insulted Okamoto and dragged him out of the truck. Okamoto was walking to the rear of the truck, as he had been ordered to do, when the sentry swore at him. Okamoto turned around, and the sentry shot him in the head.[38] After the army investigation, the sentry was acquitted of committing a crime but was fined $1, the cost of the bullet that was fired in an "unauthorized use of government property."[39]

ACQUITTALS

In all seven documented cases, the perpetrators were acquitted of wrongdoing.[40] These cases point out the obvious conclusion, which the internees and inmates quickly realized. Whatever their conduct, whatever the ostensible rules, a genuine death threat hung over them from guards and sentries who were armed and capable of pulling the trigger. Little or no restraint was practiced that might temper this ultimate action, and the only punishment meted out to those who committed the homicides was the fine of $1.

THE 1929 GENEVA CONVENTION

Not all Nikkei internees and inmates experienced physical harm during their wartime incarceration or internment. However, there appears to be sufficient corroborative information to show that many internees suffered, others died, and probably all were affected negatively in some way by their imprisonment.

After their arrests in early 1942, the Issei believed they had no means of protesting or changing the often brutal and inhumane treatment enforced upon them. An important document surfaced in the Justice Department camps in mid-1942 and eventually tempered some of the severe mistreatment of the internees. This instrument was the Geneva Convention of July 27, 1929, Relative to the Treatment of Prisoners of War, more commonly known as the 1929 Geneva Convention. The United States signed and ratified the original document, and it was proclaimed as law on August 4, 1932. In an effort to obtain fair treatment for the many prisoners of war captured by the Japanese military in Southeast Asia, U.S. government officials sent a message through the Swiss government on December 18, 1941, that it not only "intended to abide by the [1929] Geneva Prisoner of War Convention and the Geneva Red Cross Convention, it further intended to extend and apply the provisions of the Geneva Prisoner of War Convention to any civilian aliens that it might intern, that it hoped that the Japanese Government would apply the provisions of these conventions reciprocally as indicated."[41] It is worth underscoring here that in agreeing to observe the Geneva accords, the U.S. government stated specifically the articles' applicability to civilian internees.

Japan signed the Geneva Convention but had not ratified it by the start of World War II. On January 29, 1942, however, Foreign Minister Shigenori Togo answered the American inquiry and promised that Japan would observe the articles of the convention and apply them *mutatis mutandis,* or "with the necessary changes," to the treatment of prisoners of war.[42] *Mutatis mutandis* meant that the Japanese would treat troops they captured as they expected other nations to treat Japanese prisoners of war.

The Issei felt that the Justice Department and the army violated many articles of the Geneva Convention. Article 2 states in part that captors must always treat prisoners humanely and protect them, particularly against acts of violence, insults, and public curiosity. A prisoner of war, according to Article 5, cannot be coerced into giving any information beyond his name, rank, and serial number. Prisoners who refuse to answer other questions may not be threatened, insulted, or exposed to unpleasant or disadvantageous treatment. Article 9 stipulates that prisoners will not be kept in unhealthful regions or places where the climate is detrimental to their well-being. In addition, as far as possible, prisoners will not be kept in a single camp with prisoners of other races or nationalities.

The Issei and the imprisonment organization probably disagreed most strongly on Article 31. This article prohibits requiring prisoners to work on projects directly related to war operations, specifically the manufacturing and transporting of arms and munitions and the transporting of materials intended for combat units. If prisoners feel that they are being forced to do work in contravention to Article 31, they are allowed "to have their protests presented through the mediation of the agents whose functions are set forth in Articles 43 [prisoners' elected officials] and 44 [access of these officials to the military authorities], or, in the absence of an agent, through the mediation of representatives of the protecting power [which represents one enemy country to another]."

Article 42 grants prisoners the right to inform their captors about the conditions of their imprisonment. Moreover, they have the right to address representatives of the protecting power with complaints about their conditions of confinement. The captors are to transmit immediately such complaints and requests, and they are prohibited from punishing the prisoners for making unfounded requests and complaints. Article 43 recognizes the right of prisoners to elect officials to represent them to the military authorities and the protecting power, although appointments are subject to the approval of military authorities. Article 46, in part, specifically forbids corporal punishment, imprisonment in quarters without daylight, and any form of cruelty in general.

Article 47 deals with offenses against prison discipline and attempted escapes. Prisoners attempting to escape would be subject to the absolute minimum of "preventative arrest," while Article 54 stipulates that arrests are not to exceed thirty days and are the most severe disciplinary punishment that can be imposed.

There is little doubt today that Japan violated the Geneva Convention during World War II, but the purpose here is not to explore Japan's treatment of military and civilian prisoners. The prisoner populations of the two nations differed in a very important way. Most of the Justice and War Departments' Nikkei internees had lived in the United States for decades before World War II; they were law-abiding, hardworking civilians, mainly older married men with American-citizen children. In contrast, cases of Japanese cruelty to prisoners usually involved enemy soldiers captured in combat zones, although this does not in any way excuse the actions of the Japanese military. The point is that unwarranted mistreatment of prisoners by the Justice Department, the army, and the W R A had heretofore been relatively unknown. And as we will see in the next chapter, various factors prevented this information from becoming public in the decades following the war.

THE GENEVA CONVENTION AND THE INTERNMENT CAMPS

From early December 1941, various Issei internees believed themselves to be the victims of cruelty and abuse. They felt they were mistreated not only by the I N S but by F B I agents, local police, and army personnel as well. If such untoward actions did occur, these agencies were either unaware of the applicability of the 1929 Geneva Convention or knew of the violations and chose to ignore them.

There is some question as to when the internees first learned about the Geneva Convention. Beginning with arrests made from early December 1941 to January 1942, Justice Department administrators dealt forcefully with behavior they perceived as unacceptable or threatening to their authority. At the I N S internment camp at Missoula, Montana, for example, when the spokesperson for the Japanese internees protested to I N S officials that certain internees had received harsh treatment in the initial holding areas, the officials told him that his objection was a form of interference. In addition, when he continued to question past events, he was told that he faced disciplinary solitary confinement.[43]

Moreover, during these early months at the Missoula camp, the army ordered internees to work on labor projects outside their compound area. The Issei internees felt they could not refuse the work order and complied without receiving pay or any other compensation. The army also ordered the internees to work in temperatures as low as fifteen degrees below zero. The internees sent a letter of complaint in early 1942 to the Japanese ambassador to the United States, Kichisaburo Nomura, who was then confined in a State Department internment hotel awaiting an exchange ship to return him to Japan. Nomura relayed the complaints to the State Department, and agents of the Justice and State Departments flew to the Missoula camp to investigate sometime after April 1942.

Perhaps because of this complaint, the Justice Department distributed Instruction Number 58 to the I N S administration on April 28, 1942. In the document, the Justice Department reiterated its directive that the Geneva Convention of 1929 defined the proper standard of conduct toward its civilian alien internees: "The minimum standards of treatment which have been established and which must prevail throughout this Service are based upon the provisions of the Convention between the United States of America and forty-six other Powers. . . . The government of the United States has agreed with the belligerent powers to apply those provisions to civilian alien enemy internees wherever applicable."[44]

This particular memo arrived at the Santa Fe Internment Camp in New Mexico on May 7, 1942, and there is little reason to doubt that other INS camp directors, for instance, at Missoula, also received this general "instructional" memo at the same time. The importance of this issue for the United States is obvious. Nomura, the Japanese ambassador, was returning to Japan and would probably make a statement about the treatment of Japanese nationals. His report could be crucial in preventing detrimental treatment of American prisoners held by the Japanese. The INS administrators at Santa Fe, where this particular memo was found filed, and thus in all the camps, were now formally apprised that they were to follow the articles of the 1929 Geneva Convention. Administrators also would have known that the convention required the posting of the full articles where prisoners could see them. Yet, the internees at Santa Fe apparently first heard of the convention's existence and relevance to their situation in late May or early June, even though the Santa Fe administrator had been informed on May 7. On June 17, 1942, the INS reported that the German, Italian, and Japanese internees had copies of the Geneva Convention at each of the camps.[45] With the text of the articles in their hands, the internees had a gauge against which to measure their treatment; this constituted a powerful weapon that allowed them to argue forcefully about the correctness of their captors' behavior.

In June 1942, the relationship between the Missoula internees and administration became more settled. There were three reasons for this change. First, the INS removed some of its officials from the various camps; according to the internees, in June, the INS dismissed or transferred three immigration officials from Missoula. A second reason was the overt introduction of the 1929 Geneva Convention into camp relations. And third, after the internees went before the hearing boards, the Justice Department started to empty its camps, either paroling internees to WRA relocation centers or sending them to the army for permanent internment.

LORDSBURG CONFLICTS AND THE GENEVA CONVENTION

In 1942, a terrible situation developed at the army internment camp in Lordsburg, New Mexico. This conflict between the internees and the army is important for two reasons: first, it shows the detrimental effects of a camp commander using his full military powers to maintain control of the internees, and second, the incident reflects the united efforts of a camp's entire internee population, despite internal disagreements, to resist treatment it saw as unlawful. We have here a Rashomon-like narrative related from three perspectives: those of the Issei internees, the camp commander, and the outside world represented by the Spanish protecting power and the War Department.

On June 18, 1942, a group of Issei internees, mostly from Hawaii and Alaska, arrived at the Lordsburg Internment Camp from Fort Sam Houston, Texas. The army formed them into the Tenth Company, Third Battalion, and ordered them to elect a leader. Sotaro Kawabe, from Alaska, was duly chosen as mayor by the internees. The next day, the army ordered the group to work both inside and outside the enclosing fence on heavy-labor projects—transferring live ammunition, helping to construct a nearby army airport, and cleaning the horse stables, mess hall, and dance hall.[46] The military made no provisions to pay for this work. In addition, the afternoon temperatures surpassed 100 degrees, making for an extremely uncomfortable work environment.

On June 20, another group of 140 internees arrived from the camp at Santa Fe, New Mexico. The army organized them into the Ninth Company, Third Battalion, and the internees elected Yaimichi Sugimachi as their representative. When the army ordered this group to work on projects outside the fence, they objected, saying that the order was an improper and unacceptable use of their labor. The Ninth and Tenth Company mayors then submitted a joint letter of protest to the Lordsburg camp commander, Lieutenant Colonel Lundy. (This same officer was still in charge of the Lordsburg camp during the July murders of Issei internees Isomura and Kobata, which were described above.)

Lundy rejected the letter and refused to meet with the two mayors. Undaunted, Kawabe and Sugimachi sent a second protest letter the next day. The letters made no specific reference to the articles of the Geneva Convention, and it is quite possible that the Issei internees did not have a copy of the articles in hand.

Regardless of what the internees knew or did not know about the Geneva Convention, Lundy should have been aware of its existence and prescribed application. As early as April 23, 1942, the army issued instructions to its camp commanders governing the treatment of civilian internees and requiring compliance with the Geneva Convention. The regulations divided civilian-internee and prisoner-of-war labor into Class I and II categories. Class I labor, which the army could require without pay, consisted of labor necessary for the repair and upkeep of the basic camp and for the internees' health and welfare. Such tasks included work in the kitchen, hospital, tailor shop, bank, and so on. Class II labor covered all other work and was to be done on either a paid or voluntary basis. Examples of unacceptable labor were direct assistance to military projects and operations and working as servants. Since the camp commander refused to meet with the internees, they asked that a telegram be sent to the Spanish consulate in New Orleans requesting an investigation.[47]

On June 26, the arrival of 177 Japanese internees—86 from Missoula, and 91 from a temporary camp at El Paso, Texas—changed the situation. The army organized the newcomers into the Eleventh Company, Third Battalion, and Genji Mihara of Seattle was elected as mayor. The three mayors—Kawabe, Mihara, and Sugimachi—requested a meeting with Lundy and presented him with a copy of the Geneva Convention, which Mihara had brought from the Missoula Internment

Camp. The mayors asked that the army treat the internees according to the articles of the convention, saying that they were most concerned with the order to work on military projects, which they believed constituted a violation of Article 31.

They also objected to three other specific violations of the convention. First, many internees were elderly, averaging sixty years of age, and were ill prepared for manual labor and the extremely hot climate; second, the army did not furnish work clothes or shoes; and, third, the internees were served an insufficient quantity of food.[48] According to the internees, Lundy refused to honor the articles of the Geneva Convention but gave them no reason for his action. If this account is true, then the earlier work orders by Lundy, which the internees found objectionable, and his subsequent behavior might reflect a deliberate violation of the internationally recognized rules of conduct.

The three mayors countered by saying that they would determine whether to send internees to work on projects ordered by the military, and on June 29, they met with Lundy to discuss the type of work he wanted the internees to perform. Lundy would not discuss the situation, took their questions as tantamount to a refusal to work, and arrested the three mayors. Kawabe, Mihara, and Sugimachi were placed in an empty barrack and were thus separated from the other internees. Lundy also closed the internee canteen and recalled all unused canteen coupons that were used to buy personal items.

On June 30, the camp commander called an 8:00 A.M. meeting of the Ninth, Tenth, and Eleventh Companies' internees. Without receiving any explanation about the fate of their mayors, the internees were instructed by Lundy's spokesman to elect three new mayors. The internees voted instead to reelect their missing mayors.

In the ensuing discussion about what constituted appropriate internee work under the Geneva Convention, it soon became apparent that there were differing opinions among the internees. Members of the Eleventh Company thought that any labor was a violation of the convention and pointed out that the army had not required them to work while they were at the El Paso camp. The Tenth Company agreed in principle with the Eleventh Company's position but expressed willingness to voluntarily police and maintain the area within the internee enclosure. However, they saw the area from the front gate to the military offices as outside the camp and not an acceptable site for voluntary internee labor. They then called for an immediate work strike.[49] The Ninth Company felt that appropriate types of voluntary labor were essentially a form of exercise and voted to accept some work orders from the military. Aside from these differences, the internees agreed to demand the release of their mayors and the reopening of the canteen and to ask that the Spanish consul visit Lordsburg to hear their complaints.[50]

Lieutenant Colonel Lundy stated that the area outside the fence enclosing the Third Battalion was still within the Lordsburg camp and was therefore to be considered a work area for the internees. He insisted that the internees' refusal to obey his work order was improper and constituted grounds for disciplinary action. That night, after dinner, while the Ninth Company met to determine its next course of action, Lundy released the mayors. On his return, Mayor Sugimachi of the Ninth Company told his group that they should not accede to the work order, even if it meant they must continue to struggle with the camp commander.[51]

The internees agreed to a partial return to work in areas outside their enclosure if Lundy would send their telegram to the Spanish consul. When the military ordered the internees to work in the afternoon as well, they objected and gave as their reason the extreme afternoon temperature; they asked for work only in the mornings. Lundy interpreted this objection as a failure to obey his orders and, on July 2, ordered all the internees into barracks arrest. He placed armed guards on patrol duty within the grounds and allowed the internees to leave the barracks only to walk to the mess hall or the latrine. In the latter case, the guards permitted only one person to leave at a time and limited occupancy to four persons.[52]

Hoping that the telegram to the Spanish consul would result in the swift arrival of an investigator, some internees decided to work outside the compound as long as the work was done in the mornings. From July 2 to 13, 75 to 130 internees assembled for work outside the fenced areas. On July 11, the internees gave Lundy another telegram for the Spanish consulate, reiterating their request for assistance. One day later, the internees asked Lundy to rescind his barracks confinement order; he replied that he would do so only if they obeyed his work orders.

The situation deteriorated on July 13, when Second Lieutenant Ervin Mitchell ordered that seventy-two internees be made available for the afternoon work detail. The internees refused to comply, although the mayors did send several men to the cabbage fields to harvest vegetables for their meal. In an effort to force the internees back to work, Lundy instituted additional penalties on July 13: the barracks confinement continued, with all doors kept closed day and night; all lights were to be turned off after 8:00 P.M.; the canteen remained closed; the use of canteen coupons was discontinued; all radios had to be surrendered; and all mail service was halted. Furthermore, Lundy forbade the use of electric fans and stopped the delivery of drinking water to the barracks. This last action created an especially excruciating situation for the internees, as the temperature quickly rose to 70 degrees in the morning, peaked at more than 100 in the afternoon, and stayed near 90 until 7:00 P.M.[53]

Lundy rearrested mayors Kawabe, Mihara, and Sugimachi along with the chief secretary of the Third Battalion, confining and isolating them once again in an unused barrack. Although Lundy later released the chief secretary, the mayors were kept in isolation. Mayor Mihara recalled that the guards posted to watch them spent their time inflicting verbal abuse. Lundy prohibited any communication between the mayors and the rest of the camp population, so the three mayors kept in contact by slipping messages under the mess-hall trays that were brought to them.[54]

On July 17, the internees gave Lundy a third telegram to be sent to the Spanish

consulate: "WE WIRED TO YOU TWICE URGENT STOP CONDITIONS GET-
TING SERIOUS SINCE THEN STOP ALL JAPANESE INTERNEES CONfiNED
IN BARRACKS UNDER SPECIAL GUARD WE REQUEST TO SEND YOUR
REPRESENTATIVE AT ONCE PLEASE ANSWER."[55] Army policy was to route all
internee telegrams through the Alien Division of the provost marshal general's
office, which then sent a copy to the State Department before forwarding it to the
intended recipient. When the internees' telegram came to the provost marshal general's attention, Lundy was ordered to explain the situation. He replied that the internees refused to work in the afternoon and that they considered labor outside the
compound voluntary, which required the army to provide financial compensation
for the work it mandated in that area. He went on to say that since July 13, the internees had refused to perform any work, and necessary disciplinary actions had
therefore been taken. Lundy also falsely stated that the internees' barracks confinement was relieved by two hours of daily outside exercise.

On July 21, at 10:00 A.M., Lundy suddenly provided the internees with copies
of the Geneva Convention translated into Japanese.[56] The lieutenant in charge of
the Ninth Company came to each barrack and asked each group: "Do you understand the reasons for the work you have engaged in up to now?" and "Will you
work eight hours per day from today?" The internees interpreted these two questions as soliciting a promise to work and refused to answer in the affirmative.[57]

On July 22, Lundy restored a few curtailed rights—the military delivered personal letters and lifted the confinement to barracks so that anyone could go outside
the building between 1:00 and 3:00 P.M. One internee interpreted these concilia-
tory gestures as a consequence of the rights specified in the Geneva Convention—
Lundy could not ignore the law.[58]

The next day, the lieutenant reappeared and asked each internee whether he approved of the Geneva Convention. He next asked whether the internees would be
willing to return to work under the convention articles when necessary. He told
them that Japan had also signed the Geneva Convention, which made the internees feel they had little choice but to accede to the army's orders. After much
discussion, the Ninth and Eleventh Company internees agreed to return to work,
although the Ninth Company spokesperson stipulated that they would continue
to negotiate the amount of time to be spent on labor.[59]

The Tenth Company internees maintained their position that the military had
violated various articles of the Geneva Convention, and they refused to respond
positively to the lieutenant's inquiry. They signed a statement saying that they were
unable to agree on a particular interpretation of the various articles. They again
requested that the camp commander send a telegram to the Spanish consul asking
him to come and adjudicate the situation. On July 24, Ninth Company internees
discussed both the option of siding with the Tenth Company by not reporting for
work in the afternoon and the alternative strategy of returning to work but using
it as leverage to negotiate their release from barracks arrest. They decided on the

latter strategy, apparently because they had already agreed to return to work in the first place. To do otherwise, some argued, would be to dishonor their promise—or, in effect, to "lose face."[60] The internees were under no illusions, however, about Lundy's opinion of them. One internee likened their situation to that of "unwanted mutts" that are either cast aside or kept in cages.[61]

Lundy interpreted the Tenth Company's position as an open refusal and gave them fifteen minutes to change their minds. The penalty for refusing this order, he said, was a continuation of the barracks confinement and additional penalties. The army called on two internees to respond—Shingo Abe, former president of the Los Angeles Japanese Association, and Reverend Yoshiaki Fukuda of the Konko-kyo church in San Francisco. According to Fukuda, two soldiers pointed unsheathed bayonets at his and Abe's stomachs.[62] However, the two men refused to back down, repeating their belief that the Geneva Convention specifically proscribed Lundy's order. Lundy declared the company's action unlawful and placed them all, except for the very old and infirm, under barracks arrest. Within the hour, the Tenth Company was transferred to a nearby vacant barrack and kept in isolation.[63]

Although the Ninth and Eleventh Companies had been released from barracks arrest, they remained concerned about their compatriots in the Tenth Company. On that same day, they discussed ways of showing solidarity with the Tenth Company internees and raised two main issues: first, whether everyone should or should not work in the afternoon, and, second, what would be the best strategy for negotiating their friends' earliest release. The internees could not resolve these issues, and camp conditions remained unchanged.

It was during this troubled time, in the early hours of July 27, that Isomura and Kobata arrived in Lordsburg and met their untimely deaths, as described in an earlier section of this chapter. And on this same day, Lundy gave the internees a letter and a telegram from the Spanish consul with a July 5 postmark.[64] Both correspondences said that the Spanish consul in New Orleans would soon be in contact with them. The internees decided to write individual statements for delivery to the consul or his agent when he arrived. They discussed the apparent contravention of the Geneva Convention regarding the speedy delivery of personal mail.

The next day, without explanation, Lundy informed the internees that he would abide by the Geneva Convention and released the Tenth Company from barracks confinement. Even with this action, however, the conflict did not subside. Lundy continued to issue other orders that the internees believed to be illegal or unacceptable according to the convention, but these disputes did not create as much conflict as the incident that had begun in mid-June.

Finally, on August 9 or 10, the Spanish consul and two representatives from the State Department arrived to investigate the protests.[65] After talking with the internees, the State Department spokesmen promised that they would report back on the interpretation of various articles of the convention. The Spanish consul asked the internees to accept the work orders of the military unless they had health problems. The internees agreed to this request and ended their work strike. Lundy released the three imprisoned mayors on August 15—they had been in isolation for more than a month.[66]

On August 26, 1942, the Spanish embassy in Washington, D.C., sent a copy of the internees' request for redress of grievances under the Geneva Convention to the State Department. The War Department's Alien Division chief in the provost marshal general's office sent Lundy a memorandum on September 18 regarding the camp commander's actions during the month of July. The army stated that the difference between Class I and Class II labor lay in whether or not the work benefited the internees, not where the work occurred. The army approved certain work outside the fence—for example, unloading quartermaster's supplies in town—if it was connected to the camp or the internees. The army concluded that the internees were not justified in refusing to work during certain hours of the day. As for Lundy's unwillingness to meet with the internees' mayors, the army said that such interviews "should be granted when the matter involved is in dispute or considered to be of importance." Lundy was told that regardless of whether the internees were under disciplinary punishment, they "should be allowed to read and write, as well as to send and receive letters, as provided for by Article 57 of the Geneva Convention."[67]

In regard to his forcing internees to clean army mess halls, latrines, and dance halls, Lundy admitted on October 10 that he required internees to work on projects that were seemingly unconnected to themselves but justified his actions by saying that such work was related to internee matters: "Japanese are required to dig post holes for the cemetery in which many of them will ultimately be buried; Japanese are required to police administration buildings and latrines; Japanese are required to police the Recreation Hall; Japanese are sent to Lordsburg, under adequate guard and suffering no indignities to load and unload their own supplies; Japanese are required to level grounds, dig necessary ditches for new utilities installations, etc."[68] Perhaps the internees would have objected further if they had known that they were going to benefit from the cemetery post holes they were digging.

As for their confinement to barracks, Lundy admitted that as part of the disciplinary punishment, the "internees were confined to barracks during the daylight hours, with free access to latrines." He implied by omission that the internees were free to move about the camp at night, although they were confined at that time as well. And he disagreed with the complaints about the mail service, saying: "Mails were as usual except that packages were held up."[69]

After receiving Lundy's response, the War Department replied to the State Department about the correspondence it had received from the Spanish consulate. Colonel Bryan reiterated the army's position that some labor, although performed outside the internee compound, was acceptable without individual or collective pay if it was for the maintenance or benefit of the internees. The army did admit that the cleaning of mess halls, dance halls, and latrines was not justified. This letter, however, did not specifically address items raised by the internees, for example, being required to work in the afternoon heat, the camp commander's obligation to meet with the mayors when requested, or the internees' right to send and receive mail.[70]

The Lordsburg internees received a report from the Spanish consul on December 5. He informed them that the State Department had agreed with many of their allegations, especially regarding the proper employment of their labor. A crucial portion of the report stated that internees should work only on projects from which they would receive benefits, such as cleaning their barracks and growing their own vegetables. Internees would not have to do work they thought of as odious and unlawful—cleaning the army's mess halls, latrines, and noncommissioned officers' or officers' clubs.[71] It had taken six months to resolve this particular point of major conflict.

CONTINUING CONFLICT AT LORDSBURG

Even with the safeguards provided by the Geneva Convention, life was not idyllic. The internees continued to encounter what they considered to be abusive and unacceptable conditions. One incident, for example, shows the government's inability to distinguish between internee and military POW populations. On November 3, 1942, the FBI reported that the Japanese internees within the Lordsburg camp had raised a Japanese flag to celebrate a national holiday: "The [Army] Officer of the Day or someone dispatched by him went into the camp to remove the flag and was chased out by the Japanese. Special guards were then called and after a considerable time they were successful in getting the flag lowered."[72] The FBI noted that an informant reported this incident along with the earlier internee strikes and predicted, "Sooner or later, there is expected to be a riot or an attempted escape."[73]

The FBI memorandum incorrectly concluded that the earlier internee strike and the flag incident were the acts of the same Issei group. According to army records, the Issei did not raise the Japanese flag. The army had placed fifty captured Japanese sailors who were military prisoners of war in a nearby compound, and "on the morning of November 3, 1942, a group of Japanese Naval prisoners of war in Compound 2, Lordsburg Internment camp, displayed a Japanese flag on their clothesline pole near the back-stop of the baseball field in the rear of the compound. First Lieutenant Clarence E. Jack, Officer of the Day, immediately went into the compound to remove the flag and as he approached, the Japanese took the flag down and ran inside the barracks building."[74] The War Department discovered its error and, within a day or two, transferred the military POWs out of Lordsburg.[75] The FBI's and the Lordsburg officer's failure to differentiate the resident civilians from Japanese military prisoners may have reinforced the authorities' prior suspicions about the Issei. There is nothing in the file to indicate that the FBI ever corrected its initial conclusion or was even aware of the misapprehension. The broad brush of suspicion tarred the Issei internees, despite their innocence.

Issei internees also had reason to fear attacks from other army prisoners held at

Lordsburg, a circumstance that heightened their stress. For unknown reasons, Lundy placed army soldiers convicted of various offenses in the compound area occupied by the Issei internees. Although the military convicts were assigned a separate barrack, the internees protested their presence in the same area as a violation of Article 9 of the Geneva Convention, but nothing happened to change the situation. On Thanksgiving 1942, a U.S. Army prisoner got drunk and stabbed Dr. Uyehara, an Issei internee.[76] A few days after this incident, Lundy moved the convicts out of the area. The assailant received a general court-martial (the outcome is unknown). The army also gave Lundy, who had been promoted to colonel just three days before the stabbing, a written reprimand for his handling of the episode.

On December 17, 1942, the army relieved Lundy of the Lordsburg command and transferred him. The transfer, however, apparently was not simply for actions related to the Japanese internees. Questions had arisen about irregularities concerning profits from the canteen and the improper use by Lundy's officers of musical equipment that had been donated to the Japanese internees by the International Red Cross. After an investigation, Lundy was transferred to Fort Sam Houston, Texas, and the army, rather than initiating disciplinary action, recommended his retirement.[77]

Even after Lundy's departure, his legacy—the atmosphere of fear and intimidation—haunted the internees. They knew they could be threatened with bodily harm even under the most normal circumstances. For example, Daisho Tana reported that on February 17, 1943, an army captain at Lordsburg drew and fired his pistol to intimidate the internees:

> Today, whether because of the [hot] weather or not, . . . some people . . . started to slow down in their work in repairing the road. Their guard probably misunderstood their actions and reported to his superiors that, "The Japanese are on a sit-down strike." His Captain came out on his motorcycle and asked the internees, "Who is the leader?" in a very nervous tone. He then pulled out his pistol saying, "If you don't work, then this will happen," and he fired a shot toward the ground. The internees, who did not have any intention of going on strike didn't know what was happening. After the Captain fired his pistol, some internees started to laugh while others were very surprised. And all of a sudden the guards pointed their rifles toward the laughing Japanese and the situation became suddenly very tense. And the Captain probably thought that if he left the bullet, it might be used as evidence against him, so he tried to look for it. He couldn't find the bullet and he went away.[78]

These internees were kept on the roadwork detail until 4:00 P.M. but were able surreptitiously to look for and find the expired bullet before returning to the camp. Their representative informed the camp commander of the incident and asked for the guard duty roster. The commander rejected the request, after which the internees reported the incident to the Spanish consul. Nothing more seems to have occurred in connection with this incident.

Lordsburg internees also documented other occasions of army personnel drawing weapons and firing at them. On June 4, 1943, two internees were walking along the inner compound fence when they suddenly heard a rifle shot and saw the dirt kick up near them. The next day, another internee was exercising as usual by hitting a golf ball. One landed just outside the fence, and as he tried to retrieve it with a long stick, the watchtower guard raised his rifle and fired at him. Tana reports that the internee was very surprised, since he and others frequently hit their golf balls out of the compound and routinely used the stick to retrieve them. The internee spokesman talked with the camp commander about both incidents and was told that the guards regarded anyone who came within twelve feet of the fence as a would-be escapee. The internees protested that they had never been told of this rule and that the guards had not given any warning before firing their weapons.[79]

The important point here is the mentality of the Lordsburg soldiers and its effects on the internees. As in most authoritarian institutions, internees quickly tried to learn the best method of surviving while incurring minimal injury to themselves. Those in the imprisonment organization understood this point; for example, an INS official at Santa Fe, New Mexico, commented on the difference in the way the Japanese internees behaved after they returned from army control in 1943:

> Last year [1942] the attitude of the [Japanese] detainees toward the administration of the camp was as though they were on good behavior and under constant observation. Since their internment by the Army this attitude has changed appreciably, partly, of course because of their continual internment, but also, I believe, because of the rigid system designed for prisoners of war, which the Army imposed on civilians.[80]

The internees were the same; their incarcerators were different. The internees' fears are easy to understand, since they did not know who would be inflicting their next punishment.

CONFLICT AT SANTA FE

Chapter 6 introduced the INS internment camp at Santa Fe, New Mexico, along with its internee populations. The conflict that arose at this Justice Department camp differed from the Lordsburg troubles in several ways. Initially, the dispute did not involve the entire camp population. It began with an existing antagonism between some Kibei and Nisei inmates and the WRA officials at the Tule Lake Segregation Camp in California; this hostility was brought to the INS camp when the Tule Lake renunciants were transported to Santa Fe. The new group of former WRA inmates, now INS internees, was thought to be more dangerous than the usual Issei internee and was treated accordingly. The crisis that broke out at Santa Fe disrupted the lives of all internees and inmates at the camp; it was so serious that the INS had to use extraordinary measures to bring it under control.

Between December 29, 1944, and July 1945, the project director of the segregation camp at Tule Lake sent to Santa Fe 866 Nisei (some of whom were Kibei) identified as renunciants along with 313 Issei.[81] The WRA and Justice Department officials identified the Nisei as members of Hokoku Seinen-dan—a so-called dissident organization that had led the resistance movement at the WRA segregation center. Upon their arrival at Santa Fe, some of the members displayed what the INS felt was an uncooperative, anti-administration attitude. The Justice Department singled out three new inmates—two Kibei, Tsutomu Higashi and Jitsushige Tsuha, and one Issei, Zenshiro Tachibana—and charged them with disobeying Santa Fe camp orders. In Higashi's case, the alleged incident involved his insolence to the head nurse at a hospital and to an INS officer-in-charge. In February 1945, the INS quickly sentenced all three men to serve twenty days in a separate detention cell. After spending ten days there, the camp authorities removed Higashi and offered him a suspended sentence if he promised to obey the camp rules. Higashi refused, saying that he had no intention of behaving in accord with regulations, and the INS returned him to the detention cell. Hearing of this, the officer in charge recommended Higashi's removal to the high-security Justice Department camp established at Fort Stanton, New Mexico, a camp discussed briefly in chapter 6. The INS assistant commissioner for alien control, W. F. Kelly, agreed with the recommendation on March 8.[82]

Meanwhile, a new contingent of WRA segregation camp inmates entering the INS camp had brought with them sweatshirts decorated with a rising-sun emblem. The camp administrators told them on March 7 that they would have to relinquish the shirts or be subject to disciplinary action. Although these former WRA inmates had not agreed to take a united stand, one of them told the administration, "We are going to defy you."[83] The INS brought in thirty additional Border Patrol guards on March 9; the next morning, they searched the internees' barracks and seized a dozen or so shirts.

After serving their twenty-day sentences, Higashi and the two other internees were released on March 12, and preparations were made for their removal to Fort Stanton. The administration put all camp guards on alert, armed them with submachine guns and riot shotguns, and posted fifteen additional Border Patrol guards. After learning of the planned removal of these three men, 250 internees gathered at the front gate to await their departure. When one internee asked permission for himself and another to accompany the three inmates to their new destination, the officer of the guard refused and ordered the internees to disperse. When the internees refused to comply with the order, which was repeated five times, the officer ordered the guards to fire tear-gas grenades. Sixteen guards carrying billy clubs and armed with tear-gas grenades charged into the milling internees and started to beat them. The internees fled, but four were left seriously injured and required hospitalization. The INS isolated 350 internees, mostly Nisei from the segregation camp, and placed them in a separate fenced enclosure.

One Issei internee from Hawaii, Yasutaro Soga, who had not been at the WRA segregation camp, offered, in Japanese, a vivid eyewitness account of the incident:

In 1945, March 12, the clash between the [WRA] segregation camp *bozu* [shaved-heads] and the military police officers reached its climax, and it finally ended with a sorry incident. Early that morning, Langston [phonetic], chief of the *renraku* [liaison office], escorted by several guards, inspected various buildings excluding the barracks and crafts room. As we were returning from our breakfast, from the mess hall, going to "downtown area," we encountered Tsuha and Tachibana, who were surrounded by guards and being escorted with their baggage to the uptown area. Many Tule Lake people were following them. There didn't seem to be any sign of violence, but when the internee group approached the "uptown area," they were met with dozens of guards who had been waiting for them. Suddenly, the guards threw tear-gas grenades, but the wind blew [the gas] back towards the guards, so the Tule Lake youths shouted for joy. This was the beginning of the incident. And the guards, carrying nightsticks, chased the *bozu* group and tried to catch them by attacking them from both sides with other guards stationed near the entrance to the downtown area. The lower-area guards also threw tear-gas grenades, and all the guards started to hit the internees with sticks. Since the *bozu* group did not have any weapons to defend themselves, they fell down, one after another. Gontaro Ono, Akira Osuji, Isamu Uchida, Motoi Hirashina all suffered head injuries, and much blood was shed. The guards put these four into a truck and sent them to the hospital area, and I saw this kind of cruelty. And this incident took place within a second.

I heard that the military police expected that something would happen on this day. . . . [After the beatings,] all activities inside the internee fence were prohibited and all work was stopped except inside the mess halls, hospital, and stores. In the afternoon, only emergency meetings of the barracks chairmen were allowed; we decided to select seven committees to help improve this situation. An INS officer informed us that they would separate the Tule Lake people, about 300 and some dozens more, from the other internees. The barracks chairpersons negotiated with the camp office to rescind that order.

The next morning, March 13, we were surprised to find military police surrounding barracks numbers 63 to 69, seven barracks nearest the baseball fields, while Mexican laborers were used to construct a double iron fence around them. The next morning, the 14th, in this segregated area, about 300 from Tule Lake, plus some dozens more, were now brought here and confined to this area, and those who were not from Tule Lake would be taken out and placed into other barracks. The military police also are watching the mess halls as well. . . . And after, the Tule Lake internees were confined in that isolated area, surrounded by a double iron fence, for a two-week period.[84]

This was a show of brute force—guards inside the compound swinging clubs and others standing outside the fence holding submachine guns to intimidate the internees. The message was clear: every aspect of the internees' behavior was subject to the dictates of the INS and the U.S. Army. These agencies demonstrated their power to interpret any rules governing the internees and made clear their willingness to wield it. The use of this power might and did result in separation, isolation, physical harm, or even death.

SEPARATION FROM WIVES AND FAMILIES

There is little doubt that married internees with families faced difficulties, anxieties, and fears not experienced by single men. Former heads of households, they languished in makeshift prisons after their arrests, separated from wives, children, and other relatives. Those family members, in turn, lost an important source of support. When the men learned that the army had ordered their families into WCCA assembly centers, their anxieties were compounded.

Wives and children suffered as much as did husbands and fathers. Both groups were powerless to affect their situations, although they appealed to government officials for help. In late 1942, for example, internees at Santa Fe, New Mexico, besieged a visiting INS official for assistance. Although he did not have the authority to solve their problems, he promised to pass on their petitions to higher authorities:

> Some twenty-five Japanese, young and old, were lined up in front of me. . . . I listened to each of their stories. Nearly all of them revolved around the tribulations of families who had been cruelly separated by the petitioners' internment. . . . One man was too filled with emotion to talk. He wept as he showed me a copy of a letter his wife had written to the Attorney General: "My husband is still detained. I am not in good health and have two children, 8 and 10 to look after. My sisters are in different [WRA-run] camps and my brother is in the American Army. I do not know why my husband is detained there, but could you please tell me if it is possible for him to be with us?"[85]

The INS official found that many of these heads of families were fishermen whom the INS had arrested at the outbreak of the war because their boats were equipped with radios. He wrote, "A paranoiac United States Attorney in California was able to convince the Attorney General's office that the fishermen could conceivably communicate with and assist any Japanese submarine which might be operating in those waters. On the basis of such flimsy conjecture, 545 Japanese fishermen were ordered interned as potentially dangerous to the national security."[86] Later, the INS transferred these fishermen to WRA-run camps or to the INS camp at Crystal City, Texas, where their families could join them.

Another petitioner, writing to the INS, exemplifies the lonely situation:

My wife, who is ill and under a doctor's care in the Hunt [Minidoka] relocation center, has patiently been waiting for my return for over two long years, forlorn and de-
spaired. She is physically weak and mentally unstable on account of our prolonged
and forced separation. She is so strained and nervous that she cannot write me
often. During the last 12 months I received only two letters from her. This condition
of hers always worries me very much about her, especially in these winter months
when flu epidemic is rampant. As she is alone, she must do everything herself in
these cold days. . . . I don't like her to be tortured like this on account of my being
detained here. . . . As we never lived apart in our married life for 23 years before my
apprehension, it is simply unbearable to have to live like this so long. . . . Eight
months have already elapsed since the filing of my petition to you but as there seems
to be little hope of getting a rehearing here shortly, I respectfully implore you to give
me and my poor, sick wife your compassion and repeat your sympathetic recommendation to Ennis for special permission to let me join my wife soon.[87]

Another year of separation went by before the INS allowed the couple to meet.

Shizuyo Yasui's story relates the determination and efforts of one wife to maintain contact with her husband. After her release from the WRA camp at Minidoka,
Idaho, she settled in Denver and learned that she could visit her husband who was
then held at the INS camp at Santa Fe, New Mexico. The trip, however, required
taking a late-afternoon bus from Denver, riding all night, and finally arriving in
Santa Fe the next morning. She was allowed to see her husband in the visitors area.
She would then return to her children in Denver. Although Mrs. Yasui was in frail
physical condition and could barely speak English, she made this arduous trip
every month for three years.[88]

An indefinite sentence, added to separation from loved ones who were also behind barbed wire, could grievously change a person. A Nisei, James Akutsu, tells of
the tragic circumstances of going to greet his father who was recently released
from an INS camp:

News came that my father was sent to the maximum-security prisoner of war camp
in Louisiana, and that he was very sick. This was a most trying time for my mother.
I could see it tearing her apart mentally, physically, and yet there was nothing I
could do. In the winter of 1943, we got a wire instructing someone to meet my father
at the gate by noon. On the way, an old man asked me where the Akutsus lived. I
pointed the direction for him. After waiting three hours at the gate, I returned to my
barrack. I couldn't believe my eyes. The old man whom I had directed earlier in the
day was my father. We hadn't recognized each other. Although my mother felt relieved that my father was back, it was a shock to see him in such emaciated condition. Shortly thereafter, she started to get weaker and finally succumbed to a total
physical breakdown. . . . My mother's death, a few years later, was directly attributed
to the evacuation.[89]

The interned Issei pressed continually for "rehearings," hoping that they would be released from the INS camps to join their wives, families, and friends. More than a year after these Issei were interned, in February 1943, the Justice Department's Alien Enemy Control Unit detailed a four-person board, an assistant attorney general, and a stenographer to Lordsburg to rehear eighty-five cases from Southern California and twenty-two from Washington State.[90] If the rehearings for these limited cases resulted in a recommendation for release or parole, the internee could then join his family in a WRA camp. If the judgment was for continued internment, the next step was to have his family join him under the family reunification program instituted at the internment camp at Crystal City. Next, the administration began rehearing the cases of unmarried internees who wished to join their relatives or friends in the WRA centers or who sought release to locations outside the restricted areas.[91]

CONCLUSION

The incidents offered in this chapter are not the only reported cases of physical and mental abuse in World War II internment and incarceration camps for persons of Japanese ancestry. Unless otherwise indicated, these are incidents acknowledged by U.S. governmental units.

In examining these cases, one conclusion seems inescapable. The imprisonment officials' power over their inmates and internees was overwhelming, and they were quite willing to use force to maintain control over their charges. Still, as we have seen, the internees themselves—as individuals or in groups—were willing to oppose this power and vehemently protest what they saw as their mistreatment at the hands of their captors.

It is not the case, however, that such protests were typical. Rather, the Nikkei internees and inmates showed notable restraint in their objections, often disagreeing among themselves about the appropriate behavior in times of strife and conflict. The number of known protest incidents is remarkably small. This should not necessarily be seen as a reflection of humanitarianism or benevolence on the part of the officials of the imprisonment organization. Rather, one could argue that the agencies' willingness to administer physical punishment and other punitive measures stood as a constant threat, deterring the formation of resistance movements. Given this oppressive situation, one might be surprised that these imprisoned people voiced any objections to their plight.

10

Imprisonment and Stigma

D uring and after World War II, the U.S. government imprisoned nearly 120,000 Nikkei, the majority of whom were American citizens. They were detained in imprisonment centers without being charged with the commission of crimes, deprived of legal counsel and trials, and incarcerated, in most instances, for no stated justifiable reason or specified duration. Most of the Issei who were imprisoned have died, while the Nisei are in or approaching their retirement years. The passage of time has helped to blunt the most painful memories of their personal and collective tragedies, yet the social effects of the wartime ordeal are still felt. I assert that these effects continue today in the form of the stigma of that wartime imprisonment.

DEVELOPMENT AND STRUCTURE OF THE IMPRISONMENT PROCESS

The central purpose of this study is to disclose the process by which U.S. authorities were able to imprison almost the entire group of West Coast and Alaska Nikkei plus many from Latin American countries and individuals from the territory of Hawaii. The reasons for the wartime imprisonment have not been examined here. Various studies have dealt with this issue and offer six basic causes. First, the Western Defense Command (WDC) and its apologists have declared throughout the years that military necessity was the only reason.[1] Two other theories propounded in the late 1940s placed responsibility on pressure groups and politicians. Carey McWilliams, for example, states the case for the pressure group theory: "That the federal government was pressured, or perhaps more accurately 'stampeded,' into the adoption of this unfortunate precedent [mass incarceration] by the noisy clamor of certain individuals, groups and organizations in the three West Coast states does not minimize the seriousness of the precedent itself."[2] The politician theory is aptly expressed by Morton Grodzins when he states that "state and local political leaders played no subsidiary role in the movement to bring about Japanese evacuation."[3]

Three other reasons are presented in the well-regarded 1982 report of the Commission on Wartime Relocation and Internment of Civilians (CWRIC).

After reviewing the events, actions, and impact of Executive Order (EO) 9066 on Japanese residents and Japanese Americans, the commission found that the justification of military necessity was not tenable. The historical causes, it maintained, that led to the creation and signing of the executive order were "race prejudice, war hysteria and a failure of political leadership."[4] Many scholars on this subject would agree on the importance of race prejudice as a cause of the mass imprisonment. This study accepts it as a fundamental factor. Certainly, another vital factor is the failure of political leadership, encompassing the actions of the executive branch of government, represented by the president, and those of the legislative area, namely the U.S. Congress.[5]

War hysteria as a base cause for imprisoning the Nikkei, however, is another matter. I would define *war hysteria* as uncontrolled actions resulting from a wartime situation and, in this specific case, as those actions directed toward Japanese nationals and American citizens *after* December 7, 1941. From that date until the signing of EO 9066 on February 19, 1942, certain military officials, media pundits, political leaders, and the public demanded that some type of action be taken against those of Japanese ancestry. The reasons for their later actions can be ascertained through government documents and private and public declarations. For example, the military shortcomings of Lieutenant General John L. DeWitt of the wdc must be understood as playing a part in his later actions, and Edward Ennis of the Justice Department's Alien Enemy Control Unit cited public relations as a paramount concern.

This study shows, however, that the main architects of the imprisonment process met, discussed, conceived, and formalized plans while they were thousands of miles from the West Coast states, long before the attack on Pearl Harbor. Moreover, they reached these decisions despite differences of opinion among agencies and officials over exactly which persons of Japanese descent ought to be examined, surveyed, and finally imprisoned. Many U.S. officials before and after December 7 did not distinguish between permanent-resident Japanese nationals, the Issei, and their citizen children, the Nisei. Before the war, the designers of the internment put the Nisei in the same category as their parents—that of suspect Americans. Thus, the forces leading to the mass imprisonment were not born after December 7 but, I contend, resulted from rational planning conducted in prewar meetings and discussions. The plans targeted potential enemy aliens, a grouping that included not only Japanese nationals but also, as we have seen, persons of German and Italian ancestry along with Communist, Fascist, and Nazi supporters. In addition to potential enemy nationals, some American citizens were targeted as well.

It was during this time that a nascent imprisonment organization arose. Various government agencies collectively constituted a loosely structured organizational network, in essence, a meta-organization. A de facto rather than formal organization, it had as its chief purpose the identification, imprisonment, and subsequent control of its prisoner population. The main elements of this imprisonment organization during the prewar period were the Justice, Navy, State, and War Departments. Later, in 1942, the War Relocation Authority was included as well. These agencies, plus others that played less obvious roles, differed in the nature of their involvement and the length of time devoted to the imprisonment process. Most of the imprisonment organization's activities transpired in the executive branch and under the authority of the chief executive, President Franklin D. Roosevelt, but Congress and the judicial branches of government played important parts in sustaining and sanctioning the process.

Units of the imprisonment organization both cooperated and competed with one another. A significant example of cooperation was the frequent exchange of internees and inmates among the many agencies under the president. Yet, since the organization had no single unified command, it was rife with internal competition, lack of coordination, and ad hoc decision making. Because the Nikkei were placed in different types of imprisonment centers, with varying degrees of coordination of authority, numerous anomalous situations arose. And unforeseen events sometimes upset the prewar plans—for example, the army decided to return its civilian internees to the Justice Department so that it could deal with the increasing numbers of military prisoners of war arriving in the United States.

In order to make this complex imprisonment process understandable, this study utilizes a two-part structure. The first focuses on the prewar preparations for internment that resulted in arrests on December 7, 1941, and for months afterward. The attack on Pearl Harbor triggered the prewar plans; even as Japanese warplanes were strafing their targets, members of the imprisonment organization began to arrest people, many of whom were named on previously prepared lists, and intern them in already existing detention centers. This first phase of the imprisonment process, the internment phase, was conducted under the authority of the Alien Enemies Act. The second part of our study focuses on events after the United States entered the war—the incarceration phase, during which the remaining Nikkei population was excluded en masse from designated areas under EO 9066. Since the prewar discussions had failed to specify a mechanism by which to incarcerate American citizens who had not committed any crime or engaged in any untoward act against their country, this executive order took care of the rest of the Japanese American population much as the Alien Enemies Act provided the means of handling the Issei, various Nisei, and other aliens.

This two-part structure has enabled us to differentiate the responsible agencies, authorities, types of prisoners, and regulations; in addition, it shows how the lines between the two segments of the imprisonment process blurred and often disappeared entirely during the wartime period. My assertion here is that internment under the Alien Enemies Act flowed smoothly into incarceration authorized under EO 9066.

The incarceration phase quickly followed the internment stage. Although no single plan to arrest the remaining Nikkei had been formed before the war, prior memorandums and discussions among various government agencies revolved around doing just that. We saw that from the 1920s, American citizens of Japanese ancestry were included in any plans for Issei internment. President Roosevelt and various army and navy officers on the West Coast, for example, categorized the entire ethnoracial population as one group but were much more discriminating in their plans for Americans of German and Italian ancestry.

As a case in point, consider the racial attitudes of Lieutenant General DeWitt, commanding general of the WDC:

> The Japanese race is an enemy race and while many second and third generation Japanese born on United States soil, possessed of United States citizenship, have become "Americanized," the racial strains are undiluted. . . . It, therefore, follows that along the vital Pacific Coast over 112,000 potential enemies, of Japanese extraction, are at large today. There are indications that these are organized and ready for concerted action at a favorable opportunity. The very fact that no sabotage has taken place to date is a disturbing and confirming indication that such action will be taken.[6]

DeWitt's remarks, which betray a particular racial hostility, show that accusation alone was enough to confirm dangerousness. All people of Japanese descent—citizen or not—were presumed dangerous from the outset. Although there was no prewar plan to imprison all Nisei, this and other similarly sweeping racial generalizations indicate a predisposition to do so.

President Roosevelt, key military and government officials, and imprisonment agencies did consider certain individuals of German ancestry potentially dangerous. As a group, however, most German and Italian nationals were not viewed with such alarm. Indeed, as we have seen, by Columbus Day 1942, Italian nationals were removed from the category of enemy aliens. Certain Italian aliens were initially arrested but soon released—the opera star Enzio Pinza and the father of baseball great Joe DiMaggio are two noted examples. And there was little sentiment, public or private, official or otherwise, in favor of incarcerating many American citizens of German or Italian ancestry.

Anyone of Japanese ancestry who lived in the West Coast states or the territory of Hawaii was another matter. During and after the arrest of enemy aliens, DeWitt and other military officers argued for the imprisonment of all Nikkei on the West Coast. Officials such as Secretary of the Navy William Franklin Knox wanted to do the same in Hawaii. But the army needed laborers in the islands, and instead of a mass incarceration, individual arrests took place. This study questions the basis on which even these few Hawaii inmates were taken. During the period of Issei internment, the Justice Department refused to accept citizens from Hawaii, although it did take predesignated and nondesignated Nisei on the West Coast.

The Justice Department objected on constitutional grounds to a mass exclusion of the remaining Nikkei population, most of whom were citizens. Nevertheless, the army was able to finesse the Justice Department's concerns by arguing for mass exclusion as a military necessity. From the days before World War II, then, this concern included Japanese nationals and their citizen children alike. My assertion is that the authorities were worried about the entire ethnoracial group. Other foreign enemy nationals were subjected to a selective procedure, not a wholesale incarceration process.

The two most active imprisonment agencies, the Justice and War Departments, substantially agreed on the treatment of German and Italian aliens and their citizen children. They disagreed, however, on how to handle the Nikkei population. Citizenship was the crucial factor in the imprisonment process. But ultimately, all three branches of government worked together to incarcerate the citizen Nisei: President Roosevelt signed EO 9066; Congress passed Public Law 503, which contained the punishment provision; and the Supreme Court later approved the forced removal as a military necessity.

The focus of the imprisonment process then shifted to keeping the internee and inmate populations docile and manageable. Each agency created its own centers and camps with separate rules and enforcement procedures. When inmate tensions rose and protests broke out, isolated high-security containment centers were created for the "troublemakers." WRA center directors could remove inmates of their choice by sending them to isolation camps, if they were citizens, or the Justice Department internment camp, if they were aliens. The rest of the WRA inmates learned the lesson, and there were few further disruptions in the peace and harmony of the ten WRA incarceration camps.

The imprisonment organization next set about obtaining volunteers for a segregated army unit and releasing inmates to fill labor shortages on farms, in the Midwest, and on the East Coast. The army and the WRA then instituted a process, utilizing what became known as the Loyalty Questionnaire, for separating inmates whom they believed to be loyal from other dangerous supposedly disloyal individuals in the WRA camps. After forcing all adults to answer the questionnaire, the WRA had a self-identified group that could be segregated because of its suspect loyalty to the United States. At the high-security Tule Lake Segregation Center, inmate schisms arose, and the actions of the WRA, the army, and the Justice Department exacerbated the tense situation.

These governmental units, with the approval of Congress, completed the circle of prewar anti-Japanese sentiment. Issei immigrants to the United States, especially those who arrived in the 1900s, faced extreme prejudice and discriminatory actions on the West Coast. Unable to become naturalized citizens after the 1922 *Ozawa v. United States* decision, they were henceforth branded as aliens "ineligible for citizenship"; their children, however, did not face that barrier because they had been born citizens on U.S. soil. Enemy aliens could be legally and quickly deported, but citizens—even if the imprisonment organization branded them a threat to national security—could not be treated in the same manner.

Prior procedures were available by which U.S. citizens could renounce their citizenship, although there were no explicit instructions for doing so while citizens were in their own country. In a highly unusual move, the government created a situation that made renouncing one's citizenship within the United States a viable option. The passage and enforcement of Public Law 405, which recognized the renunciation of U.S. citizenship, enabled the imprisonment organization to transform U.S. citizens into deportable aliens. A significant number of Nisei at the fear-ridden WRA segregation camp at Tule Lake, California, signed the renunciation forms with the encouragement of, and perhaps under coercion from, officials from the army, the Justice Department, and the WRA. The deportation of citizens became the ultimate control mechanism, and homicide was the most extreme means of controlling these same prisoners. The imprisonment organization added these two elements to the earlier process by which it identified, arrested, interned or incarcerated, and finally expelled unwanted persons from the country.

THE STIGMA OF IMPRISONMENT

Up to this point, our discussion has focused on the conditions and situations faced by people of Japanese ancestry during World War II, but the tragedy of the imprisonment experience extends to its long-lasting effects. Sociopsychological trauma has affected succeeding generations of Japanese Americans in a phenomenon identified here as the *stigma of imprisonment.*

Whatever personal decisions an internee or inmate made at various turning points, friends and family members often chose different courses. This fact resulted and still results in intense sensitivity to particular aspects of the imprisonment experience. Repercussions of the many sociopsychological reactions to the experience can be seen in intrafamilial, interpersonal, and intergenerational areas of present-day life.

After the signing of EO 9066, all families on the West Coast and in the territory of Alaska, and others in Hawaii and Latin America, were either interned or incarcerated. Many households were fractured when fathers were arrested in the first FBI sweeps. Family members who wished to remain together had to gather and make plans to coordinate their movements. Numerous decisions, both large and small, demanded immediate attention—what to do with personal possessions, farm crops, real estate and other property, and even pets. Once in the camps, important as well as mundane issues continually arose, and discussions between parents and children often ended in conflict. The Loyalty Questionnaire, possible repatriation for the Issei, the Nisei response to Selective Service summonses, and the renunciation of American citizenship were significant points of contention. Other crises centered on the separation of families or a Nisei wishing to leave for educational or work opportunities. These are but a few of the myriad problems, but they show the magnitude of the situations faced by each individual and family.

These same dilemmas also created difficulties in interpersonal arenas. Whatever the family sentiments, whether unanimous or splintered, inmates did not necessarily know where their neighbors stood in regard to these issues. For years after the war, whenever former inmates met, it was important to ascertain the particular camp or camps in which they had lived. Any hint that the other person might have been at Tule Lake after it became a segregation camp, or that he or she held controversial opinions on the draft or renunciation conflicts, usually produced a serious rift in the conversation if not the relationship. Another delicate matter still unresolved today concerns those who were remembered or mistakenly identified as informers for camp authorities. For years after the camp period, Japanese Americans would occasionally bring up the names of suspected government informants, or *inu*. Such social labeling indicates that a strong tie to past events continues and intrudes on the present—to this day, these subjects remain open sores sensitive to verbal probing.

In addition to intrafamilial and interpersonal effects, the imprisonment trauma has had an impact on intergenerational relationships. It is in this complex area that we see the ongoing nature of the imprisonment experience, that is, that wartime events survive the original situations and those who participated in them. When the Sansei (third generation), Yonsei (fourth generation), and later generations who were not in the camps attempt to learn of the incarceration, they discover the Nisei's deep reluctance to speak of the period:

[Jeanne] said that the book [*Farewell to Manzanar*] was a result of her twenty-five-year-old nephew coming to her and saying, "I was born in Manzanar and I know nothing about it. Will you please tell me?" And [Jeanne] said, "Why didn't you talk to your parents?" And he replied, "They won't talk about it." And she said, "I looked at him and opened my mouth and nothing came out."[7]

David Takami, a Sansei, said: "My mother was in a camp, but she didn't talk about it, . . . All she'd say was it was the most humiliating experience in her life. That would end the discussion."[8] And another Sansei reported:

"When I first learned of the internment as a youth, I found that it was a difficult matter to discuss with my parents. My perception of them was that they did not speak honestly about the camp experience. Positive aspects were mentioned, if anything at all, but there always seemed to be something that was left out. My feeling was that there was much more to their experience than they wanted to reveal. Their words said one thing, while their hearts were holding something else deep inside."[9]

Not all Nisei were or are as reticent about their experiences, yet a significant number even now are unwilling or unable to confront the past. It appears that the more personal and social difficulties an individual or family underwent in the camps, the more hesitant they are to resurrect the past.

When many Sansei discovered that their parents had not told them about the World War II portion of their family histories, reactions varied. Some Sansei became angry and criticized their parents' silence, some felt frustrated and alienated from their parents, and still others became more curious about the wartime events. A number of Sansei even wondered if their parents had been guilty of some wrongdoing—why else would the government have imprisoned them? Their parents' reluctance to divulge facts reinforced the suspicion that they indeed had something to hide. Thus, many younger Japanese Americans did not understand what had transpired during the war period or why their parents and grandparents were so secretive. The inability of the Sansei to comprehend their parents' and grandparents' behavior stems from the sociopsychological dynamics of the imprisonment experience.

The stigma phenomenon, I contend, affects more than just those who were imprisoned and the later generations who were not. The stigma strikes at the basic identity mosaic of the Japanese American. Unlike other immigrant groups from Europe that were able to become naturalized citizens if they wished, the Issei were precluded from becoming full-fledged Americans and were forced to retain their identity as Japanese. By 1940, because their sons and daughters were citizens of the United States and they themselves had established homes and businesses, many had adopted America as their country. Wartime events, however, caused some Nisei to question their identities as Americans. They felt that their government not only had refused to protect them from outside prejudices but had created a mechanism for withdrawing their citizenship in order to deport them from their birthplace.

Because many of the internees and inmates could not mitigate or rationalize their imprisonment, they responded with various emotions. There were instances in all the camps of attempted and successful suicides, and some internees and inmates became mentally unstable. Others expressed clear signs of anxiety and fear or displayed overt or latent hostility toward authority figures. Many felt deprived and alienated after being denied contact with their fathers in the internment camps or kept apart from families and friends who were lingering in WRA centers. Everyone asked the administrators questions that went unanswered regarding the reasons for their imprisonment, the duration of their stay, and provisions for their future once the war ended. For example, an Issei husband who was still in an internment camp after the war ended spoke of his family's condition to the assistant commissioner for alien control:

> My health is degenerating mentally and physically owing to the long internment life. I am now suffering from kidney trouble and must go to the toilet very often every night. Therefore, I cannot sleep well and become very nervous thinking of my unfortunate status and also the miserable and lonesome life of my family. I am afraid that

further internment life might break down my health completely. My wife is living with five children [in] . . . Los Angeles, California. . . . My wife fainted twice, in April and December of last year on the street due to her extreme asthenia. . . . Such poor condition of her health might have been caused by her over-worriness about my present status and heavy burden to make their daily living and to bring up five children with her weak hands.[10]

The physiological and psychological problems described here were not unusual. Other inmates and internees reported suffering extreme weight loss, impaired vision, and fainting spells.

From the time of their release and through the intervening years, formerly imprisoned Japanese Americans have been noticeably unwilling to express their deep feelings or emotions about the cataclysmic events they had endured. This reluctance to articulate the painful aspects of camp life to outsiders—and often even to their children who were born afterward—can be conceptualized as *social amnesia*. Social amnesia is here defined as a group phenomenon marked by attempts to suppress feelings and memories of particular moments or extended periods. It is not a psychological pathology but a conscious effort to screen memories and, as manifested here, to suppress unpleasant experiences. For years after the war, conversations about the camps revolved around trivial, humorous, and nonthreatening topics.[11] This does not mean people repressed the camp experiences in a psychoanalytic sense, but many Issei and Nisei found it exceedingly difficult to discuss any significant camp episode.

Japanese Americans have conducted their lives for decades under the social cloud of the incarceration and, unable to banish it, have lived with the stigma. Up to the 1980s, there was very little assistance available for healing the long-standing wounds to the individual's psyche and the group's collective consciousness.[12] As one notable California Sansei stated in 1987:

My mother and father who were in their twenties were both born and raised in Sacramento CA. . . . For some reason because of Pearl Harbor in 1942, their lives and futures were shattered. They were given 72 hours notice that they had to leave their home, their neighborhood, abandon their business, and show up at the Memorial Auditorium which is in the heart of Sacramento and then be taken, like cattle, in trains to the Tule Lake Internment Camp.

My father was not able to talk about this subject for over 40 years and I was a 6-month-old child that they happened to have. So I really did not even understand what had happened until the 1980's. It was very interesting because when he finally was able to articulate it he said, "You know what the problem is, why I can't discuss this issue is because I was in one of those internment camps, a prisoner of war camp and if I talk about it the first thing I have to say is, 'Look, I wasn't guilty. I was loyal to my country,' because the specter of disloyalty attaches to anybody who was in those camps." And that stigma exists today on every one of those 60,000 Americans of Japanese ancestry who happened to have lived in one of those camps.[13]

This Sansei, Congressman Robert T. Matsui, was one of many Japanese Americans who began in the 1970s to help relieve the burden created by the imprisonment experience.

CONCLUSION

From the 1980s, certain events led to a growing sense of release for those who were incarcerated a half-century earlier. Fragmented developments at the national level were precursors to this relief. In 1948, the government passed the Japanese American Evacuation Claims Act, resulting in extremely limited monetary compensation for proven losses.[14] Beginning in 1967, Japanese Americans became active in a national movement to repeal Title II of the Internal Security Act, or the Emergency Detention Act. This act allowed the government to detain persons who were *expected* to engage in acts of espionage in the event of an insurrection, war, or invasion. Title II was repealed in 1971. On February 19, 1976, President Gerald R. Ford formally rescinded EO 9066, stating, "We know now what we should have known then—not only was the evacuation wrong, but Japanese Americans were and are loyal Americans."[15]

Three important court decisions must be mentioned as well. Gordon Kiyoshi Hirabayashi, Fred Toyosaburo Korematsu, and Minoru Yasui individually protested the wartime orders directed at Japanese Americans. After they deliberately disobeyed curfew and evacuation orders, they were arrested, charged, and brought before an established tribunal and were represented by counsel. Judgments against them were pronounced and were then appealed to the U.S. Supreme Court. The Supreme Court ruled that regulations concerning curfew and eviction based on military necessity were constitutional. Later, in the 1980s, the three cases were reheard in federal courts under the rarely used legal procedure of a petition for a writ of error *coram nobis*. In all three cases, their major convictions were vacated.[16] Although the Supreme Court rulings still stand, the legal precedents they set will in all likelihood not be used to justify the expulsion of a group in a similar situation. It is now acknowledged that the government's argument in these Japanese American Supreme Court cases rested on suppression and misuse of vital information.

Another milestone event occurred in 1980, when Congress created the Commission on Wartime Relocation and Internment of Civilians. The commission's task was to examine the actions and impact of EO 9066; its findings offered specific remedies for the personal injustices endured by the Nikkei and the Aleut Indians. The commission recommended that Congress and the president apologize for the wartime action and give symbolic monetary payments to those who had been incarcerated. Congress accepted the recommendations, and President

Ronald Reagan signed the Civil Rights Acts of 1988 and offered an apology on behalf of the nation. In 1990, President George Bush issued the first symbolic redress
payment with the following words: "A monetary sum and words alone cannot restore lost years or erase painful memories; neither can they fully convey our Nation's resolve to rectify injustice and to uphold the rights of individuals. We can
never fully right the wrongs of the past. But we can take a clear stand for justice
and recognize that serious injustices were done to Japanese Americans during
World War II. In enacting a law calling for restitution and offering a sincere apology, your fellow Americans have, in a very real sense, renewed their traditional
commitment to the ideals of freedom, equality, and justice."

This is a significant statement. Every living person who was directly affected by
EO 9066 received a formal apology and $20,000, a sum of $1.25 billion for the entire group. And yet the story is far from over.[17] Although Nikkei teachers and government workers who lost their jobs because of their ancestry received apologies
in California and Washington, another group of 54 Nikkei railroad and mining
workers and their families, out of 381 others who suffered the same fate, were denied redress by early 2001. In addition, internees from Latin American countries
who were brought to the United States were offered an apology and $5,000 in sym-
bolic redress, but not every individual so affected received the letter or payment.
The government did not accept particular applications for redress for various reasons and for particular individuals. Their struggles continue, even as late as February 2001.[18]

Certainly the presidential apology and monetary reparations help to amend, in
part, the injustices done to the Nikkei during World War II. These positive steps
are reason for momentary celebration and much reflection. That a small minority
group could mount a successful campaign with the assistance and support of
other Americans from many sectors of society shows that this is a national issue of
great importance. The three branches of government now formally acknowledge
their errors, doing much to restore faith in the government and the strength of the
U.S. Constitution, which was shaken during World War II. For Japanese Americans, however, all is not finished. The imprisonment stigma lingers today.[19]

In 1986, District Court Judge Donald S. Voorhees offered a relevant thought: "It
is now considered by almost everyone that the internment of Japanese-Americans
during World War II was simply a tragic mistake for which American society as a
whole must accept responsibility."[20] That it was tragic is beyond question. In a
larger sense, however, to characterize the mass imprisonment as a mistake is to re-
duce it to a simple error. This calamity must be seen as more than just an error.
The group imprisonment was conceived before the United States entered the war
by high-level officials who planned to remove both alien and citizen Nikkei, and
once the imprisonment process began, all branches of the government sanctioned
it. Moreover, mistake or not, the repercussions continue to this day.

As we have seen, the government's actions resulted in the devastation of lives,

livelihoods, families, and communities. It especially complicated the Nisei generation's fundamental status and identity as Americans. Thus, an event of this magnitude cannot be easily expunged with an apology, and the people affected cannot be
expected to forget.

This is an American story, and the real challenge is to all Americans. If one
group can be singled out, so can another that is perceived as different. All Americans have ties to some foreign national or ethnic group, and these differences can
be used to discriminate against individuals.

Yet, simply sharing the ethnoracial ancestry of an enemy nation does not create
an entire population of pariahs, as was demonstrated by the government's treatment of German and Italian nationals and their descendants. Familiarity with and
understanding of Germans and Italians led to individualized consideration of these
groups. Unfamiliarity and lack of understanding resulted in blanket treatment for
the Nikkei. Additional negative factors for the Nikkei included a long history of
racial and ethnic animosity and derogatory stereotypes rooted in an earlier era of
"yellow peril" fear-mongering, especially on the West Coast. There is little doubt
that these prejudices were readily evoked and exaggerated during the months from
December 7, 1941, up to the actual incarceration. In Hawaii, where people of Japanese ancestry were not a minority and had for some time been an accepted part of
island communities, the group (with the exception of the Kibei) was treated as were
Germans and Italians on the mainland. Unfortunately, such anti-Asian attitudes
still linger as part of American cultural values, although they are subtler and just
below the surface. They could, perhaps, be triggered once again by a precipitating
catastrophic event and then manipulated by public authorities.

Of the many lessons to be learned from the imprisonment experience, the following are most prominent. The United States has practiced equality for some
since its founding days, yet equality for all is the stated goal. Obtaining this lofty
end requires at least a modicum of understanding of others. We as a nation must
take care not to base our actions on prejudice and stereotypes. The doors to equal
treatment have widened in the last half-century of the United States' history, but
securing equality for all is still a distant but, we hope, an achievable goal. It is
therefore important to know not only why the expulsion and imprisonment of
Japanese Americans took place during World War II but also how that terrible
process unfolded. Understanding the process requires insight into the methods by
which a nation could embark on such a large-scale miscarriage of justice. Only by
making the American populace aware can we ensure that such injustices will never
affect another group of Americans.

NOTES

1 / THE IMPRISONMENT PROCESS

1. Yasutaro Hibi and Taju Koide, interviewed in their homes in San Diego, Calif., December 1983, by the author. Interviews are presently in the author's possession and will be placed in Manuscripts, Special Collections, University Archives of the University of Washington Libraries, Seattle. Mr. Koide, born April 15, 1888, died on April 28, 1991, in San Diego; I am indebted to Tamiko Iwashita, Coronado, Calif., for this information.

After spending years in the WRA camps with their families, both men were eventually released and allowed to return to San Diego. They lost most of their possessions during the war years, and since the Issei were denied commercial fishing licenses, they could not return to their prewar occupations until 1948. They became landscape gardeners in order to feed their families. Mr. Hibi's love of fishing continued, but in the postwar years he pursued it only as a sport, while Mr. Koide devoted his recreational time to oil painting.

2. Tadashi Yamaguchi, interviewed at his home in Seattle, 1979, by the author. Interview is in the author's possession and later will be placed in the University of Washington Libraries.

3. Eugene V. Rostow, "Our Worst Wartime Mistake," *Harper's Magazine* (September 1945), pp. 193-201.

4. Listing the available literature on the incarceration of Japanese Americans is beyond the scope of this presentation. However, many of the available works are listed in the bibliography.

5. The army occasionally changed the designations of units dealing with intelligence matters. From 1939 to 1945, the Military Intelligence Division (MID) was the overall branch, and the MID-Intelligence Branch was a subsidiary unit until 1942. In either January or March 1942, the Intelligence Branch name was changed to Military Intelligence Service (MIS), and the branch was charged with collecting, evaluating, and disseminating intelligence information. The Counterintelligence Corps was a component of the Intelligence Branch, and when the Intelligence Branch became the MIS, the Counterintelligence Corps became the Counter Intelligence Corps (CIC). In this book, for the sake of consistency and clarity and unless it is important to specify a particular unit within a branch, the army's intelligence branch will be referred to as the Military Intelligence Division and the navy's branch as the Office of Naval Intelligence.

6. Dorothy S. Thomas, *The Salvage* (Berkeley: University of California Press, 1952), p. 581.

2 / PRE–WORLD WAR II PREPARATIONS

1. Edward K. Strong, *The Second Generation Japanese Problem* (Palo Alto, Calif.: Stanford University Press, 1934; reprint, New York: Arno Press and The New York Times, 1970), p. 150.

2. Marcus Garvey, *The Marcus Garvey and Universal Negro Improvement Association Papers,* ed. Robert A. Hill, 7 vols. (Berkeley: University of California Press, 1985), 4:702.

3. Lee Kennett, *For the Duration . . . The United States Goes to War* (New York: Charles Scribner's Sons, 1985), p. 64.

4 Memorandum, U.S. State Department, quoted in Bob Kuramoto, "The Search for Spies: American Counter-intelligence and the Japanese American Community 1931–1942," *Amerasia Journal* 6, no. 2 (fall 1979): 49.

5. Quoted in Gary Y. Okihiro, *Cane Fires* (Philadelphia: Temple University Press, 1991), p. 173.

6. William O. Douglas, *The Court Years* (New York: Random House, 1980), p. 271.

7. Ibid., pp. 271–72.

8. The difference in numbers from the original 411 is accounted for by two deaths, five transfers, and two paroled to the German embassy. Memorandum, W. F. Kelly, Assistant Commissioner for Alien Control, to Lemuel B. Scofield, Special Assistant to the U.S. Attorney General and Director of the Immigration and Naturalization Service of the Justice Department, 14 October 1942, Justice Department, Record Group (hereafter RG) 85, File Number (hereafter F.N.) 56125, National Archives, Washington, D.C. (hereafter N.A.).

9. Richard G. Powers, *Secrecy and Power* (New York: The Free Press, 1987), p. 127.

10. Garvey, *Marcus Garvey Papers,* 3:47.

11. Ibid., 4:236. Emphasis added.

12. Reference is to an undated F B I headquarters file on Naka Nakana, or Satohata Takahashi, quoted in Karl Evanzz, *The Messenger* (New York: Pantheon Books, 1991), pp. 126, 536. Since few sources exist on this enigmatic figure, I have relied on Evanzz's writings. Mention of Takahashi is also in C. Eric Lincoln, *The Black Muslims in America* (New York: Beacon Press, 1961), p. 18: "[Takahashi] tried to persuade the Muslims to swear allegiance to the Mikado, and succeeded in splitting off some members of the movement."

13. Memorandum, Hayne Ellis, Director of the O N I, to J. Edgar Hoover, March 1932, quoted in Evanzz, *The Messenger,* p. 108.

14. F B I memo, St. Louis Special Agent in Charge to J. Edgar Hoover, 24 June 1933, quoted in Evanzz, *The Messenger,* p. 108.

15. I am indebted to Albert Black, Seattle, for alerting me to this issue. On September 22, 1942, the *Chicago Tribune* reported that eighty African Americans, including the leaders of three organizations, were arrested and brought to trial. The main charges against them were refusal to submit to the military draft and influencing others to do the same. Additional ac-

cusations alleged sedition and conspiracy. Their indictments contained the statement that a few organizations were "alleged to have taught negroes that their interests were in a Japanese victory, and that they were racially akin to the Japanese." Noted persons among them included Elijah Muhammed, leader of the Black Muslims and Minister of Islam, and Lenzie Karien; both admitted sympathy for Japan. Although Chicago FBI Special Agent Johnson reported that "no definite connection" had been found between Negro organizations and Japanese activity in this country, Elijah Muhammed went to the Milan, Mich., federal prison, where he remained until 1946. Lincoln, *Black Muslims,* pp. 16, 26.

16. After World War I, the intelligence-gathering activities of the United States were severely curtailed. "The Army's Military Intelligence Division was cut from 1,441 men in 1918 to just 90 in 1922 and a budget of only $225,000. The ONI was cut from nearly 1,000 men to 42. In 1927 the State Department's U-1 Bureau, its chief intelligence-gathering division, was eliminated altogether.... There was growing awareness of the dangers, but precious few resources to understand them. Even the resources available were woefully inadequate: because of miniscule budgets, the Army's Military Intelligence ruled that officers assigned to military attache duty overseas—the front line of intelligence collection—would be required to defray the expenses of life on the diplomatic circuit out of their own pockets." Ernest Volkman and Blaine Baggett, *Secret Intelligence* (New York: Doubleday, 1989), pp. 23–24.

17. Ibid., p. 228

18. Ralph DeToledano, *J. Edgar Hoover* (New Rochelle, N.Y.: Arlington House, 1973), pp. 184–203; see also William Breuer, *Nazi Spies in America,* reprint (New York: St. Martin's Paperback, 1990), pp. 198–99.

19. Breuer, *Nazi Spies,* p. 31.

20. For example, Bernard Julius Otto Kuehn and his wife Friedel, or Ruth, worked for a few years in Hawaii before 1941 on behalf of the Axis powers. Kuehn was apparently a member of the German navy's secret police from 1928 to 1930 and joined the Nazi party in 1930. After contacting the Japanese naval attaché in Berlin in 1935, he worked for the Japanese navy. In 1940, a Japanese agent wrote about the dubious quality of Kuehn's espionage work: " . . . his ability as a spy was so poor and primitive that it was feared he would not be able to get sufficient information for our intention of launching an air strike upon Pearl Harbor. He was not bold enough, too, to commit espionage activity in the face of danger" (quoted in Gordon W. Prange, *At Dawn We Slept* [New York: Penguin Books, 1981], p. 311).

Sources differ on various details, such as giving the couple's name as Kuehn or Kuhn and identifying Otto and Ruth as husband and wife or father and daughter. After the pair's capture, a military court convicted Kuehn of espionage and sentenced him to death. Later, this sentence was commuted to fifty years at hard labor. His wife or daughter received a lighter sentence, and in 1948, the government deported both of them to Argentina. See DeToledano, *Hoover,* pp. 158, 186, and Nathan Miller, *Spying for America* (New York: Dell Publishing, 1989), p. 292.

21. U.S. Department of Justice, *Annual Report of the Attorney General of the United States* (hereafter *ARAG*) *1937* (Washington, D.C.: U.S. Government Printing Office), p. 76.

22. Whitehead, *FBI Story,* p. 193. In June 1938, for example, the FBI and the ONI investi-

gated several cases leading to indictments against two German war ministry officials and sixteen others. Only four persons were convicted, while fourteen others escaped the FBI's dragnet and avoided trial.

23. *ARAG 1939*, pp. 61–62.

24. Volkman and Baggett, *Secret Intelligence*, pp. 22–29.

25. Ibid., pp. 24–25, and Miller, *Spying for America*.

26. Nicholas Dawidoff, *The Catcher Was a Spy* (New York: Pantheon, 1994).

27. The particular agency holding this authority is important. J. Edgar Hoover, FBI director, wrote, "... I informed [the Attorney General] of the conference which I had with the President on September 1, 1936, at which the Secretary of State was present, and at which time the Secretary of State, at the President's suggestion requested of me, the representative of the Department of Justice, to have investigation made of the subversive activities in this country, including communism and fascism. I transmitted this request to the Attorney General, and the Attorney General verbally directed me to proceed with this investigation and to coordinate, as the President suggested, information upon these matters in the possession of the Military Intelligence Division, the Naval Intelligence Division, and the State Department. This, therefore, is the authority upon which to proceed in the conduct of this investigation, which should of course be handled in a most discreet and confidential manner." Whitehead, *FBI Story*, pp. 159–60.

28. Powers, *Secrecy and Power*, p. 230.

29. *ARAG 1940*, p. 153.

30. Memorandum, J. Edgar Hoover, Director, Federal Bureau of Investigation (hereafter FBI), to Lawrence M. C. Smith, Chief of the Justice Department's Special Defense Unit, 23 October 1941, FBI, F.N. 62-63892-4, Washington, D.C.

31. Scott P. Corbett, *Quiet Passages* (Kent, Ohio: Kent State University Press, 1987), p. 26.

32. Kennett, *Duration*, p. 65.

33. Corbett, *Passages*, p. 26.

34. Kennett, *Duration*, p. 65.

35. *ARAG 1940*, p. 153.

36. Roosevelt's directive stated: "To this end, I request all police officers, sheriffs, and all other law-enforcement officers in the United States to promptly turn over to the nearest representative of the FBI any information obtained by them related to espionage, counterespionage, sabotage, subversive activities, and violations of the neutrality laws" (*ARAG 1940*, p. 152).

37. The FBI continued to increase its activities and size during these prewar years. For example, it reported 16,885 national defense investigative matters pending in June 1940; a year later, the number increased to 78,509. Its investigative staff more than doubled in size, from 1,000 in 1940 to 2,100 in 1941. Moreover, the agency reported by July 1941 that 11,307 nationals and citizens of German ancestry were under investigation for possible espionage violations and 192 persons for possible sabotage violations. One estimate in 1941 assigned about 80 percent of all FBI investigative work to matters of national defense. Memoran-

dum, not dated (probably July 1941), Justice Department, Immigration and Naturalization Service (hereafter I N S), RG 85, F.N. 44-3-31, N.A.

38. Corbett, *Passages,* p. 27.

39. Curt Gentry, *J. Edgar Hoover* (New York: W. W. Norton and Co., 1991).

40. Paul Spickard, "The Nisei Assume Power," *Pacific Historical Review* 52, no. 2 (May 1983): 157.

41. Bill Hosokawa, *Nisei* (New York: William Morrow and Co., 1969), p. 216. Tokutaro Slocum, a national J A C L leader, accompanied F B I agents when they arrested leaders of the Central Japanese Association on the night of December 7, 1941. In his own words: "Just as in World War I, again I went over the top. This time it was on the home front, and I led our F B I and Intelligence officers right into the den of disloyal and traitorous elements, the Central Japanese Association" (quoted in Spickard, "Nisei Assume Power," p. 157).

42. For others, the situation is more complex. Information obtained from any particular informant is initially questionable. Whenever possible, intelligence agents try to secure confirmation from more than one source. Moreover, not all people are willing to talk, even when the F B I calls them in for questioning. Intelligence agents might mix innocuous questions with more important ones for interviewees who are not known informants. Attempts to uncover specific information may be hidden within these conversations, and the interviewee may not know the real purpose of any particular question. Interviewees were sometimes frightened or flattered when the F B I asked to speak with them. For example, some were called and told they had been chosen for their "expertise" regarding the community; after a few sessions, they might then be asked to obtain specific information for the F B I. Agents might counter interviewees' refusals by hinting that their friends would be told they were official informants. Other tactics included fear, offers of money, or appeals to pride, the desire for revenge, and patriotism. Based on the personal observations of the author, who served as an intelligence officer on active duty with the U.S. Army from 1963 to 1965.

43. Saburo Muraoka, interviewed in San Diego, Calif., 1983. Interview tape is in the author's possession.

44. *Los Angeles Times,* November 13, 1941, pp. 1, 11.

45. Memorandum, 28 January 1942, F B I, F.N. 100-2-29-139, Washington, D.C.

46. Memorandum, 19 July 1940, U.S. Army, Records of the Adjutant General's Office, RG 407, Entry 360, Box 23:2, N.A.

47. Ibid., p. 1.

48. Memorandum, Francis Biddle, 18 July 1941, Justice Department, I N S, RG 85, F.N. 56125/Gen: 1, N.A.

49. Memorandum, Major General Allen W. Gullion, Provost Marshal General, to Assistant Chief of Staff, G-1, 12 May 1941, U.S. Army, Records of the Adjutant General's Office, RG 407, F.N. Entry 360, Box 21, N.A.

50. Memorandum, 14 August 1941, F B I, F.N. 62-63892-10, Washington, D.C.

51. Memorandum, Biddle, 18 July 1941, Justice Department, I N S, RG 85, F.N. 56125/Gen: 4, N.A.

52. Ibid., p. 4.

53. Memorandum, Karl R. Bendetson, Chief Aliens Division, 10 October 1941, War Department, Records of the Office of the Provost Marshal General, RG 389, F.N. 452.1362-014.311, N.A.

54. Memorandum, J. I. Miller to Provost Marshal General, 21 November 1941, ibid.

55. Norman Littell, *My Roosevelt Years* (Seattle: University of Washington Press, 1987), p. 110, and memorandum, 4 October 1939, Justice Department, I N S, RG 85, F.N. 44-3-31, N.A. During the 1930s, the United States enacted laws that became known as the Neutrality Acts, which would keep it out of foreign wars. The Neutrality Act of 1935 (Public Res. 67) banned trade with belligerents for one year; the 1936 act (49 Stat. 1152) extended the 1935 act for another year and banned loans to belligerents. The Neutrality Act of 1937 (Public Res. 27) extended the 1936 act indefinitely and required all sales to belligerents to be strictly cash-and-carry. The Neutrality Act of 1939 (Public Res. 54) incorporated the previous Neutrality Acts and prohibited American ships from entering war zones.

56. Memorandum, 16 May 1940, Justice Department, I N S, RG 85, F.N. 44-3-31, N.A.

57. Memorandum, 4 October 1939, ibid.

58. Powers, *Secrecy and Power*, p. 233.

59. Memorandum, no date, Justice Department, I N S, RG 85, F.N. 44-3-31, N.A.; memorandum, 1 August 1941, F B I, F.N. 62-63892-1x; and memorandum, 23 October 1941, F.N. 62-63892-4, Washington, D.C.

60. Corbett, *Passages*, p. 18.

61. Memorandum, "Special Defense Unit Estimate," 19 September 1941, Justice Department, I N S, RG 85, F.N. 62-63892-4, N.A.

62. Memorandum, 21 August 1941, Justice Department, I N S, RG 85, F.N. 44-3-31, N.A.

63. Memorandum, 28 June 1943, Special Defense Unit (hereafter S D U), Justice Department, I N S, RG 85, F.N. 44-3-31, N.A.

64. Memorandum, 22 August 1941, and memorandum, 8 September 1941, S D U, Justice Department, I N S, RG 85, F.N. 44-3-31, N.A.

65. From Minutes of Joint Conference, 26 July 1940, War Department, Military Intelligence Division files, RG 165, F.N. 9794-186A/12, N.A., quoted in Okihiro, *Cane Fires*, p. 178.

In his excellent article "Search for Spies," Bob Kuramoto also examines the ABC list: "Since the beginning of the surveillance, the number of Japanese under investigation had grown considerably. By early 1941, over 2,000 suspects had been identified and divided in three classifications. Group A suspects were 'known dangerous' and demanded intense observation" (p. 18). He does not, however, identify the agency assigning the ABC classifications. My contention is that the O N I probably was the originator of the first ABC list as early as 1938. Kuramoto does refer to the O N I but does not make a connection between the ABC list and the O N I. Nowhere in his article does he mention the Special Defense Unit or the abbreviation S D U.

66. Memorandum, 8 September 1941, S D U, Justice Department, I N S, RG 85, F.N. 44-3-31, N.A.

67. Memorandum, James Rowe Jr. to U.S. Attorneys, 2 February 1942, Justice Department, INS, RG 85, N.A. Emphasis in the original.

68. Ibid. The other nine organizations are the Cherry Association (Sakura Kai), composed of veterans of the Russo-Japanese War; Imperial Japanese Reservists (Hinode Kai); Japanese Overseas Central Society (Kaigai Dobo Chuo Kai); Japanese Protective Association (recruiting organization for Japanese army); Military Friends' Corp (Nanka Teikoku Gunyu Dan); Military Virtue Society (Dai Nippon Butoku Kai); North American Reserve Officers' Association (Hokubei Zaigo Shoko Dan); Reserve Officers' Association (Suiko Sha), Los Angeles; and Rising Sun Flag Society (Hinomaru Kai).

Regarding the Black Dragon Society, a California congressional committee heard testimony that this organization had an American arm, the Imperial Comradeship Society, with 4,800 members at the start of the war. Report, Joint Fact-Finding Committee on Un-American Activities in California to the Fifth-fifth California Legislature, Sacramento, Calif., 1943: 337.

69. Memorandum, 100-2-51-50. Emphasis added.

70. Okihiro, *Cane Fires*, p. 178.

71. Michael Sayers and Albert E. Kahn, *Sabotage! The Secret War against America* (New York: Harper and Bros., 1942), p. 65.

72. Evanzz relates that a Pan-African organization, the Peace Movement of Ethiopia (PME), founded in 1935 by former United Negro Improvement Association officers for the purpose of repatriating black Americans to Africa, was an "unwitting front" for the Black Dragon Society, since most of its funds came from the Japanese consuls general in San Francisco and New York. By 1938, Takahashi was supposedly running the PME. *The Messenger*, pp. 125–26.

A file on the Black Dragon Society exists in the Central Records Facility (CRF) of the U.S. Army intelligence branch Counter Intelligence Corps (CIC). In 1953, Henry Miyatake, now residing in Bellevue, Wash., was a CIC special agent working at the CRF at Fort Holabird, Md., and he examined the World War II files on this organization. The records show that a group of Los Angeles Kibei created the organization as a way to cover their repeated absences from their wives and homes. Their activities were confined to drinking, gambling, and carousing. When Agent Miyatake talked with other CIC agents, one officer told him that the subversive nature of this organization was a government creation. By defining the group as "dangerous," Miyatake stated, "intelligence agencies could charge a Japanese ancestry person with membership or participation in it to justify an initial arrest and incarceration." Discussion with Henry Miyatake, Pacific Rim Disease Prevention Center office, Seattle, September 20, 1999.

73. Memorandum, J. Rowe to U.S. Attorneys, 2 February 1942, Justice Department, INS, RG 85, N.A. Other organizations listed in the B category were the Central Japanese Association (Beikoku Chuo Nipponjin Kai), Northwest Japanese Association, and Central Japanese Association of Southern California and their various branches, all formed by the Issei; Kibei Association (Kibei Seinen Kai), which had four alternate names; and Shinto temples and

the Konkokyo Federation of North America, which was mistakenly identified by the s d u as part of the Shinto temples.

74. Memorandum, J. Rowe to U.S. Attorneys, 2 February 1942, Justice Department, i n s, RG 85, N.A.

75. Memorandum, 13 July 1943, Justice Department, F.N. 44-3-31, RG 85, N.A.

76. Memorandum, 14 October 1941, f b i, F.N. 62-63892-4, pp. 2–9, Washington, D.C.

77. Ibid.

78. The Justice Department's stated rationale for creating the War Division was to coordinate the work of "war planning, alien enemy control and alien enemy property." To this end, the division incorporated other previously autonomous Justice Department units, including the Alien Enemy Control Unit, the Special War Policies Unit, and the Alien Property Divisions. Memorandum, Order 2507, Supplement 14, 19 May 1942, Justice Department, i n s, RG 85, F.N. 44-3-31, N.A.

79. Memorandum, no date (probably July 1941), Justice Department, i n s, RG 85, F.N. 44-3-31, N.A.

80. Memorandum, 25 October 1938, f b i, F.N. 62-63892-X5, Washington, D.C. Emphasis added.

81. Testimony, John L. Burling, "General Instructions [on the] Handling of Aliens," 30 July 1943, i n s, RG 85, Justice Department, F.N. 56125/26/b&c, p. 56, N.A.

82. Memorandum, W. E. Shedd for Chief of Staff, 13 January 1941, U.S. Army, Records of the Adjutant General's Office, RG 407, F.N. Entry 360, Box 21, N.A.

83. Memorandum, CG Ninth Corps Area to Adjutant General, 14 April 1941, U.S. Army, Records of the Adjutant General's Office, RG 407, F.N. Entry 36, Box 22, N.A. The original six sites were Fort Lewis, Wash.; Camp Killpack, Wash.; Fort McDowell, Angel Island, Calif.; Camp San Clemente, Calif.; Fort Ord, East Garrison, Calif.; and Camp Williams, Utah. An unused Civilian Conservation Corps camp in Griffith Park in Los Angeles later took the place of San Clemente.

84. Memorandum, W. E. Shedd for Chief of Staff, 13 January 1941, U.S. Army, Records of the Adjutant General's Office, RG 407, F.N. Entry 360, Box 21, N.A.

85. Miller, *Spying for America,* p. 248.

86. Ken Ringle, "What Did You Do before the War, Daddy?" *Washington Post Magazine,* December 6, 1981, p. 56.

87. Ibid., p. 57. Ringle states that the o n i and the f b i used the information obtained by his father to deport Tachibana for attempting to purchase military secrets. This apparently was not the only time the o n i employed burglary as an intelligence-gathering tactic: "The major targets of o n i's covert activities . . . were Japanese consular and business officers in the United States. Over five successive nights in September 1929, a team headed by [Lieutenant Commander] Glenn Howell, the district intelligence officer in New York City, burglarized the offices of the Japanese Inspector of Machinery. They cracked the office safe and photographed code books and secret documents containing valuable information on Japanese aircraft and weaponry. . . . A similar raid was made against the offices of the Impe-

rial Japanese Railway in Manhattan. Howell did not confine his activities to the Japanese. The offices of the pacifist Federal Council of Churches were also burglarized, as were those of the Communist Party" (Miller, *Spying for America*, p. 248). The quality of the intelligence obtained from the break-ins is not reported.

88. Ringle, "What Did You Do . . . ?" p. 57.

89. I am indebted to Stanford Lyman for pointing out that some Issei did work successfully as spies for a number of years. Their espionage target, however, was Japan, not the United States.

For example, from late 1933 until his capture, Yotoku Miyagi was part of Richard Sorge's ring, which was devoted to obtaining information for Russia, with Sorge masquerading as an agent for Nazi Germany. Miyagi was born in Okinawa in 1903 and was raised by his grandparents while his father tried farming in the Philippines and Hawaii before settling in Southern California. Miyagi came to California when he was sixteen, seeking a more hospitable climate after contracting tuberculosis, and met up with his father in the desert town of Brawley. After short stays in various California cities, he arrived in 1926 in Los Angeles, where he worked as an artist and ran the Owl Restaurant with three other Issei. They formed a Marxist study group and joined the Communist Party USA in 1933. Miyagi's social and political beliefs were different from those of many Issei. He remembered the exploitation of Okinawan farmers by Japanese bankers, doctors, and petty officials and observed similar treatment being meted out to the Japanese by Euro-Americans. His views thus were a mixture of anti-Japanese and anti-American sentiments. He apparently was recruited by two American communist agents, an Issei and a Caucasian, to go to Japan for not more than three months for the purpose of establishing a Comintern group in Tokyo. Miyagi died in a Japanese prison on August 2, 1943, before his sentencing. The husband-and-wife team of Yoshisaburo and Tomo Kitabayashi were also members of the Sorge ring and the Communist Party USA. Chalmers Johnson, *An Instance of Treason* (Stanford, Calif.: Stanford University Press, 1990), pp. 92–97.

90. U.S. Army Report, 1947, U.S. Army, Records of the Adjutant General's Office, RG 407, Appendix II, Tab 1, p. 130, N.A.

91. The full definition of an A designation is: "The existence of the Japanese organizations listed herein is deemed to constitute an actual threat to the internal security of the United States. All officers and members, whether full or associate, of these organizations should be given serious consideration before employment in any position of confidence or trust in this country" (ONI, quoted in ibid.).

92. The full definition of a B designation is "The existence of the Japanese organization listed herein is deemed to constitute a potential threat to the internal security of the United States. All officers and those members who are considered to be especially active should be investigated before admission to a position of confidence or trust in this country" (ibid.).

93. Ibid.

94. See Department of Defense, *The "Magic" Background of Pearl Harbor,* vol. 4, *October 17, 1941–December 7, 1941* (Washington, D.C.: U.S. Government Printing Office, 1978), and Angus MacBeth, "Addendum to Personal Justice Denied," in Commission on Wartime

Relocation and Internment of Civilians, *Personal Justice Denied,* reprint (Seattle: University of Washington Press, 1997), pp. 471–79.

95. MacBeth, "Addendum," p. 474.

96. See Jacobus tenBroek, Edward M. Barnhart, and Floyd W. Matson, *Prejudice, War, and the Constitution* (Berkeley: University of California Press, 1954), pp. 304, 393.

97. The best source on the Special Division is Corbett, *Passages.* Initially, the s d u functioned as the protecting power for Germans and Italians trapped in Allied territories and worked to assist Americans in Europe. The division succeeded in repatriating 75,000 Americans, but by 1941, there were still 50,901 Americans in Europe. The s d u was also concerned about the lives of 24,443 citizens who remained in Asia: 6,700 in China, 124 in French Indochina, 1,280 in Hong Kong, 15,295 in Japan, 476 in Netherlands East India, 450 in the Straits Settlements, 90 in Thailand, and 28 in various Pacific islands (ibid., p. 17). This number does not include thousands of Americans trapped in the Philippine Islands.

98. Ibid., pp. 27, 112.

99. Greg Robinson, *By Order of the President* (Cambridge: Harvard University Press, 2001), p. 65, and Michi Weglyn, *Years of Infamy* (New York: William Morrow and Co., 1976), p. 284, n. 4.

100. Corbett, *Passages,* pp. 28–29, and Ringle, "What Did You Do . . . ?" pp. 56–57.

101. Curtis B. Munson, "Japanese on the West Coast," 7 November 1941, Commission on Wartime Relocation and Internment of Civilians, RG 220, F.N. 3670-89, N.A.

102. Ibid. Emphasis added.

103. Ibid.

104. Robinson, *By Order,* pp. 71–72.

3 / THE INTERNMENT PROCESS OF THE JUSTICE AND WAR DEPARTMENTS

1. Prominent Americans, such as Charles A. Lindbergh and Father Caughlin, a popular radio priest, were notably opposed to the United States entering into the ongoing overseas war.

In 1941, Roosevelt was actively preparing for war in Europe, in support of the British, and did not want a hostile distraction in the Pacific. He nonetheless refused to treat seriously Japan's wishes to negotiate settlement of U.S. and Japanese differences over Japan's entry into Asian countries; in addition, he froze Japanese assets in the United States and severely limited the sale of petroleum products to that country. Greg Robinson, *By Order of the President* (Cambridge: Harvard University Press, 2001), pp. 62–64.

2. Memorandum, District Director to Immigration and Naturalization Service (hereafter i n s) offices, 7 July 1942, Record Group (hereafter RG) 85, File Number (hereafter F.N.) Entry 89, Box 3, National Archives, Washington, D.C. (hereafter N.A.).

3. The San Diego f b i office sent a telegram on February 11 to f b i headquarters requesting authorization for the arrest: "San Diego [f b i] office recommends that the follow-

ing Japanese aliens on whom custodial detention memoranda have been submitted but no custodial detention cards have as yet been forwarded to the San Diego office by the FBI ... be immediately arrested ... Saburo Muraoka, [along with ten other Japanese names]" (Teletype, 11 February 1942, Federal Bureau of Investigation [hereafter FBI], F.N. 100-2-50-55, Washington, D.C.).

4. Saburo and Haruko Muraoka, interviewed at their residence in Chula Vista, Calif., December 1983, by the author. Mr. Muraoka was born in Japan on August 16, 1900, and died in Chula Vista on August 17, 1983. Interview is in the author's possession.

5. Gordon W. Prange, *At Dawn We Slept* (New York: Penguin Books, 1981), p. 558.

6. Telegram, 7 December 1941, FBI, F.N. 100-2-20-23, Washington, D.C.

7. One source offers the following reasons for the arrests: "the nature of the attack and the quickly spreading rumors that resident Japanese had assisted the attackers at Pearl Harbor led [the Justice Department] summarily to arrest all Japanese nationals in all classes of suspicion" (Jacobus tenBroek, Edward N. Barnhart, and Floyd W. Matson, *Prejudice, War, and the Constitution* [Berkeley: University of California Press, 1954], p. 102). The contention that rumors played a major role in the Justice Department's decision is questionable, since arrests began well before any rumors could have reached the department in Washington, D.C. The FBI telegram ordering the agents to arrest all Japanese on the custodial detention list, regardless of classification, was sent and delivered on December 7. It is therefore doubtful that "quickly spreading rumors" had any bearing on implementation of plans.

8. Don Whitehead, *The FBI Story* (New York: Random House, 1956), p. 182.

9. Through the decoding of the Magic cables (see chapter 2), the United States had strong intimations of a possible Japanese attack in the Pacific, although the date and time were unknown. It is unlikely that J. Edgar Hoover knew of the existence of the secret code, given the short list of persons privy to the information. The FBI, however, wiretapped the Japanese consulate's office in Hawaii and knew that unusual actions had occurred there, such as the precipitous burning of documents.

10. Quoted in Richard G. Powers, *Secrecy and Power* (New York: The Free Press, 1987), p. 245.

11. Radiogram, Adjutant General to Army and Corps Commanders, 7 December 1941, U.S. Army, Records of the Adjutant General's Office, RG 407, Provost Marshal General, F.N. PMG 014.311-81, N.A. Classified "Secret." Emphasis added.

12. Circular No. 3643 Amended, 28 February 1942, Justice Department, in War Department, Records of the Provost Marshal General's Office, RG 389, F.N. Entry 451, Box 1217, N.A.

13. Francis Biddle, *In Brief Authority* (New York: Doubleday and Co., 1962), p. 206.

14. Teletype, 11 February 1942, FBI, F.N. 100-2-50-55, Washington, D.C. The total of thirty-one is derived from FBI reports from West Coast cities, F.N. 100-2-x, Washington, D.C.; specific references are given in note 43.

15. Circular No. 3643 Amended, 28 February 1942, Justice Department, in War Department, Records of the Provost Marshal General's Office, RG 389, F.N. Entry 451, Box 1217, N.A.

16. W. Makabe, quoted in John Tateishi, ed., *And Justice for All* (New York: Random House, 1984), p. 251.

17. Biddle, *In Brief Authority,* p. 206; Justice Department memorandum, 24 March 1942, FBI, F.N. 100-2-60-171, Washington, D.C.

18. K. Iwamoto, quoted in William Hohri, *Repairing America* (Pullman: Washington State University Press, 1988), p. 179.

19. Code of Federal Regulations, Title 3, The President, 1938–1943 Compilation, Presidential Proclamation No. 2525, dated December 7, 1941, pp. 273–76.

20. Ibid., Presidential Proclamation No. 2526, dated December 8, 1941, pp. 276–78, and Presidential Proclamation No. 2527, dated December 8, 1941, pp. 278–79.

21. Norman M. Littell, *My Roosevelt Years* (Seattle: University of Washington Press, 1987), p. 57.

22. Peter Irons, *Justice at War* (New York: Oxford University Press, 1983), p. 5.

23. Biddle, *In Brief Authority,* p. 207.

24. Memorandum, 9 December 1941, FBI, F.N. 100-2-2387, Washington, D.C.

25. INS files, 9 December 1941, in the Commission on Wartime Relocation and Internment of Civilians (hereafter CWRIC) papers, RG 220, No. 10372, N.A.

26. INS memorandum from Lemuel B. Schofield, 10 December 1942, F.N. 56125, No. 29, in the CWRIC papers, RG 220, No. 10373, N.A. By December 13, the Justice Department reported to the War Department the following numbers of persons apprehended from selected Pacific Coast cities under the Alien Enemies Act:

	Nationalities				
Places	Jpn	Grm	Ital	Others	Total
1. Los Angeles and San Diego	353	83	6	0	442
2. San Francisco	102	58	17	7	184
3. Seattle and Portland	131	43	3	16	193
4. Spokane	9	3	0	0	12
TOTAL	595	187	26	23	831

NOTE: Compiled from memorandum, H. Bundy, 13 December 1941, War Department, Records of the Provost Marshal General's Office, RG 389, F.N. 014.311, Entry 452, Box 1362, N.A.

Of the 595 arrested Japanese nationals, 258 were classified by the Justice Department as belonging in category A, 13 in category B, and 324 in category C. Of the 187 German nationals, 121 were in category A, 61 in category B, and 5 in category C. Of the Italian nationals, 9 were in category A, 8 in category B, and 9 in category C. No rationale is given for the extraordinary number of Issei included in Japanese category C-the "least dangerous" category-especially when compared proportionally to the other groups. Compiled from memorandum, H. Bundy, 13 December 1941, War Department, Records of the Provost Marshal General's Office, RG 389, F.N. 014.311, Entry 452, Box 1362, N.A.

27. Total arrests by the Justice Department up to various dates in 1942 were as follows:

	2/18/42	3/13/42	5/11/42	11/4/42
Japanese	2,311	3,615	4,659	5,334
German	1,450	1,816	2,742	4,769
Italian	271	533	1,292	2,262
Other	—	—	—	10
TOTAL	4,032	5,964	8,693	12,375

NOTE: Compiled from FBI memorandum, 18 February 1942, F.N. 100-2-60-213; Justice Department memorandum, 1942, F.N. 100-2-60-171; and FBI memorandum, 4 November 1942, F.N. 100-2-60-1088, FBI and N.A. The "other" category for November 4, 1942, included 8 Hungarians, 1 Bulgarian, and 1 Romanian.

28. Memorandum, 2 June 1942, FBI, F.N. 100-2-51-243, Washington, D.C.

29. William K. Klingaman, *1941* (New York: Harper & Row, 1970), p. 429.

30. Edward Ennis, interviewed during Gordon Hirabayashi's *coram nobis* hearings at the Seattle Hilton Hotel, June 20, 1985, by the author. Ennis was told that the purpose of the interview was to resolve various questions concerning the Justice Department's handling of enemy alien matters during World War II. Interview is in the author's possession.

31. Stephan Fox, *The Unknown Internment* (Boston: Twayne Publishers, 1990), p. 162.

32. Interview, E. Ennis.

33. Memorandum, Provost Marshal General's Office to Chief Engineer, U.S Army, 22 May 1942, War Department, Records of the Provost Marshal General's Office, RG 389, F.N. Entry 434, Box 414, N.A.

34. Biddle, *In Brief Authority*, p. 207; Geoffreys Smith, "Racial Nativism and Origins of American Relocation," in Roger Daniels, Sandra Taylor, and Harry H. L. Kitano, eds., *Japanese Americans,* 2nd ed. (Seattle: University of Washington Press, 1991), pp. 84–85.

35. Interview, E. Ennis.

36. Arnold Krammer, *Undue Process* (Boulder, Colo.: Rowman and Littlefield Publishers, 1997), p. 57.

37. President Roosevelt's sentiments about Japanese and German nationals were seconded by California's law enforcement officers. On February 18, 1942, California attorney general Earl Warren sent a questionnaire to all state district attorneys, sheriffs, and chiefs of police, asking them to describe the group they felt was most likely to commit sabotage and espionage. The following quotes, all dated February 19, 1942, were obtained from CWRIC, Record Group 220, No. 10649-10656, N.A.

Of the 116 who replied, 54 felt that Japanese nationals constituted the greatest threat. For example, one wrote: "My experience with the Japanese has been, that taken as a whole, the great majority can't be trusted at any time and very much less at the present time" (E. C. Mehl, Chief of Police, Upland, to E. Warren). Another responded: "Our State and Federal laws, supported by a bill of rights, are entirely inadequate to meet the situation. If we are not to run the risk of disaster we must forget such things as the writ of habeas corpus, and the prohibition against unreasonable searches and seizures. The right of self-defense, self-preservation, on behalf of the people, is higher than the bill of rights" (G. Mordecai, District

Attorney, Madera County, to E. Warren). Only four officers thought the German and Italian nationals were more dangerous. This respondent specified the Germans: "It is my belief that the Germans constitute the greatest threat in this area. A considerable number of Germans reside in this county and many more San Francisco Germans own summer homes and congregate on the slopes of Mount Tamalpais above Mill Valley. I believe most of these people have become naturalized American citizens. Despite that fact their allegiance to Nazi-Germany has remained prevalent and apparent . . ." (A. E. Bagshaw, District Attorney of Marin County, to E. Warren). Most of the respondents (94 out of 118) said they favored a plan that would remove individuals by force from particular areas as a means of dealing with the potential "problem." Four opposed the measure, while eighteen gave no opinion.

These California-based officers' viewpoints exemplify one element in the prevailing opinion about West Coast Japanese Americans. It also underlines the belief of both the Justice Department and the military that other residents of the state would approve of their actions against Japanese Americans.

38. Memorandum, no date, "Instructions to United States Attorneys," Justice Department, in Records of the Provost Marshal General's Office, RG 389, F.N. 014.311, N.A.

39. Memorandum, 1 January 1942, F B I, F.N. 100-2-29-129, Washington, D.C.

40. Ibid.

41. Letter, Edward Ennis to Milton Eisenhower, 18 June 1942, quoted in Richard Drinnon, *Keeper of Concentration Camps* (Berkeley: University of California Press, 1987), p. 280.

42. Memorandum, 14 September 1942, I N S, RG 85, F.N. 56125/Gen/B, N.A.

43. Basic arrest data from December 7, 1941, to the end of the war are available for major West Coast cities. For example, for San Diego, Calif., December 7, 1941–February 11, 1942, the F B I arrested 59 Issei and 2 Nisei, 19 German nationals (2 of whom were born in Germany but had Mexican citizenship), and 2 Italian nationals. The hearing boards recommended interning 53 Issei and 1 Nisei, releasing 1 Issei and 1 Nisei, and paroling 5 Issei. The fate of the interned Nisei is unreported. The board paroled 2 persons of German ancestry and released 3 others plus 1 person of Italian ancestry. From February 1942 and through the war years, arrestees totaled 270 Issei, 2 Nisei, 35 German nationals, 2 German-born Mexican citizens, and 6 Italian nationals in this area, which stretched from San Diego eastward to the Arizona border. Teletype, 11 February 1942, F B I, F.N. 100-2-50-55, and memorandum, 4 January 1942, F B I, F.N. 100-2-5-244, Washington, D.C.

For Los Angeles, on December 10, 1941, the Los Angeles F B I reported the arrest of 311 Issei, 3 Nisei, 59 German nationals, 12 citizens of German ancestry, 10 Italian nationals, and 1 citizen of Italian ancestry for a total of 396 persons. Memorandum, 10 December 1941, F B I, F.N. 10-2-21-21, Washington, D.C. By the end of the war, the arrests totaled 2,024 Japanese nationals, 15 Nisei, and 3 non-Japanese nationals (Russian, Polish, and Filipino) who were suspected of being sympathetic to Japan. There were as well 180 German nationals, 16 citizens of German ancestry, 8 non-German nationals suspected of having sympathies with Germany, 142 Italian nationals, and 1 citizen of Italian ancestry. Memorandum, 10 July 1946, F B I, F.N. 100-2-29-445, Washington, D.C.

The profile of those Issei arrested in the Los Angeles jurisdictional area is similar to that of Mr. K.A. His FBI dossier included the allegation that he was "a member of the Riverside, CA, unit of the Japanese Association. He was an officer of the Japanese Language Institute [*sic*]. He is a Buddhist. Subject has two daughters and an 18-year-old son presently residing in Japan. He also has a sister in Japan. Subject contributed to the Japanese Language School for the purpose of constructing a school. Subject owns a half acre of land in Japan" (memorandum, 25 March 1944, Alien Enemy Control [hereafter AEC] Unit, Justice Department, INS RG 85, F.N. 39.053, N.A.). Mr. K.A. was interned for more than two years before being paroled to join his wife and family at the WRA center at Poston, Ariz.

For San Francisco, in the Northern California area, by December 20, 1941, the FBI had arrested 109 Issei, 11 Nisei, 57 German nationals, 5 citizens of German ancestry, 19 Italians, and 2 citizens of Italian ancestry. In addition, they arrested 2 nationals from Austria, 1 from Canada, 1 from Chile, 1 from Czechoslovakia, 1 from Hungary, 1 from Sweden, and 1 from Switzerland. Memorandum, 20 December 1941, FBI, F.N. 100-2-51-65, Washington, D.C. By the end of the war, the total reported arrests included 654 Issei and 13 Nisei, 332 German nationals and 7 citizens of German ancestry, 453 Italian nationals and 5 citizens of Italian ancestry. Memorandum, 7 January 1946, FBI, F.N. 100-2-51-399, Washington, D.C.

In Portland, Oreg., the FBI had arrested 39 Issei, 35 Germans, and 1 Italian by February 18, 1942. Memorandum, 18 February 1942, FBI, F.N. 100-2-60-213, Washington D.C. The total number of arrests during the war came to 103 Issei, 1 Nisei, 133 Germans, 1 citizen of German ancestry, 33 Italians, and 1 Romanian. Memorandum, Portland Special Agent in Charge to FBI Bureau, 20 February 1946, FBI, F.N. 100-2-43-241 and 100-2-43-245, Washington, D.C.

The account of Mr. Umata Natsushima, a Portland internee, is reported in a Japanese source. Natsushima states that the FBI placed his small store under surveillance after the attack on Pearl Harbor. On December 10, agents entered his store near closing time and arrested him and his brother-in-law. Without giving them any further information, the FBI took them to jail, where they remained for eighteen days. There, the guards placed Natsushima's breakfasts of mush and coffee, and equally meager lunches, on the floor outside the cell, instructing him to reach through the bars and eat his food with his hands. Natsushima likened this ignominious situation to being treated like a chicken. Kazuo Ito, *America shunju hachijunen* (America spring-fall eighty years) (Tokyo: PMC Publishers, 1982), p. 59.

For Seattle, by February 18, 1942, the FBI had taken into custody 178 Issei, 52 Germans, and 8 Italians. A Seattle resident, Mr. S. K. was interned for a year and a half because of his three trips to Japan in 1911, 1929, and 1940 and because "he was a member of the Seattle Japanese Association, the Seattle Japanese Meat Retail Association, and the Hiroshima Kenjinkai [Hiroshima Prefectural Association]." Besides having relatives in Japan, he also "donated to the Japanese language school." Memorandum, AEC Unit, 29 June 1943, Justice Department, INS, RG 85, F.N. 39.052, Box 288, p. 6, N.A.

Ito (*America shunju*, p. 64) also reports that the FBI arrested and interned Mr. Tokichi Uyehara in the mistaken belief that he was Tokuya Uyehara, an employee of the Seattle branch of the Japan Shipmail Company. It also arrested Mr. Tora Miyake, believing him to be Toro Miyake, a former director of the *Northwest Jiho,* a Japanese-vernacular newspaper. In fact, Toro Miyake had passed away before the war started. Both Issei were interned for a year and half before being paroled to the W R A.

The story of another foreign national contains some unique features. Samuel Ichiro Yamate (a pseudonym) was born and raised in Vancouver, British Columbia, but was of Japanese ancestry and carried a Japanese passport. He received a B.Sc. degree in forest engineering from the University of British Columbia and, as worldwide depression took hold in the early 1930s, accepted the only engineering position available to him, with Mitsubishi Shoji Corporation, a Japanese company operating in Seattle. Since it was difficult for a Japanese Canadian to immigrate to the United States, he obtained a Japanese passport as a treaty merchant and worked for Mitsubishi in Seattle from 1930 until December 1941.

He was playing golf when he heard news of the attack on Pearl Harbor on the public address system. Astonished and disconcerted, he returned home to call a few of his Japanese business friends, only to find that the F B I had already arrested many of them. Believing it was just a matter of time before his own arrest, he packed a suitcase and waited for the inevitable. After a week or so, the F B I telephoned him with some questions and ordered him to appear for further talks. Although he does not recall the questions exactly, he knows they concerned his overall attitude toward the war and whether his basic loyalty was to the United States or to Japan. Yamate recalls the common belief within the Nikkei community that any person summoned to the F B I office would not return. In an attempt to prevent this from happening, he took his youngest son, an American citizen, with him whenever he was summoned. He endured several interviews over a period of three months. Most often, the interviewers were F B I agents, although on one occasion, a representative of the district attorney's office was present.

Finally, without offering any reason, the F B I arrested him in March 1942. He was taken to the Seattle I N S station and later transferred to a makeshift holding area near the Seattle Boeing Airfield camp, where there were a few other Issei. He knows of no reason why he and these Issei were treated differently from other Japanese nationals. The Justice Department kept Yamate there for nine months until he was released. He was given no further information about his case nor did the agency offer any apology for the time he had spent behind barbed wire. Yamate's story is unique: he was a Canadian carrying a Japanese passport and working in the United States. His nine-month internment was probably a result of his immigrant status as an alien carrying a Japanese passport and working for a Japanese company. That he was not taken for permanent internment and treated as other Issei perhaps reflects his uniqueness. S. Yamate (pseudonym), interviewed at his office in Seattle, 1979, by the author. Interview is in the author's possession.

44. Genji Mihara, interviewed at his home in Seattle, 1979, by Janet Inahara. Interview is in the author's possession.

45. Memorandum, A E C Unit, September 1943, Justice Department, I N S, RG 85, F.N. Box 288, 39.052, N.A.

46. Eugene M. Culp, "Alien Enemy Paroles," Department of Justice, *Immigration and Naturalization Monthly Review* 3, no. 4 (October 1945): 205.

47. Telegram, John L. DeWitt to Attorney General Biddle, 12 December 1941, and memorandum, General A. Gullion to War Department, 23 December 1941, U.S. Army, Records of the Adjutant General's Office, RG 407, F.N. Stack 17, W3, Row 3, Box 21, N.A.

48. Telegram, 11 December 1941, F B I, F.N. 100-2-29-234, and memorandum, 11 December 1941, F B I, F.N. 100-2-29-23, Washington, D.C.

49. Telegram, 11 December 1941, F B I, F.N. 100-2-29-234.

50. Herbert V. Nicholson, *Treasures in Earthen Vessels* (Whittier, Calif.: Penn Lithographics, 1974), p. 65.

51. Interview, E. Ennis.

52. Memorandum, 23 February 1942, War Department, Records of the Provost Marshal General's Office, RG 389, F.N. Entry 451, Box 1217, N.A.

53. Memorandum, A E C Unit, September 1943, Justice Department, I N S, RG 85, F.N. Box 288, 39.052, N.A.

54. Nicholson, *Treasures in Earthen Vessels,* p. 65. In a reported German alien hearing, the questions had a similar flavor. "Did I like Hitler? Did we attend German-American Day at Cincinnati's Coney Island amusement park? . . . -every question was designed to make me [then a fifteen year old youth] look like a wild-eyed Nazi. One question asked of me was: If your German cousin came up the Ohio river on a U-boat [submarine] and asked for shelter, what would you tell him?" Eberhard Fuhr, interview, quoted in Krammer, *Undue Process,* p. 79.

55. Nicholson, *Treasures in Earthen Vessels,* p. 65.

56. Minoru Yasui, "Minidoka," in John Tateishi, ed., *And Justice for All* (New York: Random House, 1984), p. 67.

57. Ibid. pp. 67–68.

58. Interview, Herbert V. Nicholson, in Arthur A. Hansen and Betty E. Mitson, eds. *Voices Long Silent* (Fullerton: Oral History Program, California State University, 1974), p. 131.

59. Nicholson, *Treasures in Earthen Vessels,* p. 124.

60. Interview, E. Ennis.

61. Ibid.

62. Letter, E. Ennis to L. B. Schofield, July 2, 1942, Justice Department, I N S, RG 85, p. 2, N.A.

63. Interview, E. Ennis.

64. Memorandum, 14 September 1942, I N S, RG 85, F.N. 56125/Gen-B, p. 2, N. A.

65. Littell, *My Roosevelt Years,* p. 75.

66. Parolees were usually required to report on a monthly basis. Culp, "Alien Enemy Paroles," p. 207. In 1943, the Justice Department eliminated this particular agency and reorganized it as the Alien Control Division.

67. Teletype, 11 February 1942, F B I, F.N. 100-2-50-55, Washington, D.C.

68. In most instances, the Justice Department's policy was not to accept American citizens of enemy-nation ancestry for permanent internment. However, many were apprehended and detained, some for long periods of time in the Justice Department camps. By the end of the war, the Justice Department was holding some forty American citizens of

German ancestry and eight citizens of Italian ancestry. How long each person was kept, where these American citizens were held, and what became of them is not easy to determine from the available files. The cases of Samuel Yamate (see n. 43 above), Yoshiju Kimura (discussed at the end of this chapter), and the Kibei arrested in Hawaii (see chapter 4) are illustrative examples. Each case is different.

69. Yoshiju Kimura, *Arizona Sunset* (Glendale, Ariz.: Y. Kimura, 1980), pp. 55–56.

70. Ibid. pp. 63–64.

71. Interview, E. Ennis.

72. *Los Angeles Times*, November 13, 1941, p. 11, and memorandum, 28 January 1942, F B I, F.N. 100-2-29-193, p. 13, Washington, D.C.

73. The topic of dual citizenship received little recognition or emphasis during the war. Some Nisei were citizens of both the United States and Japan, but they were few in number, and this issue never became an important one to Japanese Americans or the U.S. government. Some readers may conclude from this that the Nisei thus were basically loyal to Japan rather than to the United States. It is probably safe to say that such was not the case.

The issue of citizenship here concerns a legal category. Japan, as did many European nations, relied on a *jus sanguinis* principle whereby the child of a father who has Japanese citizenship at the time of birth is considered to be Japanese. The United States, basing its rule on a *jus soli* principle, stipulates that U.S. citizenship is acquired through birth on U.S. soil. Therefore, according to international law, the Nisei, who were born in the United States, could be Japanese nationals based on ancestry and U.S. citizens by reason of birthplace.

Japan, however, has never strongly claimed that the Nisei were Japanese citizens. Indeed, by 1924, the Japanese had revised their law to require that parents of children so eligible for Japanese citizenship register their offspring within fourteen days after birth with the express intent of retaining Japanese citizenship. Moreover, provisions were made for Nisei born before December 1, 1924, that would enable them to renounce their Japanese citizenship.

Three points should be made. First, the conflicting nationality laws of the two countries resulted in a legal category over which the dual citizen had no control. Second, dual citizenship had little bearing on the basic loyalty of the Nisei, since these categories were legal definitions on an international rather than a personal level. And finally, if an Issei parent registered an infant as a Japanese citizen, the Nisei could not have known about or acquiesced to the act.

By 1943, a W R A survey found 15–20 percent of the Nisei were dual citizens. Although the proportion seems high, a number of factors make dual citizenship a moot factor with respect to basic loyalty. Foremost is the suggestion that if a person holding dual loyalties were to opt for either Japan or the United States, there is just as much reason, if not more reason, to assert that the Nisei would choose the United States over Japan. The *jus sanguinis* principle is also followed by Italy and Germany, both Axis allies of Japan, but dual citizenship never became an issue for the American-born offspring of those countries' citizens. Much of this information comes from tenBroek et al., *Prejudice, War and the Constitution*, pp. 271–73.

4 / THE TERRITORY OF HAWAII

1. See, for example, Lawrence Fuchs, *Hawaii Pono* (New York: Harcourt, 1961), and Dennis Ogawa, *Kodomo no Tame-ni—For the Sake of the Children* (Honolulu: University Press of Hawaii, 1978).

2. Roland Kotani, "The Japanese in Hawaii: A Century of Struggle," program booklet of the Oahu Kanyaku Imin Centennial Committee (Honolulu: Hawaii Hochi, 1985), p. 90.

3. Memorandum, R. C. Shivers to J. E. Hoover, 4 December 1941, Federal Bureau of Investigation (hereafter FBI), File Number (hereafter F.N.) 100-2-20-26, National Archives, Washington, D.C. (hereafter N.A.).

4. Ibid.

5. Memorandum, A. P. Sullivan to Commanding General (hereafter CG), Hawaiian Dept., 13 March 1941, U.S. Army, Records of the Provost Marshal General's Office, RG 407, F.N. Entry 360, Box 28, N.A.; memorandum, W. P. Short to Adjutant General, 18 April 1941, U.S. Army, Records of the Provost Marshal General's Office, RG 407, F.N. Entry 360, Box 28, N.A. In response, the Hawaii CG submitted a plan on April 18, requesting that two establishments be turned over to its control—the INS Immigration Building on Ala Moana Road and the Public Health Service Quarantine Station at Sand Island, both on the island of Oahu, in Honolulu. Although the INS agreed, the Public Health Service refused to relinquish its station. When war did break out, the army simply requisitioned it. Meanwhile, during this prewar period, the army looked for additional sites for holding the internee population. It proposed construction of another internment facility with three separate compounds, at a cost of $319,000, on the Schofield Barracks Military Reservation on Oahu, one mile away from the barracks near the village of Wahiawa.

6. Memorandum, W. P. Short to Adjutant General, 3 July 1941, U.S. Army, RG 407, F.N. Entry 360, Box 28, N.A.

7. Norman M. Littell, *My Roosevelt Years* (Seattle: University of Washington Press, 1987), p. 11.

8. Ibid., p. 117.

9. Ibid.

10. General Order Number 5, dated December 8, 1941, ordered in part that all Japanese nationals refrain from hostile acts or otherwise aiding or abetting the enemy, comply with expanded curfew hours, and surrender or refrain from using various items, including weapons, explosives, radio transmitters, cameras, or codes. In addition, the Issei could not change their addresses or occupations without permission from local authorities.

11. Radiogram, Adjutant General to CG, Army and Corps Commanders, 7 December 1941, U.S. Army, RG 407, F.N. PMG 014.311-8, N.A.

12. J. Edgar Hoover, "Alien Enemy Control," *Iowa Law Review* 29 (March 1944): 402.

13. Memorandum, 17 December 1941, FBI, F.N. 100-2-20-x, pp. 2–3, Washington, D.C.

14. Kazuo Miyamoto, *Hawaii* (Rutland, Vt.: Charles E. Tuttle, 1964), p. 335.

15. Memorandum, R. Shivers to J. E. Hoover, 4 December 1941, FBI, F.N. 100-2-20-26, Washington, D.C.

16. Ibid.

17. Memorandum, E. S. Tamm to J. E. Hoover, 8 December 1941, F B I, F.N. 100-2-20-x, Washington, D.C.

18. Memorandum, 9 December 1941, F B I, F.N. 100-2-20-x, Washington, D.C.

19. Memorandum, Townsend to Amberg, Special Assistant to Secretary of War, 9 December 1941, F B I, F.N. 100-2-20-x, N.A.

20. Memorandum, 10 December 1941, U.S. Army, Adjutant General's Office, RG 407, F.N. Entry 360, Box 28, N.A.

21. Memorandum, A. W. Gullion to Chief of Staff, 13 January 1941, U.S. Army, Adjutant General's Office, RG 407, F.N. Entry 360, Box 28, N.A.

22. The islands and places where those apprehended were detained are as follows: Hawaii, Kilauea Military Camp and Volcano Internment Camp; Kauai, Wailua County Jail, Kalaheo Stockade, and Waimea County Jail; and Oahu, I N S Immigration Building, Sand Island Detention Station, and Honouliuli Gulch Internment Camp. From Maui, Molokai, and Lanai, detainees were taken initially to the Maui County Jail and Haiku Internment Camp. Compiled from Allen Gwenfield, *Hawaii's War Years* (Honolulu: University of Hawaii Press, 1950), pp. 136–37; Andrew Lind, *The Japanese in Hawaii under War Conditions* (Honolulu: American Council Institute of Pacific Relations, 1942), p. 23; Hank Sato, "Honouliuli Camp: Footnote to a Dark Chapter," *Honolulu Star-Bulletin*, March 18, 1976, pp. A-1–A-8; Nakano and Nakano, eds. and trans., *Poets behind Barbed Wire* (Honolulu: Bamboo Ridge Press, 1983), p. 4; memorandum, 6 December 1941, F B I, F.N. 100-2-20-38; Kotani, "Japanese in Hawaii," p. 91.

23. Kotani, "Japanese in Hawaii," pp. 89–90.

24. Miyamoto, *Hawaii*, p. 314.

25. Kotani, "Japanese in Hawaii," p. 92.

26. Patsy Saiki, Commission on Wartime Relocation and Internment of Civilians (hereafter C W R I C) hearing, September 9, 1981, Seattle, and Kotani, "Japanese in Hawaii."

27. Quoted in Yukiko Kimura, *Issei* (Honolulu: University of Hawaii Press, 1988), p. 222.

28. Gordon W. Prange, *At Dawn We Slept* (New York: Penguin Books, 1981), p. 586. Secretary of the Navy Knox, a Republican, was brought into President Roosevelt's cabinet as a symbol of bipartisanship. His past positions included publisher of the *Chicago Daily News,* but before that, Knox "had been general manager of the Hearst Newspaper during the shrill racist blasts against Chinese and Japanese immigration on the West Coast" (John Hersey, "A Mistake of Terrifically Horrible Proportions," in John Armor and Peter Wright, *Manzanar* [New York: Times Books, 1988], p. 18).

29. Knox's position on Japanese Americans again underscores an important point—the refusal of this high-ranking, influential official to differentiate between Issei and Nisei.

30. C W R I C, *Personal Justice Denied*, reprint, with a new foreword (Seattle: University of Washington Press, 1997), p. 264.

31. Radiogram to CG, Hawaiian Dept., 10 January 1942, U.S. Army, Records of the Provost Marshal General's Office, RG 407, F.N. Entry 360, Box 28, N.A.

32. Radiogram, Delos C. Emmons to Adjutant General, 12 January 1942, U.S. Army,

Records of the Provost Marshal General's Office, RG 407, F.N. Entry 360, Box 28, N.A. Other individuals in Hawaii did not agree with the War Department's orders. According to the former territorial attorney general: "The Army wanted to move people of Japanese ancestry to Molokai, but [Major General Thomas H.] Green [Executive Officer to the Military Governor, Lieutenant General Emmons] argued against it. I passed this on to Governor Poindexter, who helped prevent the move.... The Japanese owe a lot to both Green and Poindexter." *Honolulu Star-Bulletin*, May 3, 1977, p. 10.

33. Radiogram, Delos C. Emmons to Adjutant General, 12 January 1942, U.S. Army, Records of the Provost Marshal General's Office, RG 407, F.N. Entry 360, Box 28, N.A.

34. Greg Robinson, *By Order of the President* (Cambridge: Harvard University Press, 2001), p. 147.

35. FBI Agent Shivers, in Hawaii, reports on Emmons's view: "Commanding General has given up idea of interning all Japanese aliens and or all Japanese aliens and citizens of Japanese extraction. He now desires continuation of present policy of picking up those where information and facts justify this action. He is working out plans to immobilize all persons of Japanese ancestry on the island of Oahu at the time of another attack which means people of Japanese ancestry will be required to remain stationary at place found when attack occurs. This appears sensible and intelligent solution." Telegram, 16 January 1942, FBI, F.N. 100-2-20-66, Washington, D.C.

36. Memorandum, Gerow to Chief of Staff, Army, 31 January 1942, U.S. Army, Records of the Provost Marshal General's Office, RG 407, F.N. Entry 360, Box 28, N.A.

37. Memorandum, Karl L. Bendetsen to Assistant Chief of Staff, 30 January 1942, U.S. Army, Records of the Provost Marshal General's Office, RG 407, F.N. Entry 360, Box 28, N.A.

38. Telegram, D. E. Emmons to Adjutant General, 10 February 1942, U.S. Army, Records of the Provost Marshal General's Office, RG 407, F.N. Entry 360, Box 28, N.A.

39. Memorandum, 16 December 1941, F.N. 100-2-20-18, Washington, D.C. Yet, their share of the total arrests far exceeded their proportion of the Hawaii population—70 percent were Issei and 12.7 percent were Nisei, accounting for nearly 83 percent of the entire interned group. A person could be released for a variety of factors, such as extreme age, gender, hearing board recommendation, and an unspecified category of "other circumstances."

40. Memorandum, 30 March 1942, F.N. 100-2-20-155, Washington, D.C., and memorandum, A. W. Gullion to Chief of Staff, 28 February 1942, U.S. Army, Records of the Provost Marshal General's Office, RG 407, F.N. Entry 360, Box 28, N.A. A second group with 167 Issei, 1 Nisei, and 2 German nationals left Honolulu for the Justice Department camps on the mainland on March 21, 1942. Radiogram, 28 March 1942, FBI, F.N. 100-2-20-156, Washington, D.C.

Two sources disagree on the number of prisoners first taken to the mainland and the sailing date. In an FBI memorandum listing the transported internees, there are 174 recognizably Japanese names in a total of 200, and Sub-lieutenant Sakamaki, the Japanese navy POW, is listed as number 201. Memorandum, R. L. Shivers to the FBI Bureau Director, 22 February 1942, F.N. 100-2-2-115, Washington, D.C. Saiki, on the other hand, reports that 172 Japanese left the immigration station on February 20, 1942, at about 9:00 A.M. Patsy Saiki,

Gambare! An Example of Japanese Spirit (Honolulu: Kisaku, 1982), pp. 46–47, 222. One solution to the date discrepancy is to assume that the army loaded the internees on February 20 but waited until the next day to set sail.

Sub-lieutenant Sakamaki commanded a midget submarine that was damaged during the attack on Pearl Harbor. He escaped from his submarine and swam to Waimanalo Beach on Oahu, where he was captured by a military patrol that was waiting in preparation for a Japanese invasion. The army transported him to the mainland, and he was apparently the lone Japanese POW until nine others joined him in July 1942.

Besides those of Japanese ancestry, other U.S. citizens were transported to the mainland. Their hearing board recommendations stated that two persons were "definitely pro-Nazi and considered dangerous" and that a Norwegian was an "outspoken Nazi sympathizer" who used his home for pro-Nazi meetings. Telegram, D. E. Emmons to Adjutant General, 2 March 1942, U.S. Army, Records of the Provost Marshal General's Office, RG 407, F.N. Entry 360, Box 28, Washington, D.C.

41. Saiki, *Gambare!*, pp. 221–26.

42. Memorandum, A. L. Lerch for the Adjutant General, 30 March 1942, U.S. Army, Records of the Provost Marshal General's Office, RG 407, F.N. Entry 360, Box 28, N.A.

43. Radiogram, 1 December 1942, FBI, F.N. 100-2-20-175, Washington, D.C.

44. Sato, "Honouliuli Camp," p. A-8.

45. Saiki, CWRIC testimony.

46. Miyamoto, *Hawaii*, pp. 314–98.

47. Memorandum, Frank Knox to Franklin D. Roosevelt, 23 February 1942, reproduced in Kotani, "Japanese in Hawaii."

48. Quoted in Ted Morgan, *FDR* (New York: Simon and Schuster, 1985), p. 629.

49. Memorandum, General Staff, 18 March 1942, U.S. Army, Records of the Provost Marshal General's Office, RG 407, F.N. Entry 360, Box 28, N.A.

50. Memorandum, A. W. Gullion to Chief of Staff, 26 March 1942, U.S. Army, Records of the Provost Marshal General's Office, RG 407, F.N. Entry 360, Box 28, N.A.

51. Telegram, D. E. Emmons to Adjutant General, 28 March 1942, U.S. Army, Records of the Provost Marshal General's Office, RG 407, F.N. Entry 360, Box 28, N.A.

52. Telegram, Chief of Staff to D. E. Emmons, 28 June 1942, U.S. Army, Records of the Provost Marshal General's Office, RG 407, F.N. Entry 360, Box 28, N.A.

53. Karleen Chinen, "Return to Tule Lake," *Hawaii Herald*, supplement, October 7, 1988, p. B-4.

54. Ibid., pp. B-4–B-7.

55. Memorandum, E. J. Crane, HQ, Maui Service Command, 27 October 1942, FBI, F.N. 100-2-20-173, Washington, D.C.

56. Memorandum, K. Kanazawa, HQ, Maui Service Command, 26 October 1942, FBI, F.N. 100-2-20-172, p. 2, Washington, D.C.

57. Hajime Takemoto, Ewa, Oahu, Hawaii, interviewed at the home of Donald T. and Lynn (Takemoto) Mizokawa, Bellevue, Wash., 1987, by the author.

58. Memorandum, E. J. Crane, HQ, Maui Service Center, 20 October 1942, FBI, F.N. 100-2-20-1xx, Washington, D.C.

59. Ibid.

60. Ibid.

61. Memorandum, E. J. Crane, HQ, Maui Service Command, 27 October 1942, F.N. 100-2-20-1xx, p. 3, Washington, D.C.

62. Letter, Richardson to J. J. McCloy, 2 February 1944, War Department, Records of the Adjutant General's Office, RG 389, F.N. Box 1511, File 2, N.A.

63. Sato, "Honouliuli Camp," p. A-6, and *Hawaii Herald,* October 7, 1988, p. 10.

64. The army also kept women at this camp. At least seven females, with names indicating apparent Japanese ancestry, such as Nakagawa, Takahashi, and Suzuki, were sequestered in their own section. They were separated from the men by a barbed-wire fence. See Sato, "Honouliuli Camp," p. A-6.

65. In June 1944, the navy arrested four Japanese civilian adults and six children in the Marshall Islands as enemy aliens and transported them to the army's Hawaiian command. Later, five more were also brought, for a total of fifteen persons. The CG, Pacific Oceans Area, wrote to the army's provost marshal general to ascertain whether they should be designated as enemy aliens or prisoners of war. Another question concerned the appropriateness of transporting them to the mainland for internment. The Justice Department replied that their status and the necessity for removal from the Marshall Islands were decisions for the commanding general. Nevertheless, the Justice Department stated that it was prepared to accept these civilians for internment at the mainland family internment center. Memorandum, Provost Marshal General to CG, Pacific Oceans Area, 13 November 1944, CWRIC Papers, Numbers 531–535A.

66. Theodore Tamba, "Secrets of U.S., Peruvian Wartime Intrigue Revealed in This Article," *Hokubei Mainichi Newspaper* (San Francisco), March 30, 1972, p. 1.

67. Sato, "Honouliuli Camp," p. A-8.

68. Ibid., p. A-1.

69. Henry Tanaka, CWRIC testimony, September 9, 1981, Seattle.

70. James Okahata, ed., *A History of Japanese in Hawaii* (Honolulu: The United Japanese Society of Hawaii, 1971), p. 265; Allen, *Hawaii's War Years,* p. 134.

71. Saiki states that 697 Japanese nationals were moved to the mainland and gives ten departure dates in 1942 and 1943. This 697 number does not represent all those transported since it omits the Nisei, Kibei, and "voluntary internees." Saiki, *Gambare!,* pp. 221–26.

72. Quoted in CWRIC, *Personal Justice Denied,* p. 274.

73. Files, 14 September 1943, FBI, F.N. 62-69023-532, Washington, D.C.

5 / THE TERRITORY OF ALASKA AND LATIN AMERICA

1. Memorandum, Army Adjutant General, 21 March 1941, U.S. Army, Record Group (hereafter RG) 407, File Number (hereafter F.N.) 014.311, Box 21, Stack 17, W.3, Row 3, National Archives, Washington, D.C. (hereafter N.A.).

2. Memorandum, 5 May 1941, Federal Bureau of Investigation (hereafter FBI), F.N. 100-2-25-x, Washington, D.C.

3. Memorandum, 5 December 1941, FBI, F.N. 100-2-25-3, Washington, D.C.

4. Telegram, A. W. Gullion to Commanding General (hereafter CG), Alaska Defense Command, 7 December 1941, U.S. Army, Records of the Adjutant General's Office, RG 407, F.N. Box 21, Stack 7, W.3, Row 3, N.A.

5. Memorandum, 7 December 1941, FBI, F.N. 100-2-25-4, Washington, D.C.

6. Radiogram, 25 January 1942, FBI, F.N. 100-2-25-28, Washington, D.C.

7. Radiogram, 8 December 1941, ibid.

8. Memorandum, J. E. Hoover to Juneau Special Agent in Charge (hereafter SAC), 10 December 1941, FBI, F.N. 100-2-25-6, Washington, D.C.

9. Memorandum, 11 December 1941, FBI, F.N. 100-2-25-7, Washington, D.C.

10. Memorandum, J. E. Hoover to staff, 13 December 1941, FBI, F.N. 100-2-25-9, Washington, D.C.

11. Radiogram, J. E. Hoover to Juneau SAC, 13 December 1941, FBI, F.N. 100-2-25-8, Washington, D.C.

12. Radiogram, 17 December 1941, FBI, F.N. 100-2-25-11, Washington, D.C.

13. Memorandum, R. C. Vogel to J. E. Hoover, 22 December 1941, FBI, F.N. 100-2-25-12, Washington, D.C.

14. Radiogram and memorandums, 29 December 1941, FBI, F.N. 100-2-25-19, 20, and 21, Washington, D.C.

15. Memorandum, CG, Alaska Defense Command to Adjutant General, 14 February 1942, located in Commission on the Wartime Relocation and Internment of Civilians (hereafter CWRIC) papers, Number 6128, RG 220, N.A.

16. Claus-M. Naske, "The Relocation of Alaska's Japanese Residents," *Pacific Northwest Quarterly* 74, no. 3 (1983): 124–32.

17. Memorandum, 10 June 1942, FBI, F.N. 100-2-25-37, Washington, D.C.

18. Naske, "Relocation of Alaska's Japanese Residents," p. 130.

19. Radiogram, 25 February 1942, FBI, F.N. 100-2-21-29x, Washington, D.C.

20. Radiogram, 26 February 1942, FBI, F.N. 100-2-25-30, Washington, D.C.

21. Naske breaks down the total number incarcerated in Alaska by the cities from which they originated: 57 from Ketchikan, 38 from Petersburg, 35 from Juneau, 14 from Sitka, 13 from Seward and Wrangell, 8 from Fairbanks, 7 from Cordova, 5 from Kodiak and Clarks Point, 4 from Deering, 3 from Killisno and Ekuk, 2 from Angoon, Wiseman, and Beaver, and 1 each from Tenakee Springs, Pilot Point, Kotzebue Tanana, and Bethel. "Relocation of Alaska's Japanese Residents," pp. 124–32.

22. This incident was reported to the author by a Nisei informant who wished to remain anonymous. He lived in Anchorage until he was brought to Seattle and placed into the WCCA assembly center at Puyallup, Wash., in 1942. Unrecorded interview by author, Bellevue, Wash., 1989.

23. Jacobus tenBroek, Edward N. Barnhart, and Floyd W. Matson, *Prejudice, War, and the Constitution* (Berkeley: University of California Press, 1954), p. 135; Michi Weglyn, *Years of Infamy* (New York: William Morrow and Co., 1976), p. 57; and Naske, "Relocation of Alaska's Japanese Residents," p. 127.

24. Paul R. Spickard, "Injustice Compounded: Amerasians and Non-Japanese Ameri-

cans in World War II Concentration Camps," *Journal of American Ethnic History* 5, no. 2 (spring 1986): 17.

25. Naske, "Relocation of Alaska's Japanese Residents," p. 128.

26. From June 1942, the United States also removed residents of the Aleutian Islands; 881 Aleuts, including some 30 non-Aleuts, were taken to various camps in southeast Alaska, where all but 50 remained until 1944 and 1945. CWRIC, *Personal Justice Denied*, reprint, with new foreword (Seattle: University of Washington Press, 1997), pp. 317–59.

27. Naske, "Relocation of Alaska's Japanese Residents," p. 13.

28. Ibid.

29. Ibid.

30. Quoted in John K. Emmerson, *The Japanese Thread* (New York: Holt, Rinehart and Winston, 1978), p. 126.

31. Although all fifteen countries sent some number of German, Japanese, and other foreign nationals to the United States for internment, an accurate count of all such persons is difficult to present. On June 30, 1945, there were 2,253 interned persons, but this number does not represent everyone involved in the program, since some people came earlier and were sent as exchanges to their homelands, others were paroled, a few died, and some children were born in the United States. There were also 835 Germans (484 males, 148 females, 203 minors) and unspecified others (62 males, 15 females, 9 minors) in custody on this date. Compiled from memorandum, 30 June 1945, Immigration and Naturalization Service (hereafter INS), RG 85, F.N. 125 General, N.A.

32. See Emmerson, *Japanese Thread*, p. 127.

The FBI was actively interested not only in internal security matters but in intelligence matters outside the United States. Hoover and the chiefs of military intelligence met with President Roosevelt and a State Department representative in June 1940 to discuss a world-wide strategy. The FBI proposal asked for jurisdiction over foreign intelligence investigations in the Western Hemisphere—including the Caribbean, Central America, Mexico, and South America—upon request from the State Department. The navy would be given jurisdiction over the Pacific, and the army was to be responsible for Africa, Europe, and the Panama Canal Zone. Sanford J. Ungar, *FBI* (Boston: Little, Brown and Co., 1976), pp. 103, 225, and Don Whitehead, *The FBI Story* (New York: Random House, 1956), pp. 166–67.

From July 1, 1940, to March 31, 1947, the SIS identified 887 persons suspected of being Axis espionage agents, resulting in 389 arrests and 105 convictions. The SIS identified suspect Axis propaganda agents, had them arrested, and convicted 20 "saboteurs" and 11 "smugglers" of war materials. Ungar, *FBI*, p. 225.

33. Memorandum, W. F. Kelly to D. Schedler, 24 May 1948, INS, RG 85, F.N. 56125/Gen., N.A. Krammer gives slightly different numbers—a total of 6,610 persons from Latin America brought to the United States. Of this number, 4,058 were of German ancestry, 2,264 were of Japanese ancestry, and 288 were of Italian ancestry. Arnold Krammer, *Undue Process* (Boulder, Colo.: Rowman and Littlefield Publishers, 1997), p. 95.

34. See Weglyn, *Years of Infamy*.

35. Within the State Department, the Special War Problems Division had responsibility

for this area. See Scott P. Corbett, *Quiet Passages* (Kent, Ohio: Kent State University Press, 1987), p. 141.

36. Jerri Mangione, *An Ethnic at Large* (New York: G. P. Putnam's Sons, 1978), p. 322.

37. Emmerson, *Japanese Thread,* pp. 143–44.

38. Memorandum, "Report of Internee from Latin America," 30 June 1945, INS, RG 85.

39. Chizuko W. Hougen, "The Japanese Immigrant Community in Mexico: Its History and Present," M.A. thesis, California State University, Los Angeles, June 1983, p. 64.

40. Hougen, "Japanese Immigrant Community," pp. 65–66.

41. Karl G. Yoneda, *Ganbatte* (Los Angeles: Asian American Studies Center, University of California, Los Angeles, 1983), p. 120.

42. Interview of A. K. Yamane, quoted in Hougen, "Japanese Immigrant Community," p. 206.

43. Hougen, "Japanese Immigrant Community," p. 67.

44. Quoted in ibid., p. 77.

45. Ibid., pp. 77, 86. I am indebted to Erasmo Gamboa, University of Washington, Seattle, personal correspondence, April 6, 2001, for pointing out the existence of the third site.

46. Ibid., pp. 78–79. My appreciation goes to Elizabeth Salas and Erasmo Gamboa, University of Washington, Seattle, personal correspondence, April 6 and 15, 2001, for clarifying points in the Mexico section.

47. Ibid., pp. 79–80.

48. Corbett, *Quiet Passages,* pp. 141, 150, 161, and Hougen, "Japanese Immigrant Community," p. 78.

49. Edward Ennis, interview held during Gordon Hirabayashi's *coram nobis* hearings at the Seattle Hilton Hotel, June 20, 1985. Interview is in the author's possession.

50. Corbett, *Quiet Passages,* p. 143.

51. C. Harvey Gardiner, *The Japanese and Peru* (Albuquerque: University of New Mexico Press, 1975), p. 85.

52. Emmerson, *Japanese Thread,* p. 145.

53. Gardiner, *Japanese and Peru,* p. 78.

54. Corbett, *Quiet Passages,* p. 146.

55. Ibid., p. 140.

56. Kakuaki and Otari Kaneko, interviewed at their home in Lemon Grove, Calif., June 1977, by the author. Interview is in the author's possession.

57. Memorandum, State Department, RG 59, in CWRIC papers, Numbers 5641–45, RG 220, N.A.

58. Emmerson, *Japanese Thread,* pp. 148–49.

59. Corbett, *Quiet Passages,* p. 147; Edward N. Barnhart, "Japanese Internees from Peru," *Pacific Historical Review* 31, no. 2 (May 1962): 169–78.

60. Edward Ennis, September 29, 1942, quoted in Corbett, *Quiet Passages,* pp. 148–49.

61. Ibid., p. 155.

62. Memorandum, L. L. Lewis to C. E. Waller, 14 February 1944, INS, RG 85, F.N. 89-3, N.A.

63. This number of Peruvians does not equal 1,771 because some were subsequently repatriated or expatriated to Japan on an early exchange ship.

64. Relaxed internment status required that an internee sign an agreement before being allowed to leave the INS's Crystal City Internment Camp. The internee agreed not to leave the Seabrook Farms property except for authorized purposes—recreational, medical, religious, business, or for visits less than six miles away and for up to six hours at a time. Memorandum, "Internee War Project and Agreement" form, 2 October 1946, Crystal City, Tex., INS, RG 85, "Crystal City, TX file," N.A., and Mitziko Sawada, "After the Camps: Seabrook Farms, New Jersey, and the Resettlement of Japanese Americans, 1944–1947," *Amerasia Journal* 13, no. 2 (1986–87): 128.

During World War II, Seabrook Farms Company became a major producer of frozen foods. Much of its achievement rested on manual labor. Labor shortages during the war required the company to take whomever was available, even children on school breaks or people on vacation. From May to October 1943, the United States transported 1,202 Jamaicans to work there, and in February 1944, 150 German prisoners of war arrived as workers. Seabrook hired workers of Japanese ancestry through the WRA and by December 1, 1944, employed 831 Nikkei. A year later, the number had grown to 1,688 and included interned Japanese Peruvians by the end of December 1945. In January 1947, there were 2,300–2,700 Nikkei laborers out of a total workforce of 5,000. Sawada, "After the Camps," pp. 117–36.

65. Sawada, "After the Camps," p. 127.

66. Theodore Tamba, "Secrets of U.S., Peruvian Wartime Intrigue Revealed in This Article," *Hokubei Mainichi Newspaper* (San Francisco), March 30, 1972, p. 1.

67. Kakuaki and Otari Kaneko, interviewed in their home in Lemon Grove, Calif., June 1, 1971; Mrs. Otari Kaneko interviewed in her home in Lemon Grove, Calif., September 27, 1992. Both interviews by author.

68. Tamba, "Secrets of U.S., Peruvian Wartime Intrigue," p. 1.

According to Barnhart, in the immediate postwar years, 79 Japanese, two-thirds of whom were wives and children, returned to Peru while 300 Japanese Peruvians remained in the United States. Later, "in the mid-1950's, when Peru finally indicated that it would allow them to return, only a few chose to go" ("Japanese Internees," pp. 174–75, 177). Most went to Japan. Gardiner states "that of the approximately 1,771 deportees to the United States, only thirty-four were allowed to reenter Peru while 364 remained in the United States, all others having been sent to Japan" (*Japanese and Peru*, p. 174).

69. E. Ennis, interview.

6 / JUSTICE DEPARTMENT AND ARMY CAMPS

1. For more on the Buddhist Churches of America, see Tetsuden Kashima, *Buddhism in America* (Westport, Conn.: Greenwood Press, 1977).

2. Daisho Tana, *Santa Fe, Rozubagu, senji tekikokujin yokuryujo nikki, dai-ikkan* (Santa Fe, Lordsburg, wartime enemy internment place diary, vol. 1) (Tokyo: Sankibo Busshorin Seisaku, 1976), p. 111. Translated with the assistance of Yasuko Iwai Takezawa. After the war,

Reverend Tana served the Hawaii Buddhist community from 1948 to 1951 and returned to the mainland to serve the Buddhist Churches of America from 1951 to 1959.

3. Ibid., Herbert V. Nicholson, *Treasures in Earthen Vessels* (Whittier, Calif.: Penn Lithographics, 1974), p. 66. Women foreign nationals designated as enemy aliens in the Los Angeles area, in weeks after December 7, 1941, were held until their hearing boards convened at the Los Angeles Federal Building. Memorandum, E. Shaughnessy to Willard F. Kelly, Assistant Commissioner for Alien Control, 14 July 1942 and 23 September 1942, Immigration and Naturalization Service (hereafter I N S), Record Group (hereafter RG) 85, File Number (hereafter F.N.) Entry 89, Box 3, 14 July 1942 and 23 September 1942, National Archives, Washington, D.C. (hereafter N.A.).

4. File, 13 December 1943, I N S, F.N. 15944/17, 15942/75, National Archives, Pacific Southwest Regional Center. The Tuna Canyon camp also accepted other Issei brought from W R A camps for unspecified "violations of immigration laws." On October 8, 1943, the apparently last nine persons of Japanese ancestry at this camp were sent to the I N S internment camp at Santa Fe, N.M., and preparations were made to close the camp.

5. The seven permanent I N S stations were located at East Boston, Mass.; Ellis Island, N.Y.; Gloucester City, N.J.; Detroit; Seattle; San Francisco; and San Pedro, Calif. The three prewar internment camps holding stranded German and Italian seamen were located at Fort Stanton, N.M.; Fort Missoula, Mont.; and Fort Lincoln, N.D.

6. Across the Atlantic Ocean, England instituted its own program for the control of various foreign nationals. Since Britain had been at war with Germany since 1939, the country's actions provide an interesting point of comparison. England had a large population of German and Austrian nationals along with a sizable number of Jewish refugees, and after the war started, the government used a selective program to intern 568 foreign nationals. It authorized its actions with the British Defence of the Realm Act, which provided for detention of foreign nationals and British citizens when such action was deemed essential to the country's security. Memorandum, 21 December 1943, I N S, RG 85, F.N. 56125, N.A.

With the discovery of Nazi espionage agents at work in Europe, the British government initiated wholesale arrests and mass internment procedures for particular groups of people. By August 1940, it had jailed some 74,000 foreign nationals, including German and Austrian Jews. As it became clear that many of these internees were actually enemies of the Nazi state, public sentiment generated reaction against the large-scale process. The British changed their system and released thousands of internees, leaving about 15,000 in confinement throughout the war years. Francis Biddle, *In Brief Authority* (New York: Doubleday and Co., 1962), pp. 207–8.

In other British territories, the government arrested enemy nationals from Trinidad and West Africa and transported them to Jamaica, British West Indies. On November 12, 1942, some 1,400 persons were held captive there—including about 200 females and their families. Other countries also took action against their enemy aliens. For example, in Surinam, the Dutch arrested and detained 154 mostly foreign nationals and planned to take them to the Dutch island of Bonaire. Memorandum, General Staff, 12 November 1943, War Department, Records of the Adjutant General's Office, RG 389, F.N. Entry 452, Box 1362, 14.311, Provost Marshal General, N.A.

The Commonwealth countries of Canada and Australia also instituted programs to intern enemy aliens. In Canada, almost all persons of Japanese ancestry, some 22,837, lived in the province of British Columbia in 1942. The Canadian government restricted the movements of or removed 21,079 of them to inland ghost towns, road construction projects, sugar beet farms, or other agricultural projects, all located 100 miles inland from the Pacific coast. There, they faced considerable difficulties, including bitter winters, inadequate shelter, personal deprivation, and other demoralizing events. See Ken Adachi, *The Enemy That Never Was* (Toronto: McClelland and Stewart, 1976); Forrest E. LaViolette, *The Canadian Japanese and World War II* (Toronto: University of Toronto Press, 1948); Ann Gomer Sunahara, *The Politics of Racism* (Toronto: James Lorimer & Co., 1981); and Patricia E. Roy et al., *Mutual Hostages* (Toronto: University of Toronto Press, 1990).

From Australia comes another story. The Japanese first came to Australia in 1871 and found work in the pearl-diving industry in Queensland and Western Australia. Special emigration provisions allowed sufficient Japanese immigration to establish a small settlement with a "Japanese town"in Broome, surrounding the pearl-fishing docks. By World War II, many of the Nisei were reaching adulthood. The Australian government arrested and interned some resident Japanese nationals and some Nisei and placed them in prisoner-of-war camps in remote parts of South Australia and Victoria. Other Nisei volunteered for military service and became part of an underwater demolition task force because of their pearl-diving experience. Apparently, one group of Nisei was given the mission of attaching magnetic mines to Japanese ships harbored in Manila Bay, and their accomplishment of this feat earned them hero status on their return to Australia. Charles Kubokawa, "Australians Relate WW2 Heroics of Nisei Divers Raiding Manila Bay," *Pacific Citizen,* June 27, 1986, p. 3; I am indebted to Brian Tanaka for providing this information. See also Yuriko Nagata, "'A Little Colony on Our Own': Australia's Camps in World War II," and Kay Saunders, "'Taken Away to Be Shot?': The Process of Incarceration in Australia in World War II," in Kay Saunders and Roger Daniels, eds., *Alien Justice* (Queensland, Australia: University of Queensland Press, 2000), pp. 152–67, 185–204.

7. By July 19, 1942, the I N S held the following number of persons:

Nationality	Males	Females	Total
Japanese	1,832	42	1,874
Germans	688	202	890
Italians	222	2	224
Misc.*	16	4	20
TOTAL	2,758	250	3,008

NOTE: Compiled from memorandum, Willard F. Kelly, Assistant Commissioner for Alien Control to E. Shaughnessy, "Report of Alien Enemies in Temporary Detention, July 14, 1942," 23 September 1942, I N S, RG 85, F.N. Entry 89, Box 3, 56125/Gen., N.A.

*Miscellaneous category for Bulgarians, Hungarians, Romanians, and a few other nationalities.

On July 14, 1942, Issei males were also held as follows: Fort McPherson, Ga., Army Post, 1 male; Fort Sam Houston, Tex., Army Post, 2 males; Fort Logan, Colo., Army Post, 8 males; and Fort Bliss, Tex., Army Post, 13 males.

By September 1942, the INS decreased its forty-nine centers to twenty-three and mostly called them "detention stations." But despite releasing or paroling some internees, the INS consolidated the remainder at various sites and continued to hold thousands of others. The INS designated five sites as permanent detention stations and eleven as temporary detention stations, downgrading the Miami site to temporary status, and made five others detention or internment camps. These latter camps were located at Kenedy, Tex.; Fort Lincoln, N.D.; Fort Missoula, Mont.; Fort Stanton, N.M.; and Santa Fe, N.M. Ibid.

   8. Ibid.

   9. Ibid.

   10. INS permanent detention stations were located in the following areas:

Facilities	Population (as of July 14, 1942)				
	Jpn	Ger	Itl	Misc*	Total
Detroit	0	7	0	0	7
East Boston	4	3	0	1	8
Ellis Island, N.Y.	13	519†	39	10	581
Gloucester City, N.J.	4	52	3	2	61
Miami	0	9	6	0	15
Seattle	16	23	8	1	48
TOTAL	37	613	56	14	720

NOTE: Compiled from memorandum, Willard F. Kelly, Assistant Commissioner for Alien Control to E. Shaughnessy, "Report of Alien Enemies in Temporary Detention, July 14, 1942," 23 September 1942, INS, RG 85, F.N. Entry 89, Box 3, 56125/Gen., N.A.

*Miscellaneous category included Bulgarians, Hungarians, Romanians, and a few other unspecified nationalities.

†German seamen captured before 1942.

The Miami facility was later downgraded to a temporary detention station. The Gloucester City station served a special purpose—the INS remodeled it in June 1942 and kept fifty-five women internees there for a short period rather than shipping them to the Seagoville Internment Camp in Texas.

   11. INS Temporary Detention Stations, 1942 (Population as of July 14, 1942):

Place	Description	Capacity	Population			
			Jpn	Ger	Itl	Misc*
Algiers, La.	(not avail.)	150	0	6	4	0
Chicago	private residence	158	2	12	0	1
Cincinnati	part of Parcel Post bldg.	75	0	18	7	1
Cleveland	former police precinct	45	0	11	23	0
Florence, Ariz.	(not avail.)	(not avail.)	(not avail.)			

Ft. Howard, Md.	old army barracks	200	22	8	0	0
Hartford, Conn.	community center	50		(not avail.)		
Houston	former police station	26		(not avail.)		
Kansas City, Mo.	municipal bldg., fl.	20	0	3	2	0
Miami	part of sports stadium	80	0	9	6	0
Nanticoko, Pa.	state armory	100		(not avail.)		
Niagara Falls	former immigra. sta.	40	0	1	0	0
Pittsburgh	state armory	400		(not avail.)		
Portland, Ore.	county jail, wing	60	1	18	1	0
Saint Louis	county jail, wing	30		(not avail.)		
Saint Paul	county jail, floor	30		(not avail.)		
Salt Lake City	county jail, wing	100	8	3	2	1
Sharp Park, Cal.	former state relief camp	450	191	83	105	0
Stringtown, Ok.	(not avail.)	(not avail.)		(not avail.)		
Syracuse	former fire station	25		(not avail.)		
Tuna Canyon, Cal.	former CCC camp	200	67	23	14	0

NOTE: Compiled from INS memorandum, E. Shaughnessy to Willard F. Kelly, 23 September 1942, INS, RG 85, F.N. Entry 89, Box 3, "Report of Alien Enemies in Temporary Detention, July 14, 1942," N.A.

*Miscellaneous category included Bulgarians, Hungarians, Romanians, and a few other nationalities that were not specified.

Memorandum, Willard F. Kelly, 14 October 1942, INS, RG 85, F.N. 89-3, 56125/Gen., p. 6, and 15 August 1944, p. 9, N.A.; and U.S. Department of Justice, Immigration and Naturalization Service (hereafter INS), *Monthly Review* 3, no. 4 (October 1945), and 2, no. 6 (December 1946): 74.

12. U.S. Department of Justice, *Annual Report of the Attorney General of the United States for the Fiscal Year Ended June 30, 1941* (Washington, D.C.: U.S. Government Printing Office, 1942), p. 234. For the 1940–41 fiscal year, for example, the INS admitted 1,436 Chinese claiming U.S. citizenship, refused admission to 127 Chinese nationals, and deported 58 others. Later, especially after the Japanese were apprehended and sent to inland camps, the INS continued to use Sharp Park to hold arrested persons and those awaiting immigration proceedings.

13. C. Harvey Gardiner, *Pawns in a Triangle of Hate* (Seattle: University of Washington Press, 1981), pp. 77–78.

14. Near the end of the war, on February 13, 1945, Sharp Park held twenty-seven internees, mainly German nationals; the population decreased to four Germans by February 19. The INS expected to close this camp on May 15, 1945, but did not do so until 1946. During these months, any remaining German nationals were sent to Fort Lincoln, N.D. Memorandum, S. W. Anderson to L. L. Lewis, 20 February 1945, INS, RG 85, F.N. Entry 89, Box 5, N.A.; memorandum, N. D. Collaer to T. B. Shoemaker, 2 April 1945, INS, RG 85, F.N. 56125/Gen., N.A.; and memorandum, 20 April 1945, INS, RG 85, F.N. Entry 89, Box 5, N.A.

15. The INS opened the Kenedy Internment Camp, in Texas, on the site of a former CCC camp, on March 30, 1942. Kenedy, an all-male facility, was located about fifty miles southeast of San Antonio, in Karnes County. The 2,900 townsfolk of Kenedy lobbied the federal

government to use the closed CCC facility to hold enemy nationals since doing so would result in jobs and revenue for the town. Thomas K. Walls, *The Japanese Texans* (Austin, Tex.:
Institute of Texan Culture, 1987), p. 178. As the existing facility had a capacity of 200 persons,
the INS erected additional temporary barracks and in April 1942 received 456 Germans, 156
Issei, and 14 Italian nationals. In addition, 141 Japanese nationals from Peru became the first
contingent of Latin Americans to come to Kenedy. The INS held twice-daily inmate counts
and three or four bed checks at night. The outer perimeter was patrolled by guards on
horses, and apparently only one internee, a German national, ever tried to escape. He was
quickly recaptured. Ibid., p. 179.

On August 1, 1944, Kenedy held 277 Germans, 215 Japanese, 10 Italians, 2 Hungarians, and
21 others of various nationalities. The INS closed the Kenedy camp in September 1944; it
sent the remaining Issei to the camp at Santa Fe, N.M., and the German nationals to Fort
Lincoln, N.D. Memorandum, Willard F. Kelly, 14 October 1942, INS, RG 85, F.N. 89-3,
56125/Gen., N.A.

16. The INS kept other categories of internees in places designated as detention camps.
German and Italian seamen were kept at the following sites:

Facilities	Seamen Population July 14, 1942		
	German	Italian	Total
Fort Lincoln, N.D.	269	0	269
Fort Missoula, Mont.	0	981	981
Fort Stanton, N.M.	260	0	260
Due to arrive at Fort Stanton from Fort Howard, Md., and Gloucester City, N.J., by July 14	143	0	143
TOTAL	672	981	1,653

NOTE: Memorandum, Willard F. Kelly to E. Shaughnessy, 23 September 1942,
INS, RG 85, F.N. Entry 89-3, 56125/Gen., N.A.

Although the INS designated two camps as detention stations in July 1942, neither was
specified as permanent or temporary. By September, the facility at Kenedy, Tex., became a
detention camp, while the INS designated the Seagoville camp, also in Texas, as a temporary
detention station.

17. See memorandum, E. Shaughnessy to Willard F. Kelly, 23 September 1942, as well as
memorandum, Willard F. Kelly, 14 October 1942, INS, RG 85, F.N. 89-3, 56125/Gen., N.A.,
and 15 August 1944, INS, RG 85, F.N. 89-3, p. 9, N.A.; and memorandum, 25 March 1944,
FBI, F.N. 62-63892-215, Washington, D.C.

A schism developed within the Italian group. The FBI reported that two factions were in
constant conflict. The pro-Fascist group, allegedly composed of the Italian seamen, had two
subgroups: Squadristi, a secret terrorist group supposedly handpicked by Benito Mussolini,
and Ovra, the secret police of the Fascists. Apparently, posturing by members of these two
groups plus some wearing black shirts infuriated the anti-Fascists. A fight ensued on September 3, 1943, which resulted in medical attention or hospitalization, but no reported
deaths, on both sides. Since Fort Missoula was scheduled to close in a few months, nothing

was done about the incident; a notation was simply placed in the dossier that went with each participant to his next internment camp or parole officer. Memorandum, 9 June 1944, FBI, F.N. 62-63892-220, Washington, D.C.

18. Testimony, Masato Uyeda, in the Commission on Wartime Relocation and Internment of Civilians (hereafter CWRIC) hearings, Seattle, September 9–11, 1981, CWRIC, RG 220, N.A.

19. John Christgau, *"Enemies"* (Ames: Iowa State University Press, 1985), pp. 144–76.

20. Security conditions were similar to those of any military prison: "Guards in the towers were equipped with .45 caliber side arms, .30 caliber rifles and, on occasion, gas equipment. Each tower was equipped with a hand operated spot-light which could be used by guards to direct a sharp, penetrating beam for several hundred yards in any direction from the towers" (memorandum, 20 January 1944, INS, RG 85, F.N. 13249, N.A.).

The Santa Fe camp included facilities for guard personnel, a mess hall for 450 men, one kitchen, one officers' mess for 50 men, eight barracks (20' by 80'), one barrack (20' by 60'), 100 "Victory Huts" (16' by 16'), a hospital for 32 persons, laundry, two barracks for assigned personnel, an administration building, warehouses, a canteen, truck sheds, and latrines. Internees were counted twice daily, once in the morning and by bed check in the evening. File, 13 September 1944, INS, RG 85, F.N. 13430.10, N.A.

21. Report, 20 January 1944, INS, RG 85, Selected Records, Old Raton, N.M., F.N. 13249, N.A., and Report, 29 April 1942, INS, RG 85, F.N. 13430-10, N.A.

22. Jerry Mangione, *An Ethnic at Large* (New York: G. P. Putnam's Sons, 1978), pp. 326–27.

23. Report, August 1942, INS, RG 85, F.N. 13430.10, N.A.

24. INS memorandum, E. Shaughnessy to Willard F. Kelly, 23 September 1942, INS, RG85, F.N. Entry 89-3, 56125/Gen., N.A., and memorandum, L. L. Jensen to J. Mangione, 19 October 1943, INS, RG 85, F.N. Old Raton Ranch, N.M., Box 3, File 1300, N.A.

25. See John J. Culley, "World War II and a Western Town: The Internment of the Japanese Railroad Workers of Clovis, New Mexico," *The Western Historical Quarterly* (January 1982): 43-61, and Paul Frederick Clark, "Those Other Camps" (M.A. thesis, California State University, Fullerton, 1980), p. 18.

In his description of the Old Raton Ranch Camp, Culley writes: "While the campsite might have appealed to an outdoorsman, as a detention camp for a community of seventeen children and fifteen adults, its most distinguishing feature was its imposed isolation—physical, social, and psychological. . . . The facilities of the fourteen-acre camp included nine buildings, two electric generators, an abundant water supply, and an inadequate sewage disposal system. The physical isolation and the nature of the internees eliminated any need for a fence or rigid security measures. Living conditions were crudely adequate; the government expended no money to repair or remodel the camp" (Culley, "World War II and a Western Town," p. 54).

26. Culley, "World War II and a Western Town," pp. 59–60.

27. Ibid., p. 52.

28. Memorandum, E. Shaughnessy to Willard F. Kelly, 23 September 1942, INS, RG85, F.N. Entry 89-3, 56125/Gen., N.A. The Seagoville women's penitentiary had a permanent hospital,

an auditorium, and other service facilities for 352 internees. The internees resided in six in-
dependent dormitories composed of forty to sixty-eight rooms. Each cottage had its own
bathing, kitchen, and dining facilities. The INS later erected fifty temporary barracks to accommodate whole families, and the Latin American internees soon filled the available rooms.

29. Nicholson, *Treasures in Earthen Vessels,* pp. 68–69.

30. The War Department planned internment camps as follows:

Permanent Facilities	Capacity	Estimated Completion Date
Camp Clark, Mo.	3,000	July 15, 1942
Camp Forrest, Tenn.	3,000	May 1, 1942
Camp Livingston, La.	5,000	June 8, 1942
Chickamauga Park,		
Snodgrass Dyer Field, Ga.	3,000	May 15, 1942
Florence, Ariz., used by WRA	3,000	May 31, 1942*
Huntsville, Tex.	3,000	August 20, 1942*
Lordsburg, N.M.	3,000	June 10, 1942
McAlester, Okla.	3,000	July 15, 1942*
Rosewell, N.M.	3,000	August 20, 1942
Stringtown, Okla.	1,700	April 20, 1942*

Temporary Facilities**	Capacity	Present Internees May 4, 1942				
		Jpn.	Ger.	Itl.	Misc.	Total
Camp Blanding, Fla.	200	5	335	3	0	343
Camp McCoy, Wis.	860	183	95	6	0	284
Camp Shelby, Miss.	1,200	0	0	0	0	0
Camp Upton, N.Y.	1,000	0	0	0	0	0
Fort Bliss, Tex.	1,350	20	11	5	0	36
Fort Bragg, N.C.	140	0	0	0	0	0
Fort Devens, Mass.	1,000	0	0	0	0	0
Fort Lewis, Wash.	315	28	10	4	0	42
Fort McDowell, Calif.	500	0	7	17	0	24
Fort Meade, Md.	1,680	136	216	32	0	384
Fort Oglethorpe, Ga.	948	0	69	18	22	109
Fort Sam Houston, Tex.	1,000	16	66	23	1	106
Fort Sill, Okla.	700	705	2	0	0	707
Fort McArthur, Calif.	500	0	5	1	0	6
TOTAL		1,093	816	109	23	2041

NOTE: This list does not include camps in the territories of Hawaii or Alaska. Memorandum, J. Lansdale to FBI,
2 May 1942, War Department, F.N. 62-63892-27, N.A.

*Letter, Provost Marshal General B. M. Bryan to War Relocation Authority (hereafter WRA), 21 November 1942,
INS file, RG 85, F.N. 88, 39.030, N.A.

**Memorandum, A. L. Lerch to Director of Operations, 4 May 1942, War Department, Records of the Adjutant
General's Office, RG 389, F.N. Entry 451, Box 1217, N.A.

31. Memorandum, Bryan, Provost Marshal General's Office to Chief of Engineers, 22 May 1942, War Department, Records of the Adjutant General's Office, RG 389, F.N. 434.414, N.A.

32. Listed below are sixteen of the twenty-three War Department internment camps in the continental United States with the total number of foreign nationals in custody on March 12, 1943.

Place	Jpn	Ger.	Itl.	Msc.	Total
Camp Blanding, Fla.	0	14	0	0	14*
Camp Chaffee, Ariz.	0	481	0	0	481*
Camp Clark, Mo.	0	0	499	0	499
Camp Crossville, Tenn.	0	182	197	0	379
Camp Forrest, Tenn.	2	681	2	1	686
Camp Livingston, La.	1,123	0	0	0	1,123
Camp McCoy, Wis.	2	40	0	1	43
Fort Leonard Wood, Mo.	0	0	660	0	660
Fort Lewis, Wash.	3	1	1	0	5
Fort McDowell, Calif.	26	12	0	0	38
Fort Meade, Md.	75	195	21	0	291
Griffith Park, Calif.	9	8	2	0	19
Lordsburg, N.M.	1,523	0	0	0	1,523
McAlester, Okla.	0	0	172	24	196
Rosewell, N.M.	0	395	0	0	395
Stringtown, Okla.	0	407	0	2	409
TOTAL	2,763	2,416	1,554	28	6,761

NOTE: Camps in the territories of Hawaii and Alaska are not included. Figures also include some early prisoners of war held by the army; these sites are marked with asterisks. Memorandum, 12 March 1943, FBI, F.N. 62-63892-136, p. 23, Washington, D.C.

33. File, 27 October 1942, FBI, F.N. 62-63892-87, p. 24, Washington, D.C.

34. The Justice Department and the army had responsibility for Angel Island, or Fort McDowell, which was its less common but proper name. Known as the "Ellis Island of the West," this 740-acre island in the middle of San Francisco Bay opened in 1910 as an immigration station. In 1939, it housed the German seamen taken from the SS *Columbus* until they were shipped to the camp at Fort Stanton, N.M. The army took responsibility for Fort McDowell in 1940, and after the United States entered the war, internees from Hawaii were kept there until they were transported to inland army camps. Jeffrey Burton et al. assign this camp to the Justice Department during World War II; however, it operated under the army during the crucial early war years. See Jeffrey F. Burton et al., *Confinement and Ethnicity* (Tucson, Ariz.: Western Archeological and Conservation Center, National Park Service, Department of the Interior, 1999), p. 380.

35. The army established an enclosure at Griffith Park, in Los Angeles, in March 1942 to keep INS-designated enemy aliens for later transfer to internment camps. On August 28,

1942, the Lordsburg, N.M., camp reported receiving one Issei from Griffith Park, and on October 1, 1942, the Griffith Park facility held only six persons of unspecified nationality. Telegram, 5 September 1942, War Department, Records of the Adjutant General's Office, RG 389, F.N. 434.414, N.A., and memorandum, R. B. Hood to J. E. Hoover, 24 November 1942, FBI, F.N. 62-63982-106, Washington, D.C.

36. Descriptions of army sites holding Nikkei nationals follow:

Camp McCoy Temporary Internment Camp, Wis.: Situated about nine miles west of Tomah, Wis., Camp McCoy was initially a CCC camp in 1935. It was selected as an internment center site for two reasons: its relative isolation and its location close to the Milwaukee Railway and on a branch line of the Chicago and Northwestern Railway. Arnold Krammer places the camp five miles from Sparta, Wis. ("Japanese Prisoners of War in America," *Pacific Historical Review* (1983): 76). Opened in March 1942, McCoy initially housed 293 foreign nationals—181 Japanese, 106 Germans, 5 Italians, and 1 Japanese POW, Sub-lieutenant Kazuo Sakamaki.

Reports about conditions at Camp McCoy are scarce. One internee recalled a lunch that consisted of a single potato with two slices of unbuttered bread. Dinner that night was a serving of dumpling soup with bread. Suikei Furuya, *Hashio ten ten* (From camp to camp) (Honolulu: Hawaii Times, 1964), p. 104. Later in the war, after the Issei returned to INS control, Camp McCoy held some 3,000 Japanese prisoners of war, 500 Koreans captured while serving with the Japanese military, and 1,000 Germans soldiers.

Fort Sill Temporary Internment Camp, Okla.: The camp, located in Comanche County, about three miles north of Lawton, was surrounded by a two-row, twelve-foot-high fence topped with barbed wire in 1942. Four guard towers, equipped with .30 caliber machine guns, shotguns, and searchlights, looked down on the camp, and additional lights along the perimeter illuminated the fence. The compound itself included 173 four-man army tents, four kitchens, a medical facility, and a recreation hall (40 feet by 10 feet). Prisoner amenities were few; there were no recreation grounds or garden. Memorandum, W. G. Banister to J. E. Hoover, 18 May 1942, FBI, F.N. 62-63892, Washington, D.C.

The weather was severe, with April windstorms that threatened to blow down the internees' tents and summer temperatures above 100 degrees, with no shade available to provide escape from the heat. Shinichi Kato, ed., *Beikoku Nikkeijin hyakunenshi* (America's persons of Japanese ancestry 100-year history) (Los Angeles: Shinnichibei Shimbunsha [New Japanese American News], 1961), p. 337.

As of May 18, 1942, 700 Issei plus three German nationals lived at Fort Sill. The camp was run military style; internees were not allowed to nap or rest on their own beds during the day, they policed the areas both inside and outside the tents, and they were expected to keep themselves occupied during the day. Their outgoing weekly correspondence was limited to two letters of thirty lines each and one postcard of ten lines, with at least two of the three pieces written in English. Fort Sill was a small camp, and as more internees were expected, the army arranged for the newcomers to be taken to a larger settlement. By June 24, 1942, all Issei internees had been transferred to Camp Livingston, in Louisiana. Kato, *Beikoku Nikkeijin hyakunenshi*.

Fort Lewis Internment Camp, Wash.: Situated in a designated portion of the sprawling Fort Lewis army base, within sight of Mount Rainier, near Tacoma, Wash., the camp had a capacity of 315 persons; by early 1942, it held twenty-eight Japanese, ten Germans, and four Italian nationals. By March 30, 1943, the Japanese and Italians were sent to the INS camp at Fort Missoula, Mont., and the German internees to Fort Lincoln, N.D. Memorandum, 30 March 1943, War Department, Provost Marshal General, Records of the Adjutant General's Office, RG 389, F.N. Entry 461, Box 2481, N.A.

Camp Forrest Permanent Internment Camp, Tenn.: This site was in a wooded area and consisted of mainly five-man huts for a total capacity of 300 persons. In 1942, it held 190 Japanese, its largest Nikkei population. By June 22 of that year, 11 had been repatriated to Japan, 174 transferred to Camp Livingston in Louisiana, and 5 are unaccounted for. Memorandum, 30 June 1942, War Department, Records of the Adjutant General's Office, RG 389, F.N. Entry 451, Box 1217, N.A., and 22 June 1942, Records of the Adjutant General's Office, RG 389, F.N. Entry 461, Box 2481, N.A.

Fort McDowell Camp, or Angel Island, Calif.: This facility, in San Francisco Bay, became a transit point for Issei and other foreign nationals from the territory of Hawaii before their transfer to INS camps. At least 180 Issei were there in 1942.

Other camps were as follows: Fort Meade, Md., which held mainly German nationals with a few Issei. Fort Sam Houston, Tex., which served as a temporary holding place for an unknown number of Japanese internees until permanent internment camps were constructed. Fort Bliss Detention Camp, Tex., held at least ninety-one resident Japanese in October 1942. Memorandum, D. S. Myer to E. G. Harrison, 21 October 1942, War Relocation Authority (hereafter WRA), RG 210, F.N. 39.039, N.A. Stringtown, Okla., was built as a sub-prison in 1933 to hold overflow prisoners from the Oklahoma State Penitentiary, was transformed into the Oklahoma State Technical Institute in 1937, and in 1942 held at least 176 Issei. German naval prisoners of war were later confined there, and after the war, it reverted to the prison system. Burton et al., *Confinement and Ethnicity,* p. 404, and memorandum, 14 August 1942, War Department, Records of the Adjutant General's Office, RG 389, F.N. 464-414 253.91, Lordsburg, NM file, N.A. Rosewell Permanent Internment Camp, N.M., was completed on August 20, 1942, and had a capacity of 3,000 persons; although a few Issei probably were held here during the early part of the war, no verifiable information is available. A few Issei were also brought to the Fort MacArthur camp in Long Beach, Calif., to Griffith Park, in Los Angeles, and to Camp Shelby, Miss.

37. The distance given comes from Kato, *Beikoku Nikkeijin hyakunenshi,* p. 338, although Tana, *Santa Fe, Rozubagu,* p. 241, says that it is seven to eight miles from the town. The plans for Lordsburg included twelve mess halls, twelve lavatories, twelve storehouses, twelve recreation rooms, three post exchange buildings, three administration buildings, and a hospital unit. The order authorizing the purchase and transfer to the military at an estimated cost of $13,000 came in February 1942. Memorandum, L. A. Duley to Army and Navy Munitions Board, 7 February 1942, War Department, Records of the Adjutant General's Office, RG 389, F.N. 434.414, 601.1, N.A. The hospital unit held one administration building, one mess and supply office, one patients' mess building, two standard ward barracks, two com-

bination ward buildings, one detention ward, one storehouse, one morgue, one surgery clinic building, and one heating plant building. Memorandum, 13 May 1942, War Department, Records of the Adjutant General's Office, RG 389, F.N. 434-414, 254, N.A. There were also forty-three Japanese prisoners of war there on October 28, 1942.

38. Kato, *Beikoku Nikkeijin hyakunenshi,* p. 338.

39. The INS assigned each internee a serial number for identification purposes. The numbers differed according to whether the internee was arrested in the continental United States, within its territories or possessions, or abroad as a prisoner of war or from U.S. Navy sources.

The largest number of internees came from the United States. Such an internee could have, for example, the designation ISN-18-4-J-36-CI. The letters ISN stand for Internment Serial Number. The second part designates the immigration district where the prisoner is held before being transferred to army control: 18 means Seattle. The third element reflects the residential state of the prisoner at the time of arrest. The forty-eight states are arranged alphabetically, with Alabama as 1, Arizona as 2, and so on: 4 is California. The fourth component designates ethnicity: G for German, I for Italian, and J for Japanese. The fifth element indicates the consecutive internee number assigned by the INS within each district. Our hypothetical internee was the thirty-sixth person ordered interned. The sixth component, CI, indicates a civilian, not a military prisoner of war.

Those arrested by the War Department in U.S. possessions or territories were issued a four-component serial number—for example, ISN-AJ-20-CI. The last two ISN elements convey the same information as do the corresponding elements in the example above—consecutive internee number and civilian status—but the first letter of the second component provides additional identification of the possession or department involved: A for Alaska, H for Hawaii, and P for the Philippines. The second letter again designates ethnicity, in this case Japanese.

Internees arrested outside the United States or its possessions also had a four-element serial number, for example, ISN-XJ-32-CI. The only difference from the first two types of identifications is the first element of the second component. The letter X indicates an arrest outside the United States. A prisoner of war might be given the designation ISN-3-36-MI, with the second element designating the capturing army or command; in this case, 3 stands for Third Army. The third element is a consecutively assigned war number, and the fourth component represents Military Intelligence. Those brought in by the U.S. Navy would bear NA as the fourth element, and the second element would then represent the particular naval district in which the internee landed and began the processing phase. File, Civilian Enemy Aliens and Prisoners of War, 27 October 1942, FBI, F.N. 62-63692-87, pp. 12–16, Washington, D.C.

40. Tana, *Santa Fe, Rozubagu,* p. 250.

41. Report, N. Rainbolt, 1–3 December 1944, War Department, Records of the Adjutant General's Office, RG 389, F.N. 1617.255, Camp Lordsburg, NM file, N.A.

42. Furuya, *Hashio ten ten,* p. 210.

43. Interview, Herbert Nicholson, in Arthur A. Hansen and Betty E. Mitson, eds., *Voices Long Silent* (Fullerton: Oral History Program, California State University, 1974), pp. 126–27.

44. Kato, *Beikoku Nikkeijin hyakunenshi,* p. 337.

45. Letter, 20 February 1945, Justice Department, RG 85, F.N. Box 5, 89, N.A.

46. Memorandum, 22 February 1943, F B I, F.N. 62-63892-130, Washington, D.C. Although the first group of POWs can be said to be the German seamen captured in 1939, others were brought to the United States beginning in 1943. To house POWs captured after December 7, 1941, the army in early 1943 proposed using sixty-nine different sites for this purpose. For example, in the Fourth Service Command Area, by February 22, 1943, Camp Blanding, Fla., held 14 sailors taken from a German submarine, and Camp Crossville, Tenn., held 253 German and Italian soldiers brought from the North African front. By March 1943, the army counted twenty-three sites as "Present Internment Camps," eighteen as "Prospective [completed] Internment Camps," and twenty-eight as "Prospective [under construction] Internment Camps." The prisoner count for Present Internment Camps was 6,763, although most of these were actually Issei and civilian German nationals arrested earlier in the United States. Memorandum, 12 March 1943, F B I, F.N. 62-63892-136, Washington, D.C. By May 1945, the prisoner-of-war population reached 425,871, held at seventy-eight different locations. This total included 5,424 Japanese and 50,273 Italian, with the remainder—about 370,000—made up of German military prisoners.

Krammer, "Japanese Prisoners," pp. 69–70, gives two main reasons for the small number of Japanese POWs. First, the Japanese military trained soldiers to prefer death to surrender, and second, the U.S. Department of War turned over the majority of its Japanese prisoners to the United States' Australian or New Zealand allies. Japanese POWs brought to the United States either were of special intelligence value or had been captured in locations closer to the United States than to the other two allied nations. The army shuffled the small number of Japanese military prisoners among various sites but kept the largest number in four camps: Camp McCoy, Wis.; Clarinda, Iowa; Kenedy, Tex.; and Angel Island, Calif. In addition, a small number were kept at the Honouliuli Gulch Camp in the territory of Hawaii.

During the war, there were few escapes attempted from the POW camps. Krammer reports that a total of 1,036 German prisoners made the attempt; the Japanese prisoners made fourteen escape attempts, all from Camp McCoy, and were all recaptured. Moore and the F B I report that 1,583 prisoners, mostly German, tried to escape and that by April 1946, 16 Germans and 6 Italians were still at large. Krammer, "Japanese Prisoners," p. 60; John H. Moore, "Hitler's Wehrmacht in Virginia, 1943–1946," *The Virginia Magazine of History and Biography* 85, no. 3 (1977): 259–73; and memorandum, 8 August 1946, F B I, F.N. 62-63892-234, Washington, D.C.

In April 1945, as the war started to wind down in Europe, the provost marshal general's office established a special project division that started as the Intellectual Diversion, or indoctrination, program for prisoners of war. By mid-1946, some 30,000 German soldiers had been forced to hear lectures extolling the virtues of the U.S. Constitution and enumerating the failures of the Weimar Republic. The program's aim was to instill appreciation of the American way of life and American democracy before the soldiers were repatriated to their homelands by means that included, for example, viewing movies such as *Abe Lincoln in Illinois*. For the Japanese, "the project was secretly authorized by the Secretary of War on July 18, 1945, after which the prisoners were screened, evaluated, and the most cooperative among them selected for reeducation. The potential converts to democracy, a total of 205 men, were sent to one of three specially designated, 're-orientation centers': Camps Huntsville, Kenedy or Hearne, Texas" (Krammer, "Japanese Prisoners," p. 88).

Beginning in December 1945, the army returned the Japanese POWs to their homeland. Most were gone by January 1946, although a few stayed until July. The few who had escaped and continued to elude the FBI occasionally surfaced in later years. The army closed all the POW camps by August 8, 1946, with 250 prisoners remaining in the United States. The 215 disciplinary cases were held mainly at the U.S. Army's Fort Leavenworth Penitentiary, in Kansas: 141 German, 20 Italian, and 1 Japanese soldier. All served their sentences for crimes committed while imprisoned, and the remaining 35 prisoners recuperated in hospitals. The army later reviewed the cases and eventually repatriated the soldiers to their homelands. Memorandum, 8 August 1946, FBI, F.N. 62-63892-234, Washington, D.C. The last Japanese prisoner recovered from his wounds and returned to Japan on June 1, 1948.

Krammer states that of the original 5,424 Japanese prisoners, 24 died in captivity, "three are still buried in the Fort Sam Houston National Cemetery, 3 at Fort Riley, Kansas, and 1 at the Presidio of Monterey, CA. . . . Of those who died in captivity, two apparently killed themselves, three were shot during an escape attempt at Denver's Fitzsimons General Hospital, one died in an agricultural accident, and the remaining eighteen succumbed to earlier war wounds or natural causes" ("Japanese Prisoners," p. 90). The army returned the other bodies to Japan.

Various sources, however, do not agree on the number of POWs brought to the United States during World War II. As stated earlier, the provost marshal general cites the Japanese total as 5,424, the FBI gives 3,915, and Krammer states 4,821. Krammer contends that a total of 53,000 Italian POWs and 425,000 German POWs were here, and that by mid-1943, the army had established 500 main and branch POW camps in the United States in which to hold them. The FBI gives 490 as the total number of camps in the United States and Hawaii.

The majority of Japanese POWs were kept in the United States at six main camps:

Camps	Officers	NCO	Enlisted	Total
Angel Island, Calif.	24	71	312	407
Clarinda, Iowa	—	73	982	1,055
McCoy, Wis.	3	10	2,749	2,762
Meade, Md.	1	—	1	2
Kenedy, Tex.	91	499	—	590
Madigan Hospital, Wash.	3	—	2	5
TOTAL	122	653	4,046	4,821

NOTE: Compiled from memorandum, 15 September 1943, FBI Bureau Bulletin No. 45, and Krammer, "Japanese Prisoners," pp. 67, 76. These numbers do not include those kept in the territory of Hawaii.

47. Issei and other Nikkei internees in the custody of the INS as of July 1944 were as follows:

In custody as of July 1, 1943	9,341
Additional received in 1943–July 1944	2,425
TOTAL received by July 1944	11,766
Repatriated	2,141
Paroled (includes 1,731 Issei sent to WRA camps)	1,838
Internment at large	258
From Latin America and similar to parole status	
Deaths	53
Other unspecified	1,238
TOTAL departed by July 1944	5,528
REMAINING by July 1944	6,238

Compiled from Justice Department, *Monthly Review* 2, no. 6 (December 1944): 74.

The INS released substantial numbers of prisoners of Italian ancestry in 1944. Unfortunately, the statistics do not coincide with various population figures because Italian nationals were often released under parole status. Some 250 were paroled or released by February 14, and 150 more were expected to depart the INS in March. Memorandum, L. L. Lewis to C. E. Waller, 14 February 1944, INS, RG 85, F.N. 89-3, N.A.

By February 1944, the INS held 6,382 internees: 2,960 Germans, 2,927 Japanese, and 87 of other nationalities. Viewed more specifically, this 6,382 figure breaks down as follows: from the continental United States, 2,466 Germans, 1,695 Japanese, 386 Italians, and 55 others; from Alaska, 47 Japanese and 9 Germans; from Hawaii, 702 Japanese and 7 Germans; and from Latin America, 483 Japanese, 478 Germans, 31 Italians, and 23 of other nationalities. Other foreign nationals residing in public health service hospitals or working at railroads or on road projects were not considered in this total. Memorandum, Willard F. Kelly to N. D. Collaer, 4 March 1944, INS, RG 85, F.N. 56125/Gen., N.A.

48. The following is a complete roster of INS facilities for holding detainees and internees during the years 1943–45. City name is followed by county name when available.

Temporary detention stations: Miami, Dade, Fla.; Algiers, Orleans, La.; Niagara Falls, Niagara, N.Y.; Chicago, Cook, Ill.; Salt Lake City, Salt Lake, Utah; Sharp Park, San Mateo, Calif.; Tuna Canyon, Los Angeles, Calif.; Cleveland, Ohio; Cincinnati, Ohio; Kansas City, Mo.

Detention/immigration stations: East Boston, Suffolk, Mass.; Ellis Island, New York, N.Y.; Gloucester City, Camden, N.J.; Detroit, Wayne, Mich.; Seattle, King, Wash.; San Pedro, Los Angeles, Calif.

Internment camps: Fort Missoula, Missoula, Mont.; Fort Lincoln, Burleigh, N.D.; Fort Stanton, Lincoln, N.M.; Kenedy, Karner, Tex.; Santa Fe, Santa Fe, N.M.; Seagoville, Dallas, Tex.; Crystal City, Zavala, Tex.; Kooskia, Idaho, Idaho.

Jails/prisons: Chicago, Cook County Jail, Ill.; Salt Lake City County Jail, Utah; Phoenix Jail, Ariz.; New Orleans Parish Prison, La.

Hospitals: Chicago, U.S. Marine Hospital; San Francisco, Marine Hospital; Agnew State

Hospital, Calif.; Washington, D.C., Doctor's Hospital; Brighton, Marine Hospital, Mass.; Tauton, Massachusetts State Hospital; North Grafton, Massachusetts State Hospital.

Hotels/homes: Staunton, Ingleside Hotel, Va.; Chicago, House of Good Shepherd, Ill.; Los Angeles, House of Good Shepherd, Calif.; East Boston, House of Good Shepherd, Mass.; Cleveland, House of Good Shepherd, Ohio; Milwaukee, House of Good Shepherd, Wis.; Cascade Inn, Hot Springs, Va.

Railroads: Great Northern Railroad (GNR), Gang #3, Flathead, Mont.; Gang #2, Mineral, Mont.; Gang #5, Powell, Mont.; Crew #5, Lewis and Clark, Mont.; Crew #6, Granite, Mont.; Chicago–Milwaukee–St. Paul Railroad (Gang #109, Missoula, Mont.).

Forest Service projects, German nationals: Headquarters, Clearwater, Idaho; Priest River, Bonner, Idaho; Warland, Lincoln, Mont.; Brown's Creek, Clearwater, Idaho; Troy, Lincoln, Mont.; Kingston, Shoshone, Idaho; Big Creek Valley, Idaho, Idaho; Green Creek, Idaho, Idaho; Sullivan Lake, Pend Oreille, Wash.; Potter Creek, Idaho; Blister Rust Control Headquarters, Bonner, Idaho.

Army posts: Fort McPherson, Ga.; Fort Howard, Md.; Fort DeMoines, Iowa; Fort McClellan, Calhoun, Ala.; Fort Screven, Chatham, Ga.

Compiled from Letter, N. D. Collaer to J. C. Capp, 16 November 1943, INS, RG 85, F.N. 56125/Gen.C., N.A.; memorandum, N. D. Collaer to Willard F. Kelly, 4 March 1944, INS, RG 85, F.N. 56125/Gen.C., N.A.; memorandum, W. F. Miller to J. E. Hoover, 26 August 1943, INS, RG 85, F.N. 56125/Gen.C., N.A. ; and memorandum, S. W. Anderson to L. L. Lewis, 20 February 1945, INS, RG 85, F.N. 5.89, N.A.

49. For example, 161 people came to the INS from WRA centers between January and mid-February 1944, and 107 other Issei arrived later with 342 family members. File, 13 September 1944, INS, RG 85, F.N. 13430.10, N.A., and File, 20 January 1944, INS, RG 85, F.N. 13249, N.A.

50. Memorandum, 13 September 1944, INS, RG 85, F.N. 13430.10, and File, 20 January 1944, INS, RG 85, F.N. 13249, N.A. Some 1,623 internees came from the continental United States, the majority from army internment camps and 85 from the INS station at Sharp Park, Calif.; 521 were sent from Hawaii, and a few others arrived from Alaska, the Pacific islands, and Latin American countries. Memorandum, L. L. Jensen to J. Mangione, 19 October 1943, INS, RG 85, Old Raton Ranch, NM, F.N. Box 3, File 1300, N.A.

51. Quoted in Clark, "Those Other Camps," p. 24.

52. P. Scott Corbett, *Quiet Passages* (Kent, Ohio: Kent State University Press, 1987), p. 123.

53. Memorandum, 15 August 1944, INS, RG 85, F.N. 89-3-56125/33, pp. 2–3, N.A.

54. Quoted in memorandum, I. Williams to Willard F. Kelly, 1 September 1945, INS, RG 85, F.N. 56125/165, 1300/B-3045, N.A. There is no indication as to whether this is the complete text of the letter or whether the last sentence was taken out of context.

55. Ibid.

56. File, 31 December 1945, INS, RG 85, F.N. 13430.10, N.A.

57. Mangione, *Ethnic at Large*, p. 327.

58. N. D. Collaer, "The Crystal City Internment Camp," *Immigration and Naturalization Service Monthly Review* 5, no. 6 (December 1947): 75.

59. Memorandum, Family Internment Camp File, 11 January 1943, W R A , RG 210, F.N. 39.039, p. 3, N.A.

60. The population of the I N S internment camp at Crystal City as of August 1, 1944:

Internees from the continental United States, U.S. possessions, Puerto Rico, Latin America

	German ancestry	Italian ancestry	Japanese ancestry
Adults, male	165	—	224
Adults, female	47	—	8
Children, male	24	—	1
Children, female	12	—	0
Subtotal	248	—	233

Voluntary internees from the continental United States or Puerto Rico

	German ancestry	Italian ancestry	Japanese ancestry
Adults, male	0	—	32
Adults, female	113	—	232
Children, male	83	—	216
Children, female	74	—	223
Subtotal	270	—	703

Those brought from Latin America and the West Indies

	German ancestry	Italian ancestry	Japanese ancestry
Adults, male	76	1	216
Adults, female	80	1	209
Children, male	67	0	293
Children, female	60	2	288
Subtotal	283	4	1006

Internees from Alaska, Hawaii, and other Pacific islands

	German ancestry	Italian ancestry	Japanese ancestry
Adults, male	0	—	37
Adults, female	2	—	41
Children, male	1	—	41
Children, female	0	—	43
Subtotal	3	—	162
TOTAL	804	4	2104

N O T E : Compiled from memorandum, 15 August 1944, I N S , RG 85, F.N. 89-3, pp. 6-7, N.A. Children are defined as those under twenty-one years of age.

61. See "The Fukudas," by M. Fukuda, in Joy N. Gee, ed., *Crystal City [Texas] 50th Anniversary Reunion Album* (Monterey, Calif.: By the editor, 1993), p. 103.

62. Memorandum, Willard F. Kelly to Edward J. Ennis, 7 March 1945, INS, RG 85, F.N. 56125, 39/14869, N.A.

63. Memorandum, Ivan Williams to Willard F. Kelly, 8 March 1945, INS, RG 85, F.N. 56125/51, 39/14869, N.A.

64. Memorandum, Willard F. Kelly, 31 August 1945, INS, RG 85 F.N.89, 56125/Gen., N.A., and U.S. Department of Justice, INS, *Monthly Review* 3, no. 4 (October 1945): 212.

65. The INS placed some interned Japanese with road construction projects during the war. In Idaho, thirty-eight miles east of the town of Kooskia, the Federal Bureau of Prisons operated a prison camp using inmate labor to help build Idaho's Lewis and Clark Highway. In February 1943, because of the diminishing prison population, the INS offered the Public Roads Administration use of Japanese internee labor, and in May 1943, 175 Japanese were brought to the work camp. The site, known as Kooskia, was an old CCC camp in the Clearwater National Forest. On August 1, 1944, 124 Issei were still working there along with 1 German national from Bolivia, a physician who had volunteered to take care of the internees' medical needs. Memorandum, 15 August 1944, INS, RG 85 F.N. 89-3, p. 6, N.A. Burton et al. report that "256 Japanese aliens, 24 male and three female Caucasian civilian employees, and one Japanese American interpreter lived at the Kooskia camp between May 1943 and May 1945" (*Confinement and Ethnicity,* p. 387). The Kooskia Internment Camp closed in May 1945, and the INS transferred the remaining internees to the camp at Santa Fe, N.M. Memorandum, N. D. Collaer to T. B. Shoemaker, 2 April 1945, INS, RG 85 F.N. 56125/Gen., N.A.; memorandum, 20 April 1945, INS, RG 85, F.N. Entry 89 Box 5, N.A.

Between March and May of that year, there were 1,091 German nationals in residence, and by August 1, 1944, 644 German and 9 other foreign nationals remained. Along with this group were 22 others working on nearby railroad maintenance projects and 243 German nationals working on seven INS Forest Service projects in Idaho and Montana. Memorandum, E. Shaughnessy to Willard F. Kelly, 14 July 1942 and 23 September 1942, INS, RG 85, F.N. Entry 89, Box 3, N.A., and memorandum, Willard F. Kelly, 15 August 1944, INS, RG 85, F.N. 89-3, 56125/Gen, p. 1, N.A.

66. Biddle, *In Brief Authority,* p. 209. This number was also used by Gentry: "Of the 16,062 enemy aliens arrested during World War II, fewer than a third were interned or repatriated. The majority were either paroled or released" (Curt Gentry, *Hoover* [New York: W. W. Norton and Co., 1991], p. 278).

67. Memorandum, U. Carusi to Attorney General, 24 August 1945, INS, RG 85, F.N. 56125/Gen., N.A.

68. Memorandum, Willard F. Kelly to D. Schedler, 24 May 1948, INS, RG 85, F.N. 56125/Gen., N.A.

69. The 185 number is the sum of the 141 taken from the mainland and 44 from South American countries. Calculations based on Kelly's figures come from ibid.; memorandum, L. L. Lewis to Willard F. Kelly, 17 April 1946 and 27 December 1946, INS, RG 85, F.N. 56125/Gen., N.A.

70. Tana, *Santa Fe, Rozubagu,* p. 261.

7 / THE ARBITRARY PROCESS OF CONTROL

1. The number of people of Japanese ancestry residing in the United States was never large. By 1940, the population totaled 284,852 persons, 126,947 on the mainland and 157,905 in Hawaii. Most were American citizens—63 percent on the mainland and 76 percent in Hawaii. Within the continental United States, most lived in only four western states: California, 93,717; Washington, 14,565; Oregon, 4,071; and Arizona, 632. These states accounted for a total of 112,985, or 89 percent of the mainland population. Dorothy S. Thomas, *The Salvage* (Berkeley: University of California Press, 1952), pp. 575–77.

2. Memorandum, 2 February 1942, Federal Bureau of Investigation (hereafter F B I), in the Commission on Wartime Relocation Internment of Civilians (hereafter C W R I C) papers, Record Group (hereafter RG) 220, Numbers 5794–5803, National Archives, Washington, D.C. (hereafter N.A.)

3. Although thorough exploration is beyond the scope of this presentation, some insight into the personalities of key personnel involved with the imprisonment of Japanese Americans is instructive. Provost Marshal General Allen W. Gullion is characterized by Ted Morgan as the "man who made himself the main apologist for the evacuation of the Japanese" and apparently was known for his racist views. In April 1943, Gullion was under investigation by the F B I "for allegedly forming an organization inside the Army known as SGs, for Slim (his nickname) Gullion, which aimed, according to an F B I informant, to 'save America from FDR, radical labor, the Communists, the Jews, and the colored race'" (Ted Morgan, *FDR* [New York: Simon and Schuster, 1985], p. 626). Greg Robinson describes Captain Karl Bendetsen, an aide to Gullion, as someone quickly promoted to the rank of Colonel "as a result of his championship of mass removal"(*By Order of the President* [Cambridge: Harvard University Press, 2001], pp. 86, 136–37).

4. Francis Biddle papers, in C W R I C, RG 220, Numbers 5741, N.A.

5. Forrest C. Pogue, *George C. Marshall* (New York: The Viking Press, 1973), p. 142.

6. Greg Robinson asserts that President Roosevelt did not differentiate the Japanese in Japan from the resident Issei and their citizen children. He documents Roosevelt's racial antipathy toward the Nikkei as well as those actions that subverted the constitutional rights of the Nisei. See *By Order of the President*, p. 257.

7. See Morton Grodzins, *Americans Betrayed* (Chicago: University of Chicago Press, 1949), pp. 19–128. The economic implications of the removal of Japanese Americans from West Coast states are explored in other sources. See, for example, Gary Okihiro and David Drummond, "The Concentration Camps and Japanese Economic Losses in California Agriculture, 1900–1942," in Roger Daniels, Sandra Taylor, and Harry H. L. Kitano, eds., *Japanese Americans,* 2nd ed. (Seattle: University of Washington Press, 1991), pp. 168–75.

8. Grodzins, *Americans Betrayed,* p. 267.

9. E. Ennis, quoted in Grodzins, *Americans Betrayed,* pp. 268, 271.

10. Francis Biddle, *In Brief Authority* (New York: Doubleday and Co., 1962), p. 213.

11. As the W D C's commanding officer writes, "Included among the evacuees were persons who were only part Japanese, some with as little as one-sixteenth Japanese blood; others who, prior to evacuation, were unaware of their Japanese ancestry; and many who had

married Caucasians, Chinese, Filipinos, Negroes, Hawaiian or Eskimo" (John L. DeWitt, *Final Report. Japanese Evacuation from the West Coast, 1942* [Washington, D.C.: U.S. Government Printing Office, 1943], p. 145).

12. See CWRIC, *Personal Justice Denied,* reprint, with a new foreword (Seattle: University of Washington Press, 1997), pp. 47–92.

13. The remaining three categories of exempted person were "a) German and Italian aliens, parents, wives, husbands, children of (or other person residing in a household whose support is dependent upon) any officer, enlisted man, or commissioned nurse who on or since December 7, 1941, has died in line of duty with the armed forces of the United States. . . . b) German and Italian aliens awaiting naturalization who have filed a petition for naturalization and who had paid the filing fee therefore on or before December 7, 1941. c) Patients in hospitals, or confined elsewhere, and too ill or incapacitated to be removed therefrom without danger to life" (DeWitt, *Final Report,* p. 305).

14. John Hersey, "A Mistake of Terrifically Horrible Proportions," in John Armor and Peter Wright, *Manzanar* (New York: Times Books, 1988), p. 15.

15. Ibid., pp. 15–16.

16. *San Francisco News,* April 13, 1943. John Hersey makes an even stronger case regarding DeWitt's racist views: "The mere fact of having Japanese blood and skin was, to General DeWitt, enough basis for suspicion—a paranoic suspicion of (in his words) 'some vast conspiracy.' 'Because of the ties of race, the intense feeling of filial piety, and the strong bonds of common tradition, this population presented a tightly-knit racial group.' When he wrote in his Final Report of the way the ethnic Japanese population had been scattered through his Defense Command, he used the military term 'deployed'—'in excess of 115,000 persons deployed along the Pacific Coast'—as if these farmers and merchants and house servants had been posted by plan, poised for attack" ("A Mistake," p. 23).

17. On December 21, 1943, the Immigration and Naturalization Service (INS) reviewed the language of EO 9066 and EO 9102 authorizing the formation of the WRA. The INS analyst points out: "I am however, unable to read into either regulation any authority for holding any person at a relocation center . . . I cannot find . . . any authority in these two Executive Orders for moving these persons to any certain location and preventing them, by force of arms, from leaving that location. In other words, I find plenty of authority for the operation of the camps but none for preventing those designated persons from leaving the camps" (memorandum, L. L. Lewis to W. F. Kelly, 21 December 1943, INS, RG 85, File Number [hereafter F.N.] 56125/Gen., N.A.).

18. The ten camps were known as or located at Tule Lake and Manzanar, Calif.; Minidoka, Idaho; Topaz, Utah; Gila River and Poston, Ariz.; Heart Mountain, Wyo.; Rohwer and Jerome, Ark.; and Granada (Amache), Colo.

19. Pamphlet, "The War Relocation Work Corps," no date, WRA, in FBI file, F.N. 62-69030-61, p. 2, Washington, D.C.

20. Civilian Restriction Order Number 1, issued on May 19, 1942, provided that no person of Japanese ancestry could leave established relocation centers without permission from the headquarters of the Western Defense Command. Similar prohibition was con-

tained in Public Proclamation Number 8, issued June 27, 1942. Public Proclamation Number W[estern] D[efense] 1 contains a provision prohibiting persons from leaving War Relocation Areas except as authorized by the secretary of war or by the director of the W R A. Departure from any of these areas without the required authorization constituted a violation of Public Law 503, and persons who did so would be subject to prosecution by the U.S. district attorney. Memorandum, E. Ennis to J. E. Hoover, 19 October 1942, F B I, F.N. 62-69030-9x, Washington, D.C. See also DeWitt, *Final Report*, pp. 241–42.

21. File, 14 September 1943, F B I, F.N. 62-639030-530, Washington, D.C.

22. DeWitt, *Final Report*, p. 147.

23. Ibid., pp. 146–47, and Paul R. Spickard, "Injustice Compounded: Amerasians and Non-Japanese Americans in World War II Concentration Camps," *Journal of American Ethnic History* 5, no. 2 (spring 1986): 6.

24. Those so exempted included "1) Families consisting of a Japanese wife, a non-Japanese husband, citizen of the U.S. or of a friendly nation, and their mixed-blood unemancipated children, 2) Families consisting of a Caucasian mother, citizen of the U.S. or of a friendly nation, and her mixed-blood children by a Japanese father (either dead or separated from the family), 3) Mixed blood (1/2 Japanese or less) individuals, citizens of the U.S. or of friendly nations whose backgrounds have been Caucasian, 4) Japanese unemancipated children who are being reared by Caucasian foster-parents, and 5) Japanese wives of non-Japanese spouses serving in the armed forces of the U.S. . . . During the execution of the Mixed-Marriage Program, 465 persons of Japanese ancestry were released for residence in the evacuated area. Of those, 290 were mixed-blood children, 34 were mixed-blood parents, 72 were Japanese mothers and 68 were mixed-blood adults with no children. Only one full blooded Japanese male, a citizen of the U.S. was authorized to reside in the evacuated area. A special exemption was made in his case because of long and honorable service in the U.S. Navy" (DeWitt, *Final Report*, pp. 145–47).

An individual eligible for exemption from incarceration could also stay at the assembly center and go with his or her spouse or family to the W R A camp. W C C A reports that out of 465 persons eligible under the Mixed-Marriage Program, 206 went to a W R A camp while 259 persons elected to stay out.

25. Spickard, "Injustice Compounded," p. 14.

26. Letter, D. Myer to J. McCloy, 1 June 1943, W R A, RG 210, F.N. Series 16, 39.053, N.A.

27. U.S. W R A, U.S. Department of the Interior, *The Evacuated People* (Washington, D.C.: U.S. Department of Interior, 1946b), p. 8.

28. Those who were already interned, however, were not released under this proclamation.

29. U.S. W R A, *Evacuated People*, p. 180.

30. U.S. Army, "Supplemental Report on Civilian Control Exercised by Western Defense Command," January 1947, U.S. Army, RG 338, pp. 841, 849, N.A.

31. Edward N. Barnhart, "The Individual Exclusion of Japanese-Americans in World War II," *Pacific Historical Review* 29, no. 2 (May 1960): 113.

32. U.S. W R A, *Evacuated People*, p. 184.

33. U.S. Army, "Supplemental Report," pp. 841–42.

34. Ibid., p. 853.

35. Further details can be found in ibid., pp. 854, 855.

36. Quoted in *New York Times*, May 8, 1943, pp. 1, 17, and August 21, 1943, p. 13, in Peter B. Sheridan, "The Internment of German and Italian Aliens Compared to the Internment of Japanese Aliens in the United States during World War II: A Brief History and Analysis," 24 November 1980, CWRIC, RG 220, F.N. 25896, N.A.

37. U.S. Army, "Supplemental Report," p. 52.

38. Lieutenant General DeWitt was not given a promotion, and his next assignment was the then obscure position of Commandant of the Army and Navy Staff College. See Roger Daniels, *The Decision to Relocate the Japanese Americans* (Philadelphia: J. B. Lippincott Co., 1975), p. 17, and Pogue, *George C. Marshall*, pp. 146–47.

39. U.S. Army, "Supplemental Report," p. 852.

40. For important exceptions, see Arthur A. Hansen and Betty E. Mitson, eds., *Voices Long Silent* (Fullerton: Oral History Program, California State University, 1974); Richard Drinnon, *Keeper of Concentration Camps* (Berkeley: University of California Press, 1987); and Michi Weglyn, *Years of Infamy* (New York: William Morrow and Co., 1976; reprint, Seattle: University of Washington Press, 1996).

41. According to Karl Yoneda, the Manzanar recruitment effort on August 6, 1942, resulted in a talk with more than ninety Issei, Nisei, and Kibei in attendance. On November 28, the Military Intelligence Service Language School recruiters talked to about fifty inmates. Fourteen passed the physical, oral, and written tests and were inducted into the U.S. Army on December 2, 1942. Among the fourteen were six Kibei, a group viewed by various governmental agencies such as the navy's Office of Naval Intelligence and the army's Military Intelligence Division as holding some of the most suspect and "pro-Japan" individuals. See Karl Yoneda, *Ganbatte* (Los Angeles: University of California, Los Angeles, Asian American Studies Center, 1983), pp. 145–48; James Oda, *Heroic Struggles of Japanese Americans* (North Hollywood, Calif.: KNI, 1980), pp. 61–66. For a description of the Military Intelligence Service Language School, see Tamotsu Shibutani, *Derelicts of Company K* (Berkeley: University of California Press, 1978), and Joseph D. Harrington, *Yankee Samurai* (Detroit: Pettigrew Enterprises, 1979).

42. The army reports that five persons were arrested. See U.S. Army, "Supplemental Report," p. 53. For a discussion of the Manzanar trouble, see Harry Ueno, "Manzanar," in John Tateishi, ed., *And Justice for All* (New York: Random House, 1984), pp. 186–207; Sue K. Embrey, Arthur A. Hansen, and Betty K. Mitson, *Manzanar Martyr* (Fullerton: California State University Oral History Program, 1986); Case History, n.d., Leupp Relocation Center, University of California, Bancroft Library, Berkeley; and memorandum, Sigler to Provinse, 12 April 1943, WRA, RG 210, F.N. Series 16, 39.053, N.A.

43. The army reports that the crowd numbered 2,000 persons. U.S. Army, "Supplemental Report," p. 53.

44. Inmates used the deprecatory term *inu* to refer to persons who were informants for

the W R A, F B I, or other governmental agencies. At the Tule Lake center in late May 1943, "The term *inu* during this period referred to not only dissenters, fence sitters, collaborationists, and informers, but it was frequently used by various individuals to blacken the name of any person they might dislike" (Donald E. Collins, *Native American Aliens* [Westport, Conn.: Greenwood Press, 1985], p. 183). For a discussion of the term, see Wayne M. Collins, "Brief for Appellees, J. Howard McGrath v. Tadayasu Abo et al., and J. Howard McGrath v. Mary Kanome Furuya et al., Nos. 12251 and 12252," *U.S. Court of Appeals for the Ninth Circuit Court,* February 27, 1950, pp. 1–128, San Francisco. Why the word *inu*, which literally means "dog," was chosen is unknown. One theory is that in Japan, certain police officers would go from house to house to "sniff out" incriminating evidence.

There is little doubt that there were some informers within the Japanese American group. Not all persons so labeled, however, were collaborating with or working for the W R A or the army against other inmates. For example, Dorothy S. Thomas, a noted sociologist, formed a group composed of young Nisei social scientists to gather data inside the camps. She received their reports with the assurance that there would be no interference from W R A administrators and that she would not be obligated to report to them. One Nisei investigator said that he typed his field notes at night; the typewriter's clacking alarmed other inmates and word spread that he was an *inu*. In situations marked by ever-present anxiety and uncertainty, it is understandable that some inmates would interpret such occurrences in this way. Inmates in the camps passed on rumors of every kind, and it was not difficult to spread the notion that a particular person was an *inu* and be taken seriously.

45. Two Nisei working at the camp hospital had earlier moved Fred Tayama and hidden him under an unused bed. The group entering the hospital did not find him. See Audrie Girdner and Anne Loftis, *The Great Betrayal* (London: The Macmillan Co., 1969), p. 264.

46. U.S. Army, "Supplemental Report," p. 56.

47. Ueno, "Manzanar," p. 199.

48. Ibid.

49. U.S. Army, "Supplemental Report," p. 57.

50. Embrey, Hansen, and Mitson, *Manzanar Martyr,* Appendix 13.

51. U.S. Army, "Supplemental Report," p. 58.

52. Frank F. Chuman, "Manzanar," in Tateishi, *And Justice for All*, pp. 227–38.

53. U.S. Army, "Supplemental Report," p. 58.

54. Ueno "Manzanar," p. 201.

55. Joe Y. Kurihara, "Murder in Camp Manzanar," April 16, 1943, University of California, Bancroft Library, Berkeley, F.N. R8.10, p. 17, typescript.

56. Ralph P. Merritt Jr., "Death Valley—Its Impounded Americans," *Keepsake: 38th Annual Death Valley '49ers Encampment, Death Valley, CA*, no. 27 (November 5–8, 1987): 8.

57. U.S. Army, "Supplemental Report," p. 59.

58. James Komai, editor and publisher of the Los Angeles newspaper *Rafu Shimpo*, quoted in Oda, *Heroic Struggles*, p. 72. The number of persons actually taken to Cow Creek

is open to question. Komai reports sixty persons going there, of whom six were Issei. Ibid. Merritt states that there were sixty-five. Merritt, "Death Valley," pp. 5, 12. The FBI reports sixty-six persons (memorandum, 23 March 1943, FBI, F.N. 62-69030-113, Washington, D.C.), and Yoneda reports sixty-seven (*Ganbatte*, p. 149). Komai describes the camp area: "As early as 1870, the Chinese came to Death Valley to build the Charcoal Kilns in Wildrose Canyon. They were reported to be the first Orientals in this region. The Chinese furnished the labor to build 10 beehive kilns, each 30 feet in diameter and 30 feet tall, constructed of stone. The kilns are still standing amid an encroaching wild plant growth. They were built here to produce charcoal for the Modoc Mine smelter 25 miles away. After the kilns, designed by Swiss engineers, were built by the Chinese, the Indians worked them" (Oda, *Heroic Struggles*, p. 72).

59. Merritt, "Death Valley," p. 6.

60. Report, 22 January 1943, FBI, F.N. 62-69030-30x3, Washington, D.C.

61. Merritt, "Death Valley," p. 10.

62. Yoneda, *Ganbatte*, p. 149.

63. Elaine Yoneda, wife of Karl Yoneda, in Hansen and Mitson, *Voices Long Silent*, p. 38.

64. Yamazaki, quoted in in Oda, *Heroic Struggles*, p. 91.

65. Merritt, "Death Valley," pp. 1, 18.

66. Letter, D. Myer to R. Best, 30 December 1942, WRA, RG 210, F.N. Series 16, 39.053, N.A.

67. Memorandum, D. Myer to J. E. Hoover, 11 September 1943, FBI File 62-69030-419, pp. 8–9, Washington, D.C. The memorandum continued: "At the present time some 76 individuals from seven different projects, including the leaders in the Manzanar trouble of last December and 11 individuals recommended by the FBI officers from Topaz [Utah] are at the isolation center under conditions approximating internment."

68. Memorandum, D. Myer to Directors, 5 June 1943, WRA, RG 210, F.N. Series 16, 39.055, N.A.

69. Ueno, "Manzanar," pp. 202–3.

70. Later, on March 14, 1943, the WRA returned one inmate to Manzanar and kept six in the isolation center until they were released to other WRA camps between July and October 1943. Their stay at the isolation center lasted from seven to ten months. The WRA kept the remaining five at Moab and then at Leupp until the latter camp closed on December 14, 1943. Letter, D. Myer to Merritt, 12 February 1944, WRA, RG 210, F.N. Series 16, 39.055, N.A.

71. Case history, F. S. Frederick, n.d., University of California, Bancroft Library, Berkeley.

72. Ibid.

73. Letter, R. Best to D. Myer, 28 February 1943, WRA, RG 210, F.N. Series 16, 39.055, N.A.

74. U.S. WRA, U.S. Department of the Interior, *Legal and Constitutional Phases of the WRA Program* (Washington, D.C.: U.S. Department of the Interior, 1946e), p. 34.

75. Letter, P. Robertson to D. Myer, 11 August 1943, RG 210, F.N. Series 16, 93.055, p. 3, N.A.

76. Ueno, "Manzanar," pp. 193–97.

77. The following shows the WRA camps from which the eighty-three isolationists originated, dates of arrival, number, and final destinations from January 11 to December 4, 1943.

| Originating | | | Departure | |
WRA Camp	Date	Number	To This Center	Other
Manzanar, Calif.	1-11-43	16		
Manzanar, Calif.	2-24-43	10		
Manzanar, Calif.	7- 4-43	1		
Manzanar, Calif.	(various dates)		5	
Gila River, Ariz.	2-18-43	13		
Gila River, Ariz.	6-13-43	1		
Gila River, Ariz.	6-16-43	1		
Gila River, Ariz.	8-24-43	1		
Gila River, Ariz.	(various dates)		3	
Tule Lake, Calif.	4-2-43	15		
Tule Lake, Calif.	5-6-43	5		
Tule Lake, Calif.	(various dates)		55	
Topaz, Utah	6-11-43	1		
Topaz, Utah	7-3-43	11		
Topaz, Utah	7-10-43	1		
Topaz, Utah	(various dates)		3	
Jerome, Ark.	6-17-43	3		
Jerome, Ark.			1	
Rohwer, Ark.	5-29-43	1		
Heart Mountain, Wyo.	7- 8-43	2		
Heart Mountain, Wyo.			1	
Granada (Amache), Colo.	7-22-43	1		
Poston, Ariz.			4	
Minidoka, Idaho	(various dates)		6	
(To the FBI)	(3-14-43)			4
(To Secret Service)	(10-25-43)			1
TOTAL		83	78	5

NOTE: Compiled from WRA Leupp Relocation Center Files, University of California, Bancroft Library, Berkeley, F.N.- S.120A, 67/14, and memorandum, 1943, WRA, RG 210, F.N. Series 16, 39.055, N.A.

The average age of these inmates was 26.8 years. Of the seventy-four Nisei or Kibei as of July 31, 1943, the youngest was nineteen and the oldest was forty-eight; 89 percent had visited Japan at least once in their lives, although the duration of their stay was not reported. Computed from memorandum, 31 July 1943 and 21 December 1943, WRA, RG 210, F.N. Series 16, 39.055, N.A.

In one unusual case, the WRA charged a Manzanar Nisei with the crime of counterfeiting. He was arrested for making lead dies of a quarter and was brought to the Moab center. The Secret Service took him into federal custody there: "[H]e was released and after the release, he went to Denver, picked up a 19 year old Cherokee Indian girl whose husband is in the South Pacific, took her to Chicago where he was arrested for violation of the Federal

Mann Act. He is being held in Chicago for $5,000 bail" (correspondence, J. Frederick to R. Spencer, 9 January 1945, University of California, Bancroft Library, Berkeley, p. 2).

78. Letter, P. Robertson to D. Myer, 11 August, 1943, W R A, RG 210, F.N. Series 16, 93.055, p. 3, N.A.

79. Letter, R. Best to D. Myer, 28 February 1943, ibid.

80. Case history, F. S. Frederick, 23 August 1943, University of California, Bancroft Library, Berkeley Calif.

81. Ibid.

82. Memorandum, Review Board to D. Myer, 25 March 1943, W R A, RG 210, F.N. Series 16, 39.055, N.A.

83. Letter, Raymond Best to Dillon Myer, 3 April 1943, W R A, RG 210, F.N. Series 16, 39.053, N.A.

84. Memorandum, 21 December 1943, W R A, RG 210, F.N. Series 16, 39.055, N.A.

85. Letter, F. S. Frederick, undated, W R A, in University of California, Bancroft Library, Berkeley.

86. Letter, P. Robertson to D. Myer, 11 August 1943, W R A, RG 210, F.N. Series 16, 39.055, p. 2, N.A.

87. W R A Administrative Instruction No. 85, p. 1, and II, p. B:6, in F B I File, F.N. 62-69030-169, Washington, D.C.

88. Memorandum, F. S. Frederick to R. R. Best, 19 April 1943, University of California, Bancroft Library, Berkeley.

89. S. F. Frederick, quoted in Drinnon, *Keeper of Concentration Camps*, p. 100.

90. File, E. Ennis to J. E. Hoover, 8 March 1943, F B I, F.N. 62-69030-102, Washington, D.C. Emphasis added.

91. Memorandum, 4 March 1943, F B I, S.N. 62-69030-95b, Washington, D.C.

92. Memorandum, 10 March 1943, W R A, RG 210, F.N. Box 289, 39.053, N.A.

93. Letter, D. Myer to J. McCloy, 1 June 1943, W R A, RG 210, F.N. Box 289, 39.053, N.A. The forty-five inmates included the seven who had earlier been confined in the Moab Grand County Jail. After the move to Leupp, the W R A kept four of the latter inmates in a nearby jail at Winslow, Ariz., and confined the remaining three at the Leupp project jail. On May 1, the Leupp administration finally brought the four jailed inmates back to the Leupp center. Memorandum, 14 December 1943, W R A, RG 210, F.N. Series 16, 39.055, N.A.

94. Letter, D. Myer to P. R. Davidson, 15 May 1943, W R A, RG 210, F.N. Box 289, 39.053, N.A.

95. Ibid.

96. Ueno, quoted in Drinnon, *Keeper of Concentration Camps*, p. 100 n.

97. Correspondence, F. S. Frederick, 29 July 1943, University of California, Bancroft Library, Berkeley.

98. Letter, F. S. Frederick to R. Spencer, 20 April 1943, University of California, Bancroft Library, Berkeley.

99. Case History, F. S. Frederick, 27 July 1943, University of California, Bancroft Library, Berkeley.

100. Mr. Y's was not the only one in which administrative error brought an inmate to the isolation center: "[Mr. C] was not and never has been an officer in the G.Y.P.A. He was president of the [Gila River w r a Center's] Canal Young Peoples' Association for a short time. These two organizations were separate and distinct associations and had no connection with each other. Since both organizations enjoyed official sanction at Gila, holding an office in either of them would not constitute a crime or violation of camp rules and regulations. The writer investigated both organizations while employed at Gila and found the Canal organization to be a quiet, weak body that was purely a social organization. The only speech [he] ever made to the public was to extend them New Years' Greetings from his organization." Mr. C. had spent six months at the isolation center at the time the security officer wrote this report; another month elapsed before he was transferred to the w r a 's center at Minidoka, Idaho. Case History, F. S. Frederick, 18 August 1943, University of California, Bancroft Library, Berkeley.

Another Gila River inmate was a Hawaii-born Nisei who had never been to Japan. His transfer to Moab was apparently the result of a w r a informant "who complained that [he] was doing a considerable amount of anti-United States and anti-w r a talking prior to [the] time of his removal" (memorandum, Williamson to Bennett, 18 June 1943, w r a, RG 210, F.N. Series 16, 30.055, N.A.). No other "derogatory" information exists in his file, yet the w r a kept him at the isolation center for six months until he was transferred to the w r a camp at Poston, Ariz. Memorandum, 21 December 1943, w r a, RG 210, F.N. Series 16, 39.055, N.A.

101. Letter, P. Robertson to D. Myer, 11 August 1943, w r a, RG 210, F.N. Series 16, 39.955, p. 2, N.A.

102. Letter, L. A. Sigler to Solicitor General, 14 August 1943, w r a, RG 210, F.N. Series 16, 39.055, N.A.

103. Gordon Brown, "w r a, Gila River Project, Community Analysis Section, May 12 to July 7, 1945, Final Report," *Applied Anthropology,* no. 4 (fall 1945): 11.

104. Memorandum, D. Myer to H. Coverly, 19 June 1943, w r a, RG 210, F.N. Series 16, 30.055, N.A.

105. Letter, P. Robertson to D. Myer, 11 August 1943, w r a, RG 210, F.N. Series 16, 39.055, p. 1, N.A.

106. Letters, R. Best to D. Myer, 5 July 1943 and 24 August 1943, w r a, RG 210, F.N. Series 16, 39.055, N.A.

107. Letter, D. Myer to H. Coverly, 22 June 1943, w r a, RG 210, F.N. Series 16, 39.055, N.A.

108. Memorandum, 14 December 1943, w r a, RG 210, F.N. Series 16, 39.055, N.A.

109. Letter, P. Robertson to D. Myer, 11 August 1943, w r a, RG 210, F.N. Series 16, 39.055, p. 2, N.A.

110. Memorandum, D. Myer to w r a Directors, 5 June 1943, w r a, RG 210, F.N. Series 16, 39.055, N.A,

111. Ibid.

112. Memorandum, C. F. Ernst to D. Myer, 13 July 1943, w r a, RG 210, F.N. Series 16, 39.055, N.A.

113. Letter, F. S. Frederick, 17 October 1943, University of California, Bancroft Library, Berkeley.

114. Letter, P. Robertson to D. Myer, 11 August 1943, WRA, RG 210, F.N. Series 16, 39.055, p. 2, N.A.

115. Ibid., p. 1.

116. Ibid., pp. 2–3.

117. Memorandum, L. A. Sigler to Solicitor General, 14 August 1943, WRA, RG 210, F.N. Series 16, 39.055, pp. 1–2, N.A.

118. Memorandum, Review Committee to D. Myer, 12 October 1943, WRA, RG 210, F.N. File 41.142, N.A.

119. Memorandum, P. Robertson to D. Myer, 23 October 1943, WRA, RG 210, F.N. Series 16, 39.055, N.A.

120. Memorandum, 21 December 1943, WRA, RG 210, F.N. Series 16, 39.055, and Weglyn, *Years of Infamy*, p. 131.

121. Memorandum, D. Myer to P. Robertson, 30 December 1943, WRA, RG 210, F.N. Series 16, File 41.142, N.A.

122. Letter, Styler to D. Myer, 18 April 1944, WRA, RG 210, F.N. Series 16, 41.040, N.A., and memorandum, D. Myer to Secretary of Interior, 20 April 1944, WRA, RG 210, F.N. File 41.142, N.A.

123. Letter, D. Myer to J. McCloy, 11 April 1944, WRA, RG 210, F.N. Series 16, 41.142, N.A.

124. WRA press release, April 26, 1944, University of California, Bancroft Library, Berkeley.

125. Memorandum, Committee to D. Myer, 12 October 1943, WRA, RG 210, F.N. 41-142, N.A.

126. Richard Drinnon's *Keeper of Concentration Camps* is an important exception. His focus is on actions taken by the WRA and its director, Dillon Myer. The presentation here significantly differs from that of Drinnon, since the WRA centers are viewed within the context of the entire control process used during World War II.

127. Memorandum, Committee to D. Myer, 12 October 1943, WRA, RG 210, F.N. 41-142, N.A.

8 / SEGREGRATION CENTERS AND OTHER CAMPS

1. See Michi Weglyn, *Years of Infamy* (New York: William Morrow and Co., 1976; reprint, Seattle: University of Washington Press, 1996); Dorothy S. Thomas and Richard Nishimoto, *The Spoilage* (Berkeley: University of California Press, 1946); and Wayne M. Collins, "Brief for Appellees, J. Howard McGrath v. Tadayasu Abo et al., and J. Howard McGrath v. Mary Kanome Furuya et al., Nos. 12251 and 12252," *U.S. Court of Appeals for the Ninth Circuit Court*, February 27, 1950: 1–128, San Francisco.

2. Thomas and Nishimoto, *Spoilage*, p. 60, n. 13.

3. Weglyn, *Years of Infamy*, p. 144.

4. J. T. Terry, June 1945, quoted in ibid., p. 145.

5. Ibid., p. 149.

6. *San Francisco Chronicle,* May 27, 1943, quoted in ibid., p. 151.

7. Teruko I. Kumei, "Skeletons in the Closet: The Japanese American *Hokoku Seinan-dan* and Their 'Disloyal' Activities at the Tule Lake Segregation Center during World War II," *Japanese Journal of American Studies* 7 (1996): 70; Commission on Wartime Relocation and Internment of Civilians (hereafter CWRIC), *Personal Justice Denied,* reprint, with a new foreword (Seattle: University of Washington Press, 1997), p. 159.

8. War Relocation Authority (hereafter WRA) "Responses to Question 28," May 1, 1943, in Federal Bureau of Investigation (hereafter FBI), File Number (hereafter F.N.) 62-69030-116, Washington, D.C.

9. Allen R. Bosworth, *America's Concentration Camps* (New York: W. W. Norton and Co., 1967), p. 167; Jacobus tenBroek, Edward N. Barnhart, and Floyd W. Matson, *Prejudice, War, and the Constitution* (Berkeley: University of California Press, 1954), pp. 150–51.

10. Bosworth, *America's Camps,* p. 189.

11. Ibid.

12. Ibid., p. 168.

13. Memorandum, WRA, in FBI, F.N. 62-69030-419, p. 1.

14. tenBroek et al., *Prejudice, War,* p. 163; Thomas and Nishimoto, *Spoilage,* pp. 84–89.

15. Thomas and Nishimoto, *Spoilage,* pp. 94–106.

16. The office stayed closed until June 1945. Tatsujiro Nakamura, affidavit, in Wayne M. Collins, "Plaintiffs' Affidavits in Support of Their Motions for Summary Judgment . . . Tadayasu Abo et al. versus Tom Clark and Mary Kanome Furuya et al. versus Tom Clark, Nos. 25294-S and 25295-S," Tatsujiro Nakamura affidavit, November and December 1946, p. 6.

17. Anne R. Fisher, *Exile of a Race* (Seattle: F. and T. Publishers, 1965), p. 164, and Bosworth, *America's Camps,* p. 193.

18. Fisher, *Exile of a Race,* p. 165.

19. Dillon Myer, quoted in Weglyn, *Years of Infamy,* p. 163.

20. W. Collins, "Brief for Appellees," p. 64.

21. W. Collins, "Plaintiffs' Affidavits," Nakamura affidavit.

22. Letter, F. S. Frederick, November 29, 1943, University of California, Bancroft Library, Berkeley.

23. Weglyn, *Years of Infamy,* p. 165.

24. W. Collins, "Brief for Appellees," p. 66. See Thomas and Nishimoto, *Spoilage,* pp. 283–303.

25. Ernest Besig, in W. Collins, "Plaintiffs' Affidavits," Nakamura affidavit.

26. W. Collins, "Plaintiffs' Affidavits," Nakamura affidavit, pp. 7–8.

27. W. Collins, "Plaintiffs' Affidavits," Nakamura affidavit, p. 8.

28. W. Collins, "Brief for Appellees," p. 75.

29. Quoted in Weglyn, *Years of Infamy,* p. 212.

30. Ibid., p. 243.

31. Edward Ennis, interviewed during Gordon Hirabayashi's *coram nobis* hearings at the Hilton Hotel, Seattle, June 20, 1985. Interview in the author's possession.

32. See Kumei, "Skeletons," p. 73, for discussion concerning the precursor to this Issei organization.

33. John Christgau, *"Enemies"* (Ames: Iowa State University Press, 1985), p. 57.

34. See Weglyn, *Years of Infamy,* and Donald E. Collins, *Native American Aliens* (Westport, Conn.: Greenwood Press, 1985).

35. Kumei, "Skeletons," p. 81.

36. Christgau, *"Enemies,"* p. 158.

37. Nisei and Kibei renunciants shipped to Justice Department camps from December 27, 1944, to March 20, 1946:

Departure Date	Number	WRA Departure Camp	Justice Destination Camp
December 27, 1944	70	Tule Lake	Santa Fe
January 26, 1945	171	Tule Lake	Santa Fe
February 11, 1945	650	Tule Lake	Fort Lincoln
March 4, 1945	125	Tule Lake	Santa Fe
March 16, 1945	70	Tule Lake	Santa Fe
June 24, 1945	399	Tule Lake	Santa Fe
July 3, 1945	100	Tule Lake	Santa Fe
Sept. 1–8, 1945	12	Granada	Santa Fe
Sept. 1–8, 1945	6	Manzanar	Santa Fe
Sept. 9–15, 1945	69	Poston	Santa Fe
Sept. 9–15, 1945	17	Gila River	Santa Fe
Feb. 2–9, 1946	9	Topaz	Santa Fe
Feb. 2–9, 1946	1	Heart Mountain	Santa Fe
Feb. 2–9, 1946	2	Manzanar	Santa Fe
Feb. 2–9, 1946	7	Minidoka	Santa Fe
Feb. 2–9, 1946	2	Rohwer	Santa Fe
March 10–20, 1946	650	Tule Lake	Fort Lincoln
TOTAL	2,360	*	

NOTE: Compiled from WRA Weekly Reports, e.g., no. 143, "Net Absences on Leave, Week ending February 9, 1946," in FBI File, F.N. 62-69030-703, Washington, D.C.; Christgau, *"Enemies,"* pp. 160–61; Weglyn, *Years of Infamy,* pp. 242–45. Not included in these numbers are 318 Issei removed from Tule Lake on March 17, 1945, and sent to an unspecified camp, most likely Santa Fe, since Fort Lincoln was filled to capacity. Memorandum, 11 April 1945, FBI, F.N. 52-69030-574, Washington, D.C.

38. See Title 8, U.S. Code 1481 (c), June 27, 1952. Subsection (c), an amendment added to Public Law 87-301 in 1962, might reflect the results of Wayne Collins's and Theodore Tamba's legal work to assist these American citizens.

39. TenBroek et al., *Prejudice, War,* pp. 166–67. Not all Nisei on active duty prior to De-

cember 7, 1941, were removed. Two examples are Lieutenant Colonel Arthur Kaneko, Silver Springs, Md., and Mr. Thomas Miyoshi, Auburn, Wash.

40. TenBroek et al., *Prejudice, War,* p. 169. There were also at least forty-seven Nisei women who attended or graduated from the language school. See *MISLS Album, 1946,* p. 91.

41. See "20 JA WWII Heroes to Get Medal of Honor," *Rafu Shimpo* (Los Angeles), May 10, 2000, p. 1; "President OKs Medal of Honor for WW II Heroes," *Rafu Shimpo* (Los Angeles), May 15, 2000, pp. 1, 3; Lynn Crost, *Honor by Fire* (Novato, Calif.: Presidio Press, 1994).

42. This figure is quoted in Clifford Uyeda, "The Forgotten Resolution," *Rafu Shimpo* (Los Angeles), July 19, 1990: 1. TenBroek et al., *Prejudice, War,* p. 170, gives the number as 164. An hour-long documentary film on the draft resisters and Japanese Americans, Frank Abe's *Conscience and the Constitution,* was previewed on May 6, 2000, in Seattle.

43. Richard Drinnon, *Keeper of Concentration Camps* (Berkeley: University of California Press, 1987), p. 300. See also Eric Muller, *Free to Die for Their Country* (Chicago: University of Chicago Press, 2001).

44. Drinnon, *Keeper of Concentration Camps,* p. 301.

45. Ibid.

46. Uyeda, "The Forgotten Resolution," p. 1.

47. Interview conducted by the author in Seattle, 1979.

48. Quoted in Frank Abe, "Report Says Wartime JACL Leader Collaborated," *Rafu Shimpo* (Los Angeles), June 12, 1990, p. 1.

49. Pamphlet, "The War Relocation Work Corps," no date, WRA, in FBI File, F.N. 62-69030-61, Washington, D.C.

50. Edward N. Barnhart, "The Individual Exclusion of Japanese-Americans in World War II," *Pacific Historical Review* 29, no. 2 (May 1960): 119.

51. Ibid., p. 130.

52. U.S. WRA, U.S. Department of the Interior, *The Evacuated People* (Washington, D.C.: U.S. Department of the Interior, 1946b), p.187.

53. Herbert V. Nicholson, *Treasures in Earthen Vessels* (Whittier, Calif.: Penn Lithographics, 1974), p. 84, and Nicholson, interviewed in Arthur A. Hansen and Betty Mitson, eds., *Voices Long Silent* (Fullerton: Oral History Program, California State University, 1974), p. 126.

54. WRA, *Evacuated People,* p. 189.

55. Jeffrey F. Burton et al., *Confinement and Ethnicity* (Tucson, Ariz.: Western Archeological and Conservation Center, National Park Service, 1999; reprinted, with a new foreword by Tetsuden Kashima, University of Washington Press, 2002), p. 409.

56. Ibid., pp. 335–38.

57. David S. Wyman, *The Abandonment of the Jews* (New York: Pantheon Books, 1984), and Marvin Tokayer and Mary Swartz, *The Fugu Plan* (New York: Paddington Press, 1979).

58. E. Cellers, quoted in Ruth Gruber, *Haven* (New York: New American Library, 1983), p. 30.

59. Gruber, *Haven,* pp. 21–43.

60. Wyman, *Abandonment of the Jews,* p. 209.

61. Ibid., p. 285.

62. Ibid., pp. 267–68.

63. Gruber, *Haven*, pp. 163–171, and Wyman, *Abandonment of the Jews*, p. 270.

64. Wyman, *Abandonment of the Jews*, p. 274, and U.S. w r a, U.S. Department of the Interior, *Token Shipment* (Washington, D.C.: U.S. Department of the Interior, 1946c).

65. Wyman, *Abandonment of the Jews*, p. 231.

66. Eugene Moosa, "Jewish Refugee Here to Honor Diplomat Who Saved Thousands," *Japan Times* (Tokyo), September 18, 1992, p. 3, and "Jews Recall Rescue by Japanese Envoy in Lithuania, *Rafu Shimpo* (Los Angeles), May 13, 2000, p. 1. See also Tokayer and Swartz, *Fugu.*

67. Wyman, *Abandonment of the Jews*, pp. xiv–xv.

68. Gwen Terasaki, *Bridge to the Sun* (Chapel Hill: University of North Carolina Press, 1957), pp. 70–71.

69. B. Long, quoted in P. Scott Corbett, *Quiet Passages* (Kent, Ohio: Kent State University Press, 1987), pp. 31–32.

70. Memorandum, W. F. Kelly, 14 October 1942, i n s, RG 85, F.N. 56125, p. 9, N.A.

71. Bosworth, *America's Camps*, p. 107.

72. Norman Littell, *My Roosevelt Years* (Seattle: University of Washington Press, 1987), p. 55. At the Greenbriar Hotel, W. Va., the State Department kept about 2,000 Japanese diplomatic personnel from December 1941 to June 1942. The Justice Department posted twenty-five Border Patrol inspectors and fifty i n s guards. The Japanese who came from the Homestead Hotel, Va., found "much wining and dining and a number of gay cocktail parties among the higher ranking people of [the German and Japanese] embassies" (Terasaki, *Bridge to Sun,* p. 82). In addition to all the regular amenities, the residents purchased goods through Montgomery Ward and Sears Roebuck catalogs to take with them when they were repatriated. Bosworth, *America's Camps*, p. 111. The Grove Park Inn, N.C., held 63 Japanese and 155 Germans from South American embassies and consulates. Here, the guests played shuffleboard, lawn bowling, badminton, and bridge under the watchful eyes of forty-eight special guards and twenty-eight f b i agents. Bosworth, *America's Camps*, p. 109. The Grove Park Inn continued to house 131 nationals from Latin American countries after September 8, 1942.

73. Memorandum, E. G. Harrison to Adjutant General, 8 September 1942, i n s, RG 85, F.N. Box 3-56125, N.A.

74. Ibid. Other establishments that were used included the Ingleside Hotel, Staunton, Va., where German diplomats were housed, the Cascade Inn, Hot Springs, Va., where French diplomats were held, and the Shenvalee Hotel, New Marken, Va., where Italian diplomats were housed.

75. See c w r i c files, No. 14645a, RG 220, N.A.; memorandum, L. L. Lewis to C. E. Waller, 14 February 1944, i n s, RG 85, F.N. 56125/Gen., N.A.; Bosworth, *America's Camps*, p. 110; and Terasaki, *Bridge to Sun.* There is little consensus about the actual number of persons transported throughout the war years. A Justice Department memorandum offers the following numbers. It probably does not reflect individuals joining the ships who were not under the department's jurisdiction:

	Japanese	German	Italian	Ship
May 7, 1942	0	58	19	MS *Drottningholm*
June 3, 1942	0	212	25	MS *Drottningholm*
June 14, 1942	0	7	0	*Yasui*
June 18, 1942	184	0	0	MS *Gripsolm*
July 3, 1942	0	117	0	*Serpa Pinta*
July 15, 1942	0	334	80	MS *Drottningholm*
Sept. 2, 1942	890	0	0	MS *Gripsolm*
Jan. 6, 1944	0	1	0	*Marquis deComili*
Feb. 15, 1944	0	1,115	0	MS *Gripsolm*
May 2, 1944	0	85	0	MS *Gripsolm*
Jan. 7, 1945	0	723	0	MS *Gripsolm*
TOTAL	1,074	2,652	124	

Also, 336 Italian seamen taken before December 7, 1941, were returned to Italy during the war. C. Harvey Gardiner, *Pawns in a Triangle of Hate* (Seattle: University of Washington Press, 1981), p. 48. Another source states that the first exchange of enemy nationals consisted of German and Italian aliens. Bosworth, *America's Camps,* p. 111. On May 7, 1942, one source reports that 948 officials sailed on the Swedish liner MS *Drottningholm* from Jersey City, N.J.

On June 18, 1942, the MS *Gripsholm* left New York with 1,065 Japanese and 18 Thai nationals and stopped in Rio de Janeiro to pick up 417 additional Japanese nationals from South American countries. The ship sailed into Lourenco Marques (now Maputo), on the east coast of Africa, on July 20, 1942. Two Axis ships, *Asama Maru* and *Conte Verde,* met the *Gripsholm,* and the exchange took place. The *Asama Maru* sailed the Japanese passengers to Singapore on August 9, 1942, and then to Japan. On September 2, 1943, the *Gripsholm* sailed again from New York with 1,340 Japanese nationals. There were thirteen originating areas, with the largest group coming from Peru and the United States. The actual number, however, is difficult to ascertain. Gardiner, *Pawns in a Triangle,* p. 48.

76. W. Collins, ""Brief for Appellees," p. 18; see W. Collins, "Plaintiffs' Briefs," Nakamura affidavit.

9 / ABUSES, PROTESTS, AND THE GENEVA CONVENTION

1. Earl G. Harrison, "Civilian Internment—American Way," *Survey Graphic* 33 (May 1944): 229. Emphasis added.

2. Kazuo Ito, *America shunju hachijunen* (America spring-fall eighty years) (Tokyo: PMC Publishers, 1982), p. 99.

3. Ibid., p. 58.

4. See Ito, *America shunju;* Yoshiaki Fukuda, *Yokuryu seikatsu rokunen* (Detention life six years) (San Francisco: Konko Kyo Kai, 1957), and English version, *My Six Years of Internment*

(San Francisco: Konko Church of San Francisco, 1990); Daisho Tana, *Santa Fe, Rozubagu, senji tekikokujin yokuryujo nikki, dai-ikkan* (Santa Fe, Lordsburg, wartime enemy internment place diary, vol. 1) (Tokyo: Sankibo Busshorin Seisaku, 1976); and Shinichi Kato, ed., *Beikoku Nikkeijin hyakunenshi* (America's persons of Japanese ancestry 100-year history) (Los Angeles: Shinnichibei Shimbunsha [New Japanese American News], 1961).

5. Memorandum, L. M. Schofield to J. Savoretti, 17 June 1942, Immigration and Naturalization Service (hereafter I N S), Record Group (hereafter RG) 85, File Number (hereafter F.N.) Entry 89, Box 3, 56136, National Archives, Washington, D.C. (hereafter N.A.).

6. Fukuda, *Yokuryu seikatsu,* pp. 60–61 (in English, *My Six Years,* p. 39).

7. Arnold Krammer, *Undue Process* (Boulder, Colo.: Rowman and Littlefield Publishers, 1997), p. 49.

8. Quoted in ibid., p. 47.

9. Memorandum, J. Savoretti to L. B. Schofield, 11 July 1942, I N S, RG 85, F.N. Entry 89, Box 3, N.A.

10. Memorandum, E. G. Harrison to Attorney General, 29 August 1942, I N S, RG 85, F.N. Entry 89, Box 3, N.A.

11. Memorandum, D. W. Brewster to E. G. Harrison, 3 February 1943, I N S, RG 85, F.N. Entry 89, Box 3, N.A.

12. Quoted in P. Scott Corbett, *Quiet Passages* (Kent, Ohio: Kent State University Press, 1987), p. 118.

13. Record of Trial by General Court-Martial, "United States vs. Private First Clarence A. Burleson, Serial Number: 38132019, Military Police Escort Guard Company,'" Case No. 226083, convened at Fort Bliss, Texas, on September 10, 1942 (hereafter "U.S. vs. Burleson"), Department of the Army, U.S. Army Judiciary, Falls Church, Va. Testimony, S. Nishizaki, September 2, 1942, p. 12.

14. Testimony, F. Hishiya, September 2, 1942, "U.S. vs. Burleson," p. 10.

15. Testimony, J. A. Beckham, First Sergeant, September 10, 1942, "U.S. vs. Burleson," p. 11.

16. Two sources report that the soldier's name was Poston and not Burleson. Ito, *America shunju,* p. 109, has Poston in Japanese (in *katakana,* one of three writing systems, used to phonetically spell foreign words); Tsujimura reports the guard's name as Private Poston in James Tsujimura, "Six Incidents Belie Idea! We Were Detained against Our Wills As Eight Shot and Killed," *Pacific Citizen* (Los Angeles), December 21–28, 1985, p. D-8.

17. Testimony, Truman C. Fambro Jr., Sergeant, September 10, 1942, "U.S. vs. Burleson," p. 62.

18. Testimony, Senmatsu Ishizaki, September 10, 1942, "U.S. vs. Burleson," p. 39.

19. Tana, *Santa Fe, Rozubagu,* p. 290.

20. Ibid., pp. 290–91, translated from the Japanese by Yasuko I. Takezawa. See also Fukuda, *Yokuryu seikatsu,* p. 67 (in English, *My Six Years,* p. 42).

21. Translated by Takezawa, from Fukuda, *Yokuryu seikatsu,* p. 67.

22. Fukuda, *Yokuryu seikatsu,* p. 67.

23. Board proceedings, July 27, 1942, "U.S. vs. Burleson."

24. Report of investigation of Private Burleson, August 15, 1942, "U.S. vs. Burleson."

25. Testimony, Sematsu Ishizaki, "Record of Hearing" (transcript), p. 4, "U.S. vs. Burleson." For the perspectives of some inmates, see Fukuda, *Yokuryu seikatsu,* pp. 68–69, and Ito, *America shunju,* p. 109.

26. Testimony, Shiro Koike, September 2, 1942, "Record of Hearing" (typescript), p. 11, "U.S. vs. Burleson." In this record, Senmatsu Ishizaki testified that, in his opinion, the two men were shot as an example to the rest of the internees at Lordsburg. During July 1942, the Lordsburg camp was in the middle of an internee strike, and these 147 men happened to arrive during the camp struggle: "I don't believe the two were shot for trying to run away, because they were striking here [*sic*] and [they] had the internees shut up in the barracks for more than 10 days, and it was done just for an example. I think that is why the shooting was done. They were not the kind of men who would run away" (ibid., p. 5). Tensions were then high among internees and camp administration.

27. Testimony, Clyde A. Lundy, September 10, 1942, "U.S. vs. Burleson," p. 123.

28. Sworn statement of Clarence A. Burleson, Private, 309th Military Police Escort Guard Company, undated (probably July 28, 1942), of the "Report of Investigation of Charges, by Louis J. Balch, Captain, Investigating Officer," "U.S. vs. Burleson."

29. Testimony, Clarence A. Burleson, September 10, 1942, "U. S. vs. Burleson," p. 134.

30. Ibid., Burleson, pp. 17, 138. The next prosecution question was "Was there any other question besides that?" Burleson's reply was "No, sir." Q: "That was the only thing they asked?" A: "Yes, sir."

31. Testimony, P. Bond, First Lieutenant, Medical Corps, September 10, 1942, "U. S. vs. Burleson." The following constitutes the relevant questions and answers from Lieutenant Bond, pp. 116–17:

Prosecution (Q): Did you from your examination find any muscular atrophy or anything which would indicate that either or both of them might be crippled?

Lordsburg Medical Officer (A): No, sir, I found nothing to substantiate that.

Q: You found nothing to indicate that their means of locomotion might have been impaired?

A: I did not.

Q: Did you or did you not perform an autopsy?

A: I did not perform an autopsy.

Q: Then "death by gunshot wounds" is your assumption?

A: Yes, sir.

Q: You made no examination to determine whether or not they did die of gunshot wounds?

A: No further examination.

EXAMINATION BY THE COURT

Member of the court (Q): The bullets, the entrance and exit, you examined those, didn't you?

A: We accounted for nine bullet wounds on each body; whether they were entrance or exits we did not determine.

Q: Well, the small holes were where?

A: Well, those were apparently buckshot and they just produce a big hole.

Q: The holes were the same size?

A: Approximately the same size.

RECROSS-EXAMINATION

Defense (Q): Did you actually extract any of the pellets or bullets?

A: We made no attempt to.

Q: Then you have no way of determining how many pellets actually hit them?

A: We have no other way.

REDIRECT EXAMINATION

Prosecution (Q): Just for clarity, did I understand you to say that you found nine wounds in each of the bodies?

A: In each of the bodies, yes, sir.

(WITNESS EXCUSED)

The death certificates signed by the medical officer seemingly contradict his testimony on whether the wounds were exit or entrance wounds. For Toshiro Kobata, the doctor reported "Immediate cause of death: Wound, gunshot, severe, center, upper left back"; for Hirota Isomura, "Wound, gunshot, severe, neck, left shoulder" ("U.S. vs. Burleson," Prosecution's Exhibit A and B).

32. Tana, *Santa Fe, Rozubagu,* p. 381. See also testimony, H. Aisawa, September 10, 1942, "U. S. vs. Burleson."

33. Fukuda, *Yokuryu seikatsu,* p. 58.

34. Tsujimura, quoted in William M. Hohri, *Repairing America* (Pullman: Washington State University Press, 1988), p. 134. Differences arise in identifying the victim. Some sources maintain that Kanesaburo Oshima was shot at the Fort Sill Internment Camp (Tsujimura, in Hohri, *Repairing America;* Michi Weglyn, *Years of Infamy* [New York: William Morrow and Co., 1976; reprint, Seattle: University of Washington, 1996], p. 312; and Corbett, *Quiet Passages,* p. 132). Fukuda, *Yokuryu seikatsu,* p. 58, reports the death of Ichiro Shimoda with a correction in the footnote. An FBI memorandum (27 February 1943, FBI, F.N. 62-63892-134, Washington, D.C.) quotes a Japanese source as saying the victim was Kai Oshima, age fifty-seven, from Panama. Another FBI report identifies the person as "Saburo Muraoka, whose address was given as Chula Vista, California" (memorandum, W. G. Banister to J. E. Hoover, 18 May 1942, FBI, F.N. 62-63892-23, p. 2, Washington, D.C.). In the case of Saburo Muraoka of Chula Vista, the only person by that name who was arrested and interned by the Justice Department did not die until 1983, making the FBI report a probable misidentification. The internees identified the victim as Kanesaburo Oshima.

35. Memorandum, FBI, F.N. 62-69030-376, p. 14.

36. Quoted in Richard Drinnon, *Keeper of Concentration Camps* (Berkeley: University of California Press, 1987), p. 43.

37. Corbett, *Quiet Passages,* p. 133.

38. Ibid., pp. 133–34. For a brief but excellent synopsis of the shooting of James Wakasa, see Roger Daniels, ed., *Asian America* (Seattle: University of Washington Press, 1988), pp. 228–31. Daniels writes that the physical "evidence was incompatible with the sentry's story that he had shot Wakasa while the inmate was crawling through the fence. It indicates that Wakasa had been facing the guard tower from which the shot came"(Daniels, *Asian America,* p. 230).

39. Quoted in Weglyn, *Years of Infamy,* p. 312.

40. Another possible death by gunfire, the eighth, might have occurred at the w r a center at Gila River, Ariz., in the summer of 1943. The victim is not identified, and no other source materials have been found on this incident. See Tsujimura, in Hohri, *Repairing America,* p. 134.

41. Howard S. Levie, ed., *Documents on Prisoners of War: International Law Studies,* vol. 5 (Newport, R.I.: U.S. Naval War College, 1979), p. 462.

42. Ibid., p. 463. After the war, the State Department was asked for its explanation of the words *mutatis mutandis.* It "explained that the Japanese government would apply, on conditions of reciprocity, the Geneva Prisoners of War Convention in the treatment of prisoners of war." See *Tomoye Kawakita v. U.S.,* No. 12061, 1951: 519, footnote 15.

43. Ito, *America shunju,* p. 61.

44. Memorandum, Justice Department to i n s, 28 April 1942, Justice Department, RG 85, Old Raton Ranch, NM, F.N. Box 3, 1263/A, N.A.

45. Ito, *America shunju,* p. 62; Tana, *Santa Fe, Rozubagu,* p. 256; memorandum, L. S. Schofield to Savoretti, 17 June 1942, i n s, RG 85, F.N. 89-3, NND 853567, N.A.

46. Fukuda, *Yokuryu seikatsu,* p. 62.

47. Kato, *Beikoku Nikkeijin,* p 339.

48. Fukuda, *Yokuryu seikatsu,* pp. 62–64; "The Fundamental Question," Lordsburg Internee, copy, in file, no date, War Department, Records of the Adjutant General's Office, RG 389, F.N. 414.253.5, N.A.

49. Ito, *America shunju,* p. 107.

50. Tana, *Santa Fe, Rozubagu,* p. 255.

51. Ibid., p. 256.

52. Fukuda, *Yokuryu seikatsu,* pp. 63–64; Tana, *Santa Fe, Rozubagu,* pp. 257–58.

53. Tana, *Santa Fe, Rozubagu,* p. 243; Ito, *America shunju,* p. 108.

54. Ito, *America shunju,* p. 108; see also Tana, *Santa Fe, Rozubagu,* pp. 279–80.

55. John J. Culley, "Trouble at the Lordsburg Internment Camp," *New Mexico Historical Review* 60, no. 3 (1985): 230.

56. Fukuda, *Yokuryu seikatsu,* p. 64.

57. Tana, *Santa Fe, Rozubagu,* p. 280.

58. Ibid., pp. 281–82.

59. Ibid. p. 283.

60. Fukuda, *Yokuryu seikatsu,* pp. 64–65; Tana, *Santa Fe, Rozubagu,* p. 283.

61. Tana, *Santa Fe, Rozubagu,* p. 284.

62. Fukuda, *Yokuryu seikatsu,* p. 65.

63. Ibid., p. 66.

64. Corbett (*Quiet Passages*, p. 117) states that the State Department's Special War Problems Division had to remind the War Department in July 1942 about the applicability of the Geneva Convention to the relationship between protecting powers and their internees. The Special Division handled transactions between the Spanish consul and the internees at Lordsburg.

65. Kato, *Beikoku Nikkeijin*, p. 340; Culley, "Trouble at Lordsburg," p. 239.

66. Kato, *Beikoku Nikkeijin*, p. 340.

67. Memorandum, B. M. Bryan to Commanding General Eighth Service Command, 18 September 1942, War Department, Records of the Adjutant General's Office, RG 389, F.N. 414.253.5, N.A.

68. Memorandum, C. A. Lundy to L. F. Guerre, Director Internal Security, 10 October 1942, War Department, Records of the Adjutant General's Office, RG 389, F.N. 414.253.3, N.A.

69. Ibid.

70. Letter, B. M. Bryan to Special Division, 2 November 1942, State Department, in Records of the Adjutant General's Office, RG 389, F.N. 414.253.5, N.A.

71. Kato, *Beikoku Nikkeijin*, p. 340.

72. Memorandum, J. E. Hoover to AG, 19 November 1942, F B I, F.N. 62-63892-93, Washington, D.C.

73. Ibid.

74. Memorandum, L. F. Guerre to Provost Marshal General, 30 November 1942, War Department, Records of the Adjutant General's Office, RG 389, F. N. Lordsburg, Box 414, 383.7, N.A.

75. Mollie Pressler, "The Lordsburg Internment/POW Camp," Lordsburg, N.M., 1992, pp. 37–38 (typewritten).

76. Yasutaro Soga, *Tessaka seikatsu* (Life inside the iron fence) (Honolulu: Hawaii Times, 1948), p. 148.

77. The investigating officer was Colonel Louis A. Ledbetter, who replaced Colonel Lundy at Lordsburg in December 1942. Ledbetter saw the removal of the Japanese internees to the camps at Santa Fe, N.M,, and Crystal City, Tex., during the 1943 summer months. Pressler, "Lordsburg Internment/POW Camp," p. 27.

78. Translated from Tana, *Santa Fe, Rozubagu*, p. 97.

79. Ibid., pp. 259–61.

80. Memorandum, L. H. Jensen to J. Mangione, 19 October 1943, I N S, RG 85, F.N. Old Raton Ranch, NM, Box 3, 1300, N.A.

81. The dates and numbers were December 29, 1944, 70; January 26, 1945, 171; March 4, 1945, 125; March 16, 1945, 70; June 24, 1945, 190; July 3, 1945, 240. See Weglyn, *Years of Infamy*; Christgau, "Enemies"; and Culley, "Trouble at Lordsburg."

82. Culley, "Trouble at Lordsburg," pp. 64–65.

83. Ibid., quote, p. 65.

84. Translated by Takezawa, from Soga, *Tessaka seikatsu*, p. 303.

85. Jerri Mangione, *An Ethnic at Large* (New York: G. P. Putnam's Sons, 1978), p. 338.

86. Ibid.

87. Letter, Iwao Matsushita to J. C. Dennis, December 27, 1943, "Iwao Matsushita File," Suzzallo Library, University of Washington, Seattle. See Louis Fiset, *Imprisoned Apart* (Seattle: University of Washington Press, 1998), for an excellent account of the Matsushita case.

88. Minoru Yasui in John Tateishi, ed., *And Justice for All* (New York: Random House, 1984), pp. 83–85.

89. Testimony, J. Akutsu, Commission on Wartime Relocation and Internment of Civilians hearings, September 9–11, 1981, Seattle.

90. See memorandum, 17 February 1943, War Department, Records of the Adjutant General's Office, RG 389, F.N. 464-414, 250.45, N.A.

91. Memorandum, L. Jensen to W. F. Kelly, 31 March 1944, INS, RG 85, F.N. Old Raton Ranch, NM, Box 3, 1300, N.A.

10 / IMPRISONMENT AND STIGMA

1. See, for example, John L. DeWitt, *Final Report* (Washington, D.C.: U.S. Government Printing Office, 1943); John J. McCloy and Karl R. Bendetsen, "Letters from John J. McCloy and Karl R. Bendetsen," in Roger Daniels, Sandra C. Taylor, Harry H. L. Kitano, eds., *Japanese Americans,* 2nd ed. (Seattle: University of Washington Press, 1992); and Page Smith, *Democracy on Trial* (New York: Simon and Schuster, 1995).

2. Carey McWilliams, *Prejudice: Japanese-Americans* (Boston: Little, Brown, 1944), p. 4. See also Bradford Smith, *Americans from Japan* (Philadelphia: Lippincott, 1948), and Morton Grodzins, *Americans Betrayed* (Chicago: University of Chicago Press, 1949).

3. Grodzins, *Americans Betrayed,* p. 92; see also pp. 90, 109.

4. Commission on Wartime Relocation and Internment of Civilians (hereafter CWRIC), *Personal Justice Denied,* reprint, with a new foreword (Seattle: University of Washington Press, 1997), p. 18.

5. See, for example, Jacobus tenBroek, Edward N. Barnhart, and Floyd W. Matson, *Prejudice, War, and the Constitution* (Berkeley: University of California Press, 1954), and Greg Robinson, *By Order of the President* (Cambridge: Harvard University Press, 2001).

6. DeWitt, *Final Report,* p. 34. Noted columnist Walter Lippman and then California attorney general Earl Warren also offered this type of negative reasoning to support their assessments of the dangerousness of the Nikkei population. See Walter Lippman, "Today and Tomorrow: The Fifth Column on the Coast," *New York Herald Tribune,* February 12, 1942. For Earl Warren's views, see Roger Daniels, *The Decision to Relocate the Japanese Americans* (Philadelphia: J. B. Lippincott Co., 1975), pp. 25, 29.

7. Jeanne Wakatsuki Houston, quoted in Arthur A. Hansen and Betty Mitson, eds., *Voices Long Silent* (Fullerton: Oral History Program, California State University, 1974), p. 186.

8. Quote, *Japan Times* (Tokyo), April 20, 1992, p. 3.

9. Quoted in CWRIC, *Personal Justice,* p. 297.

10. Shizuo Hisamune, Alien Internment Camp, P. O. Box 788, Crystal City, Texas, March 13,1947, in Iwao Shimzu collection, "Petition—Aged and Infirmed Aliens," Japanese American Library, San Francisco.

11. Tetsuden Kashima, "Japanese American Internees Return—1945–1955: Readjustment and Social Amnesia," *Phylon Quarterly* 41, no. 2 (June 1980): 113.

12. There are many examples of this. Sharon Hashimoto (*Reparations* [Waldron Island, Wash.: Brooding Heron Press and Bindery, 1992]), for example, writes about the experiences of her mother in a W R A camp: "So I imagine her at thirteen. Her memory blurs the exact picture with the few facts she can recall, and I ask her, What do you remember? She tells me: Your grandmother made us think it was an adventure to hang blankets at night and make our own rooms, to fall asleep listening to wind and each other's coughing as floodlights filled the slits in the walls."

13. Robert Matsui, *Congressional Record* 133, no. 141 (September 17, 1987).

14. See Sandra C. Taylor, in Daniels et al., *Japanese Americans,* pp. 163–68. In 1948, Congress passed the Japanese American Evacuation Claims Act (Public Law 80-886, July 2, 1948) by which individuals could claim monetary relief if they could show proof of loss. The final outcome was grossly inadequate. Eight other congressional actions predated the 1988 Civil Liberties Act. Krammer lists them as the "Amendment to Claims Acts of 1948 (82-116), 17 August 1951; Benefits for Certain Federal Employees of Japanese Ancestry (82-545), 15 July 1952; Amendment to Claims Act of 1948 (84-673), 9 July 1956; Credit for Periods of Internment for Certain Federal Employees of Japanese American Ancestry (86-782), 14 September 1960; Social Security Amendment of 1972 (Section 142-92-603), 17 November 1972; and the Japanese American Civil Service Retirement Credit for Periods of Internment, 22 September 1978" (Arnold Krammer, *Undue Process* [Boulder, Colo.: Rowman and Littlefield Publishers, 1997], p. 168). In addition, states such as California and Washington have passed legislation symbolically correcting certain actions taken against state employees before their incarceration during World War II.

15. Proclamation No. 4417, 41 Fed. Reg. No. 35: 7741, 20 February 1976.

16. See Peter Irons, ed., *Justice Delayed* (Middletown, Conn.: Wesleyan University Press, 1989). Three major judicial cases concerning the Japanese Americans were reopened through a writ of error *coram nobis.* The grounds for a *coram nobis* petition with respect to the wartime Japanese American cases rests on the allegation that in presenting their cases before the court, the government deliberately suppressed, altered, or destroyed vital information.

Although the Supreme Court ruled in 1943 that the forced evacuation was constitutional, Fred Korematsu's original conviction was not vacated and his indictment dismissed by the U.S. District Court until April 19, 1984. Judge Marilyn H. Patel, speaking for the Northern District of California, wrote that "substantial support [exists] in the record that the government deliberately omitted relevant information and provided misleading information in papers before the court. The information was critical to the court's determination although it cannot now be said what result would have obtained had the information been disclosed. Because the information was of the kind peculiar with the government's knowledge, the court was dependent upon the government to provide a full and accurate account. . . . The judicial process is seriously impaired when the government's law enforcement officers violate their ethical obligations to the court" (quoted in ibid., pp. 242–43).

In another major case, brought by Gordon Hirabayashi, District Court Judge Donald S. Voorhees ruled on February 10, 1986, that an error existed in the original Supreme Court hearing and found that "the failure of the government to disclose to the petitioner, to petitioner's counsel, and to the Supreme Court the reason stated by General DeWitt for his deciding that military necessity required the exclusion of all those of Japanese ancestry from the West Coast was an error of the most fundamental character and that petitioner was in fact very seriously prejudiced by the non-disclosure in his appeal from his conviction of failing to report [for 'evacuation']" (quoted in ibid., pp. 374–75). The judge vacated Hirabayashi's conviction for failure to obey the exclusion order but upheld one concerning the violation of the curfew order since it was "relatively mild." In a subsequent opinion, the judge contended that "Petitioner should not, however, consider that conviction [for the curfew violation] to be a stigma. His refusal to obey the curfew order and, even more so, his refusal to obey the order to report for his imprisonment were in the tradition of those who have forged the freedoms which we now enjoy" (quoted in ibid. p. 384). Later, on September 24, 1987, the U.S. Court of Appeals for the Ninth Circuit unanimously upheld the orders to vacate the exclusion order and the conviction based on a failure to obey the curfew order.

In Oregon, Minoru Yasui also had his wartime conviction for violation of the curfew order reheard. The district court judge vacated his earlier conviction on January 26, 1984, but dismissed the *coram nobis* petition. While appealing the petition dismissal, Minoru Yasui passed away in November 1986.

17. Three excellent volumes on what has become known as the Japanese American redress movements are Yasuko I. Takezawa , *Breaking the Silence* (Ithaca, N.Y.: Cornell University Press, 1995), and Leslie T. Hatamiya, *Righting a Wrong* (Stanford, Calif.: Stanford University Press, 1993). In September 1997, Harry H. L. Kitano, Mitchell T. Maki, and S. Megan Berthold convened an important conference at the University of California, Los Angeles, "Voices of the Japanese American Redress." Major participants in the redress movement—from community action groups, representatives of the government, national organizations such as the Japanese American Citizens League, National Coalition for Japanese American Redress, and the National Coalition for Redress and Reparations plus elected officials, defendants and attorneys in the legal arena, staff and members of the C W R I C, and academicians—met and reflected on the many strands of this complex social movement. Their report, analysis, and interpretation of the redress movement is published in Mitchell Maki, Harry H. L. Kitano, and S. Megan Berthold, *Achieving the Impossible Dream* (Urbana: University of Illinois Press, 1999).

18. I am indebted to Grace Shimizu, El Cerrito, Calif., of the Campaign for Justice Committee, for the following information. Individuals denied redress include the "dependent children of railroad and mining workers who were fired from their jobs" after December 7, 1941, by the government, Japanese Americans born in an internment camp after June 30, 1946, and those who were "legally residing in the U.S. but were not U.S. citizens or permanent residents at the time of internment." The last category refers to persons brought from

Latin American countries and placed into internment camps. Congressman Xavier Becerra (Democrat-CA, 30th District) reintroduced HR 619, the Wartime Parity and Justice Act of 2001. The proposed legislation provides full funding for the public education mandated by the 1988 Civil Liberties Act, rectifies the deprivations of those denied redress under the Civil Liberties Act, ensures redress equity for Latin American internees, and provides for civil liberties applications made after the deadline date. Grace Shimizu, personal correspondence. Quotes taken from informational flyer "Campaign for Justice: Redress Now for Japanese Latin Americans!" winter 2001.

19. The commission hearings raised an additional social issue that created considerable controversy within the Japanese American community. As part of each testimony, the participants were asked to comment on any remedies they thought would be appropriate. Japanese Americans discussed the idea that monetary reparations for a wrong done by the government, a public presidential apology, and various social programs for the benefit of the Japanese American community might be worthwhile goals. However, not a few Japanese Americans argued against any monetary redress because it required placing a dollar amount on losses, which would ultimately demean the entire imprisonment experience. Others who approved of monetary redress favored various and conflicting levels of compensation. The opportunity to discuss the experience openly in the community became the vital point for many. Community sentiments long suppressed could finally be raised.

20. Quoted in Irons, *Justice Delayed*, p. 384. The statement was made on April 29, 1986.

BIBLIOGRAPHY

Abe, Frank. "Report Says Wartime JACL Leader Collaborated." *Rafu Shimpo* (Los Angeles), June 12, 1990, p. 1.

Adachi, Ken. *The Enemy That Never Was: A History of the Japanese Canadians.* Toronto: McClelland and Stewart, 1976.

Allen, Gwenfield. *Hawaii's War Years.* Honolulu: University of Hawaii Press, 1950.

Amidos, Beulah. "Aliens in America." *Survey Graphics* 30 (February 1943).

Anonymous. "The Concentration Camp Arrives in the United States." *Missions* (January 1942), p. 8.

Armor, John, and Peter Wright. *Manzanar.* New York: Times Books, 1988.

Bancroft Library, University of California, Berkeley. Robertson, Paul G. "Correspondence to S. F. Frederick," December 27, 1943.

———. Frederick, Frances S. "Correspondences, Case Histories, and Memorandums," July to December 1943.

———. Kurihara, Joe Y. "Murder in Camp Manzanar." File R8.10. April 16, 1943.

Barnhart, Edward N. "The Individual Exclusion of Japanese-Americans in World War II." *Pacific Historical Review* 29, no. 2 (May 1960): 111–30.

———. "Japanese Internees from Peru." *Pacific Historical Review* 31, no. 2 (May 1962): 169–78.

Bendetsen, Karl R. "Letters from John J. McCloy and Karl R. Bendetsen." In Roger Daniels, Sandra C. Taylor, and Harry H. L. Kitano, eds., *Japanese Americans: From Relocation to Redress,* 2nd ed., pp. 213–16. Seattle: University of Washington Press, 1991.

Bendix, Reinhard, and Guenther Roth. *Scholarship and Partisanship: Essays on Max Weber.* Berkeley: University of California Press, 1971.

Bevans, Charles I., comp. *Treaties and Other International Agreements of the United States of America, 1776–1949.* Washington, D.C.: Department of State, 1969.

Biddle, Francis. *In Brief Authority.* New York: Doubleday and Co., 1962.

Bloom, Leonard, and Ruth Reimer. *Removal and Return, the Socio-Economic Effects of the War on Japanese Americans.* Berkeley: University of California Press, 1949.

Bosworth, Allen R. *America's Concentration Camps.* New York: W. W. Norton and Co., 1967.

Breuer, William. *Nazi Spies in America: Hitler's Undercover War.* Reprint, New York: St. Martin's Paperback, 1990.

Broom, Leonard, and John I. Kituse. *The Managed Casualty: The Japanese American Family in World War II.* Berkeley: University of California Press, 1956.

Brown, G. Gordon. "W R A, Gila River Project, Community Analysis Section, May 12 to July 7, 1945, Final Report." *Applied Anthropology,* no. 4 (fall 1945).

Burton, Jeffrey F., Mary M. Farrell, Florence B. Lord, and Richard W. Lord. *Confinement and Ethnicity: An Overview of World War II Japanese American Relocation Sites.* Tucson, Ariz.: Western Archeological and Conservation Center, National Park Service, Department of the Interior, 1999; reprint, with a new foreword, Seattle: University of Washington Press, 2002.

California. *Report, Joint Fact-Finding Committee on Un-American Activities in California to the Fifty-fifth California Legislature* (1943). Jack B. Tenny, chairman, California Legislature.

Chinen, Karleen. "Return to Tule Lake." *Hawaii Herald,* supplement, October 7, 1988, pp. B-4–B-7.

Christgau, John. *"Enemies": World War II Alien Internment.* Ames: Iowa State University Press, 1985.

Chuman, Frank F. "Manzanar." In John Tateishi, ed., *And Justice for All: An Oral History of the Japanese American Detention Camps,* pp. 227–38. New York: Random House, 1984.

———. *The Bamboo People: The Law and Japanese-Americans.* Del Mar, Calif.: Publisher's Inc., 1976.

Clark, Paul Frederick. "Those Other Camps: An Oral History Analysis of Japanese Alien Enemy Internment during World War II." M.A. thesis, California State University, Fullerton, 1980. Also in National Archives, Washington, D.C., Wartime Relocation and Internment of Civilians, Record Group 220, Numerical Files, pp. 4403–55.

Coggins, Cecil H. "The Japanese-Americans in Hawaii." *Harper's Magazine* (June 1943): 193–201.

Collaer, N. D. "The Crystal City Internment Camp." U.S. Department of Justice, *Immigration and Naturalization Service Monthly Review* 5, no. 6 (December 1947): 75–77.

Collins, Donald E. *Native American Aliens: Disloyalty and Renunciation of Citizenship by Japanese Americans during World War II.* Westport, Conn.: Greenwood Press, 1985.

Collins, Wayne M. "Brief for Appellees, J. Howard McGrath v. Tadayasu Abo et al., and J. Howard McGrath v. Mary Kanome Furuya et al., Nos. 12251 and 12252." *U.S. Court of Appeals for the Ninth Circuit Court.* February 27, 1950, pp. 1–128, San Francisco.

———. "Plaintiffs' Affidavits in Support of Their Motions for Summary Judgment . . . Tadayasu Abo et al. versus Tom Clark and Mary Kanome Furuya et al. versus Tom Clark, Nos. 25294-S and 25295-S," Tatsujiro Nakamura affidavit. November and December 1946.

Commission on Wartime Relocation and Internment of Civilians. *Personal Justice Denied.* Washington, D.C.: U.S. Government Printing Office, 1982; reprint, with a new foreword, Seattle: University of Washington Press, 1997.

———. *Personal Justice Denied,* Part 2: *Recommendations.* Washington, D.C.: U.S. Government Printing Office, June, 1983. Reprinted in *Personal Justice Denied,* with a new fore-word, Seattle: University of Washington Press, 1997.

Corbett, P. Scott. *Quiet Passages: The Exchange of Civilians between the United States and Japan during the Second World War.* Kent, Ohio: Kent State University Press, 1987.

Crost, Lynn. *Honor by Fire: Japanese Americans at War in Europe and the Pacific.* Novato, Calif.: Presidio Press, 1994.

Culley, John J. "The Santa Fe Camp and the Justice Department Program for Enemy Aliens." In Roger Daniels, Sandra C. Taylor, and Harry H. L. Kitano, eds., *Japanese Americans: From Relocation to Redress,* 2nd ed., pp. 57–71. Seattle: University of Washington Press, 1991.

————. "Trouble at the Lordsburg Internment Camp." *New Mexico Historical Review* 60, no. 3 (1985).

————. "World War II and a Western Town: The Internment of the Japanese Railroad Workers of Clovis, New Mexico." *The Western Historical Quarterly* (January 1982): 43–61.

Culp, Eugene M. "Alien Enemy Paroles." Department of Justice, *Immigration and Naturalization Monthly Review* 3, no. 4 (October 1945): 204–8.

Daniels, Roger. *Asian America: Chinese and Japanese in the United States since 1850.* Seattle: University of Washington Press, 1988.

————. *The Decision to Relocate the Japanese Americans.* Philadelphia: J. B. Lippincott Co., 1975.

————. *Concentration Camps U.S.A.: Japanese Americans and World War II.* New York: Holt, Rinehart and Winston, 1970.

Daniels, Roger, ed. *Prisoners without Trial: Japanese Americans in World War II.* New York: Hill and Wang, 1993.

————. *American Concentration Camps,* vols. 1–9. New York: Garland Publishing, 1989.

Daniels, Roger, Sandra C. Taylor, and Harry H. L. Kitano, eds. *Japanese Americans: From Relocation to Redress,* 2nd ed. Seattle: University of Washington Press, 1991.

Dawidoff, Nicholas. *The Catcher Was a Spy: The Mysterious Life of Moe Berg.* New York: Pantheon, 1994. (Orig. pub., New Rochelle, N.Y.: Arlington House, 1973.)

DeToledano, Ralph. *J. Edgar Hoover: The Man in His Time.* New Rochelle, N.Y.: Arlington House, 1973.

DeWitt, John L. *Final Report. Japanese Evacuation from the West Coast, 1942.* Washington, D.C.: U.S. Government Printing Office, 1943.

Douglas, William O. *The Court Years: 1939–1975.* New York: Random House, 1980.

Drinnon, Richard. *Keeper of Concentration Camps: Dillon S. Myer and American Racism.* Berkeley: University of California Press, 1987.

Eisenhower, John. *Allies: Pearl Harbor to D-Day.* New York: Doubleday and Co., 1982.

Eisenhower, Milton S. *The President Is Calling.* New York: Doubleday and Co., 1974.

Embrey, Sue K., Arthur A. Hansen, and Betty K. Mitson. *Manzanar Martyr: An Interview with Harry Y. Ueno.* Fullerton: Oral History Program, California State University, 1986.

Emmerson, John K. *The Japanese Thread: A Life in the U.S. Foreign Service.* New York: Holt, Rinehart and Winston, 1978.

Encyclopedia of Social Sciences, 1931 ed. S. vol. 5, "Enemy Alien," by Frederic L. Schuman.

————. 1931 ed. S. vol. 12, "Prisoners of War," by E. G. Trimble.

Evanzz, Karl. *The Messenger: The Rise and Fall of Elijah Muhammad.* New York: Pantheon Books, 1991.

Fiset, Louis. *Imprisoned Apart: The World War II Correspondence of an Issei Couple.* Seattle: University of Washington Press, 1998.

Fisher, Anne R. *Exile of a Race.* Seattle: F. and T. Publishers, 1965.

Floherty, John J. *Our FBI.* Philadelphia: J. B. Lippincott Co., 1951.

Fox, Stephan. *The Unknown Internment: An Oral History of the Relocation of Italian Americans during World War II.* Boston: Twayne Publishers, 1990.

Fuchs, Lawrence. *Hawaii Pono: A Social History.* New York: Harcourt, 1961.

Fujimura, Bunyu. *Though I Be Crushed: The Wartime Experience of a Buddhist Minister.* Los Angeles: Nembutsu Press, 1985.

Fukuda, Yoshiaki. *Yokuryu seikatsu rokunen* (Detention life six years). San Francisco: Konko Kyo Kai, 1957. Translated and republished as *My Six Years of Internment: An Issei's Struggle for Justice.* San Francisco: Konko Church of San Francisco, 1990.

"The Fukudas," by M. Fukuda. In Joy N. Gee, ed., *Crystal City [Texas] 50th Anniversary Reunion Album.* Monterey, Calif.: By the editor, 1993.

Furer, Julius A. *Administration of the Navy Department in World War II.* Washington, D.C.: U.S. Navy Department, 1959.

Furuya, Suikei. *Hashio ten ten* (From camp to camp). Honolulu: Hawaii Times, 1964.

Ganor, Solly. *Light One Candle: A Survivor's Tale from Lithuania to Jerusalem.* New York: Kodansha International, 1995.

Gardiner, C. Harvey. *Pawns in a Triangle of Hate: The Peruvian Japanese and the United States.* Seattle: University of Washington Press, 1981.

————. *The Japanese and Peru: 1873–1973.* Albuquerque: University of New Mexico Press, 1975.

Garvey, Marcus. *The Marcus Garvey and Universal Negro Improvement Association Papers.* Edited by Robert A. Hill, vols. 1–2. Edited by Robert A. Hill, Emory J. Tolbert, and Deborah Forczek, vols. 3–4. Berkeley: University of California Press, 1983–85.

Gee, Joy N., ed. *Crystal City [Texas] 50th Anniversary Reunion Album.* Monterey, Calif.: By the editor, 1993.

Gentry, Curt. *J. Edgar Hoover: The Man and the Secret.* New York: W. W. Norton and Co., 1991.

Gibson, William Marion. *Aliens and the Law.* Chapel Hill, N.C.: University of North Carolina Press, 1940.

Girdner, Audrie, and Anne Loftis. *The Great Betrayal: The Evacuation of the Japanese Americans during World War II.* London: The Macmillian Co., 1969.

Grodzins, Morton. *Americans Betrayed: Politics and the Japanese Evacuation.* Chicago: University of Chicago Press, 1949.

Gruber, Ruth. *Haven: The Unknown Story of 1,000 World War II Refugees.* New York: New American Library, 1983.

Hall, David L. "Internment and Resistance: The Japanese American Experience in the Minidoka Relocation Center, 1942–1945." M.A. thesis, Washington State University, 1987.

Hansen, Arthur A., and Betty E. Mitson, eds. *Voices Long Silent: An Oral Inquiry into the Japanese American Evacuation.* Fullerton: Oral History Program, California State University, 1974.

Harrington, Joseph D. *Yankee Samurai: The Secret Role of Nisei in America's Pacific Victory.* Detroit: Pettigrew Enterprises, 1979.

Harrison, Earl G. "Civilian Internment—American Way." *Survey Graphic* 33 (May 1944): 229–33.

Harrison, Will. "The Santa Fe Internment Camp." Department of Justice, *Immigration and Naturalization Service Monthly Review* 3, no. 10 (April 1946): 298–300.

Hashimoto, Sharon. *Reparations.* Waldron Island, Wash.: Brooding Heron Press and Bindery, 1992.

Hatamiya, Leslie T. *Righting a Wrong: Japanese Americans and the Passage of the Civil Liberties Act of 1988.* Stanford, Calif.: Stanford University Press, 1993.

Hersey, John. "A Mistake of Terrifically Horrible Proportions." In John Armor and Peter Wright, *Manzanar,* pp. 1–66. New York: Times Books, 1988.

Herzig, Jack. "Japanese Americans and Magic." *Amerasia Journal* 11, no. 2 (1984): 47–65.

Higashide, Seiichi. *Adios to Tears: The Memoirs of a Japanese-Peruvian Internee in U.S. Concentration Camps.* Honolulu: E & E Kudo, 1993. Reprint, with a new foreword, Seattle: University of Washington Press, 2000.

Hodges, Antony N., and Ivan Tilgenkamp. *The Mysteries of Pearl Harbor.* Honolulu: Dimensional Graphics, International Ltd., 1981.

Hohri, William. *Repairing America: An Account of the Movement for Japanese-American Redress.* Pullman: Washington State University Press, 1988.

Hoover, J. Edgar. "Alien Enemy Control." *Iowa Law Review* 29 (March 1944): 396–403.

Hosokawa, Bill. *Nisei: The Quiet Americans.* New York: William Morrow and Co., 1969.

Hougen, Chizuko W. "The Japanese Immigrant Community in Mexico: Its History and Present." M.A. thesis, California State University, Los Angeles, June 1983.

Houston, Jeanne W., and James D. Houston. *Farewell to Manzanar.* Boston: Houghton Mifflin Co., 1973.

Hynd, Alan. *Betrayal from the East: The Inside Story of Japanese Spies in America.* New York: Robert. M. McBride & Co., 1943.

Ichioka, Yuji, ed. *Views from Within: The Japanese American Evacuation and Resettlement Study.* Los Angeles: Asian American Studies Center, University of California, Los Angeles, 1989.

International Encyclopedia of Social Sciences, 1968 ed. S. v. "Internment and Custody," by Albert Biderman.

Irons, Peter. *Justice at War: The Story of the Japanese Internment.* New York: Oxford University Press, 1983.

———, ed. *Justice Delayed: The Record of the Japanese American Internment Cases.* Middletown, Conn.: Wesleyan University Press, 1989.

Israel, Fred. "Military Justice in Hawaii, 1941–1944." *Pacific Historical Review* 36, no. 3 (August 1967): 243–67.

———. *The War Diary of Breckinridge Long: Selections from the Years 1939–1944.* Lincoln: University of Nebraska Press, 1966.

Ito, Kazuo. *America shunju hachijunen* (America spring-fall eighty years). Tokyo: PMC Publishers, 1982.

Johnson, Chalmers. *An Instance of Treason: Ozaki Hotsumi and the Sorge Spy Ring.* Stanford, Calif.: Stanford University Press, 1990.

Kamae, Takashi. "Rozubagu Nihonjin shyojo jimmelroku" (Roster of Japanese internees), Lordsburg, N.M., January 1943. Mimeographed.

Kaneshiro, Takeo. *Internees: War Relocation Center Memories and Dairies.* New York: Vantage Press, 1976.

Kashima, Tetsuden. "American Mistreatment of Internees during World War II: Enemy Alien Japanese." In Roger Daniels, Sandra C. Taylor, and Harry H. L. Kitano, eds., *Japanese Americans: From Relocation to Redress,* 2nd ed., pp. 52–56. Seattle: University of Washington Press, 1991.

———. "Japanese American Internees Return—1945–1955: Readjustment and Social Amnesia." *Phylon Quarterly* 41, no. 2 (June 1980): 107–15.

———. *Buddhism in America: The Social Organization of an Ethnic Religious Organization.* Westport, Conn.: Greenwood Press, 1977.

Kato, Shinichi, ed. *Beikoku Nikkeijin hyakunenshi* (America's persons of Japanese ancestry 100-year history). Los Angeles: Shinnichibei Shimbunsha (New Japanese American news), 1961.

Kawakita, Tomoye, v. United States 1951, 190 F 2nd 506; 3B4 US 717, 96 L ed. 1249, 72 Supreme Court 950, 1951.

Kennett, Lee. *For the Duration...The United States Goes to War: Pearl Harbor–1942.* New York: Charles Scribner's Sons, 1985.

Kimura, Yoshiju. *Arizona Sunset.* Glendale, Ariz.: Y. Kimura, 1980.

Kimura, Yukiko. *Issei: Japanese Immigrants in Hawaii.* Honolulu: University of Hawaii Press, 1988.

Kitagawa, Daisuke. *Issei and Nisei: The Internment Years.* New York: Seabury Press, 1967.

Klingaman, William K. *1941: Our Lives in a World on the Edge.* New York: Harper & Row, 1970.

Kotani, Roland. "The Japanese in Hawaii: A Century of Struggle," program booklet of the Oahu Kanyaku Imin Centennial Committee. Honolulu: Hawaii Hochi, Ltd., 1985.

Krammer, Arnold. *Undue Process: The Untold Story of America's German Alien Internees.* Boulder, Colo.: Rowman and Littlefield Publishers, 1997.

———. "Japanese Prisoners of War in America." *Pacific Historical Review* 52, no. 1 (February 1983): 67–91.

Kubokawa, Charles. "Australian Relates WW2 Heroics of Nisei Divers Raiding Manila Bay." *Pacific Citizen* (Los Angeles), June 27, 1986, p. 3.

Kumei, Teruko I. "Skeletons in the Closet: The Japanese American *Hokoku Seinandan* and

Their 'Disloyal' Activities at the Tule Lake Segregation Center during World War II." *Japanese Journal of American Studies* 7 (1996): 67–102.

Kuramoto, Bob. "The Search for Spies." *Amerasia Journal* 6, no. 2 (fall 1979): 45–76.

Kurihara, Joe Y. "Murder in Camp Manzanar." April 16, 1943, University of California, Bancroft Library, Berkeley, F.N. R8.10. Typescript.

Kutler, Stanley I. "At the Bar of History: Japanese Americans versus the United States." *American Bar Foundation Research Journal* 2 (1985): 361–73.

LaViolette, Forrest E. *The Canadian Japanese and World War II: A Social and Psychological Account.* Toronto: University of Toronto Press, 1948.

Leighton, Alexander H. *Governing of Men.* Princeton, N.J.: Princeton University Press, 1945.

Levie, Howard S., ed. *Documents on Prisoners of War: International Law Studies,* vol. 5. Newport, R.I.: U.S. Naval War College, 1979.

Lincoln, C. Eric. *The Black Muslims in America.* New York: Beacon Press, 1961.

Lind, Andrew W. *Hawaii's People,* 3rd ed. Honolulu: University of Hawaii Press, 1967.

———. *The Japanese in Hawaii under War Conditions.* Honolulu: American Council Institute of Pacific Relations, 1942.

Lippman, Walter. "Today and Tomorrow: The Fifth Column on the Coast." *New York Herald Tribune,* February 12, 1942.

Littell, Norman. *My Roosevelt Years.* Edited by Jonathan Dembro. Seattle: University of Washington Press, 1987.

Lowenthal, Max. *The Federal Bureau of Investigation.* New York: William Sloane Associates, 1950.

MacBeth, Angus. "Addendum to Personal Justice Denied [on 'Magic']." In Commission on Wartime Relocation and Internment of Civilians, *Personal Justice Denied,* pp. 471–79. Reprint, with a new foreword, Seattle: University of Washington Press, 1997.

Mackey, Mike, ed. *Remembering Heart Mountain: Essays on Japanese American Internment in Wyoming.* Powell, Wyo.: Western History Publications Book, 1998.

Makabe, Wilson. "442nd Regimental Combat Team, Italy." In John Tateishi, ed., *And Justice for All: An Oral History of the Japanese American Detention Camps,* pp. 250–59. New York: Random House, 1984.

Maki, Mitchell, Harry H. L. Kitano, and S. Megan Berthold. *Achieving the Impossible Dream: How the Japanese Americans Obtained Redress.* Urbana: University of Illinois Press, 1999.

Mangione, Jerri. *An Ethnic at Large: A Memoir of America in the Thirties and Forties.* New York: G. P. Putnam's Sons, 1978.

McCloy, John J. "Letters from John J. McCloy and Karl R. Bendetsen." In Roger Daniels, Sandra C. Taylor, and Harry H. L. Kitano, eds., *Japanese Americans: From Relocation to Redress,* 2nd ed., pp. 213–16. Seattle: University of Washington Press, 1991.

———. "Repay U.S. Japanese?" *New York Times,* 10 April 1983.

———. "Moving the West-Coast Japanese." *Harper's Magazine,* September 1942, pp. 359–69.

McWilliams, Carey. *Prejudice: Japanese Americans: Symbol of Racial Intolerance.* Boston: Little, Brown, 1944.

Merritt, Ralph P. Jr. "Death Valley—Its Impounded Americans." *Keepsake: 38th Annual Death Valley '49ers Encampment, Death Valley, CA,* no. 27 (November 5–8, 1987).

Miller, Nathan. *Spying for America: The Hidden History of U.S. Intelligence.* New York: Dell Publishing, 1989.

MIS Language School Album, 1946.

Miyamoto, Kazuo. *Hawaii: End of the Rainbow.* Rutland, Vt.: Charles E. Tuttle, 1964.

Miyamoto, S. Frank. *Social Solidarity among the Japanese in Seattle.* 1939. Reprint, with a new foreword, Seattle: University of Washington Press, 1987.

Moore, John H. "Hitler's Wehrmacht in Virginia, 1943–1946." *The Virginia Magazine of History and Biography* 85, no. 3 (1977): 259–73.

Moosa, Eugene. "Jewish Refugee Here to Honor Diplomat Who Saved Thousands." *Japan Times* (Tokyo), September 18, 1992, p. 3.

Morgan, Ted. *FDR: A Biography.* New York: Simon and Schuster, 1985.

Myer, Dillion S. *Uprooted Americans: The Japanese Americans and the War Relocation Authority.* Tucson: University of Arizona Press, 1971.

Muller, Eric. *Free to Die for Their Country: The Story of the Japanese American Draft Resisters in World War II.* Chicago: University of Chicago Press, 2001.

Nagata, Yuriko. "'A Little Colony on Our Own': Australia's Camps in World War II." In Kay Saunders and Roger Daniels, eds., *Alien Justice: Wartime Internment in Australia and North America,* pp. 152–67. Queensland, Australia: University of Queensland Press, 2000.

Nakano, Jiro, and Kay Nakano, eds. and trans. *Poets behind Barbed Wire.* Honolulu: Bamboo Ridge Press, 1983.

Naske, Claus-M. "The Relocation of Alaska's Japanese Residents." *Pacific Northwest Quarterly* 74, no. 3 (1983): 124–32.

Nelson, Douglas W. *Heart Mountain: The History of an American Concentration Camp.* Madison: State Historical Society of Wisconsin, 1976.

Nicholson, Herbert V. *Treasures in Earthen Vessels.* Whittier, Calif.: Penn Lithographics, 1974.

Oda, James. *Heroic Struggles of Japanese Americans.* North Hollywood, Calif.: KNI, 1980.

Ogawa, Dennis. *Kodomo no Tame-ni—For the Sake of the Children: The Japanese American Experience in Hawaii.* Honolulu: University Press of Hawaii, 1978.

Ogawa, Dennis M., and Evarts C. Fox Jr. "Japanese Internment and Relocation: The Hawaii Experience." In Roger Daniels, Sandra C. Taylor, and Harry H. L. Kitano, eds., *Japanese Americans: From Relocation to Redress,* 2nd ed., pp. 135–38.. Seattle: University of Washington Press, 1991.

Okahata, James, ed. *A History of Japanese in Hawaii.* Honolulu: The United Japanese Society of Hawaii, 1971.

Okihiro, Gary Y. *Cane Fires: The Anti-Japanese Movement in Hawaii, 1865–1945.* Philadelphia: Temple University Press, 1991.

Okihiro, Gary Y., and David Drummond. "The Concentration Camps and Japanese Economic Losses in California Agriculture, 1900–1942." In Roger Daniels, Sandra Taylor, and Harry H. L. Kitano, eds., *Japanese Americans: From Relocation to Redress,* 2nd ed., pp. 168–75. Seattle: University of Washington Press, 1991.

Okihiro, Gary Y., and Joan Myers. *Whispered Silences: Japanese Americans and World War II.* Seattle: University of Washington Press, 1996.

Park, Robert E., and Herbert A. Miller. *Old World Traits Transplanted.* New York: Harper and Bros., 1921.

Piccigallo, Philip R. *The Japanese on Trial: Allied War Crimes Operations in the East, 1945–1961.* Austin: University of Texas Press, 1979.

Pogue, Forrest C. *George C. Marshall: Organizer of Victory.* New York: The Viking Press, 1973.

Powers, Richard G. *Secrecy and Power: The Life of J. Edgar Hoover.* New York: The Free Press, 1987.

Prange, Gordon W. *At Dawn We Slept: The Untold Story of Pearl Harbor.* New York: Penguin Books, 1981.

Prange, Gordon W., Donald M. Goldstein, and Katherine V. Dillon. *Pearl Harbor: The Verdict of History.* New York: McGraw Hill, 1986.

Pressler, Mollie. "The Lordsburg Internment/POW Camp." Lordsburg, N.M., 1992. Typescript.

Preston, William Jr. *Aliens and Dissenters.* Cambridge: Harvard University Press, 1963.

Ringle, Kenneth D. "What Did You Do Before the War, Dad?" *Washington Post Magazine,* December 6, 1981.

———. "The Japanese in America: The Problem and Its Solution." *Harper's Magazine* 185 (1942): 489–97.

Robinson, Greg. *By Order of the President: FDR and the Internment of Japanese Americans.* Cambridge: Harvard University Press, 2001.

Rostow, Eugene V. "The Japanese American Cases—A Disaster." *Yale Law Journal* 54 (1945): 489–533.

———. "Our Worst Wartime Mistake." *Harper's Magazine* 191 (September 1945): 193–201.

Roy, Patricia E., J. L. Granastein, Masako Iino, and Hiroko Takamura. *Mutual Hostages: Canadians and Japanese during the Second World War.* Toronto: University of Toronto Press, 1990.

Russell, Edward. *Knights of Bushido.* London: Cassell and Co., 1958.

Saiki, Patsy S. *Gambare! An Example of Japanese Spirit.* Honolulu: Kisaku, 1982.

San Francisco, National Japanese American Library. Shizuo Hisamune, "Petition of Shizuo Hisamune, Alien Internment Camp, Crystal City, Texas, 13 March 1947." In Iwao Shimizu collection, "Private Papers: Petition—Aged and Infirmed Aliens."

———. Iwao Shimizu collection, "Private Papers."

Santa Fe Jihosha. *Santa Fe Nihonjin shuyojo jimmelroku* (Roster of Japanese internees at Santa Fe). Santa Fe, N.M., November 1, 1943. Typescript.

Sato, Hank. "Honouliuli Camp: Footnote to a Dark Chapter." *Honolulu Star-Bulletin,* March 18, 1976, pp. A-1–A-8.

Saunders, Kay. "'Taken Away to Be Shot?': The Process of Incarceration in Australia in

World War II." In Kay Saunders and Roger Daniels, eds., *Alien Justice: Wartime Internment in Australia and North America,* pp. 185–204. Queensland, Australia: University of Queensland Press, 2000.

Sawada, Mitziko. "After the Camps: Seabrook Farms, New Jersey, and the Resettlement of Japanese Americans, 1944–1947." *Amerasia Journal* 13, no. 2 (1986–87): 117–36.

Sayers, Michael, and Albert E. Kahn. *Sabotage! The Secret War against America.* New York: Harper and Bros., 1942.

Seattle. University of Washington, Suzzallo Library, Manuscripts and Archives Division. Iwao Matsushita, "Private Papers," 1941–43.

Seth, Ronald. *Secret Servants: A History of Japanese Espionage.* New York: Farrar, Straus and Cudahy, 1957.

Shibutani, Tamotsu. *Derelicts of Company K: A Sociological Study of Demoralization.* Berkeley: University of California Press, 1978.

Smith, Bradford. *Americans from Japan.* Philadelphia: Lippincott, 1948.

Smith, Geoffreys. "Racial Nativism and Origins of American Relocation." In Roger Daniels, Sandra C. Taylor, and Harry H. L. Kitano, eds., *Japanese Americans: From Relocation to Redress,* 2nd ed., pp. 79–88. Seattle: University of Washington Press, 1991.

Smith, Page. *Democracy on Trial: The Japanese American Evacuation and Relocation in World War II.* New York: Simon and Schuster, 1995.

Soga, Yasutaro. *Tessaka seikatsu* (Life inside the iron fence). Honolulu: Hawaii Times, 1948.

Spicer, Edward H., Asael T. Hansen, Katherine Luomala, and Marvin Opler. *Impounded People: Japanese-Americans in the Relocation Centers.* Tucson: University of Arizona Press, 1969.

Spickard, Paul R. "Injustice Compounded: Amerasians and Non-Japanese Americans in World War II Concentration Camps." *Journal of American Ethnic History* 5, no. 2 (spring 1986): 5–22.

———. "The Nisei Assume Power: The Japanese American Citizens League, 1941–1942." *Pacific Historical Review* 52, no. 2 (May 1983): 147–74.

Stephan, John J. *Hawaii under the Rising Sun: Japan's Plans for Conquest After Pearl Harbor.* Honolulu: University of Hawaii Press, 1984.

Sullivan, William C. *The Bureau.* New York: W. W. Norton and Co., 1969.

Sunahara, Ann Gomer. *The Politics of Racism: The Uprooting of Japanese Canadians during the Second World War.* Toronto: James Lorimer & Co., 1981.

Takezawa, Yasuku I. *Breaking the Silence: Redress and Japanese American Ethnicity.* Ithaca, N.Y.: Cornell University Press, 1995.

Tamba, Theodore. "Secrets of U.S., Peruvian Wartime Intrigue Revealed in This Article." *San Francisco Hokubei Mainichi,* March 30, 1972, p. 1.

Tana, Daisho. *Santa Fe, Rozubagu, senji tekikokujin yokuryujo nikki, dai-ikkan* (Santa Fe, Lordsburg, wartime enemy internment place diary, vol. 1). Tokyo: Sankibo Busshorin Seisaku, 1976.

Tateishi, John, ed. *And Justice for All: An Oral History of the Japanese American Detention*

Camps. New York: Random House, 1984; reprint, with a new foreword, Seattle: University of Washington Press, 1999.

tenBroek, Jacobus, Edward N. Barnhart, and Floyd W. Matson. *Prejudice, War, and the Constitution.* Berkeley: University of California Press, 1954.

Terasaki, Gwen. *Bridge to the Sun.* Chapel Hill: University of North Carolina Press, 1957.

Theobald, Robert A. *The Final Secret of Pearl Harbor.* New York: Devin-Adair Co., 1954.

Thomas, Dorothy S. *The Salvage.* Berkeley: University of California Press, 1952.

Thomas, Dorothy S., and Richard Nishimoto. *The Spoilage.* Berkeley: University of California Press, 1946.

Tokayer, Marvin, and Mary Swartz. *The Fugu Plan.* New York: Paddington Press, 1979.

Trooboff, Peter D., ed. *Law and Responsibility in Warfare.* Chapel Hill: University of North Carolina Press, 1975.

Tsujimura, James. "Six Incidents Belie Idea! We Were Detained against Our Wills As Eight Shot and Killed." *Pacific Citizen* (Los Angeles), December 21–28, 1985, p. D-8.

Ueno, Harry. "Manzanar." In John Tateishi, ed., *And Justice for All: An Oral History of the Japanese American Detention Camps,* pp. 186–207. New York: Random House, 1984.

Ungar, Sanford J. *FBI.* Boston: Little, Brown and Co., 1976.

U.S. Army. "Supplemental Report on Civilian Control Exercised by Western Defense Command," January 1947, Record Group 338, vols. I, II, III, National Archives, Washington, D.C.

U.S. Department of Defense. *The "Magic" Background of Pearl Harbor,* 8 vols. Volume 4: *October 17, 1941–December 7, 1941.* Washington, D.C.: U.S. Government Printing Office, 1978.

U.S. Department of Interior. *Annual Report of the Secretary of the Interior.* Washington, D.C.: U.S. Government Printing Office.

U.S. Department of Justice. *Annual Report of the Attorney General of the United States for the Fiscal Year Ended....* Washington, D.C.: U.S. Government Printing Office, various years.

U.S. Department of Justice, Federal Bureau of Investigation. Record Group 62-63892, 1941; File Numbers 100-2-25, 1941–42 through 100-2-43-245, 1946.

U.S. Department of Justice, Immigration and Naturalization Service. "Fort Stanton Internment Camp Closed by Service" *Monthly Review* 3, no. 4 (October 1945): 212.

———. "Second Group of Aliens Deported on Gripsholm." *Monthly Review* 3, no. 3 (September 1945): 202.

———. "Work Projects for Interned Alien Enemies." *Monthly Review* 2, no. 12 (June 1945): 159–61.

———. "Fort Lincoln Internment Camp Is Abandoned by Service." *Monthly Review* 2, no. 6 (December 1944): 74–76.

———. "Internment of Alien Enemy." *Monthly Review* 1, no. 12 (June 1944): 13.

———. *Immigration and Nationality Laws and Regulations: As of March 1, 1944.* Washington, D.C.: U.S. Government Printing Office, 1944.

———. "All Enemy Alien Internees Now In Custody of Immigration Service." *Monthly Review* 1, no. 1 (July 1943): 21.

———. Files, Record Group 85, National Archives, Washington, D.C.

U.S. Department of Justice, Special Defense Unit. Files, Record Group 44, National Archives, Washington, D.C.

U.S. General Services Administration. *Federal Records of WW II.* Vol. 1: *Civilian Agencies.* Washington, D.C.: U.S. Government Printing Office, 1950.

U.S. War Relocation Authority, U.S. Department of the Interior. *W R A : The Story of Human Conservation.* Washington, D.C.: U.S. Department of the Interior, vol. 9, 1947.

———. *The Evacuated People: A Quantitative Description.* Washington, D.C.: U.S. Department of the Interior, vol. 3, 1946b.

———. *Token Shipment: The Story of America's War Refugee Shelter.* Washington, D.C.: U.S. Department of the Interior, vol. 8, 1946c.

———. *Wartime Exile: The Exclusion of the Japanese Americans from the West Coast.* Washington, D.C.: U.S. Department of the Interior, vol. 10, 1946d.

———. *Legal and Constitutional Phases of the W R A Program.* Washington, D.C.: U.S. Department of the Interior, 1946e.

———. *People in Motion: The Postwar Adjustment of the Evacuated Japanese Americans.* Washington, D.C.: U.S. Department of the Interior, 1946f.

———. *The Wartime Handling of Evacuee Property.* Washington, D.C.: U.S. Department of the Interior, 1946g.

———. *Community Government in War Relocation Centers.* Washington, D.C.: U.S. Department of the Interior, 1946h.

———. Files, Record Group 210, National Archives, Washington, D.C.

U.S. Department of War. Files, Record Group 389, National Archives, Washington, D.C.

Uyeda, Clifford. "The Forgotten Resolution." *Rafu Shimpo* (Los Angeles), July 19, 1990, p. 1.

Volkman, Ernest, and Blaine Baggett. *Secret Intelligence: The Inside Story of America's Espionage Empire.* New York: Doubleday, 1989.

Walls, Thomas K. *The Japanese Texans.* Austin, Tex.: Institute of Texan Culture, 1987.

Washington, D.C. National Archives. Commission on Wartime Relocation and Internment of Civilians. Peter B. Sheridan, "The Internment of Germans and Italians Aliens Compared to the Internment of Japanese Aliens in the United States during World War II: A Brief History and Analysis," Numerical Files, No. 25886-25897, November 24, 1980.

———. National Archives. Commission on Wartime Relocation and Internment of Civilians. Record Group 220. Curtis B. Munson, "Japanese on the West Coast," Numerical Files, No. 3670-3689, November 7, 1941.

Weber, Max. *The Theory of Social and Economic Organization.* Trans. A. M. Henderson and Talcott Parsons. New York: Oxford University Press, 1947.

Weglyn, Michi. *Years of Infamy: The Untold Story of America's Concentration Camps.* New York: William Morrow and Co., 1976. Reprint, Seattle: University of Washington Press, 1996.

Whitehead, Don. *The FBI Story: A Report to the People.* New York: Random House, 1956.

Wyman, David S. *The Abandonment of the Jews: America and the Holocaust, 1941–1945.* New York: Pantheon Books, 1984.

Yasui, Minori. "Minidoka." In John Tateishi, ed., *And Justice for All: An Oral History of the Japanese American Detention Camps.* New York: Random House, 1984, pp. 62–93.

Yoneda, Karl G. *Ganbatte: Sixty-Year Struggle of a Kibei Worker.* Los Angeles: Asian American Studies Center, University of California, Los Angeles, 1983.

INDEX